SEARCH FOR THE

OF THE ATOCHA

BY EUGENE LYON

FLORIDA CLASSICS LIBRARY

Grateful acknowledgement is made for permission to reprint:

Lines from "A Pirate Looks at Forty." Words and music by Jimmy Buffet. Copyright © 1974 by Duchess Music Corporation, New York, N.Y. Used by permission. All rights reserved.

1989 Florida Classics Library
Cover design by James Baker

Library of Congress Cataloging in Publication Data

Lyon, Eugene, 1929-
    Search for the Motherload of the Atocha
    1. Nuestra Senora de Atocha (Ship) 2. Treasure – Trove – Florida I. Title.
G530.N83L95   975.9'01   89-83905
ISBN 0-912451-20-3

Cover Photo:
Nine fathoms down in Hawk Channel a solitary Mahogany Snapper swims above a king's ransom.

To Po

CONTENTS

I.	Ocean's Call	1
II.	Treasure Fever in Florida	16
III.	The Archive of the Indies	34
IV.	No Mercy in the Wind	50
V.	"We Must Find the *Almiranta*"	69
VI.	The Nitty-Gritty	86
VII.	The Bank of Spain	102
VIII.	"We've Found the Big A"	116
IX.	Squalls When You Find It	130
X.	Conmen, Mystics, and Credibility	142
XI.	Gold Shines Forever	154
XII.	The Guns of the *Atocha*	168
XIII.	A Powerful Ocean	177
XIV.	Courts, Cannons, and Silver	188
XV.	The World's Greatest Treasure Hunter	207
XVI.	"Today's the Day"	218
XVII.	The Ghost Galleon	235
XVIII.	The Mother Lode	265

Paper delivered to the Society of Historical Archaeology by Eugene Lyon	Appendix A
Communication from Marquis of Cadereita to the Crown	Appendix B
Communication from Don Louis de Cordoba to Crown Havana	Appendix C
Communication from Gaspar de Vargas	Appendix D
Communication from General Don Francisco Venegas	Appendix E
Facts and Conclusions of Law Case Nos.79-1381-Civ-JKL 80-1205-Civ-JLK	Appendix F
Tracking the *Atocha*	Appendix G
Guns of the 1622 Spanish Galleons	Appendix H
Abandoned Shipwreck Act of 1988	Appendix J

To come to know a fragment of our past
is to recognize a piece of ourselves.
—PAUL MAC KENDRICK

I. Ocean's Call

Mother, mother Ocean
  I have heard your call;
I have wanted to sail your waters
  Since I was three feet tall;
You've seen it all
  You've seen it all.

. . . In your belly you hold the treasures
  Few have ever seen . . .
Most of them dreams
  Most of them dreams.

—Jimmy Buffett

Holly's Folly was a tiny point moving across a vast, shimmering sheet of ocean in the lower Florida Keys. Astern of her, a long, wavering line of pelicans flew back toward the Marquesas Keys, out of sight in the northeast; westward, even farther away, lay the Dry Tortugas. The trim Chris-Craft plowed on southwest, out toward the Gulf Stream, but her crew were not trolling for dolphin, nor were they deep-sea fishing. *Holly's Folly* was a magnetometer boat, searching for long-buried Spanish treasure.

There was a steady, persistent wind this summer morning, and the sun glinted all across the rippled sea it had raised. It was past time to turn back onto the northeast course leg; the boat was almost out of sight of the youth in the theodolite tower on the derelict destroyer eight miles away. But the helmsman, half-hypnotized by the sun-dazzle on the sea, was dozing at the wheel.

Dozens of bright orange Day-Glo buoys were stacked in the roomy cockpit, their rope coils and concrete-block weights attached, ready for use. If the boat's track should bring its towed magnetometer head near any sunken iron, and an anomaly registered on the mag dial, the buoys would be thrown to mark the spot.

Under the shade of the cabin roof, Marjory Hargreaves squinted at the dial. As she watched, the needle dipped, then swerved hard over to the right. A peg reading! She cried out, "Anomaly!" and suddenly the boat came to life. With her brother, Bob, she wrestled a buoy with its heavy block weight onto the gunwale, threw it clear, and it fell with a splash into the churning wake of *Holly's Folly*.

When he had anchored his boat close alongside the bobbing buoy and shut his engines down, Bob Holloway prepared to dive and investigate the strong magnetometer contact. His sister and Kay Finley helped him pull on a wet-suit top; he wore it not because the water in the Keys was so cold in June, but to protect his shoulders against the straps of his scuba tanks. Next, he hefted the twin tanks onto his back, secured them, and sat on the Chris-Craft's rail to put on his flippers. Then, moving his face mask down into place, he put the mouthpiece into his mouth and moved to the rail. With a sure agility that belied his forty-nine years, Bob Holloway climbed down into the water and was lost to sight beneath the surface.

The whole world below was flooded with a dark-green light that made the white-sand bottom look dark-brown in color. He saw rippled sand bottom: *Holly's Folly* had anchored on the edge of the Quicksands, a twenty-mile shoal stretching west from the Marquesas Keys, in fourteen feet of water. As Bob oriented himself, his eyes searched the area around the buoy weight on the bottom. He saw a large, dark, circular object, partly buried in the sand, and swam to it. Fanning with his hands around its base, he cleared the whole diameter of the ring and saw that it was almost three feet across; he found that the ring was connected with a swivel to a thick iron shaft that disappeared into the sand. It was the ring of a very large and very old anchor. Bob Holloway had found the anchor of a sunken galleon; now he could tell Mel Fisher that the long search might have come to an end at last.

It was Saturday, June 12, 1971, and the news of the anchor find had brought results. Light swells rocked a little fleet of salvage boats moored over the galleon anchor: *Virgilona,* a forty-six-foot wooden diesel workboat, the fiberglass inboard *Anomaly,* and a dinghy. Three taut anchor lines held *Virgilona* in place for digging. In the middle distance, *Holly's Folly* cut a wake, searching for new contacts.

Virgilona's decks were cluttered with salvage gear: an air compressor, a rack of diving tanks, and a green plastic garbage can full of face masks and scuba regulators. In the water at the boat's stern were two blue-painted steel tubes, the "mailboxes."

Mel Fisher, a large, deeply tanned man, stood near the stern; he looked at his wife, Deo, and at the others. "That's it," he said. "I know we've got it now. We've got the *Margarita* or probably the *Atocha.* All those millions—they're right down there somewhere." Still breathing hard from his dive, Mel gestured to the small black object lying on the deck, as if to prove his point.

It was hard to believe. After four years of searching far up the Keys, and more than a year hunting down here—miles and square miles—and then *Holly's Folly* had found the galleon anchor. Now Mel had dived and found an item that he said proved it was an old shipwreck—one single lead musket ball.

Rick Vaughan bobbed up alongside *Virgilona,* his mask streaming seawater. He spat out his mouthpiece and cried, "Hey, Mel! Look at this!" He swam to the ladder and laid down two pieces of faded orange-brown pottery on the gunwale. Then Rick climbed aboard, freed a blackened thing from his right glove, and carefully handed it to Mel Fisher.

The flat, rounded object was dotted with small, coarse shells. Mel smeared these away with gentle rubbing, leaving a black stain on his fingers. There appeared a glinting grid of bright lines and bars and then a tiny silver lion.

"Hey . . . how about that?" said Mel. "A Spanish coin!" A babble of voices broke out.

"Look—it's round, not like the 1715 cobs."

"No date?"

"Here's some lettering. *Philippus IV.*"

"That's right for 1622."

Deo Fisher bent over to pick up the terra-cotta sherds from the boat's rail. "Mel," she called out in her clear voice, "these are olive-jar pieces. Spanish."

By noon the next day, the wind had freshened, and the boats faced around together into a light chop. The mailboxes had just finished a "blow," and Don Kincaid was preparing to dive. Kincaid, a slim, bearded young man, was new on the job; he had come out from Key West the night before to photograph the galleon anchor. Rick Vaughan was already down; Don adjusted his mask, picked up his camera, and somersaulted backward from the diving ladder into the water. As Don tells what happened next: "I went down through a cloud of dust from the mailboxes and could only see a foot in front of me. Then it slowly began to clear and I saw the crater. In the wall I suddenly spied these shiny links of chain—just a few links. In the green light, they looked like cheap brass. Sand sliding down the crater wall was covering them up fast, so I grabbed, and this little ball of chain came out. I signaled to Rick and started up, looking at it all the time. As I got higher and it got lighter, the chain began to look less and less like brass and more like . . . gold!"

When Kincaid climbed back aboard the *Virgilona*, nobody was on deck. Except for a diver perched on the bow, everyone was below for lunch. At Don's exultant shout, Fay Feild came up from the cabin. As he caught sight of the gold chain, still balled up in Don's fist, Fay let out a string of cheerful curses. This brought Mel and Deo from below. With mounting excitement they watched as Don strung the chain—three pieces of it—out on the engine cover. Deo, childlike, clapped her hands and began to dance. Mel picked up one of the chains. Turning the finely worked, gleaming links over in his fingers, Mel let out a long "Golllleeeeeee."

Finally Deo broke the spell by reminding Mel to call Bob Holloway and tell him the good news. Mel Fisher strode to the wheel, picked up the microphone, keyed it, and called:

"Holly, Holly, this is *Virgilona.* Come in, Bob."

In a moment the voice of Bob Holloway cut in: *"Holly's Folly* here; go ahead, *Virgilona."*

Mel's slow drawl had tautened. *"Holly, Holly,* this is *Virgilona.* This is Mel. Come over to lunch. You got that, Bob? Come over to lunch."

Those words—the code words for the finding of gold—spread the contagion of excitement to Bob and his crew. Soon *Holly's Folly* was tied up alongside *Virgilona.* Then another whole boatload arrived from Key West, with Bob Moran, Chet Alexander, and Ingrid Nilsen. Now more than twenty people crowded the cockpit of the salvage boat. The gold chains, the silver coin, the pottery, and the musket ball passed from hand to hand and were admired again and again.

Mel worked at the wired cork of the only bottle of champagne aboard. When it popped, Deo poured some into the bottom of each person's paper cup. Mel lifted his cup.

"To the *Atocha.* Here's to the rest of all that loot—that four hundred million—right down there. It's real close now."

Mel Fisher says the first Spanish treasure he saw was near the Saint Petersburg City Pier, in Tampa Bay. He says, "This diver brought it in off a ballast pile: a key, a padlock, some ballast stones, pottery, and some pieces of eight. It impressed me. The guy wouldn't tell me where his wreck was, so I went out and searched for it. But I never found it."

Mel spent his youth in Gary, Indiana. In high school he learned to play the saxophone and formed his own swing band. When he went to study engineering at Purdue University, Mel gave up the band but worked his way through college as a booking agent for ASCAP. He joined the Army Reserve, and when Pearl Harbor came, he was called to active duty. The Army enrolled Mel in its own engineering program at Purdue and then transferred him to Alabama. When the program closed down, Mel entered the Army Engineers and in 1944 was shipped to France. He landed there just after the Normandy invasion and followed the armies into Germany, "repairing," as he said, "everything we'd bombed out."

Just before he went overseas, Mel was married. Like many wartime matches, his did not long survive the coming of peace, and ended in divorce. After his Army discharge, Mel moved: first to Chicago, then to Denver, where for a year he worked as a carpenter for the Bureau of Reclamation. As restless as postwar America, he moved again—this time to Tampa, Florida, where he established himself as a general contractor. For recreation, Mel began to go spearfishing in the Bay and Gulf, but this was no idle pastime for the tall, rangy young man. He had to excel. Soon he became known among local skin divers as the man who would go farther out than anyone else and bring in more and bigger fish. He also became interested in underwater photography. As Mel said, "Some people wouldn't believe my stories about the huge fish I speared, so I took photographs to prove my stories were true."

Mel was also mastering a new technology that had been developed in wartime. After 1945, Americans invaded the water for pleasure and sport. They used flippers, face masks, and protective wet suits. They learned to dive deeper with self-contained underwater breathing apparatus (SCUBA)—the regulator and dive tanks perfected by Captain Jacques-Yves Cousteau and used by World War II frogmen. A new world had been opened up for adventure: a cool green kingdom, filled with lovely and deadly creatures—bright tropical fish, menacing sharks and barracuda. It featured coral paradises, beds of giant kelp, and sunken ships.

After seeing his first undersea treasure at Saint Petersburg, Mel continued to dive on shipwrecks. In 1950 he changed his scene of operations again, and went with his parents to that golden goal of millions of Americans, California. At Torrance, in the Los Angeles area, Mel and his father built a large chicken ranch. Although his work demanded long hours, Mel had not forgotten his underwater experiences in Florida. The nearby Pacific called to him, and he began to dive again. The skin-diving craze was just beginning in California, and Mel could see commercial advantages in the underwater field. In the feed shed of his Torrance chicken ranch, he built a dive shop—one of the first in the state. He also set up a compressor to provide a scuba-tank filling service for divers, and began to sell them equipment.

Mel's feed-shed dive shop was open only in the afternoons, but he soon realized that he made more money during those hours than from his work on the chicken farm. To encourage business further, Mel organized a diving club, which he named the Sharks, and began to give lessons in scuba diving.

One day the Hortons, a family from Montana, came to look over the chicken ranch, and when they decided to buy the Fishers out, they agreed that Mel would stay on awhile to show the new owners how to handle the chickens and market the eggs. In this way Mel Fisher met Dolores Horton, nicknamed "Deo," a tall, lovely, sixteen-year-old redhead. Deo remembers that her mother and uncle let Mel keep his shop in the feed shed, and recalls that "one night Mel invited my sister and me to a meeting of the Sharks to see some underwater movies he had made in Florida. I was fascinated. Mel taught me to snorkel out at Catalina and then showed me how to scuba dive. Although I was uneasy about using the scuba at first, I had no fear whatever of diving. The beauty and variety of underwater life thrilled me like nothing I had ever seen before."

Before long, Mel and Deo had fallen in love. In June 1953 they were married. Theirs was a divers' honeymoon. Mel took Deo to Florida, sought out a Key West fisherman, and told him, "Take us to shipwrecks—as many shipwrecks as you can." Mel was not only honeymooning—he was making a spearfishing film for the Voit Company, which makes swimfins and face masks. Big fish abound on old wrecks.

Their guide led them to a score of shipwrecks, and the Fishers reveled in the prodigal richness of the marine life in the clear summer waters of the Florida Keys. One day they were guided twenty-five miles west of Key West to the Marquesas Keys, across a long sandbar and to the hulk of a derelict ship named *Balbanera,* which had stranded on the edge of the Tortuga Channel in a storm in the 1920s. As he dived from the *Balbanera,* Mel never dreamed that he would later begin his greatest treasure quest at that same place.

When the Fishers returned to California from their honeymoon, Mel decided to give his skin-diving shop a permanent home closer to the Pacific, at Redondo Beach. To raise the money to build the shop, Mel and Deo began to dive commercially for lobster in the Santa Barbara Channel. Mel recalled that it was tough going: "The water was really cold, so we wore two sets of long johns and a dry suit over that. Outside we wore coveralls; lobsters will tear up a diving suit. But the claws and spines still cut into our suits, and we would end up cold and miserable. We rented a boat on shares, and when our share was good, I'd buy some more concrete blocks and cement and put up another wall at the shop."

Finally the store was finished and equipped; it was

named Mel's Aqua Shop. The Fishers had a zestful flair for commercial promotion, and soon Mel was selling more surfboards, scuba equipment, underwater cameras, and spearguns than anyone else around; the dive shop became a resounding success. Mel began a regular scuba school, and thousands of persons eventually took his three-day, twenty-five-dollar course. Deo was active in Mel's enterprises, although the Fisher family was now increasing. In 1954, Dirk, fair like his mother, was born; Kim, dark-haired like his father, came in 1956.

An irrepressible promoter, Mel persuaded some of his suppliers and some outside partners to stake him to diving expeditions to make films of his adventures. In 1954 he went to Haiti and to the Virgin Islands, and wrote a magazine article after his return, describing a dramatic battle in which he killed a shark underwater with his diver's knife.

Next, Mel began a venture that was peculiarly Californian: he invented a small gold dredge for use in the rocky beds of mountain streams. Bleth McHaley, a former registered nurse and stewardess, who had left her airline to work for the new magazine *Skindiver,* learned of Mel's new scheme, and says, "We began to hear that Mel was taking these huge parties—hundreds of people—up into the Sierras, hunting for gold with the dredges Mel had sold them. As far as I ever heard, nobody ever found much gold; only one guy and his wife found anything big." One day, Mel would put his gold dredges to use in the ocean instead of in the mountains.

By the middle 1950s, shipwreck salvage had come into a new era, as scuba divers began seriously to explore the wrecks they had found as spearfishermen. Sites formerly accessible only to commercial hard-hat divers had now become any diver's weekend goal. Amateurs began to study half-forgotten treasure lore. Men began to travel to places made famous in pirate legend to follow their dreams of sunken galleons and bright doubloons.

When Mel and Deo took their honeymoon trip to the

Florida Keys, divers had been actively working old ship-wrecks there for years. Arthur McKee had dived on treas-ure wrecks before the war and had found Spanish gold and silver coins and an ingot of silver. In 1949 he began to work a newly found galleon wreck, the remains of a Spanish ship that had gone down in a 1733 hurricane.

In 1951 another important find had been made in the Keys. The H.M.S. *Looe,* a forty-gun frigate lost in 1743, was found and identified by a group that included McKee, Dr. and Mrs. George Crile, Edwin A. Link (the inventor of the Link trainer), and Mendel Peterson of the Smithso-nian Institution. In 1953 the team explored other Keys sites, using a device called an airlift, which Link had built. Previously used by Cousteau in the Mediterranean, the airlift employed compressed air to clear away mud or sand accumulated over shipwrecks. The Keys salvors also used underwater metal detectors to locate anchors, cannons, and other buried metal objects.

A few years later, Link led a search for the grave of Columbus's flagship, the *Santa Maria,* which had grounded and broken up off the north Haitian coast on Christmas Eve, 1492. In this operation, Link employed an electronic device invented as an antisubmarine weapon during World War II: the flux-gate magnetometer. By not-ing differences in magnetic fields caused by iron objects in the water, the magnetometer could locate sunken ships. Thus armed, Link uncovered an ancient handwrought an-chor that was dated by Mendel Peterson at the approxi-mate age to have been lost during Columbus's voyage.

In Bermuda, a man named Edward Tucker, nicknamed "Teddy," had combed the reefs and inlets seeking modern shipwrecks. Instead, in 1950 he found a cluster of iron cannon from a colonial shipwreck site near an outlying reef. After selling the guns, Tucker did not return to the place until 1954. Once he began seriously to dive on the wreck, he brought up a breathtaking assemblage of coins, bullion, jewelry, and artifacts from a sixteenth-century Spanish vessel—the first substantial treasure recovered in modern times. When photographs of the lovely emerald-studded Bishop's cross he had found were published, treasure hunters around the world had fresh incentive for their quest.

In Mediterranean waters near Marseilles, Captain Cousteau had begun the careful excavation of an ancient Greek ship, lost there more than two thousand years before. His systematic methods of recording data on the shipwreck as it was uncovered contributed greatly to the newborn science of marine archaeology.

A whole Spanish treasure fleet had met disaster at the hands of enemy ships in Vigo Bay in Galicia, northwestern Spain, in 1702. A well-prepared expedition began in 1955 to work to recover what still remained of the treasure after contemporary Spanish salvage efforts. The group, which included John S. Potter, Jr., and Robert Sténuit, a scholarly young Belgian diver, researched the Vigo ships thoroughly in European archives and libraries before beginning their search. But they found the ships' wreckage in the bay itself to be hopelessly scattered and buried in the mud. One immensely rich vessel lost off the harbor entrance proved to have sunk too deeply for salvage. They had to give up their search.

Back in the United States, a perceptive man named Clifford (Kip) Wagner had moved to Sebastian, in the isolated Indian River section of Florida, where he supported himself as a plastering contractor. Wagner, who had a taste for history, soon heard local treasure tales and saw some of the odd, misshapen, and encrusted coins found on the Sebastian beach. He learned that these were Spanish pieces of eight. Wagner bought a war-surplus Army mine detector and began to scour the beach after storms. There he discovered one of the Spanish salvage camps which had existed from 1715 to 1717. In 1951 he found his first silver coin; then, many others. By 1955 Kip Wagner was ready to go out into the ocean to find the source of the silver.

During the 1950s, Mel Fisher continued to expand his

commercial promotions in California, but his own emphasis began to shift from sport diving and spearfishing to the search for sunken treasure. With the best divers among his friends and scuba students, Mel formed a marine salvage club. Its members began to seek out and dive on known shipwrecks. Mel bought a fifty-five-foot diesel party boat on time payments of a thousand dollars per month; he christened it *Golden Doubloon,* although he had not yet seen a doubloon.

To help meet the monthly payments on the boat, Mel took out large parties for spearfishing, underwater photography, and shipwreck hunting. Soon Mel had some valuable professional help in his search for old wrecks. He met a man named Fay Feild.

Feild, an electronics expert, had also learned to dive in Florida. At first he was a cave diver, but changed his emphasis when his wife began the hobby of collecting the shells of the thorny oyster, *Spondylus americanus.* Since the rare shell was best found on sunken hulls, Feild invented a portable magnetometer to locate lost ships. After he was transferred to California, Fay Feild needed a steel-hulled boat from which to tow and calibrate his equipment. He consulted the Yellow Pages of the telephone directory and found the *Golden Doubloon.* Owner: Mel Fisher. As Fay describes his experience, "I called and asked Mel if he minded if I went along on one of his charters to test my magnetometer. He didn't mind at all, and wouldn't take any money for it; he even served me a cocktail when I came aboard. Well, everything went just fine, and I was invited back. Next time, when I arrived, I saw that he had the boat crowded full of people. He'd sold them all a dive on a virgin wreck—which I was supposed to provide. Well, we did find a wreck."

As a further test of Feild's magnetometer and to make a trial of another type of underwater metal detector mounted on a towing sled, the diving club next undertook an expedition to the Cortez Bank, an offshore shoal. It was rumored that a Spanish galleon had sunk there in

1717. Rupert Gates, an able, intense cartographer, went along on the trip; he was also a skilled mountain climber and gold diver. For four days the divers searched with magnetometer and the towed sled. When the detector being towed imploded at a depth of 110 feet, Mel had a narrow escape; the impact pulled off his face mask. Since, however, he had the presence of mind to keep the regulator in his mouth, he came to the surface without harm. Unfortunately, the iron content of the rocks in the shoal disturbed the electronic equipment; nothing was found. However, a film made during the expedition, *Highroad to Danger,* was successfully sold.

Next, Mel and his associates undertook a trip to Caribbean waters, chartering a boat in Yucatán to take them to the waters around Cozumel. Robert Marx, a young California diver, destined to become well known in marine archaeology and to play a major role in Mel's life, came along on the trip. At Dzibilchaltún, Mel dived in the murky *cenote* (sacrificial well) and found intact a Mayan vessel, which he presented to Dr. E. Wyllys Andrews of Tulane University, who was then excavating at the site. For his part, Bob Marx was struck with the potential of the waters of Yucatán; he vowed to return again to the area.

Silver Shoals, north of the Dominican Republic, was the next salvage goal of Mel's diving associates. There, together with many others, lay the shipwreck of a richly laden Spanish vessel lost in 1641. It had been the site of history's most successful treasure salvage operation, that of Sir William Phips in 1687, when divers using primitive diving bells raised tons of coins and silver ingots. Since twentieth-century treasure hunters suspected that Phips had left much silver behind on Silver Shoals, it had been the target of several modern expeditions. Mel had found a book by Ferris Coffman, called the *Treasure Atlas,* which showed hundreds of shipwrecks around the world, real and imaginary; among them was the Silver Shoals site. On the strength of this source, which was somewhat questionable because it was based on uneven data, and with the backing of twenty-five California investors, each of whom put up a thousand dollars, Mel organized another expedition.

The *Golden Doubloon* left San Pedro in June 1960, made its way down the west coast of Mexico, and passed through the Panama Canal. At Colón, engine trouble forced Mel to hire a crew of diesel mechanics. Among the men who came aboard was a stocky black Spanish-speaking Panamanian with an unlikely name: Demosthenes Molinar. Molinar was invariably cheerful, skillful, and industrious. In order to get around the name Demosthenes, everyone called him "Moe." Mel decided that he needed a diesel mechanic aboard the *Golden Doubloon,* so, as he says, "I stuck my head down into the engine room and asked Moe if he'd like to go treasure hunting. He said, 'Yeah, mon.' I told him that whatever his wages were, I'd double 'em. So he just stowed away in the boat, and when we got out to sea, we 'found' him."

Halfway across the open Caribbean to the Dominican Republic, a storm struck, and the *Golden Doubloon* began to leak seriously. When her bilge pumps malfunctioned, the boat began to settle and go down by the stern. Clinging to lifelines, Mel and Moe worked in the swirling water around the fantail and built a plywood shield to keep out the sea until the pumps could be repaired. Then the engines quit; fiberglass resin had been mistakenly put into them instead of lubricating oil; the would-be treasure hunters drifted around for several days, got the engines going, and put back into Panama for repairs.

On the Caribbean coast of Panama lies the old Spanish fleet terminus, Portobello. Off its shores, on a likely-looking reef, Mel found his first Spanish shipwreck. After the magnetometer pinpointed a wreck site below, Moe Molinar, now a full partner in the treasure venture, made his first dive. Choking from water in his snorkel, Moe came up to report that he had spied cannons below. Instantly Mel dived down and saw the guns, resting on a mound of ballast stones; he hastened to bring down a small water jet. The jet, which Mel had developed for gold hunting in the California Sierras, pumped a stream of water from its nozzle to burrow into underwater wreckage. It turned up old nails, Spanish pottery, and musket balls; no gold or silver. Disappointed, the salvors abandoned the place, not realizing that they had probably left valuable items buried below. They were as yet too inexperienced to realize that to excavate a shipwreck thoroughly might require months, even years, of effort.

In the San Blas Islands, the next stop, Mel entered the world of Hernando Cortés when he saw Indians dressed and decorated in gold. He recalls, "Breastplates, chains, bracelets, earrings—there was gold all over them. I was impressed. When I saw them, I felt like one of the conquistadores."

The expedition soon had to come to an end; it was time to go back to California, without even getting to dive at Silver Shoals. On the last day before entering the Canal again, north of Portobello, the divers suddenly came upon several old shipwrecks. Mel had read about the pirate Henry Morgan, who had stormed Panama in the seventeenth century, and was certain that the ships were his. Some of the artifacts found in the wrecks were shipped back, but when the adventurers returned home, Mel was deeply in debt. The twenty-five thousand dollars was gone, and Mel had run up another twenty-five thousand in costs; it took him almost a year to pay it all off.

From now on, Mel decided, he would try to accumulate enough money before an expedition to carry it through to the end. But it was hard to keep salvage costs under control. Treasure hunting, he had learned, was a rough game: exciting, but expensive.

II. Treasure Fever in Florida

In Florida, Kip Wagner had made real progress in his own search for Spanish treasure. He was able to correlate his beach coin finds with a map drawn by one Bernard Romans, who had surveyed the Florida coasts in 1774. Romans had written on the map opposite the Sebastian River: "Opposite this river perished the Admiral commanding the Plate Fleet of 1715." Wagner began to research the 1715 ships; with a friend, Dr. Kip Kelso, he located other books that described the shipwrecks. They later turned up further information from microfilmed Spanish documents in Saint Augustine libraries.

With Kelso and several other men who worked in the booming American space effort at Cape Canaveral, Kip Wagner organized a salvage group named Real 8. (They took their name from the eight-*real* Spanish silver peso coin.) Working weekends and holidays, the group found several offshore wreck sites. At one of these, in the summer of 1960, they found several wedges of silver. In that same year, Real 8 obtained from the state of Florida a 50-mile-long search contract, stretching from Sebastian Inlet south to Stuart. Although it was recognized that the state held legal jurisdiction over shipwrecks in Florida waters, the controls then exercised over salvors and the materials they had recovered were not as strict as they later became. Periodically, Real 8 had to turn artifacts they found over to university archaeologists and to the State Museum.

One chilly day in January 1961, near the northernmost of their wreck sites, close to the Spanish salvage camp Wagner had found on the beach, the divers uncovered a cache of several hundred silver coins; this was the first sizable treasure discovered in Florida in modern times. Later in the year, the Real 8 men recovered eighteenth-century Chinese porcelain, gold jewelry, and many more pieces of eight; excitement began to stir among the treasure-hunting fraternity from coast to coast.

In the winter of 1962, one of the Real 8 partners visited Mel Fisher at his Redondo Beach shop. Mel, who was about to leave California for another expedition to Silver Shoals, learned how Real 8 had used airlifts to move sand from their shipwrecks. In turn, Mel advised the Florida man of the electronic expertise his own group now possessed through Fay Feild's improved magnetometer.

The new Silver Shoals expedition was better financed and organized. Mel and Deo, Rupert Gates, Fay, Moe Molinar, and Walt Holzworth went along. By now, Deo Fisher was a fine diver in her own right; in 1959, before her third son, Kane, was born, Deo had broken the world's record for a woman's endurance dive by remaining underwater for more than fifty-seven hours. The newest recruit on the treasure team, Walt Holzworth, was a construction foreman whose interest in Spanish colonial coins had drawn him into treasure hunting. John Leeper, who owned a boatyard in the area, funded the expedition and furnished the boat: a 78-foot purse seiner named *Don Pedro.*

The searchers spent two months at Silver Shoals, and their magnetometer turned up a half-dozen shipwrecks; the best of these yielded four iron cannons, cannonballs, and ceramic plates. The group had not completed its work on the wreck sites when their funds ran out, but the trip had helped firm up their organization and a broader vision of what it could do.

Soon the salvors met with a new associate, Eric Schiff, to plan yet another Silver Shoals trip; they also hoped to seek out other sunken vessels in the Caribbean and to look for the riches of El Dorado in Colombia's Lake Guatavita. The men formed a legal partnership: Mel, Rupert, and Fay would contribute their equipment and experience; Moe Molinar would dive; and they were joined by Dick Williams, an expert welder and diesel mechanic from Texas. Walt Holzworth and Schiff would put up the necessary cash, together with Arnold McLean, a physicist from Colorado. Mel Fisher's team was complete.

This time, Mel stopped in to meet Kip Wagner on his way to Silver Shoals. Kip gave Mel a seventeenth-century map of the Phips salvage site and a narrative he had found about the work, written by Phips's doctor. Even with this help, the salvors found no bonanza at Silver Shoals. They found the rudder of the ship they had previously located, and brought up many encrusted artifacts, but found no treasure. Finally they had to conclude that they had discovered an armed merchantman and not the galleon of 1641. Back in California, the group disbanded. Schiff, who had sunk thirty thousand dollars in the venture, wanted out. Mel and the others felt completely free to go on to other underwater projects. They did not then know that they would hear again from Eric Schiff.

The remaining partners had now reached a crucial decision—they would become full-time treasure hunters. They would leave their regular jobs and gamble on golden success. The Californians depended upon their skill as superb divers and upon the accuracy of their search capability, built around Feild's magnetometer. They were as yet less skilled in uncovering buried shipwrecks, but had many technical skills. Their capabilities in historical research in 1963 were rudimentary.

A key factor in the future operations of the salvage group was to be the character of their leader, Mel Fisher. His willingness to experiment freely, his reckless optimism, his relentless persistence—these were possibly ideal qualities for a treasure hunter. Now the men had decided on the focus of their next enterprise: they had chosen to pull up stakes and move to Florida. The partners planned to work there for at least a year with Kip Wagner—to bring their own expertise to the salvage of the 1715 ships, and to help Real 8 in the several sites that they now had under contract. Mel wrote Kip that he had arranged to lease his business, sell his boat and his home, and move at once; the other men, except Fay Feild, did the same. Fay agreed to furnish his skills and his magnetometer as needed during the diving seasons in Florida.

In midsummer 1963, a small caravan of cars and rental trailers carried the treasure hunters east. They arrived, laden with hopes, at Fort Pierce on July 4, 1963. Something new had come into the world of Florida salvage.

The first impact of the new group on Florida was anything but thrilling. The salvors quickly realized that conditions in the Indian River area were quite different from anything they had seen before. The 1715 ships had struck reefs or sandbars close inshore along a thirty-mile stretch of deserted shoreline. The divers often had to work in the surge of the outer surf; in many seasons the water was made murky by storms. Their access to the wreck sites came only through swift-running inlets or directly out through the breakers.

Under their agreement with Real 8, the Californians had to support themselves for a year and provide for all their own expenses; anything they found would be divided fifty-fifty with Real 8—subject, of course, to the state's share at division. The salvors bought a battered boat and dubbed it the *Dee-Gee*; soon their compressor and diving equipment were installed aboard. At first the wives and children were settled in motels in Fort Pierce and Vero Beach; then the men bought or rented houses. Mel's family had continued to grow: Kane, now three years old, had been joined by Taffi, the only girl, now less than two. Both the children had their mother's bright red hair. At nine, Dirk had already learned to dive and hoped to join his father in the treasure hunt.

Real 8 continued to work their northernmost site, called

"the cabin wreck" for its location near a summer home on the beach. Kip Wagner assigned Mel's team to a 1715 site on the Fort Pierce north beach, where silver wedges had previously been found. There the newly arrived salvage group began their work. Obviously, since the wreck was near shore, it had been diligently salvaged by the Spaniards, but the modern salvors used the magnetometer and underwater metal detectors. Fay Feild had built a discriminating detector that could distinguish between ferrous and precious metals; this they used to examine the picked-over wreckage. One day Mel, scouring the bottom with the detector, got a strong reading from an object that seemed to be just an oblong stone. When brought to the surface and cleaned, the "stone" became a silver wedge: the first real treasure the group had found.

After the "wedge wreck" had yielded only a few coins and the wedge, Mel moved to another shipwreck several miles north, off Sand Point. There, in a sand pocket, they found fifteen hundred worn Spanish silver coins and two small two-*escudo* gold pieces. One of these coins—his first gold—Mel had set in a massive ring, which he proudly wore as a badge of his new profession. At Sand Point, Mel's excitement rose again when the metal detector pointed his way to a bronze ship's bell protruding from the sand. At first, in the turgid water, Mel had thought it to be that elusive goal of all treasure hunters: a bronze cannon. At last, under the threat of rough fall weather, after no further finds of consequence, the team left Sand Point.

Their first months in Florida had not brought great success to the divers from California. It was evident that their existing tools for moving sand were distressingly inadequate, but their worst trial was murky water. Even when the surface water was clear, their visibility on the bottom might be as little as a foot or two. Mel puzzled over the problem and thought of various engineering solutions for it; he had to bring clear water down to his divers. On a trip to California, he talked it over with Fay Feild. As

Fay tells it, "Mel sat in my living room and asked if we couldn't get clear water down to the bottom by ducting the propellers. I said, 'Certainly,' and sketched it right out."

The device, which Mel then built back in Florida, was called "the mailbox" because of its appearance. It directed prop wash from the boat's propellers downward through a deflector hinged on the transom. The salvors tried the new invention out on a shipwreck in fifty feet of water near the Fort Pierce inlet. Mel describes the results: "It was inky black and you couldn't see your finger in front of your mask. We turned the mailbox on slow and watched as it pushed a column of clear water right down to the bottom. We drifted down that column to the wreck, and the mailbox had made a huge bubble of clear water all around it; we could see the whole thing."

One of the divers then discovered something even more important. The mailbox blow had had another, unplanned effect: it had dug a wide crater six feet deep into the sand! The mailbox was not only the way to get clearer diving water but was the key to moving the vast quantities of sand that continually drifted over the 1715 shipwrecks.

In 1963 the Real 8 company had acquired the rights to another 1715 location, south of Fort Pierce, where gold coins had been found on the beach. The partner firms moved there to work together with the mailbox as the 1964 diving season began with the first calm water of summer. The magnetometer had pinpointed an iron cannon, around which the divers unearthed ballast stones and then a hundred silver coins. Then, on May 8, 1964, Moe Molinar found two disks of Spanish gold. Nearby, the salvors found the first gold coins located on the site. After a mailbox blow on May 24, dazed divers surfaced to report that the sea bottom was literally "paved with gold"! On that day, 1,033 gold coins of two, four, and eight *escudos* were recovered; all told, in that week, 2,700 were found.

The salvors' greatest day, however, came the next summer. Real 8 moved its boat out from the area where they had been working with Mel and arbitrarily put their mail-box down at a random spot. The result: bonanza! They brought up 1,128 gold coins in one day.

By the end of that season, in addition to the gold, the combined treasure teams had found many thousands of silver pieces of eight, a number of lovely, fragile, and sur-prisingly intact vessels of K'ang Hsi porcelain, and several rare royal gold coins. The magnetometer and the mailbox had helped open a vein of treasure, and the salvors had struck it rich.

The 1715 treasure worked its magic upon Florida, the nation, and the world. National publicity culminated in an article in *National Geographic* magazine in January 1965. The sheer beauty of the coins and artifacts and their dollar value—estimated at several millions—awoke ad-venturers everywhere. Treasure fever struck Florida. Hundreds of eager beach walkers, hoping to emulate Kip Wagner, bought metal detectors and stalked the shore-lines. Scores of treasure companies were formed. At one time in 1966, forty-seven of them petitioned the state for permits to seek shipwrecks around the peninsula and in the Florida Keys.

The golden discoveries of 1964 and 1965 drew treasure hunters to Florida like a magnet. Among these were Nor-man Scott, who had dived in the sacrificial wells of Yuca-tán and sought sunken ships off Jamaica, and Burt D. Webber, Jr., who had explored Pedro Bank in the Carib-bean with Art McKee in 1961. McKee continued to dive actively in the Keys, where he was joined by competitors Art Hartman, Tom Gurr, and Martin Meylach. A young pilot named Goin (Jack) Haskins had abandoned flying for treasure salvage and moved to Florida. Up in the In-dian River area, a number of challengers rose to contend with Kip Wagner and Mel; among these was a canny, forceful lady salvor, Jeanne DuRand.

The treasure hunters—the "brotherhood of the coast"—are a colorful and controversial fraternity. As could be expected in one of the last bastions of virtually unrestricted enterprise, the members are distinctly individuals. Although friendships have developed among some treasure hunters, they are often fierce competitors, sometimes hurling lurid charges at one another. By nature, salvors are secretive, jealously guarding their knowledge of sunken ships. One Fort Pierce applicant failed to get a state salvage contract because he would never put the location of his shipwreck into writing! Fay Feild tells of one such incident: "We got a big laugh out of it one time. We'd given up trying to keep the mailbox secret after we found it had been patented for Mississippi River dredging in 1876. If anybody had asked, we'd have gladly showed it to him. But this one guy hired a detective to spy on us and get drawings of it."

Since treasure hunters are often men of great drive and ego who are living out their fantasies, they may color their adventures highly, and tend to dramatize their finds in extravagant terms. Mel, now beginning to loom large in the treasure fraternity, possessed all these characteristics to excess. He was ready to gamble for higher stakes, to take more risks, and to exaggerate more than anyone. These qualities, taken together with his success, made him a natural target for other salvors' envy.

The 1715 finds also stirred strong reactions among historians, archaeologists, and government officials in Florida. At one point, state officials moved in to seize some of the 1715 treasure and to institute a more rigorous system of reporting finds and placing the materials in protective custody. Under the pressure of applications sent to Tallahassee, new policies toward salvors began to evolve. Deep differences of opinion then arose over the regulation of shipwreck salvage.

The academic community generally felt that the shipwrecks off Florida were unique, irreplaceable "time capsules" whose integrity should not be violated by treasure hunters. Their deepest wish was that there be no commercial salvage at all. This view was advanced by the energetic young state marine archaeologist, Carl Clausen, and his superior, Secretary of State Tom Adams. On the other hand, Governor Haydon Burns and several other Cabinet members wanted private enterprise to rule treasure hunting in Florida. At that time, the Florida Cabinet gave final approval to all shipwreck search and salvage contracts in state waters. Carl Clausen proposed a compromise in which large preserves would be set aside where no commercial salvors could go; eventually this was done.

After a moratorium on salvage contracts during which the new policies were hammered out, an antiquities law was passed and the State Department given a limited budget to supervise salvors. Only ten contracts were granted in 1966, which bitterly disappointed the private treasure hunters. They pointed out that only private enterprise could generate the great investment needed to seek out and salvage wreck sites. On balance, the compromises of 1966 left neither side satisfied. Some of the state authorities viewed salvors as somehow unclean and their work as necessarily totally destructive. For their part, some salvors vowed to get by stealth what they were denied by law. Widespread pirating of shipwreck sites began. For Mel Fisher, as a major client of the state, who expected to continue his work in Florida waters, it was necessary to submit to the regulations, surrender the materials he found to state inspectors, and then, at final division of the treasure, yield 25 percent to Florida as its legal share.

By now the men who had come together from California had become a Florida corporation, called Treasure Salvors. In the first exuberance of their 1715 triumphs, Mel and his associates planned to expand their operations, while continuing to work with Real 8 on several of the original Indian River sites. That work was furthered by Fay Feild's development of a second-generation, far more sensitive proton magnetometer. They put this tool to work in mapping systematically all the 1715 shipwrecks. This led to the discovery that iron materials found by the magnetometer could be correlated with the outline of the scattered sunken ship itself, often found lying over a mile or more of underwater distance. This in turn led to the greater exploitation of the "cabin wreck," and resulted in the detection of another 1715 ship off Riomar at Vero Beach. To open up the reef crevices in which the remains of the Riomar wreck were found, Mel devised the *Golddigger,* a barge fitted out with huge blower propellers mounted horizontally to excavate more fully. There at Riomar, a number of gold coins, some rings, and a lovely gold cross came to light.

Rupert Gates, Fay, and Mel also evolved a plan to position their salvage craft more accurately by means of location stakes ashore. This developed further into a system of shore markers with a vernier scale, from which cross bearings were more precise. Carl Clausen used Treasure Salvors' maps and the data gained from the new positioning systems when he wrote his monograph on the 1715 shipwrecks. Clausen's work was a key piece in modern marine archaeology: the first significant work on shallow-water shipwreck analysis in the Western Hemisphere.

The improved magnetometer itself became a focus of new enterprise: Treasure Salvors formed a subsidiary company to exploit and market it. In 1964 another opportunity presented itself when Mel Fisher met another remarkable man with a dream. This was Bob Moran, who had left Florida in 1962 to ferry his boat to the Dominican Republic to go treasure hunting there. When his craft sank in a storm off the coast of Cuba, Moran and his associates were arrested and then confined in one of Fidel Castro's prisons. During more than a month of imprisonment, Moran had to keep his mind occupied; he conceived and mentally "built" a Spanish galleon replica. It was his idea to build such a ship as a movable museum, and to travel with it and a treasure display along the U.S. East Coast. At last, Moran was released from jail and allowed to return home.

Bob Moran's idea and the treasure that Mel's divers had recovered seemed to go together naturally. Another new corporation, Treasure Ship, Inc., was founded, combining the interests of Moran (who became president), Treasure Salvors, and a group of Canadian investors. Mel and Bob flew to Europe and bought a wooden-hulled Swedish lumber ship for twenty-five thousand dollars. Rupert Gates sailed the ship back across the Atlantic, and the vessel went into a Fort Pierce dockyard to be reconverted into a sixteenth-century Spanish galleon. With Bob Moran's research and the services of a marine architect, the job was done in October 1967, and the ship stocked with treasure exhibits. The galleon was renamed the *Golden Doubloon.*

Although Mel Fisher continued to work the 1715 sites under the Real 8 agreement, relations between the two companies began to deteriorate in the late 1960s. The outward drive of Treasure Salvors alone would eventually have carried it beyond the Real 8 orbit, but events hastened the process. Misunderstandings arose after new contract arrangements were made between Treasure Salvors, Real 8, and the state of Florida. Real 8 testimony in an Internal Revenue Service matter later estranged some of the Treasure Salvors group. For their part, Real 8 members felt that Mel and his partners had not always kept them fully informed or given proper credit to Real 8. In December 1969, Real 8 filed suit against Treasure Salvors, asking the Circuit Court to clarify the contractual relations between the two firms. After this time, mutual operations gradually declined until Real 8's later bankruptcy, when the connections were dissolved.

The finding of treasure had not brought instant riches to Mel and his associates. Part of their financial problems were inherent in the nature of Florida treasure hunting. It was often many months after a shipwreck recovery before salvors got a division of materials with the state. Once they actually held the treasure in their hands, the salvors still faced a marketing dilemma. Some gold and silver coins and other valuables were distributed to partners, but the company feared individual price-cutting and the deadening effect upon the numismatic market if too many

1715 epoch coins appeared at any one time. In October 1964, in New Jersey, an auction of some of the treasure had been held; others followed. But only a small part of the treasure was sold.

What aggravated the financial woes of the company was that such a slow return from finds could not keep up with the day-to-day cost of operations. Salvage is expensive work, and the company suffered periodic money droughts. Something had to be done, and Mel resorted to bank loans to bridge the money gap. He describes the practice: "I borrowed a hundred thousand dollars from a Vero Beach bank and another hundred thousand from a bank in Fort Pierce and then sixty thousand from a Fort Lauderdale bank. They took Spanish coins as collateral, and then they'd loan us about sixty percent of the retail value of those coins. Some of those coins were up as collateral for as long as ten years. I finally borrowed a larger amount— I think two hundred and seventy-five thousand—from a bank in Tampa. I paid off the other loans and moved the treasure over there as collateral for the new loan."

Relief from one serious financial pressure came when Treasure Salvors obtained an Internal Revenue Service ruling that deferred federal income taxes on treasure until it was actually sold, but soon legal trouble threatened from an unexpected source. In February 1965 Eric Schiff had heard of the discoveries in Florida; he filed suit in California seeking a partner's share of the company's finds. After his first case was dismissed, Schiff filed another pleading in 1966. In 1968 the case moved into arbitration in California. There it languished and apparently died.

To avoid the money troubles that came with the discovery of treasure, Mel and the other men in Treasure Salvors could have quit their search and gone into other work. Then, eventually, they would have received a good return from their enterprise as salvaged items were slowly disposed of. Instead, they chose to remain on the treasure merry-go-round, attempting to market their previous finds and keep their operations going while they sought a bigger "hit," a richer galleon to bail them out for good. They did attract outside investors to help back some of their new expeditions, and did some commercial dredging and for-hire magnetometer surveys. This mitigated but did not solve their underlying financial problem.

But the impetus that sent Mel out to seek more treasure was not merely monetary; he was moved by a strong inward need to surpass, to excel. Soon after the 1715 publicity, Treasure Salvors moved out to look for other shipwrecks. To better utilize the winters when waters in the Indian River area were rough and cold, Mel obtained a state search contract for all of Monroe County, in which most of the Florida Keys lie.

The Treasure Salvors' team made a rapid magnetometer search of the middle Keys and had soon found more than forty shipwrecks. Although McKee, Meylach, and others had previously worked 1733 sites, Treasure Salvors not only made a more complete electronic analysis of those shipwrecks, but they also located several new ones. Using the Spanish archival map made after the 1733 disaster, Mel was able to name and to identify some of the sites he had found. Treasure Salvors worked some and farmed others out to different salvage firms. Perhaps the most valuable shipwreck, certainly the most controversial of these, was that of the 1733 ship *San Joseph y las Ánimas,* more popularly called the *San José.*

Mel turned the site of the *San José,* which was located outside the traditional Florida three-mile limit in the Atlantic, over to salvor Tom Gurr. Gurr then uncovered a well-preserved lower hull and salvaged many valuable coins and artifacts. At this point, Carl Clausen and Secretary of State Adams began to press for extension of the old Florida boundaries to the outer reefs. This would have included the *San José* in state waters. Pressure from the state, aided by a Coast Guard boarding party and a legal decision from a Key West judge, finally forced Gurr to yield his shipwreck to state control. The new Florida Constitution of 1968 featured the new state boundaries.

As more restrictive state policies on treasure search—the bonding of salvors, the keeping of an official state log including the recording and tagging of all items recovered, and the supervision of salvage operations by state agents—came into effect, Mel continued to apply regularly for new contracts. He worked these—in the name of Treasure Salvors or that of a new subsidiary corporation, Armada Research, Inc.—finished them, and moved on to apply for more. This rapid process irritated some officials in Tallahassee. Their procedures tended to move rather slowly in any case, and some of them were philosophically opposed to private salvage, anyway.

In their rapid progress across the area of the 1733 ship losses, Treasure Salvors had realized some valuable returns in treasure. The 1733 ships, however, had been largely salvaged by the Spaniards, and the "big hit" continued to elude the treasure hunters. Soon, however, Mel was off full-tilt on another pursuit. He had found a new goal, worthy of his best efforts. He had learned of a virtually unsalvaged Spanish galleon of immense value. Mel began the search for the *Atocha*.

Mel had heard of the 1622 galleons before he ever moved to Florida, but learned more during the years that followed. In 1960 John S. Potter, Jr., published his *Treasure Diver's Guide,* which soon became the Bible for every armchair or practicing treasure hunter. In Potter's book, Mel read about the Spanish galleons *Santa Margarita* and *Nuestra Señora de Atocha,* lost in the hurricane of September 5, 1622, in the Florida Keys. He learned that the *Atocha* had been carrying a cargo of coin and bar silver of huge value: a million pesos. When his main work in the 1715 area and his initial Keys explorations had ended, Mel committed himself unhesitatingly and wholeheartedly to the search for the 1622 ships.

The Florida Keys surround the extreme lower southeast peninsula like a protective shield; they stretch out more than 175 miles from lower Biscayne Bay to the Dry Tortu-

gas. The middle Keys, which extend northeast by southwest, center around the town of Islamorada on Upper Matecumbe Key. It was there that Mel began his search for
the *Atocha,* for everything he had seen said that the 1622
ships were lost "in the Keys of Matecumbe."

With his trained search team and a fast boat called the
Buccaneer, Mel set out to cover a vast area. It was an
open-water search, done with magnetometer and buoys;
any contacts found in the marked-off areas were dived
on and then "dusted" with the mailboxes to determine
their nature. As soon as the searchers determined that
the shipwrecks were not of the 1622 epoch, they moved
on. Finally they had covered an area blanketing the Matecumbe Keys and running north to central Key Largo,
and no sign of the *Atocha* or the *Santa Margarita* had
appeared.

Puzzled, Mel tried to get better research material on
the 1622 ships. He heard that a St. Louis treasure hunter
named Roy Volker had found a printed English narrative
that described the shipwrecks. He asked Volker to come
to see him at his Vero Beach office and bring the document. There they dickered over a price for the information. Mel says, "He wouldn't let me look at it. He'd read
a few words and then he'd wave it at me. He was teasing
me, so I suddenly jerked it out of his hands and started
running around and around my desk. He chased me, trying to get his document back."

Once Mel held the document, which was an old English
translation of the Spanish original, in his hands, he found
that it added little to his knowledge of the galleons' location. It stated that the ships were lost "in the place of
the *Cabeza de los Mártires* in Matecumbe." There was
that word *Matecumbe* again. Mel knew that *mártires*
meant "martyrs," a Spanish name for the Florida Keys.
(They had been so named by Juan Ponce de León because
the numerous small islands had seemed to resemble the
heads of struggling Christian martyrs.) Mel doggedly re-

turned and searched the Matecumbe area again, but still got no result.

Next, thinking that the *Atocha* might be found farther south, Mel moved his operations base to Marathon, thirty-five miles down the Keys. From there he could search the lower-central Keys; this time the work would be done from the air. Harold Williams, a skilled fixed-wing and helicopter pilot, brought an autogiro from his Fort Pierce airfield. With Fay Feild and his magnetometer aboard, Williams could cover the search area much more rapidly and effectively than by boat. But the autogiro and helicopter search came to an end; nothing had been found that remotely resembled the galleons lost in 1622.

Again Mel consulted the few Spanish charts that he had been able to obtain. One of them showed the *Cabeza,* or "Head," of the Martyrs to have been in the northern-most of the Florida Keys, up toward lower Biscayne Bay. Undaunted, Mel relocated his base again; this time he worked out of the plush Angler's Club on the northern tip of Key Largo. After the magnetometer had spoken to indicate a strong underwater contact, the Treasure Salvors' divers found a large galleon anchor and other materials from a Spanish colonial shipwreck. Again, however, the materials did not date back to the time of the *Atocha.*

Now Mel heard that Art McKee had somehow obtained further research on the 1622 galleons. McKee had copies of documents from the Archive of the Indies in Seville, Spain, including a précis of the manifest of the *Atocha* and the *Santa Margarita* and other data on the ship-wrecks' location. Late in 1969, Mel offered Art McKee a chance to invest in his search, contribute his research data, and receive an amount of stock in Treasure Salvors. The deal never went through, for Art was directly involved in a major effort to find the 1622 ships launched by one of Mel's competitors, Burt Webber.

In seemed, in 1969, that Burt Webber's outfit, Continental Explorations, had everything going for it, that it could hardly fail to find the *Atocha* and its missing sister ship. For almost four years Webber had prepared for his search. He began by sponsoring a research team in Seville. Webber's investigators examined those parts of the archive that usually contained shipwreck information and sent him a large amount of data; all of it pointed to the fact that the ships he sought had been lost in "the Keys of Matecumbe." Armed with this data, Burt Webber applied to the state for a search contract off Matecumbe. This was granted in July 1969.

To carry out his search, Burt Webber bought the 136-foot *Revenge* and equipped it with every kind of salvage gear then available. One of his associates in the venture was Kenneth Myers, president of an electronics firm, who brought a large, advanced Varian magnetometer to use in the search. Jack Haskins and Art McKee also joined Webber in the enterprise.

To Mel Fisher, ever the pragmatist, it seemed a dubious quest. He was, admittedly, always ready to believe in a fabulous galleon, but he knew that he had searched the whole area of Webber's lease and found no trace of the 1622 ships. Mel doubted, therefore, that Webber could succeed where he had failed. What he needed now was new research, a new lead, an edge over his rivals. He thought of me.

After spending my first working years as a city manager, I settled in Vero Beach with my family and began to teach history at the local community college. This reawakened an old interest of mine in the Spanish conquest of Florida, and in 1967 I returned to graduate school to study for a doctorate in Latin American history.

At the University of Florida, I learned to read older written scripts in the extensive microfilm collections of Spanish documents there. By September 1969 I had finished my course work and qualifying examinations and was ready to leave for Spain; there I was to carry out research among the documents in the Archive of the Indies in Seville for a dissertation on Florida's Spanish origins.

My wife, Dot, met Mel when he came into the Fort Pierce library looking for shipwreck information; I first met him briefly in 1964 through a treasure-hunting group of which I was a member. We came to know the Fishers better when both our families joined a new Methodist church being founded in Vero Beach. We were struck by the romantic aura that seemed to envelop the figure of Mel Fisher the adventurer, but we also came to know Mel and Deo as friends. On his part, Mel was interested to learn that I could read Spanish archival documents.

When Mel discovered that I would be going to Spain for a year to work in the archives there, he asked me to let him know of anything I might turn up on the 1622 shipwrecks, particularly any hard data on their location. I agreed to do so, and in mid-September we left for Seville.

As the 1969 treasure-diving season ended and the new year of 1970 came, no one had yet uncovered the 1622 shipwrecks. Now they had become Florida's new treasure magnet, drawing the volatile salvors into strong competition. Somewhere in the Florida Keys they lay, their riches awaiting the finder. Why had none of the eager searchers found them as yet?

III. The Archive of the Indies

The Archive of the Indies stands beside Seville's cathedral with its graceful Giralda Tower, not far from the Guadalquivir River. Inside the thick stone walls of the archive, up a wide, pink-marble staircase and past the lobby, there is room for thirty researchers at ornate tables in the readers' hall. Except for the faint whisper of turned pages and an occasional cough, the room is silent.

Few nations have preserved their written heritage as well as Spain. The Archive of the Indies, one of its most important repositories, contains the story of Castile's prodigious expansion into America and of its four hundred years of colonial rule there. Forty thousand bundles of carefully preserved and guarded documents—fifty million pages—await the researcher.

A historian learns his craft in archival research, and the Archive of the Indies is the necessary starting point for any serious worker in Spanish colonial history. After five months, by the late winter of 1970, I had become fairly well acquainted with the archive's organization and had made considerable headway on my dissertation topic. I had learned to read the documents rapidly as well as accurately, for gathering information on any particular man or event in the Archive of the Indies can easily involve scanning thousands of pages to glean one key sentence.

The language in which the Spanish documents are written has not changed significantly since colonial times.

Anyone fluent in modern Spanish can, by adding some older words to his vocabulary, understand the language of the sixteenth- and seventeenth-century documents. But the scripts and the age of the documents offer serious barriers to the reader.

Some of the pages display chains of joined, rounded letters, called *procesal,* which look like a frieze of Arabic characters above the arched doorway of a mosque. Only a practiced reader can pick Spanish words out of the endless curves of that writing. Other writing is Gothic in appearance, while countless pages feature an illegible cursive scrawl. Further, there is little punctuation in a Spanish archival document; one must read a continuous running text and learn to supply the missing starting and stopping points of sentences. The student must also become acquainted with scores of archaic abbreviations. Lastly, the documents are written by hand upon linen paper with an ink made from oak galls. Time and the elements have stained and faded some of them. Often, over the years, the ink has bled through from opposite pages, forcing the reader to try to follow a sentence through a tangle of crossed words. One whole section—the American accounts—was damaged long ago by fire, leaving many pages charred and brittle. Finally, many documents are riddled with wormholes.

In addition to my own work on Pedro Menéndez de Avilés, the Florida founder, I had also found some material on the *Atocha.* Buried among the fleet papers, I had discovered the totals of the cargoes lost in the 1622 shipwrecks: the papers stated that the *Atocha* had carried a million pesos' worth of treasure. Seeking relief from the seemingly endless legal cases that surrounded Menéndez's efforts in Florida, I had found a packet of pages written in a strange, almost Oriental script, with numbers written in cursive Roman figures. This was a listing of each shipper of cargo aboard the *Santa Margarita* and the *Nuestra Señora de Atocha.* For tax purposes, each treasure consignment was listed; I could see that the cargoes had included tons of copper, silver bars, pieces of eight, and a considerable amount of gold. I wrote Mel immediately to tell him that no significant location data had yet turned up.

After reading the galleons' lading summaries, I realized that I was getting closer to the historical ships, if not to their final resting place. The records, I saw, disclosed the very fabric of the Indies trade. As some names began to reappear in the documents, the impersonality of the shipwrecks began to disappear. As a human story, the history of the galleons' loss began to intrigue me.

One February morning I was told by a *portero* that I had visitors. When I passed through the purple doorway curtain from the readers' hall into the lobby, I was surprised to see Mel and Deo Fisher. After getting my letter, and on the spur of the moment, they had decided to come to Spain. After a few days of vacationing in Majorca, they had flown to Seville.

After we had talked awhile, I introduced the Fishers to Ángeles Flores Rodríguez, a skilled professional researcher who had previously worked for Mel. Now he retained her again, to seek out and send him copies of documents on the 1622 ships after I left for the United States in the spring. As he prepared to leave, Mel told me that none of the searchers in Florida had yet found either of the sunken ships. He encouraged me to keep looking for any documents that might reveal their location.

When Mel and Deo left Seville, I returned to my daily sessions at the archive, seeking material on Menéndez's Florida expenses among the colonial accounting papers. One morning, ten days after the Fishers' visit, I was reading an index to the Cuban accounts. As my eyes ran quickly down the page, I suddenly spied the numbers "1622." The entry read: "Accounts of Francisco Núñez Melián, of what he salvaged from the galleon *Margarita* . . . in the Keys of Matecumbe, coast of Florida." It was an audit of the salvage of the *Santa Margarita*! My heart beating rapidly, I returned to my table and speedily returned the bundle I had been studying to the main desk, with a call slip bearing the number of the salvage account: *Contaduría* 1, 112.

In a few minutes, a *portero* dropped a packet, tied with faded pink ribbon, on the table. It seemed to take hours to untie the ribbon, knotted through a hole in the upper left corner of the documents. When finally the bundle lay open on the table, I began feverishly to scan the pages. The audit was rich in detail, and it was plain that Melián had salvaged the *Santa Margarita* for more than four years, recovering many coins and silver bars. As I turned toward the end of the bundle, I saw how worms had eaten the last pages. At the very end, the auditor's final certificate was a perforated tissue of holes. Reading the text was difficult because of the wormholes, but my eyes followed the words, seeing the familiar phrase *"Cayos de Matecumbe"*—the "Keys of Matecumbe"—but then something new. Melián, it stated, had found the shipwreck in the *"Cayos del Marqués."* Translated, this meant the "Keys of the Marquis." Carefully retracing my way through the documents, in two hours I had found the same phrase in four other places.

It was a puzzling mystery. That night, I sought to sum up the evidence and reconcile the apparently contradictory locations of the shipwrecks in the documents. Most of the accounts had stated that the 1622 galleons had been sunk in the "Keys of Matecumbe," while several had added the words *"Cabeza de los Mártires."* Now—a new element—the "Keys of the Marquis." This seemed to point to the 1622 fleet commander, the Marquis of Cadereita. Since I had learned that the Marquis had been personally in the Keys after the shipwrecks, I guessed that this island, wherever it was, might have been named after him. Where did the island lie today?

Fortunately, the Archive of the Indies has a fine map collection. When I had a seventeenth-century map of Florida laid out before me, I could see that the islands called "Tortugas" on the map were the Dry Tortugas of today.

The next island group to their east were named "Marquéz" on the old map; on another, of the eighteenth century, that atoll was named with the very words *"Cayos del Marquéz."* It referred, I could see, to the Marquesas Keys of modern charts.

Now it was clear that at the time of the shipwrecks, the term "Matecumbe" was generic and referred to all the island Keys except the Tortuga group. In their research, Mel, Burt Webber, Bob Marx, and the rest had concentrated on documents written at the time of the fleet disaster or shortly thereafter. However, as a result of the first salvage operations, one of the "Matecumbes" had been renamed, but only documents generated after that time bore the new name, "Marquéz." Even more misleading, other Keys had over the years also been renamed until only two now carry the original group designation. The modern salvors, seeing everywhere the name "Matecumbe," had leaped to the conclusion that the 1622 shipwrecks were near the modern Matecumbe Keys. Actually, they had been wrong by more than a hundred miles.

During the process of reasoning out the missing galleons' location, I sent Mel Fisher a series of letters; Norman Johnson, Treasure Salvors' research director, mailed me modern charts to facilitate the comparisons. In April 1970, I sent Mel and Norman my conclusions: the 1622 shipwrecks had occurred over a wide front from Loggerhead Key in the Dry Tortugas eastward to Sand Key near Key West. The *Atocha* and the *Santa Margarita* should be found somewhere in the vicinity of the Marquesas Keys. This was as close a location as I could give.

But Mel had already anticipated the conclusion. In March he had applied for a new state search area west of the Marquesas. He also dropped his other state contracts. As always, he was sure of his instincts, which told him that this location was right. Willing to put all his money on one throw, he prepared to move his operations base to Key West and to mount a massive effort from there. When the strong spring winds ended in the Keys and the new diving season began, Fisher would be in place and ready to go. Surely now the *Atocha* was within his grasp.

Meanwhile, I prepared to leave Seville. I had continued to gather documents about the 1622 ships, and Señora Flores had continued accumulating 1622 material as well. In June, I returned to my Vero Beach home and found a packet of transcriptions awaiting me. I sat at my desk to analyze the shipwreck data, hoping to find a closer location for the galleons by reading the transcripts and microfilm from the Archive of the Indies. But I found it difficult to concentrate on the pragmatic task of narrowing down the *Atocha*'s latitude and longitude. My work on Spanish history had been too intense the past several years to be put aside all at once. And the documents unfolded to me not only a location but a panorama that expanded my understanding of Spain's past. Researching the loss of the *Atocha* had become for me a doorway into one of Spain's great moments of crisis.

Spain's new King, crowned Philip IV in 1621, had inherited the world's greatest empire. Since 1580, Castile had controlled Portugal and, through her, vast possessions in Brazil, Africa, and Asia. In Europe, Philip's lands swept in a strategic arc from the North Sea to the heel of the Italian boot; his Mediterranean dominions included Sicily, Sardinia, the Balearic Islands, and several North African strongpoints. Across the Atlantic, the lands the conquistadores had won for Spain were the envy of the world. From the silver hill of Potosí, from the mines of Guanajuato and the New Granada goldfields, a rich stream of treasure flowed into Iberia. In Asiatic waters, the Spanish Philippines served to channel the Orient's riches to Acapulco, and thence to Europe.

Thus the sixteen-year-old King had an immensely valuable but widely scattered inheritance. Defending these far-flung territories and the Roman Catholic religion were Spain's two main aims. In formulating and carrying out those purposes, the new King's able, aggressive grandfather, Philip II, had begun a long war with his breakaway Dutch provinces. He had interfered openly in the internal wars in France and had launched the Grand Armada of 1588 against England. He had also exhausted his realm, which by 1600 staggered under a debt of a hundred million ducats.

After the death of Philip II, Spain took a badly needed breathing spell, signing peace treaties with France and England and arranging a twelve-year truce with the Dutch. Unfortunately, the peace in Europe was not destined to last for long.

It was religion, and loyalty to fellow Hapsburgs, that drew Spain back into costly war. Holy Roman Emperor Ferdinand II had vowed to restore Catholicism to all the German states, swearing to defeat the Protestants and taking as his motto "better a desert than a country full of heretics." In 1618, when he moved to counter the Protestant rebels in Bohemia, Ferdinand began the terrible struggle that would be known as the Thirty Years War. Spain entered the fray, sending twenty-five thousand Spanish troops into Germany. By 1621 the Catholic cause was progressing well, but the expenses of the war were mounting daily.

Spain's troubles were multiplied by the ending of the Dutch truce. By 1621 Dutch seafarers had expanded from their small European base into an incredible worldwide enterprise of trade and war. They had taken control of the Indian Ocean, attacked Ceylon, built a trading station in Java, and placed Manila under blockade. The Dutch had even more aggressive designs against the Spanish-Portuguese empire: they hoped to seize both Brazil and Angola and take over the profitable trade in African slaves. But their most cherished dream was to plant bases in the Spanish Caribbean and pull off the ultimate seventeenth-century coup—the seizure of a whole Spanish treasure fleet.

Within Spain, Church and military leaders, the young king and many nobles—those who sought above all else the continued grandeur of Castile—opposed the renewal of the Dutch truce. In April 1621, therefore, formal warfare with the Dutch began. Already deeply embroiled in Germany, Spain had now to face a hard and dedicated enemy, powerful on land and at sea.

On the surface at least, Spain, the greatest world power, seemed well able to meet her challengers. Her army—the famed *tercios* from Italy, Flanders, and Spain—was the finest force in Europe. Her maritime resources were still great, and provided a marine lifeline through which bullion was continually funneled to back Spanish policies around the globe. Culturally, Spanish artists, writers, and playwrights were at the peak of their Golden Age flowering. In spite of the forebodings of some Spaniards, others felt that God had ordained the eternal prosperity of Castile. Even if disaster should befall the Spanish Indies, they felt that "the Lord would surely send us another Potosí."

However, Spain's power rested upon shaky foundations. In part, her strength was an illusion, due to the momentary weakness and disunion of her enemies, including France and England. That illusion could one day vanish. But Spain's worst weaknesses were internal, and they were largely social and economic.

The Spanish court, brilliant in its display and ostentation, was improvident in its spending. The nobility made up only a small fraction of the population but enjoyed virtually all the offices, civil and military, at home and overseas. Where the aristocracy was exempt from taxation, those least able to pay—the peasantry of Castile—bore the brunt of the tax burden. There was even a crown tax upon wheat, which made dear the necessary daily bread. While the court at Madrid shone with finery, the cities of Spain filled with unemployed vagabonds, travelers in country districts had to beware of highwaymen, and Castilian villages declined in population. The country's lopsided social structure ensured that the wealth of the Indies never trickled very far down; in fact, much of the New World bullion went directly into foreign hands in return for the luxuries dear to the nobility. And the Spanish crown did not use its American revenues for public investment. The truth was that the Spanish crown was bankrupt.

The King's European and Indies revenues were never enough; the costs of war and glory, and of wasteful display, ran up a perpetual deficit. For unpaid royal debts, foreign moneylenders held effective first mortgages on all the King's income. Banking firms such as the Fuggers of Augsburg kept representatives in Seville to claim first rights on the incoming silver from Mexico and Peru.

Each year's Indies treasure came, therefore, like a cool drink to a fevered man. It was urgently needed, not to balance accounts for once and for all, but merely to keep one jump ahead of the most pressing needs. As long as it flowed in, the silver deferred the need to face up to hard facts, to take the fiscal measures that would bring sanity out of chaos. The King's Indies treasure came from many sources, but by far the most important single source was the silver mines at Potosí.

For over seventy-five years these mines on the high plateau of upper Peru had yielded great riches. By 1622 more than three hundred million pesos' worth had been drawn from that great mountain of silver. Now forty thousand Spaniards lived at Potosí, drawn irresistibly by the lure of silver. In the isolated city, life was recklessly gay and costly, fed by the great wealth that circulated through Potosí each year.

All the wealth and display of Potosí—and all that its silver meant to Spain—rested on the backs of forced labor. From dawn to dusk, thirteen thousand Indians toiled in poorly lit, ill-ventilated shafts, digging silver ore from the heart of the mountain. They were paid two and a half *reales* a day for their work, but had no choice as to whether or not they would work. Other Indians hauled the ore to grinding mills, and from there to refining areas, using thousands of llamas as beasts of burden. Indian laborers then treated the pulverized ore with a mixture of brine and mercury. This proved deadly work for many Indians, who sickened and died from contact with the lethal mercury. It produced, however, a fine silver, more than 99 percent pure.

A few years before 1622, an idealistic judge in the local court had attempted to put an end to forced Indian service. As if with one voice, the dignitaries of upper Peru—silver merchants, Church prelates, and government officials—had risen in protest. Their views had prevailed, and Indians continued to toil and die at Potosí for the glory of Spain.

Each year there came from Potosí a flood of ingots and crudely stamped coins—a silver torrent that washed through South America, reached Mexico and the Caribbean, and was felt even in the Orient. Carried to Spain by the annual fleets, the silver pulsed into Europe to add to inflation there. Fraud and corruption—counterfeiting, short-weighting, bribery, and smuggling—were widespread in Potosí. Still, the king collected vast sums from his *quinto*, or the royal fifth, of all bullion minted and cast.

To the Spanish king, beset by powerful creditors and at war on several fronts, the Potosí silver was doubly important by 1621. Philip IV and his ministers knew how poorly prepared Spain was for the underwriting of a hard and lengthy struggle. If the flow of silver carried by the fleets should ever slacken . . .

One of the most viable and important sectors of the Castilian economy was that of the Indies trade. After the discovery of the Americas, Spanish merchants had built a marine bridge to the New World, following a regularly traveled route known as the *Carrera de Indias*. At the great Andalusian city of Seville the merchants' guild established their monopoly on American trade, forming a community of interests with the Royal House of Trade there. Private profits and royal revenues flowed thereafter from the Indies, and Spanish ships also carried eastward the varied wonders of America: exquisite Aztec feather headdresses, Atahualpa's gold, the blessings of corn and the potato, the curse of syphilis.

Even though many ships were lost to storm or pirate attack, the Indies trade was immensely profitable. To protect it, the crown required by the mid-sixteenth century that ships sail in escorted convoy. Eventually, the convoys became regularly scheduled fleets. One of these sailed from Veracruz with silver, dyestuffs, and spices from Mexico, together with the silks, gold, and porcelain from the Manila galleon route. Since it came from the Viceroyalty of New Spain, this became known as the New Spain fleet.

From the South American mainland came the *Tierra Firme* (mainland) Fleet, bearing the riches of Peru and New Granada. Smaller, single ships that had gathered cargoes around the rim of the Caribbean and a flotilla from Honduras also sailed to join the convoy at Havana and voyage homeward in relative safety.

Armed convoy escorts were provided to guard the fleets; at least one lead ship—the *capitana*—and an escort to bring up the rear—an *almiranta*—sailed with each major fleet. At first, the escort ships were private vessels chartered by the crown. Philip II first organized a separate Royal Armada, and the stresses of the early seventeenth century had caused a revival of the idea. A Guard Fleet owned and operated in the royal interest provided protection for merchants and king alike, but it was paid for by private enterprise through a tax levied on Indies cargoes, known as the *avería*. The tax payments furnished the money to lease or buy ships, employ soldiers and sailors, and purchase the necessary supplies for their long sea voyage.

Defense of the fleets was a strangely mixed enterprise, for the merchants who shipped the goods aboard paid for their own protection and also served often as the taxfarmers who managed the *avería* in the king's name. Thus merchants were pulled both ways: they wanted convoy escorts strong enough to bring their cargoes through in safety, but they were also anxious to keep their tax burden low. After the Dutch truce in 1609, the number of guard galleons had been cut from nine to five.

The intimate mutual involvement of Spanish kings and the merchants in the Indies trade led to a "see-no-evil" attitude about the widespread smuggling. When wholesale fraud was found in the taxes paid for the 1598 fleet, for example, merchants paid the crown 150,000 ducats outright, and nothing more was said. By 1621 merchants and tax collectors had reached a mutual standoff. Royal officials agreed that they would not open any chests or bales to inspect the contents, but would accept the "sworn statements" of shippers. Taxes were then levied on the basis of the merchants' affidavits.

It was clear, however, that rising taxes on the Indies trade were driving many goods outside official channels to avoid even the lax administration of customs that prevailed. At the Portobello fair in 1620, the streets had been piled high with bullion and the products of Europe, but taxes had fallen to a new low. In spite of the heavy penalty for smuggling—two hundred lashes and ten years chained to an oar in the Spanish galleys—there was more customs fraud than ever.

As Spain approached her supreme test in the 1620s, the vital link with the New World silver was still intact, but everything depended upon keeping open the sea passages to America. In serious question, however, was the economic ability of the Indies merchants to continue to underwrite the costs of defense, particularly if a long war were to develop at sea. Could the system of fleets stand such a test?

In 1616 *avería* officials contracted with Captain Alonso Ferrera to build four 500-ton guard galleons in his Havana shipyard. The contractor was to have the vessels completed by July 1619. The new guard galleons were to be 110 feet in overall length, 33 feet wide, and draw 14 feet of water. They would carry square sails on fore- and main-masts and have a lateen mizzen; the ships would each set a spritsail on a massive 75-foot bowsprit. The after part of each galleon's hull was to be crowned by a towering sterncastle. As the ultimate weapons system of their day, the ships would mount twenty to twenty-four bronze cannons, most of them sited on the gun deck, one level down from the weather deck. Each ship was to come furnished with five large anchors and one smaller one, a launch, and a full set of sails and rigging.

As soon as his contract was signed, Ferrera sent to Vizcaya for anchors and fastenings, to Flanders and to Germany for spars and rigging lines, and to the House of Trade in Seville for the bronze guns, but the Havana shipbuilder did not meet his deadline. Although he turned over the first three galleons to fleet officials in Havana in August 1619, it was a full year later, on August 16, 1620, when Ferrera gave over possession of the last ship to *averia* deputies.

The fourth galleon bore, like most Spanish ships, a holy name. This ship had been christened with a particularly important name: *Nuestra Señora de Atocha*—"Our Lady of Atocha." It honored the Virgin of a great Madrid shrine, whose image had become vital to Castile. The shrine was hung with the banners of medieval armies victorious in the cause of king and Church. The kings and queens of Spain had come for many years to do weekly homage there. The new ship carried a small replica of the image of Our Lady of Atocha and bore a painted depiction of the Virgin high on her sterncastle. No better way could be devised to bring good fortune to a ship.

The new vessel's name seemed, however, to bring her little luck on her first voyage. After leaving Havana for Spain, the *Atocha* had not gone far up the Bahama Channel before returning, disabled by a shattered mainmast. Angry fleet officials charged Ferrera with using inferior materials; he provided a new mast, and the *Atocha* sailed again. Late in 1620 the galleon finally arrived at Sanlúcar, the Guadalquivir port of Seville. Unfortunately, more troubles had developed on the homeward journey; serious leaks had opened up around the ship's bow, and more repairs were needed before she could join the fleet. The maiden voyage of *Nuestra Señora de Atocha* had not been an auspicious one.

Reflecting the mood of growing international tension, the new *avería* contract provided for an expanded force of eight Guard Fleet galleons, three smaller escorts, and two courier ships. The *avería* money had also to pay for the New Spain and Honduras ships, and went to enlist and supply a force of 2,550 sailors and soldiers to man the fleets. By the last days of 1621 the work of assembling the next year's fleet was well under way. The officials had bought a fine, stout new ship, the *Santa Margarita,* from its Cádiz owners for fleet reinforcement, and arms and supplies were being loaded aboard the galleons in Sanlúcar harbor.

Aboard the *Atocha,* officers and crew were busy with the thousand details of preparing for sea. As the crown's weapon against its enemies, the galleon had been armed: the king's artillery master had inventoried her twenty bronze cannons, and cases and barrels of muskets, pikes, powder, and shot had been stored in her armory orlop below. To defend the ship and to mount a force for boarding any enemy vessel bold enough to attack the fleet, the *Atocha* would carry an entire infantry company; the men were still ashore, but their commander, Captain Bartolomé García de Nodal, was supervising the loading of arms. García de Nodal was a notable soldier and explorer; three years before, he had led a force of caravels to discover a new channel near the Straits of Magellan. The Captain was aided by his Sergeant and by the youngest member of his troop, the thirteen-year-old flag-bearer, Jaime de Aranda.

Another principal officer of the galleon, silvermaster Jacove de Vreder, was busily occupied with the ship's quartermaster in registering aboard and securing below the royal and commercial cargoes for the voyage outbound to the Indies. In the main hold below the gun deck, stacked pipes of Andalusian wine were stored with bales of fine Flemish cloth and ceramic jars of olive oil. For the king, and for the refining of the Indies silver, three hundred heavy cases of mercury from the royal mines at Almadén had been loaded aboard. The last cargoes to come swaying down the main hatch were supplies for the voyage: biscuit, salt pork, garbanzos, kidney beans, vinegar, oil, and honey.

Sailors were busy readying the largest and finest cabin aboard, located high in the sterncastle, for the official who would be the last to come aboard. *Atocha* had been designated *almiranta*; she had been posted to guard the rear of the *Tierra Firme* ships, and Vice-Admiral Don Pedro de Pasquier, *caballero* of the Order of Calatrava, would make the Indies journey with the ship. Soon, all would be in readiness, and *Nuestra Señora de Atocha* could take her place on the all-important voyage of 1622.

From Madrid as well as from Seville, anxious eyes watched the fleet preparations. During 1621, Italian bankers in Seville had advanced the crown a substantial sum in anticipation of the coming of the next year's treasure. The Fuggers' agent also waited, with little patience, for the monies due his masters. In December 1621, Philip IV received some good news and some bad news. His counselors told him: "The fleet from the Indies, bearing the silver, had arrived safely only by a miracle—the sea being so full of enemies. Even with that, there is not enough money in the treasury even for the most pressing needs. The enemies of Spain's greatness are many, and the forces needed to defend her are comparably large."

The coming of the 1621 silver temporarily satisfied the king's creditors, and Spaniards were hopeful for the new year. They knew only too well, though, that their prosperity, even their survival, might depend upon the successful passage of the coming year's fleets.

Thus far had the documents from the Archive of the Indies led me. They had made it possible for me to live at least momentarily in the seventeenth century, to feel to a degree the mood of the times. I could begin to grasp some of the motives that drove the men who prepared the ships for sailing with the 1622 fleet. Now the letters, accounts, and reports from the archive—written in incredible detail—made it possible for me to reconstruct the *Atocha*'s last voyage.

IV. No Mercy in the Wind

> . . . the passengers, when it was
> apparant they could not escape,
> saw as little mercy in the Sea,
> as they had endured in the Winde.
>
> —English account, 1623

Jacove de Vreder, silvermaster on the galleon *Nuestra Señora de Atocha,* was thankful for the scant breeze that stirred the surface of Portobello harbor. It eased the mid-July heat, even though it also carried to the ship the rotten-egg smell of mangrove from the nearby marsh. To protect de Vreder from the sun, the sailors had rigged a canvas awning over the quarterdeck table where he sat with the quartermaster, Felipe Martín. The silvermaster had spent the morning entering cargo in the *Atocha*'s homebound manifest, and just now welcomed a momentary halt in the steady parade of boats along the galleon's starboard rail.

The *Tierra Firme* Fleet had left Spain on March 23, traversed the Atlantic, and made its first American landfall at the high green island of Dominica. From there the ships had sailed six days through the Caribbean before sighting the snows on the high Venezuelan peaks. At that point, the little ship *Buen Jesús* was detached for its voyage to Maracaibo and Santa Marta. The fleet had stopped at Cartagena to unload a part of the ships' ladings. At last, on May 24, the *capitana* had led the way into the anchorage at Portobello.

For more than a month, lighters had slowly ferried ashore the rest of the fleet's cargoes—Andalusian wine, ironwork from Vizcaya, books, fine cloth, and royal mercury. The goods were stockpiled in warehouses or, as space ran out, stored in canvas enclosures on the town plaza to await the opening of the great annual *Tierra Firme* fair. Portobello seemed, in truth, a poor choice of location for such an event: a small place whose anchorage ended to the east in mud flats and a mangrove shoreline—a prime breeding ground for fevers. But for a few weeks each year, Portobello became the nexus where European goods met the bullion and other products of South America. Briefly, during the fair, the nondescript, unhealthful port was transformed into a metropolis.

The first step in Portobello's metamorphosis occurred on July 1. On that day a cannon salute, answered by Fort San Felipe, awoke the sleeping harbor. Then, one by one, a parade of ships under full sail rounded the point. The remaining four galleons of the Guard Fleet—left behind in Spain four months before—dropped anchor off the town. After that, things happened quickly, for Don Lope Díaz de Armendariz, Marquis of Cadereita, His Majesty's Captain-General of the Guard Fleet, had arrived to put an end to lethargy.

That same day, in Government House at Portobello, the Marquis met in *junta* with *Tierra firme* Fleet Admiral Juan de Lara Moran, Vice-Admiral Don Pedro de Pasquier from the *Atocha,* and all the military captains and pilots of the combined fleets. The Royal Governor at Portobello also joined the meeting. When Cadereita discovered that neither the crown treasure nor the merchants' goods and money had yet arrived from the city of Panama across the isthmus, he was enraged. He immediately interrupted the meeting to send a courier riding with the peremptory order that the president of Panama send the silver at once. The Marquis knew that the timing of the fleet cycle had already been seriously disrupted by delays in sailing from

Spain. Any further delay could prove fatal to the home-bound fleets, for it might send them through the Bahama Passage during the hurricane season.

Next, the *junta* pondered the problems of defense. They learned that a Dutch force had established a base at the Araya salt pans in the eastern Caribbean, and that thirty-six ships from there had recently been sighted off Cartagena. To strengthen his fleet, the Marquis ordered that a private galleon in the harbor, *Nuestra Señora del Rosario,* be seized for crown service as an added silver galleon. The ship, the second in the fleet by that name, belonged to Captain Gaspar de Vargas, an experienced mariner who also commanded an infantry company in the Guard Fleet.

Two days later, a train of a hundred heavily laden mules straggled into Portobello. For the next week, mule trains continued to arrive over the fifty-mile trail from the city of Panama. They carried the treasures of the Viceroyalty of Peru: thousands of silver ingots and millions of silver coins. Most of the coins—the harvest of trade and government—came from Potosí, but some were from the old Lima mint and some had come from as far away as the isolated kingdom of Chile. In other loads came Peru bark for fever, as well as rings, brooches, and other fine jewelry made by the artisans of Lima and Cuzco. As valuables continued to pour into Portobello, they were piled helter-skelter on the town square, where chests, bales, and boxes were cheek by jowl with piles of stacked silver ingots. Now the Portobello fair could properly begin, and the crowded town became a commercial madhouse.

In recent years, the trade had markedly changed. Formerly, mainly necessities had come from Europe for the fair. Now, in keeping with Spain's new taste for luxury, many higher-priced items were featured: costly embroidery and brocades, cloth-of-gold. In the first two weeks, for cash or credit, more than four million pesos' worth of goods were sold.

With thousands—soldiers, sailors, nobles, traders, and

clergymen—in the town, all bidding for food, lodging, and entertainment, prices climbed to manic levels. The heat, overcrowding, and poor sanitation in Portobello soon resulted in rampant disease: dysentery spread from the town and ran quickly through the ships' crews. Malaria brought its chills and fever to hundreds, and there was a whispered rumor of *viruela*—smallpox. During the fair's second week, alone, more than two hundred succumbed to disease. The *Atocha*'s crew began to think that theirs might, after all, be a lucky ship; only a boy and two soldiers died.

In haste to leave the noisome place, fleet officials turned over the stockpiled mercury to the king's agents in Portobello: almost 250 tons, sent to refine next year's silver. The royal officials of Portobello then released the royal revenues that had come from Peru. Left unspoken was the knowledge that all at the fair shared—that many of the European goods that had been sold at the market had evaded proper taxation in Spain and that, as always, the ships would eventually return laden with hidden contraband bullion.

Silvermaster de Vreder was called back to attention by a shout from a barge making fast on the *Atocha*'s starboard side. As the craft settled alongside, the notary picked up his quill pen and prepared to fill the next manifest page. First aboard was Lorenzo de Arriola, an important Potosí merchant, followed by four stevedores bearing his luggage. Arriola, who was returning to Spain as a passenger on the *Atocha,* was also shipping sixty silver bars—averaging sixty-five pounds in weight—on the galleon. Hedging somewhat against the risks of the sea, the merchant had also registered twenty ingots on the Marquis's *capitana* and ten more on the *capitana* of the *Tierra Firme* Fleet. But he had entrusted his person and the bulk of his silver to the *Nuestra Señora de Atocha.*

Lorenzo de Arriola formally committed his treasure to the silvermaster. The formalities were lengthy, for the manifest served both as bill of lading and as a report for taxation in Spain. Soon page after page was covered with the notary's scrawled *procesal* hand; his pen scratched as he recorded the numbers stamped into the surface of each silver bar: its weight, serial number, and silver fineness. In the manifest margin, the notary drew Arriola's mark—famous in the Indies—a joined *A* and *R* with a small diamond above. This was the mark that was cut into each ingot and burned into the wood of each shipping chest.

At the end of the manifest, the parties agreed that de Vreder would turn the silver over to Arriola in Seville when the taxes and sea freight due were paid. This of course would happen, the manifest then recited piously, "if God brings the ship safely to Spain."

When the completed manifest had been signed and witnessed, Arriola bent briefly to whisper into de Vreder's ear. At a nod from the silvermaster, the merchant passed him a small leather sack. In return, he received a scrawled receipt in de Vreder's own hand. Nothing more had been entered in the manifest, and the notary had seemed not to notice. The silvermaster had just taken a shipment "in confidence." The sack would be stored in the big chest in his cabin, but neither the king nor his tax officials would be any the wiser.

Many of the chests coming aboard the *Atocha,* however, were the property of Philip IV. Thousands upon thousands of pesos of royal revenues came across the gangway and were locked below in the silver storeroom. There were many coins from the sale of papal indulgences in Peru and Panama; thousands more from fines and crown sales taxes from the proud viceregal city of Lima. In accordance with the royal settlement with the heirs of Christopher Columbus, 21,323 pieces of eight were shipped on the *Atocha* to pay his descendant, the Duke of Veragua. Ten thousand pesos were earmarked as a royal pension for that important grandee, the Duke of Alba. It took almost a whole day to load and record another massive consignment of the king's silver. It was part of the *quinto* from

Potosí. The *Atocha*'s share came to 133 silver bars in thirty-four chests, each marked with the red crown of Philip IV. If the *Atocha* reached Spain safely, this shipment alone would enrich the king by more than four tons of silver.

Day after day, treasure passed across the silvermaster's table and into the *Atocha*'s hold: a leather sack with 828 pieces of eight for María de Aguirre, a widow of Seville; one Father Linero sent 691 pesos to the heirs of Ana del Bado; a Spaniard in the little Peruvian town of Guamanga sent three silver bars to establish a priest's living in his home city of Aleucho in Spain. Thus into the pages of the *Atocha*'s manifest flowed the record of Spain's life in the Indies: private savings and royal extravagance, swollen profits and pious gifts, the fruits of injustice and the hope of Heaven.

When the fair had ended and the last cargoes were aboard ship in Portobello, the vessels took on water and last-minute supplies and prepared to sail. Now a number of passengers were ferried out to the *Atocha*. Forty-eight had chosen to return to Spain aboard the *almiranta,* seeking the security of travel aboard the king's new ship. This meant even more overcrowding on the *Atocha;* the passengers had somehow to be fitted into the jammed cabins and staterooms, while the steerage room was packed with their baggage.

The passengers represented Castilian and Spanish-American society in microcosm. Fray Maestro Pedro de la Madriz, a notable Augustinian, had gone with three of his fellows to Peru at the orders of Philip III to undertake an investigation. Fourteen of the passengers carried the proud prefix *Don* or *Doña* before their names; they were of the nobility. One of these, Don Diego de Guzmán, was *Corregidor* of Cuzco. He held almost complete economic and political power over the Indians in his immense district. He regulated their markets, collected their tribute, and was their only judge.

Several of the passengers came from the small, educated

minority. One of these, Martín Salgado, who came aboard with his wife, María, and three servants, was returning home after a term as secretary of the prestigious *audiencia* (court) of Lima. Salgado's earnings and an inheritance—his family's future—were bound up in the fifteen silver ingots he registered on the *Atocha.* Another learned man, the *licenciado* Fragoso, was a Spanish surgeon who had become wealthy in the Indies. In addition to Arriola, several other merchants shipped aboard the *Atocha;* one of these, Miguel de Munibe, was also a trader of substance, who traveled with a large amount of private treasure.

Luis Quintero, a citizen of Callao in Peru, brought his wife, Doña Gerónima, their son, Pedro, and their teenage daughter, Doña Luisa. The last person listed by name on the passenger register was Diego de Illescas, a *mestizo,* or person of mixed Spanish and Indian blood. At the very bottom of the social scale on the *Atocha* were eight servants and slaves. Their names did not show on the ship's records, for they were, as the register proclaimed, "persons of no importance."

With the passengers came chests and boxes of rich personal belongings. They brought bolts of Chinese silks and brocades and silverware crafted in Cuzco and Lima. They carried many religious mementos: devotional books and missals, rosaries, medallions, and reliquary rings. Tiny leather and velvet caskets held their jewelry: gold chains and brooches of Baroque style, with misshapen pearls hung from circles of chased gold. In their private purses they carried the silver of the Indies and gold coins minted in Spain.

When all the passengers had embarked, the fleet was ready to leave Panama at last. Packed with human and bullion cargo, the *Atocha* was already badly overcrowded. As the ships weighed anchor on July 22, the fleet had still other stops to make on its homeward journey. A long voyage still lay ahead.

The night was split by a fiery rocket trail; another, then another, lifted and flowered red above the *Atocha*'s outlined masts and rigging. Like a tropical flower, an orange glow blossomed high above the ship's stern, and four cannons boomed salute. It was Saturday night, August 27, 1622, the eve of Saint Augustine's Day. Illuminations lit Havana harbor, and a holiday spirit ruled in the moored fleets, for the *fiesta* offered a welcome relief from the labors and tensions of recent weeks.

Since leaving Portobello, the newly combined Guard and *Tierra Firme* fleets had been driven on by the impatience of the Marquis of Cadereita. He had allowed a pause of only eight days at the important port of Cartagena, where additional quantities of treasure had entered the *Atocha*'s books. There was more coin and bar silver, but another kind of bullion as well, for this was the country par excellence of gold. In disks, bars, and shining bits, twenty thousand *pesos de oro* of gold cargo were legally registered on the *Atocha*. To prove their legitimacy, the gold items bore the king's round tax stamp.

Since the New Granada mines and goldfields were largely worked by black slaves, Cartagena was the major Indies entrepôt in 1622 of the African slave trade. As example of the impact of the human traffic, a chest of silver bars was sent aboard the *Atocha* to Philip IV in payment of the head tax on some of the 1400 blacks sold in Cartagena during the year. One Captain Duarte Márquez, who traded in slaves, sent silver bar number 569 on the *Atocha* to his partners in Seville.

Silvermaster de Vreder had also recorded one small but significant consignment of shining new silver coins. They were newly coined by the king's mintmaster, Alonso Turillo de Yebra, who had invented an improved coin press. The coins, the first ever minted in New Granada, bore the letters *RN*.

From a number of plantations along the nearby coast had come shipments of tobacco, a crop newly popular in Europe. Tobacco was a royal monopoly in Spain, and the king's agents brought 500 bales—over twelve tons—to be stowed somehow in the *Atocha*'s lower hold.

Now the small vessels that had fanned out from the outbound fleets—to Caracas, Cumaná, the pearl island of Margarita, Maracaibo, and Santa Marta—had returned to rejoin the ships for their voyage to Havana. A small Portuguese slaver, which had discharged its human freight at Cartagena, also joined the fleet there.

After leaving Cartagena for their northward journey, the ships had encountered long days of calm. The Marquis and his pilots had fretted over the added delay, but there was no way to bend the weather to the king's will, or to hasten the breeze that would speed the return of the merchants' silver. It was already August 22, well into the dreaded hurricane season, when the ships finally reached the port of Havana.

The Marquis of Cadereita then called upon all the Cuban officials and the fleet silvermasters to hasten the completion of shiploading in Havana. The New Spain ships, unwilling to wait longer, had already sailed for Spain, but according to orders they had left their treasure, dyestuffs, and other valuables to come with the Guard Fleet. From the king's Cuban mines came 582 crudely cast slabs of copper for loading on the *Nuestra Señora de Atocha*—to be sent back for casting into more bronze cannons for the wars of Spain.

Quartermaster Martín cursed and the seamen sweated as they shifted the tobacco bales loaded in Cartagena to make room for baled indigo and the slabs of copper. More private treasure—bars of gold and silver, coins from Mexico, and crated silverware—was registered on the *Atocha* at Havana. Finally, her Indies lading completed, the galleon was crammed with merchandise, registered treasure, and contraband. Her manifest now showed a total of 901 silver ingots, 255,000 silver coins, and 161 pieces of registered gold. Altogether, the *Atocha*'s cargo was worth a million pesos.

As last-minute work in the harbor continued, the Marquis called a *junta* of fleet officials and the Havana governor, Francisco Venegas, to settle the vital question of a fleet sailing date. A heated argument arose in the *junta,* as all the contradictions built into Spain's fleet system boiled up. Several speakers pointed to the lateness of the date and expressed their fear that if they left Havana during the hurricane season, the ships would be sailing directly into danger. Others remarked that any further delay in Cuba would bring the fleets into Spanish harbors at the height of the winter storms. A third point of view was that if the ships did not sail at all that year, but spent the winter in Havana, it might well cost hundreds of thousands of pesos in expenses for all concerned.

But the argument that outweighed all others was the crying need in Spain for the gold and silver. Many unseen but urgent economic lines pulled the fleet homeward: creditors demanding their money, merchants awaiting long-delayed payment, heirs hoping for the settlement of estates—above all, the desperate financial state of the crown.

Balancing the risks and advantages of the several courses of action in his mind, the Marquis of Cadereita put the question of the state of the weather to the pilots, in whose province such predictions fell. Lorenzo Vernal, chief pilot of the Guard Fleet, advised the *junta* that the conjunction of the moon would soon occur. It would take place, in fact, on September 5. (Seventeenth-century seamen believed that the movements of the planets greatly influenced the weather. They felt that weather conditions that prevailed at the time of the new moon—when earth, sun, and moon were in "conjunction"—would be especially severe and enduring.)

Finally, the Marquis agreed to wait and see. The decision to sail would be deferred until the day before the conjunction; then a decision would be made. Thus, in order better to ensure the safety of the fleet, the sailing was delayed a week. More precious time had been lost.

Sunday, August 28, was Saint Augustine's Day, a holy day for the Church. At ten in the morning, a brilliant procession, bright with colorful vestments and studded with flags and banners, left the Augustinian convent. Leading the march was the Bishop of Havana, with an escort of a score of other clergymen. Next came the Guard Fleet officials: the Marquis and his captains, Admiral Moran and Vice-Admiral Pasquier, accompanied by the royal standard and the flags of the infantry companies. The *Alcalde* (mayor), city council, and leaders of the local garrison followed.

Clouds of blue incense swirled up from swinging censers as the head of the procession passed through the great iron doors and entered the cathedral. Strident church bells began rapidly to ring as the guns of all the ships in the harbor answered in salute.

Before the ornate main altar, in front of all the assembled dignitaries, the Bishop, aided by Fray Madriz, presided at a solemn High Mass. At the mystic moment of the elevation of the Host, when Christ was truly present before the kneeling hundreds, Heaven's seal on Spain's glory had never seemed more sure. When the Bishop had ended the Mass, he gave his blessing to the Marquis and all the other officers of the homebound fleet—the best possible talisman against the uncertainties of the sea.

That same morning, far to the north and east of the Leeward Islands, an area of squalls had widened. At first like the hundreds that daily darken and disturb the tropical seas, it intensified as the morning wore on, and then began a weak circulation. Unnamed and unknown, 1300 miles from Havana, a tropical storm had been born.

Sunday, September 4, 1622. Slowly and majestically, flying all their flags, the ships of the combined fleets passed one at a time by El Morro at the Havana harbor entrance. With Guard Fleet galleons and escorts, *Tierra Firme* vessels and small craft, twenty-eight ships filed out into the open sea. They sailed a good six weeks behind schedule.

At dawning the day had been so serene, so clear, that Lorenzo Vernal and the other pilots had unanimously recommended that the fleet sail. If the morning before the conjunction of September were so fair, what possible danger could the next day bring? When he heard the pilots' recommendation, the Marquis of Cadereita felt reassurance, but still he hesitated. At last, the decision had to be made; he determined that the fleet had to sail. Too much was at stake, at home and abroad, to do otherwise. At seven in the morning, the Marquis had given the order to weigh anchor.

It took more than an hour for all the ships in the unwieldy convoy to clear the port and form into sailing order. Then the Guard Fleet *capitana* led off on a north-north-west course. As *almiranta* of the *Tierra Firme* ships, the *Atocha* brought up the rear of its fleet. Having gotten safely offshore by midafternoon, the fleet then tacked to the eastward of Havana to enable the ships to sail easily northward with the wind to the lower Florida Keys. There, where the current was strongest, the fleet would enter the Gulf Stream, which would boost them strongly homeward.

At sunset, Lorenzo Vernal estimated that the fleet had reached a point thirty miles to the northeast of Havana. Accordingly, he ordered a turn to the northward. Although the wind had changed little in strength or direction since morning, Vernal knew the weather had altered. The strikingly lovely deep-red sunset was disquieting in itself; its vivid colors were reflected in a thin veil of cirrus clouds that had overspread the sky. And Vernal saw how the sunset tint lit a towering bank of cumulus piled high in the southeast. At dusk a stronger breeze began to blow.

Through a night of steadily rising wind, the fleet held its course. Toward dawn on Monday the ships entered the center of the Gulf Stream current. The tossing motion of the vessels brought discomfort, then uneasiness, then wholesale seasickness to many passengers and crewmen of the fleets. Early morning disclosed that a strong north-east wind was raking the opposite-flowing current of the Gulf Stream, raising vicious cross-seas.

The ships reduced sail to weather the storm. Seamen went aloft to bring down the topmasts and reduce windage there. All objects on deck were strongly secured and hatch covers firmly lashed down. As the morning passed, the day darkened and the weather worsened. The wind rose to a whole gale. The height of seas around the convoy mounted to more than ten feet, and flying spray torn from wavetops by the shrieking wind obscured the horizon. Visibility fell until pilots and lookouts on the ships could scarcely make out the vessels on the convoy's edge.

Now the *Atocha*'s waist was almost continuously awash, as great seas swept around the overloaded ship. The pilot ordered the mainsail lowered so that the ship could go forward more easily under foresail alone. The sailors who struggled to comply with the order clung to the main yard, battling lashing canvas, as the extreme ends of the yard dipped regularly into the boiling sea. What most disturbed the men at work, however, was what they had seen near the ship's stern: the fins and upper bodies of two great gray sharks, following the *Atocha* through the storm.

Even with reduced sail area, the ship plunged wildly and became increasingly difficult to control. The helmsman could no longer steer properly, so the whipstaff was disconnected and the tiller lashed in place. At each heavy blow of the sea, the *Atocha*'s hull shuddered and her masts creaked in their steps. Crashes below told of shifting cargoes and broken wine and olive jars.

By the end of the long afternoon, many of the ships in the convoy had lost their mainmasts. Some had no steerage-way whatsoever, for their rudders had been shattered by huge following seas. One small ship, the *Buen Jesús,* had lost both masts and rudder; she fell farther and farther behind the other vessels and was finally lost to sight. Watchers aboard the *Atocha* saw the little *Nuestra Señora de la Consolación* struggling along under a close-reefed foresail. To their horror, they saw the small craft suddenly capsize and vanish into the angry ocean. They could launch no boat in the wild seas, nor could they turn their own ship to go to the aid of those on the stricken vessel. The gnawing feeling grew among those on the *Atocha* that the same fate might well await them all.

Long before sundown the world grew dark, and chief pilot Vernal lit the Guard Fleet *capitana*'s stern lantern. He could not tell at that point if any other ships survived to follow the lantern's gleam; as far as he could see, the *capitana* now sailed alone. Any protective sense of being in convoy had now gone, and each ship still afloat struggled in its own lonely battle against the hurricane.

Aboard the *Santa Margarita,* silvermaster Gutierre de Espinosa called his aide, Aguirre, to his cabin. Bracing against the plunging motion of the ship, Espinosa opened his official trunk and asked Aguirre to help him take out some treasure. The two men removed eight gold disks and six gold bars, three small gold pieces, a silver bar, and some silverware; they placed it in Espinosa's personal sea chest. The silvermaster then locked the chest and bound it with rope. He had made his own private preparations for disaster.

Meanwhile, below decks in the *Santa Margarita,* Captain Bernardino de Lugo shouted for silence; frightened cries and groans of despair faded, then died. Holding for support to a ringbolt, the captain motioned to the pale cleric beside him, and told his men that Chaplain Ortiz was ready to begin confessing them. He added that the two Jesuit priests aboard were in the cabins above, taking the confessions of the officers and passengers; they would also come to the gun deck to help there when they were through. Even greater than his dread of drowning at sea was a Spaniard's fear of dying in a state of sin. That could mean the loss of his soul for all eternity. The men crowded forward.

A lantern guttered, spreading light at the foot of the *Atocha's* main ladder. Fray Madriz sat astride a cannon, steadying himself with one hand. His other arm encircled the image of Our Lady of Atocha, brought below from its quarterdeck niche. The lantern's light was reflected from the holy statue's pink face, the silver trimming on her robe, and the jewels in her gold crown. The Augustinian, with Chaplain Fernández and the other three friars, led the kneeling company in the litany. The low-pitched responses of the crowd could scarcely be heard above the creaking of the pumps and the howling of the storm wind. Pilot Jiménez closed his eyes. He had sensed a gradual shifting of the wind and knew that it now blew from the south. The *Atocha* could only run before that wind, and ahead on that course, the pilot knew, lay the dreaded reefs of Florida. He joined fervently in the prayers.

By the time the wind shifted to the south, both *capitanas* and nineteen other vessels of the combined fleets had passed to the west of the Tortugas and thus out of danger of grounding. Five unlucky ships—Vargas's ship the *Rosario,* the fleet *patache* (tender), the Portuguese slaver, the *Santa Margarita,* and the *Atocha,* playthings of the wind—were swept irresistibly toward the Keys. A small Cuban coast-guard vessel was also caught up in the ill-fated group.

To Spanish mariners, Florida was an evil name. Scores of shipwrecks dotted the sea bottom along its coasts and in the Keys. In the isolated area that lay ahead of the six ships, Spain's writ scarcely ran. For more than fifty years, expeditions sent there from the Spanish capital at Saint Augustine had never succeeded in making lasting settlement. Sailors lost in the Keys had to run a double gauntlet: if they survived the ruin of their ship, they still had to face the untamed ferocity of the Keys Indians, who often killed shipwrecked men.

The first light of dawn on Tuesday, September 6, revealed an awesome sight. As the Spanish ships came into more shallow waters, the seas became even steeper. The few men left on deck beheld a sea covered with huge rollers, their fifteen-foot crests whitened by the gusting wind. Lookouts on the three westernmost of the ships saw vaguely ahead the outline of low islands—the Tortugas. The sailors heaved over their anchors to halt the ships' onward course to disaster. One by one their anchor lines broke, and the *Rosario,* the slave ship, and the fleet *patache* were grounded, wrecked in the shallows, battered by incoming storm waves.

Meanwhile, forty miles to the east, the *Santa Margarita* and the *Atocha* approached a place where the trough of each passing wave bared the reef in a welter of foam.

Only the stump of the *Margarita*'s mainmast remained; her rudder was gone and her foresail had blown away. When soundings showed rapidly shoaling water, three seamen crept forward to set a scrap of canvas on the foremast and attempt to claw back away from the reefs ahead. The makeshift sail blew out. When their anchors began to drag, the crew was helpless. The ship was pushed inevitably toward the place of danger. At seven in the morning, the *Santa Margarita* surged across the reef on the crest of a wave. As the ship swept on, Captain de Lugo looked to the east. There, to his astonishment, he saw the hull of another crippled galleon. It was the *Atocha.*

Early in the morning hours, the *almiranta*'s foremast had carried away, taking with it any hope of controlling the galleon's onward course. Only a small deck watch and a seaman and two apprentices tied in the mizzen shrouds watched the *Atocha* approach the reef. Every other soul was closed in below decks or huddled in the sterncastle cabins. Suddenly the great ship was lifted high on the crest of a towering wave. As it fell into the next trough, it crashed with sickening force upon the reef. The shock of the impact snapped the ship's mainmast above the weather deck. The rolling seas quickly carried the hulk beyond the reef, trailing its broken mast, but the *Atocha* was mortally wounded. The reef had ripped into her lower bow, and the sea poured in through the opened hull. The ship wallowed, sinking; as rising water flooded the gun deck, strangled screams, curses, and supplications came from the trapped people below. Desperate hands forced open the forecastle hatch, and a stream of figures emerged. Briefly they clung to the forecastle coaming and the stump of the foremast, but great seas combing across the hull swept them away.

The galleon was buoyant no more. The weight of her ballast, the cannons, the king's copper, and thirty-five tons of silver dragged her down to her grave. As she sank, the last thing seen of the *Atocha*'s hull was the red-and-gold painted image of Our Lady of Atocha high on the poop. Finally, only the ship's mizzenmast remained above the rolling seas.

Lorenzo de Arriola was gone, together with his silver; gone were the Salgado inheritance, the Duke of Alba's pension, the king's *quinto*. Lost among the broken crockery were gold chains, brooches of pearl, and Turillo de Yebra's bright coins. Deep below, the seaman's skill and the navigator's art lay buried with the shattered capstan and the pilot's astrolabe, while the gunners' craft was interred with their twenty guns of shining bronze.

Sunk also with the *Atocha* were religion's comfort and power: the chaplain with the friar, Doña Luisa clutching her rosary, the indulgence money from Lima, the breviary and the candlesticks of silver. In a common tomb rested *corregidor* and *mestizo,* the *audiencia*'s dignity and slavery's shame. Soldier and admiral, Captain Nodal and his flag-bearer Aranda alike slept forever in the *Atocha.* Cannons, swords, and muskets mounted vain guard over the gold and silver, the lost hope of empire, locked in the sunken hull.

Fifty-five feet deep, off a wide shoal west of a storm-swept circle of mangrove islands, lay *Nuestra Señora de Atocha.* With her, frozen in time, lay seventeenth-century Spain.

The southern sky had cleared. Except for fitful gusts, the wind had dropped, and the afternoon sun burned down fiercely on the place of disaster. With nightmare clarity, it revealed a churned and littered sea, its surface heaving with the refuse of shipwreck. The little merchant ship *Santa Cruz* had weathered the hurricane; it picked its way through floating planks and spars in the waters off the great sandbank. The small ship was already crowded with sixty-eight survivors of the *Santa Margarita,* including Captain de Lugo and twenty of his men. Shortly after the sinking of the *Atocha,* the *Margarita* had grounded against the sandbar. By midmorning, battered by the waves, the ship had begun to break up. Only those who could keep a hold on floating wreckage had survived. Gutierre de Espinosa and all the passengers had perished. One hundred forty-three persons had drowned.

A launch from the *Santa Cruz* cautiously approached the sunken hulk of the *Atocha,* marked now only by its protruding mizzenmast. There, dazed with shock and almost blinded by sun and salt, clung five persons. Gently they were lifted into the boat: Andrés Lorenzo, a twenty-nine-year-old seaman; two teenaged apprentices, Juan Muñoz and Francisco Núñez, and two black slaves. All the others, 260 souls—all those important people on *Nuestra Señora de Atocha*—were gone.

Bartolomé López, owner of the frigate *Santa Catalina,* had brought his ship to a point just off the mangrove atoll east of the great shoal. On the swells ahead, a sailor suddenly spied two barrels and a sea chest. Sailing close alongside, the ship luffed its lateen sail, and her men pulled the chest over the rail and laid it on deck. They forced its lid. Inside was a stack of neatly folded clothing: woolen breeches, cotton stockings, and a purple taffeta jacket. When the clothing had been removed, the glitter of gold struck the sailors' eyes. Eager fingers pulled out bars and disks of gold, a small silver bar, and piece after piece of silverware. A sailor found a piece of folded paper in the jacket pocket and brought it to López to read. It was a receipt for the rental of a room in Portobello and it was made out to Gutierre de Espinosa. The crew had found the sea chest of the drowned silvermaster of the *Margarita.*

The shipwrecks of 1622 lay scattered over an area of more than fifty miles. From the stranded *Rosario* and the other ships on the Tortugas eastward to the site of the sunken *Atocha* and beyond to the wreck of the Cuban coast-guard vessel *Candelaria,* six ships had been lost. None knew the grave of the two other small merchant vessels sunk during the storm. Five hundred fifty persons and cargoes worth more than two million ducats had been drowned, together with many hopes and fortunes, in the sea.

V. "We Must Find the Almiranta"

As I trust in God Our Lord,
we must find the *almiranta*.

—Lorenzo de Cabrera, 1628

Again the Marquis of Cadereita had called a *junta* to meet in the Governor's house in Havana. This time, on September 12, 1622, those present were in a grim, shaken mood, still reliving their hurricane experience. The Marquis put the same question to his surviving officers: Should the fleet attempt to return to Spain before the end of the year, or should it now pass the winter in Cuba?

A grizzled seaman of fifty-five, Gaspar de Vargas, spoke first. Vargas, who had fought in the 1588 Armada and served fifteen voyages as chief pilot of the Guard Fleet, was acknowledged to be the most experienced seaman present. The old sailor urged an immediate return to Europe as soon as weather and the condition of the ships permitted.

The Marquis indicated his agreement with Vargas, but called upon Lorenzo Vernal and the other fleet pilots for an opinion. They were unanimous in disagreement. They dwelt upon the risks the weakened ships would run from further hurricanes and the winter storms in Spanish waters. The deciding word then came from Juan de Lara Moran, General of the decimated *Tierra Firme* Fleet. Moran sided with the pilots, but for a different reason. He strongly stressed the need to salvage the sunken galleons before it was too late. He pointed out that Spain's enemies might well learn where they lay and seize all the treasure; the General also feared that the wrecks might break up and their bullion be lost forever in the sands of the Keys.

The argument convinced the *junta,* and the Marquis gave the order: first priority would be given to the location of the three missing silver galleons.

As soon as he had heard the stories of the *Atocha* survivors and Captain de Lugo, the Marquis of Cadereita commissioned Gaspar de Vargas to find and salvage the lost 1622 ships. Vargas wasted no time; on September 16 he sailed with five vessels for the lower Florida Keys.

The next day, definite news of the *Atocha*'s location reached the Marquis from another source. Bartolomé López, who had found Espinosa's floating sea chest, came into Havana to report that he had seen the sunken *almiranta* near "the last Key of Matecumbe." Captain Vargas was already beyond recall, so the Marquis sent López back to guide him to the *Atocha.*

In the meantime, while autumn rain squalls swept over the Tortugas, the *Rosario* survivors huddled together on Loggerhead Key. They had struggled to the barren islet from their ship, grounded nearby, and suffered greatly from exposure, hunger, and thirst.

López found Gaspar de Vargas and took him to the place west of the mangrove atoll where the *Atocha*'s mizzenmast protruded above the water. Vargas went alongside the sunken hull in a launch and measured the water depth at fifty-five feet. He sent his divers down to the decks of the *almiranta,* only dimly visible from the surface. They came up to report that it was impossible to break into the hull to get to the silver; the ship's hatches were still tightly secured. All Vargas's men could do was remove two small cannon from an upper deck. He vowed to return to Havana for tools and explosives to open or blow up the hull. After searching in vain for the spot where the *Santa Margarita* had broken up, Vargas passed along to the west and found the *Rosario* and her survivors.

Gaspar de Vargas immediately set to work, and decided that he had to destroy the stranded *Rosario* in order to salvage her precious cargo. He set fire to the hulk and burned it down to the waterline; then he quickly recovered all the ship's bullion, copper, and artillery out of the shallows in which the galleon's remains lay. Vargas had almost completed his work when on October 5, just one month after the first hurricane, a second storm struck the Keys. As the storm waters rose, Vargas and his crew and the twice-battered shipwreck survivors were hard put to save their lives. Retreating to the highest part of the island, they clung together for shelter against the driving wind and spray.

The second hurricane was even more powerful and destructive than the first. Forty miles from the Tortugas, surging waves lashed and swirled around the sunken hull of *Nuestra Señora de Atocha.* As the seas mounted higher, immense stresses tore at the galleon's timbers. Finally, shuddering under the impact of tremendous seas, the hull broke asunder. The lower hull, held down by the weight of the silver and copper, remained fixed on the deep bottom, but the whole bow section pulled loose, surfaced, and went dancing down the waves. The galleon's gun deck and sterncastle, like a giant, misshapen raft, broke away, still carrying many of the bronze cannons. The wreckage was swept many miles, broke up, and was covered by sand. Jumbled masses of silver ingots and broken chests of coin now rested with other shipwreck materials in an unmarked grave. When the storm tides receded and the wind returned to its steady southeast breeze, the waters around the mangrove atoll displayed no clue to the whereabouts of the lost *Atocha.*

Gaspar de Vargas finally had to face it. He was a man of action, not words, and thoroughly disliked report-writing. But the weather had turned bad again, and the January wind covered the waters around his headquarters on the mangrove atoll with whitecaps. Work was impossible for today, and Vargas had to report to the Marquis on what he had done.

After his quick success in salvaging the *Rosario,* Gaspar de Vargas had endured days of grinding frustration after his return from Havana with the equipment obtained there. Every morning he sailed out from the atoll to the place where the *Atocha* was last seen before the October storm. Often it took his crews more than three hours to reach the area; the return, rowing against the wind and currents, at times required seven or eight hours.

But reaching down to the sunken *Atocha* was more than a matter of merely conquering the problems of weather and distance. The place where the Spaniards believed it lay was in deep water—so deep that it was near, or beyond, a free diver's limit. Even if he could reach the bottom, a man's scant breath capacity allowed him only a pitifully short time to work there.

Vargas and his men dragged for the wreck with grapnel anchors, and he sent divers down to explore any underwater object that the anchors snagged. One of the divers, examining such an area, surfaced jubilantly to report that he had found the *almiranta;* other divers who followed him vowed that it was nothing but rocky bottom. In truth, the task was beyond the divers' capacity.

In his report, Gaspar de Vargas begged the Marquis to send trained Caribbean pearl divers. This, he felt, was the only hope if they wished to recover the treasures that lay tantalizingly somewhere beneath the shifting sands.

It was like a one-two punch. When messengers from Havana brought news of the fleet disaster to Spain on February 1, 1623, the report followed closely another piece of bad news. The Spanish court had just heard that several of the New Spain ships had also been sunk by storms at sea. The evil tidings swept over Spain, and many families mourned the human losses of 1622.

In Seville, agents of the Indies merchants, the *avería* deputies, and the House of Trade met to sift the news and pick up the pieces of a commercial calamity. The shipwrecks had created financial chaos. The *avería* agents faced bankruptcy; they had spent two hundred thousand ducats of borrowed money to dispatch the 1622 fleets. Now they asked the king to suspend collection on their previous loans and to allow them to borrow another hundred thousand ducats from the probate court deposits in Seville. They also decided to sell three galleons from the fleet to raise cash. They knew, however, that eventually the loss of ships, sunken or sold, would have to be made up. The Seville merchants, who had suffered a terrible blow, petitioned the king to relieve them from all claims and judgments until they could recover, to a degree, from the tragedy.

The Spanish king's financial problems were also aggravated by the shipwrecks of 1622. No royal silver, copper, or tobacco had arrived from the Indies, and much of what had been gathered there had been lost. Philip IV sent for the manifests of the two galleons still missing in the Keys to learn his exact losses. In this situation, the crown's creditors would just have to wait; the needs of war took precedence over their claims, and the military news was also bad. Spies had reported that the Dutch were arming thirteen warships for an assault on the Spanish fleet that carried the silver from Peru up the Pacific coast to Panama. Spain would have to prepare for this threat, and the recovery of the treasure lost in the Florida Keys was more important than ever.

Support for Gaspar de Vargas's salvage effort came from all over the Spanish Caribbean. Supplies and equipment came from Veracruz, and Vargas got his pearl divers: twelve blacks from the island of Margarita. But the Marquis of Cadereita grew impatient with the lack of salvage results and determined to lead the work in person. On February 22, 1623, the Marquis left Havana for the Keys. When he arrived at the group of low mangrove islands near the shipwreck sites, the fleet commander made his own base there with Gaspar de Vargas. The salvage master made the nobleman as comfortable as possible in such primitive surroundings, and in honor of Cadereita's sojourn there, the islands were given his name: *Cayos del Marqués*—"Keys of the Marquis."

The Marquis's coming stirred the divers to new labors; now more than twenty men were diving deep near Vargas's buoys, and they brought up two silver bars and other remnants of the *Atocha* from the deep water. But although the work was going well, by the end of March the Marquis of Cadereita could wait no longer. It was almost time for the fleet to sail for Spain, and he returned to Havana, leaving Gaspar de Vargas to follow him in a few days.

In Havana, the Marquis found engineer Captain Nicholas de Cardona, sent with a team of skilled divers from New Spain. This, plus the better salvage news, decided the Marquis to order the continuance of the salvage operation. He seized money from the fleet registries and left it in Havana to finance Vargas's and Cardona's work. As his vessels sailed for Spain on April 15, the Marquis was very hopeful about the success of the salvage operation in the Keys. He had every expectation that the rest of the missing treasure would follow him in a very few months.

In the end, it was the sand that defeated them. True, they had other problems: boisterous winds from cold fronts raised seas that destroyed their buoys and halted work for weeks; many divers became ill from working at the very limit of their deep-water capabilities. But when the salvors returned to the site in April, they found that five feet of sand had drifted over the wreckage. By June 1, strong currents had piled up another five full feet over the *Atocha*'s grave.

As the summer of 1623 advanced, the divers and searchers continued to work, but nothing more was found. Nicholas de Cardona became discouraged and decided to leave, but before his departure, the engineer prepared a map of the salvage area and left it with the Havana authorities.

On August 6, 1623, Captain Gaspar de Vargas also returned from the Keys. He told Governor Venegas that he, too, had lost all hope of finding either of the lost galleons, and he returned to Spain with the next fleet. In spite of hard, harrowing work and heavy expenditure—the salvage attempts had cost more than one hundred thousand pesos—Gaspar de Vargas had failed. Sand still hid the remains of the *Santa Margarita* and the *Nuestra Señora de Atocha.*

A jerk on the line told the watchers above that Juan Bañon had launched himself from the diving bell and plunged toward the sea bottom.The ship's sails were shivering gently in the light wind when the diver suddenly rose. Dollops of water scattered as his head and gleaming black shoulders burst through the surface.

In his excitement, Bañon tried to shout even while he gulped air; he gargled the words: "*Margarita, la Margarita!* Found . . . found!" Juan Bañon swam to the ship's side and hung there, gasping, looking up into a circle of astonished faces. "A rope, a rope!" the slave cried impatiently. Shaken from their trance, the men on deck moved, and one threw Bañon a line. Grasping it, he remembered that he had left his weight below. At another urgent gesture, the sailors manhandled a stone weight onto the rail and handed it down to Juan Bañon. The diver's thick arm encircled the weight, and, with the rope's end, he dived.

A long minute passed. To the salvage master, Francisco Núñez Melián, it seemed but one more pause in the long search for the 1622 galleons. After four years, little of their treasure had been found. When the fleet salvage effort had failed, Melián, a Havana citizen, had stepped in. Now, on June 3, 1626, Melián's gamble seemed about to pay off.

The diver surfaced, more slowly this time, spreading ripples over the calm blue sea. Attached to the line, but cradled in his arms, Juan Bañon held a bulky gray object. Laboriously he swam to the ship's side, while many eager hands hauled on the rope. As it rose, the heavy thing bumped against the ship; finally it was hauled over the rail.

An oblong bar lay dripping on the deck. The sight roused a feverish babble of shouts and cries. One seaman knelt and scraped a cracked thumbnail across the darkened surface of the bar. A streak of silver reflected the sun. The slave diver had brought up a silver ingot from the *Santa Margarita,* and one of the missing 1622 ships had been found.

Juan Bañon clambered wearily over the ship's rail and sat to rest on a hatch cover. He was still breathing quickly, and his heartbeat was rapid from the effort of his dive and his excitement. Suddenly, with the hammering of blood in his head there beat the word *libertad.* Freedom— he had won his freedom! Juan Bañon rose, broke into the circle gathered around the silver bar, and placed an imploring hand on Melián's sleeve. *"Señor!"* he pleaded. "I beg you to remember your promise. I claim my freedom!"

Melián shook off the man's grasp, stepped back, and said, "You have indeed had my word, Juan de Casta Bañon. I pledged on the honor of a *caballero* that the man who first discovered the lost ships would have his reward. If he were a slave, he would be free. Now I swear by Our Lord"—he touched his sword hilt—"you shall have your liberty." Melián turned to a seaman. "Give this *freedman* a drink of wine. No, serve it out to all aboard. Then we must set about our work. God has granted us this miracle, and we must not fail to seize the chance."

Francisco Núñez Melián was the man to grasp an opportunity. He had proved that in the rough-and-tumble of Havana politics. After coming to Cuba, Melián had joined the governor's faction, opposing that of the royal treasury officials. Melián involved himself in the Canary Islands wine trade; through the governor's intervention, he escaped prosecution on smuggling charges. As the years passed, Melián rose in the local hierarchy; he became an alderman, then *alcalde,* then gained the privilege of handling the crown's indulgence sales in Cuba.

In 1624 Francisco Melián's influence procured him a royal contract to salvage the 1622 galleons. Of any treasure found, the salvor and the king would each get a third, and Melián's expenses would come out of the rest. Melián then sought the best data he could about the location of the missing ships. Antonio Govea, a Havana pilot, had a copy of Cardona's map. Melián knew that the Havana governors had used the map to keep the wreck site buoyed; in 1625 one Francisco de la Luz had gone to the Keys to check the buoys. He never returned from his mission.

Melián and Govea came to an agreement on using the pilot's skills and information. But the canny politician had other cards up his sleeve. He was not only a gambler, ready to risk his money on a chance for great riches; he was also an inventor. Melián knew that water depth had severely limited the divers who had previously searched for the *Atocha*. Accordingly he devised an apparatus to serve both as search vehicle and as a divers' air station. He told the king that his invention, a diving bell with windows, could enable the man inside "to see the most hidden things." The invention, Melián claimed, was "something never before seen; it cost an infinite sum to have brought it to a state of perfection."

It cost Francisco Melián no infinite sum to make his device—he paid only five thousand *reales* to have the 680-pound bronze bell cast in Havana. But it had been his secret weapon, the tool with which the *Santa Margarita* had been found. While Melián's bell was being dragged slowly along the edge of the great sandbar, Juan Bañon had spied telltale wreckage on the sandy bottom.

After the discovery, Melián's divers had not worked long before the salvor realized that uncovering all the silver below would involve the wholesale removal of sand and ballast stones. He returned to Havana to outfit a stronger force. When he came back to the Keys, the salvage master brought Antonio Govea and four vessels; he also carried a royal auditor, Juan de Chaves, three cooks, thirteen divers, and fifty-seven seamen. The salvors built their camp and stockpiled supplies on the southwestern key in the Marquesas atoll.

Soon Indian canoes drifted motionless off the salvage camp and near the diving site not far away. The Keys Indians—long-haired, impassive, heathen—seemed to the Spaniards symbolic of the strange and hostile nature of the islands. Melián's only interest in the Indians was to keep them from disturbing the work, and in their possible utilization as divers. Through an interpreter, he agreed to bring the Indians gifts of hatchets, food, and drink each time he returned from Havana.

Working from a longboat anchored over the wreckage, the divers shortly found 312 more silver ingots, already gray from immersion in the sea, and a great mass of blackened silver coins. They also brought up a hundred irregular, rough copper slabs; digging further, they located eight of the *Margarita's* fine bronze guns. As the summer advanced, rough seas and squally winds alternated with days of blazing sun. One by one or in handfuls, thousands of coins were passed up from the divers in the water to Chaves in the longboat. The auditor counted and sorted the money and, at the end of each day, agreed with Melián on the count. The coins were then deposited in a chest on the largest salvage ship.

Soon Chaves found that the sailors and divers were secreting pieces of eight from the shipwreck. He found caches of coin on the longboat and on the other vessels, and found some coins in the divers' breeches pockets. Chaves then cut off the divers' pockets to stop the thievery.

At the end of August, word came from Havana that the fleet had arrived, and that Melián should hasten with the recovered treasure so that it could be returned to Spain. The salvors had by then found more than sixty-four thousand silver coins, in addition to the ingots, the copper, and the cannons and silverware. With their booty, the salvors sailed away from their mangrove atoll campsite for Cuba.

Controversy arose when Melián sailed into Havana with his shipload of treasure. In keeping with his usual practice, Melián had cultivated the new governor, an aging soldier named Lorenzo de Cabrera. Friendly to Melián, Cabrera left him entirely alone as the salvor set about the task of preparing the treasure for its journey to Spain. The treasury officials, however, viewed Melián's success with envy and with malice, and watched him closely. They wrote the king that Melián had refused to allow them to audit his records or even to examine the treasure. Instead, they charged, he carried the coins, ingots, and silverware to his own house "on the pretext of cleaning and counting them." The officials also reported a rumor that a thousand more coins had been found in the Keys than Chaves had officially recorded.

It was difficult, however, to quarrel with success. When Melián's silver trove left Havana for Spain and the eager hands awaiting it there, the salvor felt certain that he could count on a substantial reward from his king.

The four years since the hurricane of 1622 had seen escalating violence in the Thirty Years War. The conflict threatened to widen even further as Cardinal Richelieu assumed full control of France's destiny and began to seek allies against Spain and the Holy Roman Empire. A rising commitment and consequent increasing costs faced the Spaniards in 1626. In that atmosphere, the arrival of the *Santa Margarita*'s treasure brought, at first, unrestrained joy in Seville. The good feeling rapidly dissolved, however, as an unseemly struggle began over the ownership of the silver.

The *avería* agents put in a claim for all the money they would have been owed if the *Santa Margarita* had come safely to port; they needed the cash badly to outfit the next Indies fleet. The private merchants, who had never recovered from the 1622 disasters, slapped a lien on the *Margarita* silver for their fair share. For its part, the Spanish crown had good reason to keep its hands on all the silver recovered in the Florida Keys. The king's creditors were demanding payment of six hundred thousand ducats in past-due loans, but they would just have to wait. The king and his ministers felt it urgently necessary to equip and send a new armada to the Philippines, for a Dutch threat there had reached crisis point. The Dutch had also made other aggressive moves against the Spanish empire. In 1624 they had taken Bahia in Brazil, requiring Spain and Portugal to mount a major expedition to retake it. Earlier in 1626 they had raided Acapulco. And in the Caribbean, they had learned of the finding of the *Santa Margarita*'s silver.

Seas were choppy and winds and currents strong as the 1627 diving season began. When they arrived at the Marquesas in late May, the salvors found that Indians had burned their camp and the supplies left there. They quickly repaired the damage and set to work in the water. While crews seeking the *Atocha* dragged chains and grapnels through the deeper water, divers descended again on the *Santa Margarita* shipwreck. There they located a bronze cannon and a large galleon anchor. During the following days, they found swords, muskets, two more cannons, and several hundred corroded silver coins.

On Corpus Christi Day, work was halted while Mass was said in the largest ship. Then, over the next few days, divers uncovered another large bronze gun and four silver bars. To hold their longboat steady against the powerful undersea currents, they moored their craft over the sunken ship with six anchor lines. On Thursday morning, June 10, while divers were below, there came a shout from the other ship: "Sail! A sail!"

The Spaniards saw a large ship standing in toward them from the direction of the Gulf Stream. As the vessel drew closer, the salvors suddenly made out the strange ship's flags: the battle ensigns of the West India Company and the United Provinces. The Dutch enemy had reached the Marquesas.

As divers, summoned up from below, clambered aboard the longboat, the Spaniards cut their anchor lines and made sail to escape. They steered northward over the wide sandbank, hoping that the Dutch could not follow them there. Then they saw that the Dutchman had been towing a launch; it was cut loose, raised its own sails, and pursued them into the shallows. The Spanish ships scattered at this; later, they reassembled and returned safely to Cuba.

Now the enemy was seen everywhere in the vicinity: off Cape San Antonio, near the Tortugas, at Cape Canaveral, and in the old Bahama Channel. When Governor Cabrera sent a longboat and soldiers to reconnoiter the Marquesas, it was captured by a Dutch flotilla. The Netherlanders left the Spaniards marooned with the Indians on Key West; later they were ransomed by a rescue expedition from Havana. But it was October before Melián felt it was safe to return to the salvage site.

Thus, 1627 was not as productive a year for Melián as the previous one had been. He took legal action for his share of the treasure that had been impounded in Seville, and campaigned for royal favor in recognition of his salvage of the *Santa Margarita,* pointing proudly to his success after "immense labors, dangers, and excessive costs." Like other privilege seekers, Melián pressed his claim at court and solicited testimonial letters from notable persons. The salvor sought an important, high-paying post in the Indies government and, if possible, a title. He also proposed to become the world's greatest treasure hunter. Melián asked royal permission to salvage a galleon lost on the Yucatán coast, requested a license to search for treasure in the whole Spanish Caribbean, and asked an exclusive franchise for his diving bell. In return, he offered the king 20 percent of his discoveries.

Although there was no immediate response to his petitions, the crown did release some of the salvaged silver to Melián. He continued to press his suit for full payment and royal recognition. During the 1628 salvage near the Marquesas, Melián used Guayquiri Indian divers from the pearl island of Margarita, and nine of the Florida Indians. Ranging out from the original area, they found thirty-seven more silver bars and another quantity of silver coins. The Spaniards worked with one eye on the horizon, for Dutch ships hovered almost constantly at the Tortugas. Late in the summer of 1628, two Dutch warships sailed boldly up to the salvage ships. A miniature naval battle ensued, and the Cuban salvors were saved from certain capture by the appearance of a ship from Saint Augustine. The Florida craft bore down on the Dutch intruders and put up such a withering small-arms fire that they retreated.

But the Dutch were after bigger game. In August they waylaid the Honduras ships on their way to Havana, capturing one. Now Admiral Piet Heyn had arrived off Havana from the Netherlands with thirty strong warships. Spanish fleet General Juan de Benavides of the New Spain Fleet, mistakenly believing the coast to be clear, sailed directly into a Dutch trap with three million pesos' worth of cargo aboard.

At the moment of its greatest test, the Spanish fleet defense failed. Benavides's ships were so crammed with goods and passengers that it was impossible to clear their decks for action, and the commander failed to respond vigorously when the Dutch ships appeared around him. Admiral Heyn forced the Spanish fleet into Matanzas harbor on Cuba's north coast; to Spain's enduring disgrace, he captured the whole fleet and a great booty.

After the Matanzas catastrophe, the Spanish crown had to borrow a million ducats more to meet its most pressing military needs. After that, the king's credit was exhausted, but appearances still had to be kept up. In October 1629, Castile was obligated to pay five hundred thousand gold pesos as a dowry for the Infanta María, but there was no money in the treasury. In desperation, Philip IV wrote his Indies Viceroys for donations for the dowry so that the Spanish Hapsburgs need feel no shame among the rulers of Europe.

The summer of 1629 was a repeat of the previous one: a sizable Dutch raid disrupted the work, and little treasure was found on the Marquesas salvage site. But some good news did come to Melián: the king had appointed him Governor of Venezuela, provided that he arrange for someone to continue the search for the *Atocha.* Melián designated Captain Juan de Añuez of Havana to carry on the work.

Melián then sailed away to Caracas to take up his new post. He did not, however, escape controversy. Rumors of corruption in Havana had reached the king's ears, and he sent a special investigator. Witnesses told the king's emissary that Melián and Governor Cabrera were political cronies, and charged that twelve silver bars from the *Margarita* had been delivered to the governor but that they had never been accounted for.

The case against Cabrera and Melián eventually came to the highest court, the Council of the Indies, where a decision typical of the times was rendered. Because of past valuable services, the governor was cleared of any criminal negligence but was fined the amount of money he had supposedly embezzled. Melián's services also saved him. No charge whatsoever was sustained against him, and he continued in his governorship at Caracas.

Now Melián submitted his salvage expenses for reimbursement; since 1626, he claimed, he had spent more than a hundred thousand pesos in the Florida Keys and in Havana. The audit of the claimed expenses was forwarded to Spain for consideration; eventually it was placed in the royal archives at Simancas. More than a hundred years later, the faded documents would be transferred to the new Archive of the Indies. There they would rest undisturbed for almost two hundred years more.

In 1643 Melián began his final search for the *Atocha.* Although Melián was now governor in Yucatán, Juan de Añuez continued seeking the missing silver in the Marquesas, but with little success. With a new crown contract in hand and new intelligence from the Keys Indians about the lost *almiranta,* the salvor Melián outfitted a ship in Spain to carry men and equipment to the Keys. But the last effort failed, and in 1644 Melián died. Although he had achieved much and gained a degree of fame, he had never realized his most cherished dreams, never reached his longtime goal: the location of that rich galleon, *Nuestra Señora de Atocha.*

Spain itself was years farther down the road to its dissolution as an international power. After French and Swedish intervention in the Thirty Years War, the tide turned against the Hapsburgs. In 1639 a combined French and Dutch fleet decisively beat the Spaniards at the Battle of the Downs. By this time, the marine lifeline between Spain's Indies and the homeland was weakening. Even though the *avería* tax had been doubled, it proved insufficient to finance the naval war the Dutch had unleashed. At the same time, silver production from Mexico and Peru had declined while the costs of the Indies bureaucracy had climbed. Spain's fleets began to shrink noticeably in size, further reducing the potential for commerce and defense. In the Caribbean, the Dutch had captured the island of Curaçao, and the English had taken Barbados. Both Portugal and Catalonia had rebelled against Spanish domination, and the Portuguese had successfully gained their independence from a weakened Spain. Finally, at the Peace of Westphalia in 1648, Spain had to concede the independence of the Dutch.

The Council of the Indies' discussion in 1688 demonstrated how low Spain had fallen. By that year, England had seized Jamaica and colonized the Carolinas, further shrinking the area of Spanish control. Louis XIV's France dominated the politics of Europe. On Spain's throne sat Charles II, whose feeble and confused mind only dimly comprehended the passage of events. His council was considering an English sea captain's request to buy the rights to salvage all the Spanish New World shipwrecks.

In considering the salvor's petition, the council asked its staff to research old shipwreck records. Soon they had before them a list of famous lost galleons and the contracts issued to salvage them. Although many notable ship disasters appeared on the council's list, one early loss stood out with clarity and poignancy. It was a galleon lost in Florida's Marquesas Keys in 1622 and never recovered: *Nuestra Señora de Atocha.*

Since the year of the *Atocha*'s sinking, Europe's emphasis had shifted northward. The great powers of the sixteenth century had passed, yielding their place to others in the inexorable rhythm of history. In a lonely, isolated place at the far end of Florida, buried below water and sand, was the wreckage of *Nuestra Señora de Atocha.* Buried with her, and with the hopes of all who had searched for her, was the climax of Castile's fortunes.

VI. The Nitty-gritty

Many trim, sleek sailboats and costly motorcraft call the
Key West Yacht Club home. None of the derelict craft
that haunt some Florida marinas is ever found there. On
a June day in 1970, however, a different kind of boat slid
up to the club's fuel dock. She was clearly no yacht; her
faded, streaked topsides and worn rails proclaimed her
a working boat. Moreover, the air compressor on her deck
and the blue mailboxes hanging at her stern marked her
out for a treasure craft. It was Mel Fisher's boat *Virgilona*,
come to Key West to begin the new search for the *Atocha*.

Watchers at the club office eyed the strange craft as
Moe Molinar turned the wheel to bring the *Virgilona* in
close. The crewman who stepped to the gunwale was
dressed in cut-off jeans; he sported a gold earring and
wore a silver piece of eight on a lanyard around his neck.
As he handed over the lines and the boat was made fast
to the dock, a tall, darkly tanned man stepped off the boat.
Norman Woods, a Key West charter captain who witnessed Mel's arrival, recalled later, "I didn't know Mel
then, and I swear I didn't know just what kind of an outfit
it was. To tell you the truth, it looked kind of shady to
me. This big guy pulled a couple of gold bars and some
coins out of his pocket and laid them out on the bait box.
Then he told us how we could get into treasure hunting,
how the *Atocha* would make us all rich. He told the dock-
master he didn't have any cash, but gave him this gasoline

credit card and told him, 'Fill 'er up.' Naturally, the dock-master had to call to check on his credit. Surprisingly enough, he found it was good."

In many ways, Key West is Mel Fisher's kind of town. No longer the bone-poor island of Hemingway's *To Have and Have Not,* Key West had experienced twenty-five years of postwar prosperity. As tourists by the thousands found their way down the Overseas Highway, modern shopping centers rose in the place of old salt ponds; rows of motels and fast-food stores now line U.S. Highway 1, leading into the city. But the old town still stands, and its aura of remoteness persists. Its streets of wooden Conch houses—gleaming white or of bare gray boards—and its faded brick warehouses bear witness to another time. Then, before the highway and the water pipeline were built from the mainland, the island had been truly iso-lated.

In spite of its recent growth, an insouciant air pervades the island. Spanish lime, sapodilla, and Geiger trees line the streets; cocks crow in the glowing tropical dawn, while stray cats forage on the cracked sidewalks. Key West ac-cepts all alike: the shrimper on his night on the town, the long-haired youth with backpack, the unshaven dere-lict slumped on a bench, the affluent occupant of the $125-a-day penthouse at the Pier House. At the bitter end of the continental line, Key West is a natural gathering place for eccentrics of every kind. To these it extends an easy tolerance.

Key West has been many things: since 1821, a Navy town; a long-established center for artists and writers; the seat of a strong Latin culture; nineteenth-century head-quarters for the wreckers. Most of all, however, Key West breathes of the waters that so closely surround it. Whether the winds of winter thrash among the dry coconut fronds along Roosevelt Boulevard or summer squalls are lashing heavy rains across the island, one never feels far from the sea.

Beyond Key West, the islands are deserted, without facilities of any kind. Every last drop of fuel and water and every other necessary thing for Mel's operations would have to be brought to the Marquesas across a twenty-five-mile supply line. There are two routes from Key West to the Marquesas: one runs outside the island chain, while the other—passable only by small boats—lies through the shallows surrounding a number of small mangrove keys. As one traverses these islands—called *chiquimulas* ("brothers") by the seventeenth-century Indians because of their look-alikeness—they seem to float like dark-green blobs on the milky green sea. One follows another: Mule Key, Ballast Key, Woman Key, Man Key.

When you reach Boca Grande, the last of these intermediate islands, you see a wide channel ahead. Across this, a faint line of green appears in the west: the Marquesas Keys. Halfway across the Boca Grande Channel, the band of green separates into larger and smaller dots. As you approach, the atoll is spread out before you: a distorted oval of islets clustered around a three-mile-wide central lagoon. Narrow beaches, fringed with sea oats, line the outer shore of several of the islands. On the two southwesterly islands, coarse saw grass covers a meager upland behind the beach; in its turn, the grass yields to buttonwood and black mangrove. The whole lagoon side of the islets is a swamp of red mangrove. The atoll looks much as it must have in 1622. The islands also serve as a breeding ground for a rich variety of bird and sea life. The black swallow-tailed frigate bird has nested on the Marquesas since time unknown; now it is rare, and protected in a refuge on the atoll. For years, sport fishermen, including Ernest Hemingway and Zane Grey, have enjoyed the bountiful fishing near the atoll. The waters around the Marquesas have also served as a Navy bombing range for more than thirty years.

The islands' isolation and their position make them a dangerous place for salvage operations. Strong countercurrents to the Gulf Stream run nearby; affected by tidal

Mel Fisher

Delores Fisher, with *Atocha* gold

The Marquesas Keys

The search boat *Holly's Folly*

Don Kincaid finds the first gold of the *Atocha*—an 8½-foot chain

Theodolite towers guided the magnetometer search

Bleth McHaley and Spencer Wickens unloading pieces of eight

(Left to right) Spencer Wickens, Steve Wickens, John Brandon, and state agent Mike Wisenbaker, after bringing up 1,500 silver coins from the "Bank of Spain"

The 4.7-pound gold disc

"Bouncy John" Lewis and the gold chain he found

Links of gold

Kim Fisher holds his finds: the gold disc and a twisted gold bar

The golden "poison cup"

A Spanish gold "finger bar"; the markings indicate its carat rating and show that the royal tax had been paid

Chains of gold and a gold button

Silver bar No. 569, found on the wreck site, matched at all points the descriptions found on this page from the *Atocha*'s manifest (with permission of the Archive of the Indies)

The crew that found the 1973 treasure, aboard Mel's galleon museum

The rosary of coral and gold

Tense moment: checking the weight of an ingot of silver against the markings on the *Atocha*'s manifest—it matches!

Gene Lyon and "Moe" Molinar, aboard *Virgilona*

While Florida Marine Patrol stands guard, Robert Williams takes custody of the *Atocha* treasure from Mel Fisher

Wilburn R. "Sonny" Cockrell, Florida State marine archaeologist

The gold whistle with its chain and grooming tools

changes, the shallow waters of the Quicksands quickly become rough in strong winds.

In summer, numberless squalls march across the sea. Where their blackness touches the horizon, the waters are churned by the visible force of fierce winds. As the short winter approaches, browning the vines in the island glades, the first weak cold fronts die in a series of northeast storms. Later, stronger fronts penetrate through to the Straits of Florida, bringing the whole range of shifting winds: northwest to north and back again to southeast. When winter winds sweep across the empty waters, boats must seek refuge between the islets of the Marquesas; outside, seas mount up quickly to five, six, and nine feet or more.

In this isolated place, Mel Fisher began his search for the *Atocha*. For guidance, he had all his past experiences and those of his associates; these had now to be applied to a truly knotty problem. The only clue I had given Mel to the location of the 1622 ships was a general one: the galleons were somewhere in the vicinity of the Marquesas. Thus, Mel had to survey an area more than thirty miles long and almost five miles wide.

The proton magnetometer was the key factor in the hunt. Fay Feild came to Key West to plan the best utilization of his instrument and to direct the search. From long experience, he knew the kinds of readings a scattered Spanish shipwreck would yield. He had thus to design a search plan that would cover the vast area as quickly as possible and yet miss no vital clue that might lead to the *Atocha* or the *Santa Margarita*. Mel and Fay decided to seek primarily for galleon anchors, which would be large enough to register at long range, so Fay set a minimum distance of fifty feet between boat search runs to ensure that none would be missed.

In the Indian River area, Mel had found and worked his shipwrecks by reference to shoreline markers. Now he would be hunting in an almost trackless place; much of the time he would be out of sight of any land. In the middle and northern Keys, Mel had searched by sea and air, using buoys to mark out his area. This time he wanted a better plan. Mel was certain that, at last, he was really onto something good; he didn't want to miss his chance. To find the *Atocha,* he wanted the most accurate system possible. Electronic navigation devices were available that could fix a boat's position to within a few feet, but these cost up to a hundred thousand dollars. Mel thought of a less costly plan. He ordered a Swedish theodolite, an accurate bearing circle used by surveyors. With this device, mounted on a fixed tower, he could track his search boats accurately. Mel fitted *Virgilona* out with a tall mast, atop which was placed a plastic garbage can painted a fluorescent orange. The search vessel, visible for many miles, would be kept in the cross hairs of the theodolite, and its course corrected by radio from the tower. In this way, the boat could run close and accurate patterns. Each successive run would overlap the last by just the proper distance, so that the questing magnetometer would miss nothing.

One of the men who had stood on the yacht club dock on the day the *Virgilona* pulled into Key West was Bob Holloway. Two years before, Bob had been a busy, successful building contractor in Indiana. One day, though, he realized he was suddenly weary of the reports, the accounts, the detail—all the endless pressures of a large business. "I just got tired of the numbers," he says. Since his marriage had ended and his children were grown, there was nothing to hold him in Indiana—but where would he go? Since his greatest lifelong affinity had been for the sea, the next decision was easy; he bought a thirty-four-foot blue Chris-Craft, which he named *Holly's Folly* in honor of his new life. Soon he was on his way south, to the Florida Keys, where he had spent many a happy fishing holiday.

It was inevitable: in early June 1970 Bob Holloway found himself talking treasure with Mel Fisher. After sizing him up, Mel was highly impressed with Holloway. A friendly, soft-spoken manner could not hide the man's cool expertise and keen determination. At first, Mel chartered *Holly's Folly* to run supplies out to the search area. Finally, he designated the Chris-Craft as the primary search boat. Fay Feild and his magnetometer moved aboard *Holly's Folly*. Now the *Virgilona* could spend its time more profitably, in checking out magnetic anomalies turned up by the new search team.

Mel had begun by taking *Virgilona* along the whole of the south side of the Quicksands, seeking likely places where a galleon might have struck and sunk. One area looked good to him: it was a small rise just off the sandbank about ten miles west of the Marquesas. Mel had also heard a turtler's story that wreckage abounded there under the sea. Anchoring over the small reef, Mel and his divers surveyed the bottom but found no ballast stones or other evidence of a Spanish ship. They passed along to the west and, at the far end of the great sandbar, came to the derelict freighter *Balbanera,* where Mel and Deo had dived on their 1953 honeymoon. Since Mel's first state search contract lay below Halfmoon Shoals, the hulk of *Balbanera* was an ideal place to mount his first theodolite tower. There the search began; the eager hunters had no idea that it would last for fifteen years.

To carry out the hunt, Bob Holloway had an all-girl crew, which included Kay Finley and Bob's sister, Marjory Hargreaves, nicknamed "T." Those aboard *Holly's Folly* soon became a highly effective team, as Fay taught Bob how to operate the magnetometer.

During the search, one crew member was at the wheel, steering with one ear cocked for radio instructions from the theodolite tower. Another watched the dial of the magnetometer for the telltale jump that indicated an anomaly; a third stood by to throw a marker buoy. Bob Holloway rotated all of the tasks until everyone aboard was letter-perfect.

The work moved at a dizzying pace. In order to cover more areas quickly, Mel fitted the boats out with aircraft strobe lights; the search went on night and day. The night tower operator squinted as he tracked the faintly winking strobe through the darkness.

As area after area was crossed off the chart, *Holly's Folly* ran thousands of linear miles over the sea. The paperwork of search contract applications in Tallahassee could not keep up with the rapidity of Mel's search. From the square south of Halfmoon, Mel moved back east toward the Marquesas. Now he thought the ships might have struck the main reef southwest of the atoll; he set up his theodolite in the old Navy range spotter's tower on the Marquesas. Day after day, men sat cramped in the tower, staring as the distant boat moved rapidly in the glare of the sea.

As the hunt went on, the strain began to tell on machines as well as upon men. *Holly's Folly* was burning two hundred gallons of fuel a day, and running a thousand miles a week. Every six weeks Bob Holloway would have to tear the engines down and have the valves ground. "I got so good at it," he says, "that I could do it blindfolded. By ten o'clock in the morning I'd have them torn down, take the heads down to be ground, reassemble the engines by dusk, and be out at sea the next morning. Finally, I wore out the bolts that hold the heads to the blocks, and I had to put in a pair of new diesel engines. But I had made up my mind that I was going to stay on until I found it."

As they searched over square miles upon miles of sea bottom, the treasure hunters felt a sense of increasing frustration. When they had moved the search area eastward, their problem changed from lack of targets to a great profusion of them. The searchers found the ocean floor littered with modern refuse—anchors, winches, and fish traps. They now also fully appreciated the fact that the whole Quicksands area and the deeper waters near it had been a bombing range: scores of bombs registered on the magnetometer dial. *Virgilona*'s crew disgustedly dug up bomb after bomb.

As if that were not enough, the magnetometer also recorded a series of very strong readings, indicating great masses of metal below. Excitedly the hunters summoned *Virgilona;* divers went down and the mailbox churned. Finally came realization: the targets lay a hundred feet or more below the sea bed. They were meteorites, deeply buried by the force of their impact.

How could the searchers deal with hundreds, thousands of such misleading targets? They had to modify their first plan. Even though they had learned through long experience just what a bomb, torpedo, or meteorite looked like on the mag dial, they still decided to log every contact. If adjacent runs disclosed other nearby contacts, a buoy would be dropped and the target would be investigated. That way, the hunters hoped, they would not miss the one vital reading that spelled "galleon."

While the intensive search was going on in the Marquesas, Mel led the constant struggle to back the effort with money. Treasure Salvors' office at this time was in Vero Beach. Mel worked there with Rupert Gates and Norman Johnson, seeking to market the still-unsold remnants of the 1715 treasure and to interest investors in the enterprise of the *Atocha.* He formed several subsidiary corporations to help in the financing: Man Key, Inc.; Woman Key, Inc.; *Margarita,* Inc. Mel burned up the roads between Vero Beach and the Keys in Deo's gold-colored Cadillac, which he had bought for her with gold coins from the 1715 treasure and which was rapidly beginning to show its age.

When I returned to Vero Beach from Spain in the summer of 1970 to go back to teaching at the community college, I spent my spare time at the microfilm reader, scanning the copies of the fleet papers and the *Margarita* salvage accounts brought from the archive, seeking a more precise location for the 1622 galleons. In September, Ángeles Flores sent us a packet of transcriptions she had made from documents concerning the shipwrecks. I eagerly read her typed transcription of a long letter written by the Marquis of Cadereita in January 1623; it contained rich detail about the shipwrecks and their later salvage. In it was a short eyewitness account of the sinking by Captain de Lugo, which stated that the *Santa Margarita* had been lost on the east side of the "last key of Matecumbe." If this was correct, we had been looking on the wrong side of the Marquesas.

When I told Mel of Señora Flores's transcript, he began immediately to redirect his search. First, he moved into the Boca Grande Channel; then he requested a search contract that ran eastward all the way to Sand Key, near Key West.

When the new effort was fully under way, Mel invited all his investors and stockholders to a Thanksgiving party in the islands. I landed at Boca Grande Key on a fine, clear late-November day and found myself in the midst of a kind of reverse Dunkirk. The treasure campers disembarked from the Treasure Salvors' workboats, several cruisers, and a dozen small outboards, and struggled down the narrow beach. Soon, bright-colored tents had been set up on the grassy upland. Many of the investors had come from Vero Beach, where the company had originated, but there were also stockholders from the Keys, from other parts of Florida, and from several other states. Young and middle-aged, all seemed happy to be living a treasure adventure.

Around a driftwood campfire that night, the group gathered around Mel. He told his audience that he believed the Key to have been the haunt of English freebooter Henry Jennings; treasure, he said, might easily be buried there. He also talked to them of the search for the 1622 galleons, and of the new clues he was now following. Mel said that he estimated that the *Atocha* and the *Santa Margarita* had sunk with cargoes worth four hundred million dollars. He went on to use a favorite expression. The "nitty-gritty" of the situation, Mel assured the stockholders, was that he knew he would find it all, and soon.

Through the winter of 1970–71, *Holly's Folly* searched, hunting even in six- to eight-foot seas, and retiring within the Marquesas when it was impossible to work. Off the Boca Grande Channel, the magnetometer picked up a large target. When divers investigated, they found a sunken World War II aircraft lying on the shallow sea bed. It was a single-engine Navy trainer craft that evidently had struck hard, for the engine had been torn loose in the crash and lay far ahead of the fuselage. Since the pilot's canopy was open and the pilot had either bailed out or been removed, the salvors notified the Navy and went on. In all the weary weeks of searching, they found no sign of the *Margarita* or of the *Atocha.*

At the beginning of January, Norman Johnson urged that we send to Seville for microfilm of the original documents Ángeles Flores had copied. I thought it an excellent suggestion, and Mel strongly concurred, so I wrote to Señora Flores with the request. In a few weeks I had a small roll of microfilm; I immediately put it on the reader, and turned at once to the Cadereita letter and Captain de Lugo's account. When I ran my finger down to the place where the survivor had described the place of the *Margarita*'s loss, I saw the words *veste del último cayo.* The word had been copied wrong: *veste* meant *west.* The shipwreck of the *Margarita* did not lie *east,* but *west* of the "last key." We had been looking on the wrong side of the Marquesas. I wrote Mel, saying, "Back to the drawing board." We had to move back west again; four months' work for nothing.

South of the great shoal, the only place left to work was an area surrounding the little rise that Mel had briefly surveyed before, ten miles west of the Marquesas. Mel sent yet another contract change application to Tallahassee and moved his theodolite to the *Patricia,* the battered destroyer that served as target ship for the Navy bombers. *Holly's Folly* had not been working long out of the *Patricia* tower when she logged the "peg" magnetometer reading, the galleon anchor was found, and the first treasure from a Spanish shipwreck, including Don Kincaid's golden chain, had come to light.

Immediately upon the recovery of the gold chain, Mel petitioned the state of Florida for a salvage contract on that spot. While the request was under study, a state agent was placed aboard the *Virgilona*. He allowed only exploratory digging to fix the limits of the shipwreck, if indeed that was what it was. The investigations turned up the encrusted bulk of a matchlock musket, some iron barrel hoops, iron cannonballs, and a few ballast stones. Ranging outward from the galleon anchor, Mel found a single ballast stone and a piece of broken silverware several hundred feet away. All had been buried in deep, deep sand. Mel wrote in his log a prophetic statement: "This wreck is badly scattered and will be very tough to salvage."

One late June day, a diver brought up a small stack of nineteen blackened silver coins. A few days later in his Key West apartment, Don Kincaid projected an enlargement of his color slide of the coins onto a screen. I gasped as the photograph came suddenly into sharp focus—the coins were breathtaking! They bore clear shields and were utterly different from the 1715 pieces of eight. I made out one date—1619—and saw several *P* mintmarks, for Potosí. Don pointed out the mark *RN* on one coin—this stood for *Nuevo Reino de Granada*—but that was impossible! No coins were known from the Bogotá mint before about 1630. These coins, however, seemed to point to the 1622 ships, but which one? Since the *Santa Margarita* had been lost in shallow water, and these coins had been found in about seventeen feet of water, we assumed that it might be the wreck of the *Margarita*.

In order to obtain a state salvage contract on the anchor site, Mel's application had to be recommended favorably by an advisory commission to the Division of History, Archives and Records Management. The division, a branch of the Florida Department of State, was now headed by Robert Williams, a former state senator. On August 8, 1971, Mel met with Senator Williams and the commission in Tallahassee. Characteristically cagey, Mel attempted to protect his find and guarantee his right to others that might lie to the east of it. He asked for another area also, one that lay between the anchor site and the Marquesas. Senator Williams assured Mel that he need not be concerned, noting that his agency didn't permit two salvors to work on the same shipwreck. The meeting was routinely tape-recorded for the record.

Because an on-site inspection had to be made by the marine archaeologist before a salvage contract could be granted, three state men—Carl Clausen, Arthur Ergle, and Allen Saltus—came by boat to the galleon anchor the next day. Clausen dived by the anchor and took charge of the materials that the salvors had replaced underwater: two matchlocks, the broken piece of silverware, an encrusted sword, musket balls, potsherds, and a coin. Pressed for time and contemptuous of the salvors' wishes, Carl Clausen refused to give them a receipt for the artifacts. Pointedly, the treasure hunters wrote all this down on their state log. Angry words and gestures were exchanged as Clausen sped away with the materials. It was a poor beginning for a partnership between Treasure Salvors and the state of Florida on the wreck site. As weeks went by, the salvors still had not received their salvage contract from Tallahassee.

In the meantime, Mel placed a theodolite closer to the wreck site. He bought an old tug, the *Bon Vent,* and grounded it not far from the galleon anchor. Now he was ready to uncover whatever treasure lay beneath the sands of the wreck site.

Rick Vaughan and Scott Barron faced the camera, smiling. Both divers made the "V for victory" sign; in their other hands, each held a six-inch gold bar. It was October 23, 1971. *Virgilona*'s mailboxes had burrowed slowly toward bedrock in the coarse, deep sand. First Rick and then Scott had spied a glimmer of gold in the crater walls; within an hour, each had surfaced clutching their treasure. From the *Virgilona* to Key West and up to Vero Beach the elation spread.

The finding of the gold bars had momentous meaning for Treasure Salvors. It raised Mel's hopes that the wreck site, which he felt to be that of the *Santa Margarita,* would prove rich and fruitful. As for me, it started a whole new chain of research. Last, it stirred significant reaction in Florida and elsewhere in the nation.

As I examined photographs of the two bars, questions arose in my mind. From which shipwreck had they come? Where had they been minted? During the previous summer I had summarized the whole *avería* cargo list from the *Atocha;* from this I learned that she had carried twenty thousand *pesos de oro* (in gold), but in what form I did not know. I needed more data on the cargoes of both ships, and asked Mel to order the entire ships' registries, or manifests, from Seville, if these were available. He sent off a request for the manifests. In the meantime, about all that I could determine was that the two bars were evidently of high carat. They bore no distinct markings, only dim circles.

News of the gold bar find was printed in the Miami *Herald;* from there it was picked up by the wire services. On November 3, Paul Harvey's nationwide radio broadcast from Chicago mentioned the recovery of remnants of the 1622 ships in Florida.

Rumors about the gold bars spread just as quickly across the Florida treasure network. Carl Clausen told several people that the bars just did not seem right for the seventeenth century; he thought there was something funny about them.

In Washington on November 4, the *Alcoa Seaprobe,* a revolutionary new deep-sea research and salvage vessel, was dedicated. The elite of the underwater world gathered for the ceremonies; among those in attendance was Robert Marx. Since his Yucatán trip with the Fishers, Bob Marx had become a genuine underwater pioneer. He had discovered the shipwreck of the Spanish trading ship *Matancero* off the Mexican coast. For three years he worked in Jamaica, excavating the historic sunken city of Port Royal; off the north coast of the island he found the remains of very early vessels, possibly those of Christopher Columbus. Marx had published a valuable monograph on colonial clay pipe styles, had carried out or sponsored lengthy archival research in Spain, and had written fifteen books on marine archaeology or treasure diving.

Now, at the Alcoa ship dedication, Bob Marx told anyone who would listen that Mel Fisher had "planted," or "salted," the shipwreck in the Marquesas. The anchor there, Marx affirmed, had been stolen from a site that he himself had found; the gold bars were phonies. Since Bob Marx was widely known, his charges against Mel spread widely. Unfortunately, Mel's irrepressible huckstering and his well-known penchant for exaggeration—called the "Fisher factor"—provided a background against which such a rumor could easily flourish. As the talk spread among treasure hunters, the faithful in Treasure Salvors reacted strongly, defending Mel from people who accused him of salting the Marquesas site.

Fay Feild, for instance, had heard it all before; he pointed out that there is no way one can salt a wreck unless everybody on the site is in on it. "There's something about the psychology of treasure hunting," he said. "You can't keep secrets. Mel would never intend to salt a wreck; even if he did intend to, he doesn't have the expertise to do it. Mel never salted a wreck, and I'd bet my life on it."

Mel also faced a number of other problems. Even though valuable recoveries had been made, working the site continued to be difficult. Key West was thirty-five miles from his new location. During much of the year, high winds spawned breaking waves that battered his boats; strong underwater currents assailed his divers. Most expeditions lasted only three or four days before the boats were forced to return to Key West. *Virgilona*'s mailboxes were broken, welded, rebroken, and rewelded countless times. By far the most stubborn obstacle to the salvage, however, was the deep sand. In some places twenty feet of sand had drifted over the underlying bedrock, where heavy shipwreck objects were most likely to be found. The way the materials lay scattered in the Quicksands, moreover, conformed to no pattern Mel or Fay had seen before. The magnetometer was of little help in their recovery; many of the electronic contacts on the site were often no stronger than the normal background readings. The salvage, therefore, was essentially a matter of wholesale sand excavation, and *Virgilona*'s trusty mailboxes lacked the digging power to do the job. Mel had to seek other alternatives.

Mel first tried the larger mailboxes and the water-jetting system of the boat *Aquanaut*. The boat, which belonged to Chet Alexander, a commercial salvor in Key West, came to the site in the late summer of 1971. After initial expectations of success, the attempt was abandoned; the *Aquanaut* had accomplished little more than had the *Virgilona*. Mel still had to devise a better way to reach down through the sand to the treasures he was certain awaited him below. In the meantime, additional research came in to encourage him further.

On December 9, I received a thick microfilm roll from Seville. It was the *Atocha*'s full cargo manifest, more than a thousand pages written in the notary's rolling *procesal* hand. I had never before seen a Spanish ship manifest; as I struggled to read the difficult script, I slowly began to understand the structure and importance of a manifest. Particularly significant was the way in which the silvermaster had recorded each consignment. Hundreds of silver ingots appeard in the manifest pages, each described minutely by its weight and serial number. Suddenly, I realized that the descriptions could be used to identify a

Spanish shipwreck. I asked Ángeles Flores Rodríguez to send also the manifest of the *Santa Margarita,* and wrote Mel to tell him that the microfilm verified the great wealth aboard the *Atocha.* Adding up the totals from the scrawled pages, I found that the galleon had carried 901 registered ingots of silver, more than 250,000 silver pieces of eight, and 161 separate gold pieces, some of them several pounds in weight. I also told Mel that, if we could find numbered bullion items on the shipwreck site, "identification is possible."

VII. The Bank of Spain

By now, Mel had an office in Key West, one particularly suited to him: Treasure Salvors had moved into the galleon built by Bob Moran. Since her triumphant dedication, the *Golden Doubloon* had fallen on evil days; in 1968 thieves broke into the ship at her Fort Lauderdale anchorage and stole coins valued at seventy thousand dollars. Later, she sank at her dock, and water damaged many of the exhibits on board. Mel dickered with the other owners of the galleon and finally made a deal to buy them out for Treasure Salvors stock. In October 1971 the galleon was towed to Key West and moored at the gasoline docks. The *Golden Doubloon* opened as an attraction in Key West on Christmas Day, 1971.

From his office in the galleon's sterncastle, Mel monitored the work in the Marquesas by radio. Most of his time was spent in attempting to solve urgent financial problems. He had continually to struggle to pay off bills or stave off his most demanding creditors.

The search for the *Atocha* and the *Margarita* had already cost more than a quarter of a million dollars, and Mel desperately needed more money for the coming diving season. Laboriously he wrote out the names of possible investors on a yellow legal pad. Telephone cradled on his shoulder and cigarette smoke curling up from his ashtray, Mel placed dozens of long-distance calls—to Tampa and Fort Lauderdale, to Atlanta, to Chicago. In his slow drawl, tinged with a Western twang, Mel told of the *Margarita* site and of the riches of the *Atocha.*

Just before Christmas, Mel called me to say that he had planned a major financing effort and was coming to Vero Beach to pick up some treasure. Could I meet him at the airport? At almost one o'clock, his light plane arrived. Mel asked me to drive him to a local bank before it closed; the last of the 1715 silver was stored there. We reached the bank just before closing time, and Mel signed the necessary receipts. Guided by the bank president, we went to the vault. The treasure had been stored in boxes, but one sack of pieces of eight rested in a child's plastic beach bucket. We loaded thousands of coins into my Volkswagen and headed for home. On the way, Mel stopped off at McDonald's to pick up lunch. At my place, with the treasure locked in the car in the driveway, we ate hamburgers and French fries while Mel talked about money—big money.

He talked of forming a Curaçao corporation with capital enough to handle the 1622 search and fund a new program of research and salvage around the world. Mel mentioned the possibility of buying out the Colombian contract to search for the fabled *San José,* sunk with millions in gold off Cartagena in 1708. Then he turned to the most bizarre scheme of all: someone had offered to approach "Bebe" Rebozo and contact President Nixon; Nixon was to be offered 10 percent of the 1622 shipwrecks in return for a million dollars cash. I sat blinking at all of this. Was it real?

Later that afternoon, the little plane took off, heavily laden with its silver cargo, heading south for Fort Lauderdale. There, hopefully, the coins could be sold or used as loan collateral.

As the spring approached, a few investors did come in. Some purchased investment contracts for a percentage of the shipwreck find; others bought stock in the company. Mel also moved to put his personal affairs in order for the coming season. The Fishers put their Vero Beach house on the market, but Dirk and Kim remained in Vero to finish the school term. Kane, Taffi, and their parents moved onto a large houseboat, moored off Roosevelt Boulevard in Key West. It was only a nominal headquarters for the Fisher clan, however. Mel and Deo were often gone on marketing or fund-raising trips; even when they were in Key West, they were so busy they seldom ate a meal at home.

By late March, with some money in hand, Mel was ready to make his next move on the wreck site. Chet Alexander towed the *Gold-digger* down from Vero Beach; on March 22, it arrived at the Marquesas. Mel hoped that the barge's huge digging propeller would move the deep sands. As *Gold-digger* anchored over the galleon anchor, the Fishers and Moe Molinar were there, with Bob Holloway, "T" Hargreaves, Kay Finley, and Don Kincaid. As the great motor started, divers Scott Barron and Mickey Fitzgerald prepared to enter the water.

The first "blow" from the barge uncovered the whole of the galleon anchor for the first time; it was measured at fifteen feet long. In the week that followed, *Gold-digger* repeated the performance; when it functioned well, it could dig quickly to bedrock. Troubles plagued the barge, however; its motor tended to overheat, and seashells repeatedly clogged the pumping system. At the end of March, stormy weather struck; in ten-foot seas, the *Gold-digger* broke loose from her moorings and drifted toward Halfmoon Shoals.

The salvors rescued their barge and returned it to the site. The *Gold-digger* worked sporadically for a few more days, but on April 16 Mel asked Chet to tow it back up to Vero Beach. One more experiment had failed, but Mel had not given up.

We all thought it likely that Mel had found the wreckage of the *Santa Margarita.* Therefore, while work went forward on the anchor site, the magnetometer search for the *Atocha* continued. Bob Holloway believed that the *almiranta* might have passed northward in high storm tides over the great shoal and found a resting place there. He also held out hope for a few small areas south of the Quicksands not yet searched. Mel asked me to check on the latitude in which the shipwrecks were said to lie and to verify the relative location of the two lost galleons. By this time, we had received copies of a letter written in 1623 by Captain Gaspar de Vargas, who had located *Atocha* after the September hurricane and then worked on the first Spanish salvage attempts. After studying all the materials at hand, I advised Mel that Vargas's account of the time it took his salvage craft to return from the wreck site to the Marquesas indicated that *Atocha* should lie not more than fifteen miles from the atoll. I also told him that the *almiranta* was said to have sunk east of the *Margarita* in a latitude similar to that in which he was then searching.

Now Mel needed more money for the summer's diving. For weeks, he whistled and sang "It's the real thing," for Mel hoped for a big investment from Coca-Cola interests. The contract package he was discussing with agents included film and publication rights for the shipwreck story, an interest in the treasure, and funding of two million dollars. After some time, however, the deals just did not materialize, and Mel had been disappointed again. Shortly thereafter, however, he did succeed in making an arrangement that would prove to be tremendously helpful: he made two contracts with the National Geographic Society.

Mel had appeared in the 1965 *National Geographic* article about Kip Wagner and the 1715 treasure; since then the society had continued to follow Mel's career. Otis Imboden, a veteran *National Geographic* photographer, and Dennis Kane, chief of the society's television division, came to Key West to survey the site and talk with the Fishers. The society also retained Mendel Peterson, recently retired head of the Smithsonian Institution's underwater program, to examine the materials and talk with me about the documentation. Despite the rumors of "salting," the *National Geographic* was satisfied that a good story might develop out of the Marquesas search, and contracted with Treasure Salvors for exclusive rights to a magazine article and a television special. Photographers and film crews would be on location during the summer.

Below the beams of the upstairs room in the *Golden Doubloon,* cigarette smoke hung in a moist, warm haze that the single laboring wall air conditioner could only slightly mitigate. Stockholders of Treasure Salvors occupied every chair and bench, and many stood along the walls. They had gathered from near and far to attend the July 1, 1972, annual meeting. True to form, it was well after ten o'clock, the hour set for opening, when Mel, wearing a multicolored sport shirt, strode up to the head table.

Mel began by describing the search for the *Atocha*. He introduced Bob Holloway, who told the audience how he hoped next to take *Holly's Folly* out to New Ground Reef, some miles north and west of the galleon anchor. Mel then said that he had every expectation of breaking open the *Margarita* site at last; in furtherance of that, he introduced Art Hempstead. Art had agreed to furnish his eighty-foot salvage barge *Sandy,* whose giant airlifts would surely be the tool to uncover the sands piled deep over the shipwreck.

Norman Johnson, now company treasurer, advised the stockholders that the state had divided a small amount of treasure from the 1715 sites with the company, but nothing from the Marquesas site had yet been received. Money was still a problem, and it was abundantly clear that time and the pressures of treasure hunting had badly eroded the original 1963 Treasure Salvors group. Dick Williams and Walt Holzworth had sold out their interests; neither man came to Key West to take part in the new expedition. Rupert Gates had retired and moved to Idaho, saying, "It isn't much fun anymore—the whole thing has become an ulcer factory."

How right he was was evident from the next announcement: Fay Feild was leaving Treasure Salvors for another position in the underwater field. Exhausted by the search, bedeviled by the financial insecurity of the business, and made ill by the irregular life that characterized Treasure Salvors, Fay had developed a bleeding ulcer. To friends he admitted, "Treasure hunting is a disease; it wiped me out financially, destroyed my marriage, ruined me physically—I had to get away. I had to find a new life."

Of the original salvors, only Mel and Deo Fisher and Moe Molinar were left. Rick Vaughan and Charles Mitchell, who participated in the early stages of the *Atocha* hunt, had already left. But new people and resources, it seemed, always came forward. When these in turn were exhausted, Mel would find others. His belief, his purpose, were stronger than ever. He would go on.

Bob Holloway's interest in New Ground Reef had paid off—in a way. A magnetometer contact had led to the uncovering of an iron anchor, then an iron cannon, and finally a whole sunken ship, partly encrusted in coral. Soon, hundreds of artifacts, including stacked pewter plates, tankards, slave shackles, and two ivory tusks, had been recovered; these finds led the divers to dub the shipwreck "H.M.S. *Woolworth.*"

Moreover, the timing of the find was ideal. Howard Worth and Don Belth of New York had contracted with the National Geographic Society to film the Marquesas treasure story for television, and Howard had a full film crew on the site when the new wreck was uncovered. Even the weather had cooperated for a change, and the calm indigo water around New Ground Reef gave stable conditions for diving and camerawork.

But unfortunately, the site was not the *Atocha.* A coin and a silver spoon with the bust of William and Mary pointed to an English nationality and a dating of possibly 1697. And when the film crew went to the galleon anchor site, they could not record any treasure triumphs in the summer of 1972. The cameramen had filmed the coming of Art Hempstead with his barge and the huge, custom-made airlifts, but again a grand idea had proved a distinct disappointment. The swirling currents on the south edge of the Quicksands, changing direction with every tide, made it impossible to control the large airlifts. The attempt was finally abandoned, and Art Hempstead took his barge *Sandy* back to Miami.

But Mel had another string to his bow. All along he had been striving for size—for some powerful force to move sand. Now, he reasoned, why not build a bigger and better mailbox? To do this, he needed larger vessels than any presently in his little fleet. Mel began to negotiate with Lou Tilley, who owned two powerful Mississippi River tugboats, and in return for stock, Treasure Salvors acquired the tugs. One, fifty-four feet long, was named *Northwind;* the other, the *Southwind,* was fifty-nine feet in length. Mel had the boats brought from New Orleans to Key West, where he began to get them into condition for salvage operations by fitting them out with mailboxes. He designated his two older sons, Dirk and Kim, to be captains, respectively, of *Northwind* and *Southwind.* Even though the diving season had ended, Mel brought *Southwind* out to the site for trials in September. The tug propeller very quickly dug a hole ten feet wide by twenty feet long to bedrock. Perhaps in the next summer the remains of the *Margarita* could be uncovered at last.

The unsuccessful season had not passed without some positive benefits: new workers had come to the task. In addition to Mel's sons, other young divers had been on the wreck site: John McGaughey, Ellis Greene, and Ken Lingle. Dean Curry, from an old Key West family, had joined the team, as had Dave Hargreaves, "T" Hargreaves's sturdy son. Lingle, who got the nickname of "Ding-a-Ling," became a crack theodolite operator. Greene, a young diver from Vero Beach, found a most interesting object in the Quicksands: a glistening white quartz cannonball. While working near the galleon anchor, the divers stirred up a cloud of deep-blue color; they found small pieces of pressed indigo dyestuff. They laughed at how the dye, which had stained their fingers blue, came off on their faces and made them look like Indians on the warpath. In keeping with youthful fashion, the divers tie-dyed a T-shirt with seventeenth-century indigo.

The divers' finds gave me some further clues to the identification of the anchor site shipwreck. In the 1622 fleet papers, I had found a list of the arms and munitions carried by the Guard Fleet of which the *Atocha* and the *Santa Margarita* had been a part. I noticed that each of the missing galleons had been equipped with bronze cannon, many muskets, 540 iron cannonballs, and 60 cannonballs of stone. The stone balls were for use in the short, wide-bore cannons called *pedreros,* carried only by the major fleet ships. The indigo was also a clue that we might have one of the guard ships; the *avería* tax accounts described how indigo had been loaded aboard both *Atocha* and *Margarita* in Havana after its transfer from a Honduran ship.

Some of the investors who had helped finance the summer's work became active in the search; a few visited the wreck site many times. Among these were Jud Chalmers of Jacksonville, Edwin Hirst of Daytona Beach, and Jim Vondehaar. Vondehaar, nicknamed "Cincinnati Jim," represented the spirit of American enterprise as truly as did Mel Fisher. Jim had a bar in Cincinnati; he could build or repair almost anything. He put not only his money but his full heart into the search for the *Atocha.* When some piece of equipment was sorely needed in Key West, Jim would get in his car and head south from Cincinnati with a compressor or pump in the back seat; he would arrive with a two-day growth of beard and a happy grin. Cincinnati Jim was also a poet. To commemorate key milestones in the treasure hunt, Jim composed odes; soon he was acknowledged as the company poet laureate.

The company had acquired a real asset in Bleth McHaley, who came to Key West earlier in the year. Since her days with *Skin Diver* magazine in California, Bleth had been a publicist, writer, and most recently manager of a large Vero Beach restaurant. But she had never shaken off her fascination with the sea. After renewing her acquaintance with Mel, and meeting Bob Holloway, Bleth began to work with Treasure Salvors, running a supply boat out to the Marquesas. Soon, however, she gravitated to the main office, where she became Mel's chief publicist and troubleshooter. One of the first problems she had to face was that of Treasure Salvors' relations with the state of Florida.

In February, Carl Clausen had left his job as Florida marine archaeologist for a similar post with the state of Texas. There he went to work on the 1554 shipwrecks off Padre Island and other historic wrecks. His departure did not significantly change the Tallahassee atmosphere toward private salvors. Clausen's successor, Wilburn (Sonny) Cockrell, a professional anthropologist, was as dedicated to the protection of underwater sites as his predecessor. In September, Cockrell wrote to chide Mel about some coins that he had not deposited with the state as quickly as regulations required. In another letter he stiffly put Treasure Salvors on notice that the company was not allowed to make any statements about the history of a shipwreck unless a state representative was present to prevent any errors. Clearly, Bleth McHaley had her work cut out for her in bettering relations with the state.

Mel Fisher's other problems were drearily familiar; the worst was a dearth of money. As salvage work ceased for the year and the usual wintertime lull began, funds were shorter than ever. At this unhappy time, bad money news came suddenly one day. The Eric Schiff case had come to life again with a vengeance. A California arbitration board had awarded Schiff a judgment against Mel and his partners for $215,000. The office in Key West was badly shaken by the news, and Bleth McHaley recalled they didn't know what to do. "We were sure they would serve us with the judgment, and we were afraid they would take everything we had. We took the mags off the galleon, painted out the name 'Treasure Salvors' on the *South-wind,* and just sat there waiting for the worst." Mel called in his attorney to defend the company, and managed to stave off the judgment until a settlement could be negotiated. It was a bad shock, but worse news was coming, as the long winter of 1972 turned slowly into 1973.

From the bar across busy Queipo de Llano Street, I sat facing the gray bulk of the Archive of the Indies. I warmed my hands around a glass of hot *café con leche,* for it was again winter in Seville. I felt, moreover, a deeper chill than the weather warranted. Up to this moment, my second year of research at the archive had gone well enough. It had begun in early November when Howard Worth and Don Belth had arrived in Seville with the *National Geographic* film crew. After archive *Directora* Doña Rosario Parra granted permission, they moved their cameras into the archive itself. There they filmed me with the "worm-eaten document" that had led us to the Marquesas; then the crew returned home to continue work on the television special.

Many interesting documents about the 1622 galleons had turned up, including the *Atocha*'s construction contract, additional reports on Vargas's and Melián's salvage efforts, and the list of bronze cannon assigned to the guard ships. One account described a Dutch attack on Melián's forces at the wreck site in 1627; it told how the salvors were working close to the *"Cayos del Marqués."* I sent Mel the new data, telling him that he did right to continue his search near the Marquesas. It seemed to me that, given enough time, Mel's inventiveness and persistence would pay off; he would find the *Atocha.* Then we learned that rivals had come to the Marquesas.

That late January morning, I had met Jack Haskins, an American researcher who had just arrived in Spain from Florida. Haskins made a favorable impression. Direct and forthright in manner, he had begun five years before to seek shipwreck data in Spanish archives. Haskins was the complete salvor—he did his own research, had his own salvage boat, was both diver and seaman. He had taught himself to read the most difficult scripts and bit by bit had accumulated a fine store of shipwreck information. That morning, I knew instinctively that Jack Haskins was my strongest, perhaps my only, competitor. As we returned to work that morning, I realized that Haskins and I were involved in a race for the *Atocha*. Neither of us believed that Mel had found it yet. Neck and neck, in the weeks that followed, we sped through the *legajos,* or bundles of papers. Once we called for the same bundle at the same time; in an archive with forty thousand *legajos,* the odds against that are considerable. The intensive search led me to many 1622 survivors' reports, to data on Melián's legal troubles in Cuba, to many other things. At one point, I thought I had found the missing clue: I learned that the full 1622 salvage papers had been brought to Madrid for a lawsuit; I followed the trail until it grew cold and then was lost for good.

Another American researcher, John Berrier, a retired naval officer, then came to work in the archive; he was also studying material about the 1622 shipwrecks. When Jack Haskins and John Berrier returned home, it was to go directly to the Keys to organize their expeditions to seek the *Atocha* in the Marquesas. They, with two other men—Burt Webber and Richard MacAllaster—had asked the state of Florida for contracts to the east of Mel Fisher's.

When Mel learned that Webber, MacAllaster, and Haskins had been granted search contracts in the vicinity of his salvage area and that John Berrier had applied for an area overlapping one he had previously applied for, he was furious. He felt that Senator Williams had broken faith with him and had violated the assurances given at the August 1971 meeting. After some difficulty, he obtained a copy of the tape of that meeting and Bleth transcribed it; sure enough, the promises had been made as he remembered them. Mel protested to Governor Reubin Askew.

From Williams's standpoint, there was no question where the right to grant or deny state search or salvage contracts lay—it resided in his agency. Moreover, he could point to the fact that Mel had already held much of the area now granted to the other men—he had held it and searched it, to no avail. This, of course, did not take into account the hard-won knowledge that we had gained: it was possible to overlook an old shipwreck in waters so littered with modern refuse, and such a wreck might yield very light electronic readings.

Williams's other position had less basis in fact; he maintained that he had satisfied himself that the four men who had applied for contracts were not related in their enterprise. We had definite knowledge that the rivals were, in fact, one group, which had relied upon Jack Haskins's research to come to the Marquesas. When Jack came to Seville in 1972, he, too, had found the key word *Marqués;* Burt Webber's outfit was then reactivated and enlarged for a new expedition. The bureaucratic regulation that forbade such combinations was not really the issue to Mel Fisher—it was the way Senator Williams easily skirted it to award Mel's rivals the right to work an area that Mel felt was his by priority.

In the end, Fisher was unable to prevent the coming of Burt Webber's group to the Marquesas. The three search areas were granted, and Berrier's application was temporarily deferred, then approved. Now the pressure was really on Mel; his rivals might easily beat him to the *Atocha*'s treasure.

What none of us knew was that while Mel's competitors were preparing for their search in the Marquesas, an unknown party illegally surveyed the whole wreck site. In the spring of 1973, a New Orleans firm leased their sidescan sonar equipment to a "very secretive" group of men.

The company, contacted later, would not give us their names. They did tell us that the group chartered a fifty-five-foot boat at the Mallory Docks in Key West, proceeded to the west of the Marquesas, and searched with the sonar. Although divers were aboard, the company advised, none went overside that day, even though a "very good target" was picked up on the equipment. We could find out no more, but one thing seemed clear: during 1973, Mel might well lose the chance to be the first to find the riches of *Nuestra Señora de Atocha.*

Fine beads of sweat dotted Moe's face as he maneuvered *Virgilona* into position. Giving a last twist to the wheel, Molinar shouted, "Set the last one!" At the word, the little Whaler buzzed off beyond the port quarter, carrying an anchor tethered to *Virgilona* by its heavy line. The two men on the small craft dropped the third anchor; one dived to be certain it was firmly set. At a signal from the Whaler, Moe shut off the engines. As he prepared to lower the mailboxes and begin work, the *Virgilona* lay floating on a sheet of ocean water as calm as a northern lake.

In late April, Moe had brought the salvage boat and his team of crack divers to the wreck site. It was, however, just too early. Heavy spring winds drove the *Virgilona* to shelter in the Marquesas and, finally, back to Key West. Now, on May 25, the weather had at last calmed. With Moe on the expedition were Norman Johnson and Mike Wisenbaker, the state agent. Also aboard *Virgilona* were three skilled divers who had worked with Moe in the Indian River area: two brothers, Steve and Spencer Wickens of Vero Beach, and John Brandon of Fort Pierce.

During a month of work, punctuated by interludes of storms, the divers had moved down southeast from the galleon anchor, taking their bearings from buoys that now bobbed over the place of previous finds. The salvors began to tap a storehouse of artifacts; they had brought up a number of weapons—muskets, swords, and daggers. They had found a pair of scissors, a bar shot, a lock and key, potsherds, and barrel hoops. On May 19 they had picked up 36 silver coins; on May 21 they had found 244 pieces of eight.

Now, four days later, the twin mailbox tubes were in place, and the throbbing of the diesels began again. Like shadows, Brandon and the Wickens brothers hovered above the invisible storm as the force of the propellers bit more deeply into the sand. All at once, the shallow crater walls were studded with innumerable black blobs. One man surfaced to tell Moe the news, to ask him to shut down the engines and send everyone down to help. *Virgilona* had uncovered a fertile pocket of silver coins. Gently the divers fanned the bottom and sides of the crater with their gloves, deftly lifting the blackened coins out of their resting places in the coarse sand. At the end of this long, exciting day, the salvors counted 1,460 pieces of four and eight.

Bleth McHaley immediately called Dennis Kane of the *National Geographic* in Washington to tell him of the bonanza; Kane said he would send a film crew at once to record the finding of the treasure. In the meantime, Bleth radioed to *Virgilona* to tell the divers to stop work until the cameramen arrived. On the radio she then named the new treasure pocket. "The Bank of Spain," she said, "is closed."

After almost three years of search and salvage, the Marquesas wreck site was at last beginning to give up its wealth. Significant amounts of treasure had been found, and Mel was jubilant. Despite all his troubles, in spite of his rivals, in contradiction of rumors spread against him, Mel's quest seemed to be paying off. In a few days, *Southwind,* with its immense digging power, would be at the site. Who knew what might then come up from the Marquesas sands?

VIII. "We've Found the Big A"

"It's the Big A. We've found it.
We've found the *Atocha.*"

—Bleth McHaley

During the last of May and early June of 1973, days of dead calm alternated with periods of choppy seas. When the waters off the Marquesas were quiet, this was the very best time for diving: the shallows were a milky green in color, shading out as the depth increased to a richer hue. To the south, beyond the salvage boats where the water grew deep, the ocean was a brilliant blue.

The *Virgilona* was still anchored over the Bank of Spain, and her crew continued to discover coins and artifacts. John Lewis, nicknamed "Bouncy John," had joined the divers; he was stocky and quite strong but had a gentle manner that belied his strength. John was sensitive to every visual impression he received on the wreck site, for he was a painter in oils. Once, Lewis had worn his hair very long, well below his shoulders; he had cut it shorter after it snagged on an anchor and he almost drowned.

Southwind relieved the *Virgilona* on June 3, and Lewis and Brandon transferred over to the tug. *Southwind* was a strange-looking craft. The full depth and beauty of her hull could not be seen above the water, and from a distance she appeared to be mostly superstructure. Her three cabins, piled one atop the other, were surmounted by a square pilot house, and the whole tug was painted a bright yellow with black trim. Her whole stern was covered by the black iron framework bracing the enormous underwater deflectors that pivoted down over the tug's two massive brass propellers. The square bow was surmounted by two large iron fenders, for once she had pushed cargo barges on the Mississippi. Now the *Southwind* was no longer engaged in the prosaic work of freight hauling; she had been enlisted in Mel Fisher's treasure hunt, and for that purpose was peopled with a vibrant, youthful crew.

Those who manned, supplied, and maintained Treasure Salvors' boats and brought up treasure from the sea bottom of its salvage area were very young. True, they learned fast, for they had to do so. But as *Southwind* came to the Marquesas in early June 1973, her crew brought to their tasks all the enthusiasm of youth.

Kim Fisher, just turned seventeen, was *Southwind*'s captain; serious and quiet, he quickly became a responsible leader. His elder brother, Dirk, stalwart and handsome, came to dive with *Southwind*'s crew since his own boat, the *Northwind,* was not yet ready for sea. A young Michigan college man, Scott Hummon, had come to work with the company; in turn, he had interested an old family friend, Jo Arden Stuart, in treasure hunting. Jo came to cook aboard the *Southwind,* but, like Bouncy John, she was an artist and was skillful at sketching the artifacts the divers recovered. Mike Schneidelbach, a slight, sandy-haired Key West youth, had signed on to dive but was also a licensed pilot. Liz Holmes had also joined the crew from Key West.

Dean Curry had recruited his sister Angel; although she also shipped as a cook, Angel Curry had a systematic mind, and set about the task of keeping the ship's log and dive records. Bill Spencer, an archaeology student, had just been assigned to the company as the new state field agent.

They were living their dream of the good life. In common with the older people caught up in Mel's enterprise, the young divers and crew had been drawn by the romance of treasure. They were, perhaps, more capable

than their elders of uncomplicated enjoyment of the salvage life. The work was demanding and the hours long,
but dress and regulations were casual. The galley stocked
ample supplies for hearty appetites; besides, they had
their pick of grouper, Florida lobster, jewfish, or whatever
else the line or spear snared from the plenty around them.

Among the crew, strong affinities began to develop; Dirk
Fisher and Angel Curry fell in love; so did Kim Fisher
and Jo Stuart. No matter how diverse their backgrounds,
the young men and women of the *Southwind* were united
in a shared feeling for their medium—the underwater
kingdom beneath the tug's keel. It was to them a magic
place. Within it, they seemed infinitely removed from any
physical turmoil on the sea's surface and from the concerns and cares of the outside world. At first, the novices
had felt like intruders, but this sensation soon vanished.
As they became fully accustomed to free movement beneath the sea, and learned from their skilled peers the
safe operation of the scuba, there came to them an unut-
terable sense of peace. Some of the divers gained a mystic
impression of the sea's *rightness.* They felt that if everyone could somehow experience this influence, humankind
might be greatly improved.

It was a bright and luminous world, alive with an infinite and multihued population. Sometimes you could hear
them: through the water came faintly the bizarre creaking
and crackling of fish noises. Over the divers' shoulders
hovered all types and sizes of fish, from the tiniest vivid
tropicals to the massive bulk of a seven-hundred-pound
jewfish. Through their masks the divers could see the
streaks of brilliance that were angelfish and the speckled,
dangerous scorpionfish. They also became acquainted
with the wreck site's most deadly inhabitants.

Nurse, lemon, and hammerhead sharks were often seen
around the wreck site, but none ever made a hostile movement against any diver. With the barracuda, they were
much more intimate. It seemed that as the mailboxes
moved sand on the ocean floor, hundreds of juicy sea

worms were stirred up; these furnished rich food for shoals of small fish. The fish attracted the slim, silvery predators. Two particularly large barracudas made their home at the salvage site; the sinister-looking fish, with their vicious, underslung jaws, seemed almost human in their curiosity. Edging ever closer to the divers' work, they finally hung motionless nearby, but never molested the human intruders in their domain. The divers named one of the barracudas "Long John Silver" and gave the other, their favorite, the nickname of "Ralph." The fish became an accepted and permanent fixture of the diving operation.

Soon Kim Fisher and his crew learned to perfection the art of maneuvering and winching the *Southwind* so that they could dig precisely adjacent trenches in the sandy bottom next to the Bank of Spain. Below, the divers hovered around an underwater hurricane, moving in a seltzerlike mixture of seawater, sand, and air bubbles. It took considerable energy and consumed great quantities of compressed air just to maintain their position in the eye of the mailbox storm. It required almost a full airtank for every working hour; the compressors on deck whirred and clattered continuously to keep up with the demand.

It was, however, surprising how the deflectors' enormous power, which could blow a ten-foot hole in the Quicksands in just two minutes, could be controlled. Divers could remain in the hole even while the engines turned at the maximum power permitted by the state agent. Most important of all, the most delicate artifacts were recovered undamaged—including a fragile glazed majolica bowl and intact seventeenth-century swords and muskets. The divers were even able to pick up single links of gold chain and one tiny gold button.

Alternating with the *Virgilona,* the *Southwind* moved steadily from place to place in the great sandbank. From an aircraft flying over the site, observers could see how the boats had punched crater after crater in the sea bottom, leaving a surface pockmarked like that of the moon.

On June 17, *Southwind* was digging in a new area, while crewmen recorded location bearings from the buoys now studding the wreck site. One by one, cannonballs, 3 rapiers and 2 swords, a dagger, barrel hoops, a musket, and more than 180 silver pieces of eight were brought from their resting place in the sands. Bill Spencer tagged and itemized each artifact, laying them gently to rest in a water tank so that they would suffer no damage before their journey to the state laboratory for cleaning and preservation.

Near noon, the sea around the tug was calm. The engines had been shut down following a "blow," and Dirk Fisher had been scouring a shallow crater dug by the deflectors. Suddenly he surfaced near the stern. Dirk smiled, narrowing his eyes against the glare reflected from a glassy sea, and held out in his right hand a round circle of blackened metal.

As Dirk scrambled aboard the *Southwind*'s fantail, the recovered object went from hand to hand in mounting excitement. Mel's son had uncovered the pilot's astrolabe. Only slowly were we to understand the significance of Dirk's find. At the time, we could clearly see that the instrument was intact and had been remarkably preserved by its cover of deep sand. The astrolabe's circular body, marked off in degrees, was topped by a swiveled handle ring. Its alidade, or pointer bar, was still fastened securely, and after 350 years, it swung freely. The astrolabe worked!

When first I held the precious thing in my hands, the treasure hunt took on fresh meaning for me. True, the astrolabe's value, in money terms, was substantial—the instrument we had found was one of only two dozen in the world, of which no more than two were in as good condition. But the other values it symbolized were far richer; the device embodied centuries of man's hard-won navigational knowledge. Developed from the complex Arab astrolabes of the ninth century, and probably based on much older instruments, the astrolabe had been perfected in the Middle Ages. It was, with the mariner's compass, a basic tool of European man's courageous expansion into hitherto unknown seas while seeking a new world. Used to determine heavenly bodies' altitude and thus the latitude of the observer, the astrolabe represented a great outthrust of knowledge. Against the infinite power of superstition and the medieval fear of the unknown, man had set his mind and all of his budding science.

We sat cross-legged on the galleon deck in the hot June sunshine, with more than two thousand silver coins before us. Bleth McHaley and Curtiss Peterson, the state's skilled preservationist, counted, sorted, and bagged the money while I tallied the count. This, my first view of the mass of coins from the Bank of Spain, began as a distinct disappointment. Ever since their recovery, the coins had been stored in water, and they gave off a rank sea smell. As we handled them, they left black smears on our hands. The coins smelled also of shipwreck and mortality and of abandoned, buried centuries. It seemed a pitiful heap of underwater refuse.

But as we examined the pieces of eight and four and placed them in sealed canvas bags for transport to Tallahassee, their nature was slowly revealed to us. The coins were not regular and milled like today's coinage. Although more round than the angular 1715 money, the 1622 coins were also cobs—that is, they were cut from a bar of silver and then hand-stamped.

Most of the coins were still covered with a heavy black accretion of silver sulfide and sand, but here and there they had come up clean, their shields and crosses clearly visible. Only a few bore dates—from 1612 to 1621—but the shields indicated that they had been minted during the reign of three Spanish kings. They had come from five colonial mints: Potosí, Lima, Mexico City, Bogotá, and Santiago de Chile.

Remembering what I had seen on the ships' manifests, I realized that here lay the remnants of a rich seventeenth-century economic life. The coins were relics of the annual currents of trade that once pulsed through the great Portobello fair, the port of Cartagena, and the entrepôt of Havana. Here were surrogates for the hopes, lusts, fears, and savings of private persons, the risks taken by long-dead merchants, and the once-coveted revenues of half-forgotten kings. Yes, here was death—the dissolution of men's hopes, the fatal decline of empire, the passing of an epoch. But the coins also spoke of life: the culture and commerce of colonial Spain. And we were privileged, as we sat among the heaps of coins, to touch all this.

Next came the day of gold. Near the northwest side of the Bank of Spain, Kim Fisher unearthed a long gold bar, bent double like a woman's hairpin; it was evidently another piece of contraband gold, for it bore no official marks. The next piece that came up, however, was different—a heavy disk of gold, stamped with markings for fifteen and one-quarter carats, royal *quinto* seals, and a mint mark. It weighed four and one-half pounds.

After the bars, the divers recovered the first two gold coins found on the site—small, shining two-*escudo* pieces. The coins had been minted in Seville. It now appeared that *Southwind* had been digging on a part of the shipwreck where the belongings of wealthy persons, perhaps passengers, had come to rest. The gold coins might have been purse or pocket money brought by them or sent to them from Spain.

I was working at the kitchen table when the telephone rang. As the intensity of Mel's salvage operations picked up in the early summer of 1973, we had moved from Vero Beach to a house on Big Pine Key to be near the action. On this quiet Fourth of July morning, I had expected no interruptions in a leisurely day of working on the final draft of my dissertation. But the drawling voice on the telephone quickly dissipated my holiday mood. It was Treasure Salvors' new executive, Preston Shoup (tragically, Norman Johnson had been critically injured in an automobile accident in June). He said, "Old buddy, you'd better get down here. They've found a mess of silver bars out there. I'm rounding up the *National Geographic* film crew right now, but we'll hold the boat for you."

I have never made the thirty-mile trip from Big Pine to Key West in faster time. As I drove, my mind raced with possibilities. Had Mel finally hit the "big pile" he had sought for so long? Most of all, would the bars be so marked that we could identify our shipwreck?

I parked my car at the pierhead where the *Golden Doubloon*'s overhanging bowsprit marked Mel's headquarters. Alongside the dock lay Preston's small, fast outboard. Already it was low in the water with camera and sound equipment and film packs. Bert von Munster, the lean, expert Dutch cameraman of the *Geographic* television crew, was waiting at dockside with his associate, John Fuhr. We hastened aboard the boat, and Preston cast off; moving the throttle full ahead, he sped from Key West harbor on the first leg of our thirty-seven-mile journey to the wreck site.

The sea, which had been almost flat at dawn, became more and more choppy as the morning advanced. By the time we reached Boca Grande Channel, the boat was still running at top speed but slammed heavily into the rough, uneven seas, scattering a heavy spray. Before long, we were completely soaked, but we pushed on, drawn by the news of what had happened aboard the *Southwind* earlier that day.

At daybreak, when the *Southwind* left her Marquesas anchorage, the ocean was calm; as the sun rose higher, the crew could see that the water was very clear for diving. On arrival at the site, the tug positioned itself, anchored, and put its deflectors down. At the conclusion of the "blow," on his very first dive of the day, Bouncy John saw, nestled in the sand, a tiny, glittering heap of red and gold. Scooping it up in one glove, he made his way to the surface. Lewis had found a small but exquisite rosary.

A little later in the morning, Kane Fisher, now fourteen, and Mike Schneidelbach entered the water near the *Southwind*'s stern. Once below, they hovered over a hollow dug by the tug's propellers. Suddenly, Kane saw something unusual—a sooty-colored, oblong thing lying on the bedrock. It looked, as he said later, "like a loaf of bread." The boy tugged at the object, first with one hand and then with both, to no avail; it was surprisingly heavy. Kane went up to the *Southwind*'s stern, got someone's attention, and said the words that electrified the ship: "I think I've found a silver bar." Kane went back down with a rope, secured the object, and brought it up.

Before the crew assembled at the tug's fantail could digest the news or even examine the bar, Mike Schneidelbach found a second ingot. Excited, he summoned all his strength; he picked up the bar in his arms and began to swim toward the surface. As his head broke into the open air, he realized that it was too heavy for him, so he wrapped his arms and legs around the anchor line and yelled for help. When someone threw him a rope from the tug, Mike let go the anchor line to grasp it. At once, he and the silver bar sank 20 feet down to the bottom. At last, the second ingot was also raised. In a few more minutes, a third bar was found.

Bleth McHaley, who had been aboard for the expedition, immediately got on the *Southwind*'s radio and passed the exciting news to the galleon office. Mel, who had been on his way back to Key West from the tug, turned right around and headed back. Don Kincaid left Key West at once in the company's fast Mako inboard with Bates Littlehales, a veteran *National Geographic* magazine photographer. As the word spread in Key West, others of the faithful prepared to go to the site. Soon, Bob Holloway got the *Holly's Folly* under way with a large group and started for the Marquesas. In the meantime, Preston had located the television cameramen and called me with the news.

Exhausted, wet clean through, but triumphant, we had nearly finished our rough passage. Ahead, above the tossing seas, we sighted the yellow pilot house of the *Southwind*. As we drew nearer, we could see that a whole flotilla of small craft had gathered around the salvage boat. It was difficult to come safely alongside the tug, for waves rolled along her low sides. As we climbed aboard, the decks were sporadically awash.

The *Southwind* was jammed with an excited crowd of more than forty persons. On the lower deck I met Mel and wrung his hand. As I offered my congratulations, it seemed to me that the man might at last be near the end of his quest, that Mel Fisher might finally have found his treasure.

Mel drew me aside and held out a small plastic envelope, filled with seawater. "Take a look at the rosary," he said. Opening the envelope, he spilled out water and beads into my cupped hands.

It looked so small and fragile. It also looked as fresh in its beauty as it had on the day of the September hurricane, 351 years before. Only a few tiny shells clinging to the beads gave any hint of its age. The rosary must have been, I thought, a woman's or a child's. Around the circle of beads, groups of ten coral beads were connected by gold chain; each eleventh bead was of fluted gold. Suspended from the rosary there hung a small Baroque cross of chased gold. Bleth McHaley had come up; she spoke quietly: "I just wonder who was clutching this rosary when the ship went down?"

Quickly I climbed to the upper deck and made my way through the crowd. The film crew had preceded me there, and their camera was already rolling. I came to the place where the dark ingots lay in an open fiberglass tank, covered with six inches of seawater. Through the water I could faintly see on the bars' discolored surfaces the lines and curves of inscribed markings. I had to examine them more closely. Bill Spencer, Don Kincaid, and I manhandled the ingots out of the tank and onto the steel deck. Mel said, "They are awful heavy, aren't they? Must weigh ninety pounds apiece."

As we brushed away the sulfide coating on the bars, their markings stood out more clearly. Bates Littlehales and Don knelt to photograph them from every angle possible, while I fingered the surface of the ingots. I knew that the ships' manifests had listed a tally number, as well as the weight and fineness of silver for each bar. I had seen these on the documents but had no idea how they would look on the bars themselves. As I examined the three ingots, I saw that each bore a number in Roman numerals. The three bars were numbered 569, 794, and 4584—those must be the tally numbers. On each bar, and also in Roman numerals, was the marking *II U CCCLXXX* (2380) indicating their silver purity against a scale of 2400. Fine, pure silver from the deadly mercury process!

In addition to the numbers, the ingots also displayed the faint impression of round seals, together with strange symbols like the jumbled letters of some exotic alphabet. Those last, I thought, might be shipping marks.

The celebration had barely begun aboard the *Southwind,* but I could not linger. I had to set immediately to work to discover what I could about the silver bars. Perhaps, I thought, this was the chance of a lifetime. This might be the opportunity to identify definitively a Spanish colonial shipwreck through her cargo.

When the public library in Key West opened its doors the next morning, I was there, with three microfilm reels containing the whole of the two galleons' manifests. Sitting down at the library's microfilm reader, I threaded the shortest reel—that representing the *Santa Margarita*—onto the machine. Since we believed it most likely that it was the *Margarita*'s shipwreck that Mel had found, it seemed the logical place to begin.

I worked at top speed, but it took all of Thursday, Friday, and Saturday to scan the record of cargoes registered on the *Santa Margarita.* I recorded as I went the weight, tally number, and silver fineness of each silver bar loaded aboard the ship at Portobello, Cartagena, and Havana. Nowhere did I find a silver ingot that bore the number of any of the three brought up at the Marquesas site on the Fourth of July.

On Sunday, the library was closed, but on Monday morning, July 9, I turned to the larger of the two manifests, that of the *almiranta*. When I had completed my reading of the treasure put on the *Atocha* at Havana, and had found no record of any of the three bar numbers, I rubbed my eyes in fatigue and discouragement. What if it were not really possible to correlate the bar numbers? What if the shipwreck Mel had found was not from the 1622 fleet at all?

Putting aside my doubts, I turned the reader crank to a beautifully ornate notary's seal that marked the Cartagena lading. Flicking from one cluttered page to another, I noted the rich mixture of silver coin, ingots, and gold bars brought aboard the galleon at Cartagena.

Then I saw it—written in the seventeenth-century style a crabbed *procesal* hand—the words *quatro mill quinientos e ochenta e quatro:* 4584. It was the tally number of one of our silver bars. I also noted that the silver fineness of the ingot was 2380, and it weighed 125 marks, 3 ounces in Spanish measure.

Hastily removing the microfilm reel from the machine, I copied the page in the library's reader-printer and hurried over to the Treasure Salvors' office.

The narrow doorway into the office on the galleon opened into pandemonium. The company's usual business had been complicated by the Fourth of July treasure bonanza, and Bleth was besieged at her desk. Both telephones were busy, and no sooner was one of them set down than it jangled again. At last I managed to catch Bleth's eye. Showing her the copy of the *Atocha*'s manifest page, I told her how the bar number matched. I tried to add that we still had to verify the bar weight in order to prove the correlation, but Bleth had already snatched the microphone of the marine radio from its hook. She called up the *Southwind* and told Kim, "It's the Big A. We've found it. We've found the *Atocha.*"

The joyous shout we heard over the radio receiver was echoed and amplified by those in the office. When the clamor died down, it was agreed that *Southwind* would pull her anchors at once and come to Key West to join the celebration.

Finally I was able to get my point across: we had to weigh the bar when it came in. Converting the Spanish weight on the document to our measure would mean that the bar should weigh 63.58 pounds. We had no scale on the galleon, but Preston scoured Key West and was able to borrow an accurate freight scale. He had it loaded on a company van and brought to the galleon's deck.

As we awaited the *Southwind* that afternoon, the excitement grew rather than diminished. A crowd gathered, until the galleon's quarterdeck and foc'sle were a mass of watchers. Friends and employees of Treasure Salvors formed a circle around the scale on the main deck.

The *Southwind* came proudly into harbor, rounding the breakwater. Kim brought the tug alongside the galleon, and the lines were made fast with a flourish. Flashbulbs popped and movie cameras whirred as the unloading of the treasure began. Solemnly the youthful crew passed over the galleon's railing the fruits of their expedition: seven hundred silver coins; cradled in its plastic bag, the rosary; muskets, swords, and barrel hoops; and one by one, the ingots of silver.

The scale had been preset to 63.60 pounds. The silver bar numbered 4584 was gently carried across the deck and laid on the scale bed. Preston adjusted the scale and stepped back. It was a tense moment. For a second, the balance arm of the scale oscillated; it wavered and then settled squarely in the middle. The weights matched! So did the silver bar from the wreck site and the one in the manifest of *Nuestra Señora de Atocha.* I was convinced. It appeared certain that Mel had discovered what Preston called "everybody's rainbow wreck—the *Atocha.*"

The silver bar find and the resulting claim that we had identified the *Atocha* launched a wave of publicity that covered Florida, hit the wire services with a national impact, and spread around the world. The statement that the 1622 ships had been worth four hundred million dollars was coupled with the news stories and helped to create a month-long sensation. During fourteen-hour days, it was all that Bleth, Don, and the Fishers could do to answer the telephones, respond to inquiries that flooded in with every mail, and arrange interviews with reporters for Mel. On Sunday morning, July 15, the Miami *Herald*'s front-page story was the Marquesas treasure; the previous week, the Fort Lauderdale *News* had featured the find in a full-color spread. Two Spanish reporters came to Key West, representing dailies from Madrid and Barcelona.

From Germany came a representative of the famous magazine *Der Stern;* he brought a German-speaking photographer from Miami. The man had come to negotiate with Mel for an article on the story, and they soon agreed on a price. With Mel's approval, they interviewed me and talked to other members of the crew. Instead of returning thereafter to sign a contract, the men chartered a plane and flew over the wreck site, photographing the *Southwind,* now back at work. After that, they left Key West by plane. The next we knew, *Der Stern* had appeared with an "authorized" article about the *Atocha.* We had clearly been outsmarted.

In spite of the confusion and in the midst of the turmoil, Mel moved buoyantly. It now appeared that he might have won—won over his rivals, the skeptics, the detractors. The finding of the *Atocha* should ease his financial strictures and help him to pay his debts. Best of all, those three silver bars and all the other treasure seemed to point the way. The great bulk of the *Atocha*'s gold and silver could not be far away now.

IX. Squalls When You Find It

"Well, Silver," replied the doctor,
"I'll go one step further: Look out
for squalls when you find it."
—Dr. Livesey to Long John Silver,
Treasure Island

The morning had begun with a tropical downpour; now a steady drizzle had settled in, falling from the heavy cloud cover over Key West. Aboard Mel's treasure galleon there was, however, the subdued excitement that accompanies an important occasion. Senator Robert Williams had flown in from Tallahassee to inventory the Marquesas treasure and return it to the state capital. In the upstairs sterncastle room, Mel signed the materials over to Williams, who accepted them on behalf of the state. Agents then began to pack the treasure: into Styrofoam ice chests, sealed with tape, went several hundred pieces of eight, the astrolabe and navigators' dividers, a brass mortar, the rosary, three silver candlesticks, and hundreds of other artifacts. Guarded by four marine patrolmen with shotguns, the boxes were taken by highway patrol escort to the Key West airport.

Williams's manner, as he took possession of the treasure, was brisk but cordial. There had, however, been one incident that showed how shallow the goodwill between the salvor and the state had become. In the galleon gift shop, Williams had suddenly noticed a lead sounding weight in the display case; it carried a yellow state identification tag. The senator flared up in an instant; he assumed that the weight had come from the *Atocha,* and that Mel had failed to turn it in. The matter was settled when the lead weight was identified as one from a 1715 site, divided with the company some nine years before. As the state officials left with the treasure, cordiality— on the surface, at least—had been restored.

The first comments of the state authorities about our shipwreck identification, which we read in the newspapers, seemed cautiously favorable. After locating silver bar No. 4584 on the *Atocha* manifest, I continued to study the documents. Very shortly, also in the Cartagena lading, I found No. 569; still further in the same section, bar No. 794 turned up. I forwarded a copy of the document pages and my translation of them to Sonny Cockrell in Tallahassee. Later, I found a second bar bearing the number 794. Until I could get the precise laboratory weight of our bar, the identification of that bar was not definitive.

One of the ingots, No. 569, however, was a complete match. Not only did the tally number, silver fineness, and weight coincide with the manifest, but the same shipper's mark was engraved on the bar's surface. This strange symbol, which resembled a letter *N* laid across a *J,* also appeared on the margin of the manifest page opposite the data for bar No. 569.

But the significance of the two silver ingots lay deeper than their surface characteristics and the resultant identification of the *Atocha.* From the microfilmed pages there sprang forth a poignant echo of one of humankind's most shameful memories—the African slave trade. Bar 4584 had been consigned to Philip IV in payment of a tax upon blacks sold at Cartagena. Ingot 569 was a remittance by one Duarte de León Marquéz, a Cartagena trader. His major livelihood came from the open sale—and the clandestine smuggling—of African slaves. It occurred to me that the silver in this bar was doubly tainted with human blood: its minting, probably in the Nuevo Reino of Granada, had been done by slaves, and the transaction that had brought it aboard the *Atocha* was also related to the traffic in human flesh.

We now felt certain that we had found the *Atocha* and had identified the ship through its cargo manifest, but some disagreed. Mel's rivals quickly picked up the challenge and disputed the find. Their reactions were strong and almost immediate. In an article in the July 13 Orlando *Sentinel,* Bob Marx fired the first broadside. He laughed to scorn Mel's four-hundred-million-dollar value estimate and vowed that all the *Atocha*'s silver was worth less than two million. At top prices, Marx said, its whole cargo might conceivably bring ten million. He also contested the location of the galleon; truly, he swore, the *Atocha* lay a hundred miles from Fisher's shipwreck. It lay, he told friends, thirteen miles from the Holiday Inn at Islamorada, on Upper Matecumbe Key. In his article, Marx said that the silver bars could have been transferred one or many times, and that their presence on the wreck site proved nothing. Finally, Marx said candidly that Fisher's claim "damaged his credibility as a historian."

That same week, Burt Webber sent Senator Williams a letter denigrating Mel's *Atocha* identification. He charged that the "mine brands," as he called the bar markings, did not match those on the manifest. He went on to state: "I feel it quite premature to say they have identified the wreck as the *Atocha* and then to go on to place a wild absurd potential value of $400 million on this wreck site. This entire scheme is obviously in the interest of stock promotion." Actually, Burt Webber was terribly disappointed; he had invested years of time and more than three hundred thousand dollars in his search. At this point, it seemed to me, he could not admit, even to himself, that Mel might have beaten him to the *Atocha.*

The rivals' denials received wide publicity, but the next blow in the treasure war was struck anonymously. Treasure Salvors had been stricken from the list of valid Florida corporations by a supposed failure to file proper reports or to pay the annual corporate tax. The list was published on July 2, but we learned of it only after someone else had advised Senator Williams. He announced that since the company was no longer properly incorporated, he would have to cancel Mel's salvage contract. But the state agency was wrong; the corporate tax had been paid, and Deo Fisher flew to Tallahassee with the receipt to prove it. She returned with a written apology from the secretary of state.

Next, a customs service official came to the galleon; he brusquely told us that it had been alleged that Treasure Salvors' tugboats were not licensed and did not carry the proper papers. When the papers were produced from the files, the officer apologized. "You know how it is," he said. "When you get a complaint, you just have to check it out."

At this same time, a series of articles appeared in the *Keynoter,* a Marathon (Florida) newspaper. Inspired by unnamed rivals, the articles cast doubt upon the authenticity of the materials found in the Marquesas and upon the *Atocha* identification. They left the impression that everything Mel had done was to further a vast speculation.

Next, a blow was aimed at the company's vitals—its ability to finance its operations—when one of Mel's enemies made a formal complaint against him to the Miami office of the Securities and Exchange Commission. While the complaint was being processed, none of us in Key West knew of it. We had hoped that the firestorm of opposition had begun to die down. Everyone in the crew hoped so, for it was time for a happy occasion: on July 28, Dirk Fisher and Angel Curry were to be married aboard the *Golden Doubloon.*

Summer sunsets in the Florida Keys are uniquely beautiful; their fire often spreads across the whole of an overarching sky. On the evening of the wedding, just as the vivid colors reached their peak, Dirk and Angel stood on the galleon's quarterdeck. As they stood before Arville Renner, pastor of the Fishers' Vero Beach church, they faced out toward the Marquesas, into the setting sun. Behind the minister the mizzenmast yard had been trimmed around square with the mast to form a huge cross.

The wedding party was as vividly clad as the sunset skies. Dirk, his best man, Kim, and the other groomsmen were resplendent in specially made tropical shirts and slacks. Angel, Jo, Taffi, and her other attendants were dressed in bright sarongs. As the minister spoke the words that united them, he told the couple that their life together should be like their life upon the sea. He pledged them, as they carried on their life's search, to face the coming storms together.

Dirk and Angel's wedding, and the reception that followed, were arranged with the flair and color typical of the Fisher family. When the wedding ceremony was over, a rapid darkness descended. Lights were turned on, and a band began to play. A fountain on the main deck gushed champagne as the newlyweds cut their cake and the festivities began. Soon the party had overflowed the galleon's decks and spilled out onto the surrounding docks. Thus the Fishers—a proud clan—drew together in solidarity in a time of joy. In the same spirit they all faced up to Mel's critics and to the mounting opposition. They never doubted for a moment that they had found the *Atocha.*

While Dirk and Angel traveled west on their honeymoon, the *Southwind* was working the east side of the Bank of Spain. Although they made no major strikes like that of the early summer, the hunters continued to uncover coins, ballast stones, and olive-jar fragments. Kim Fisher had recovered a small but exquisite gold cup. Although it had been squeezed almost flat in the shipwreck and was covered on one side with shells, its opulent beauty shone through to the observers. The goblet's upper rim was covered with an incised running design that looked, at first glance, to be Oriental. Later, we decided that the motif was not dragons but Baroque dolphins. A gold dolphin formed the cup's handle, and its interior was lined with jewel settings—we could see one emerald still in one of these. Was it the private drinking cup of a wealthy person?

Seventeen of the silver artifacts resembling small candlesticks had now been found. They were decorated with religious symbols: the Lamb, a cross, the Sacred Heart. At first I thought that these might be bases for silver monstrances, which held the Communion Host. We wondered, too, what these artifacts were and whence they came.

Southwind continued to work on the site. Her crew now included Mark Hansen and Patty Strahan. On August 6, Don Kincaid was aboard with the *National Geographic* TV film crew. Mr. and Mrs. Jud Chalmers had also come aboard with Bates Littlehales, photographer for *National Geographic* magazine. Ever since the major finds in May, Bates had been close to the scene of action, filming the underwater work and photographing every item of treasure brought up. On this day, as on several other occasions, Bates had brought along his eleven-year-old son Nicholas—soon known to the crew as Nikko. Nikko was a fine swimmer and had learned to use his own set of scuba equipment.

Southwind had been delayed leaving Key West because of generator trouble. She had not sailed until that morning, and it was two P.M. before she reached the wreck site and put her anchors down. Digging began at two thirty; after the second hole was dug, at four o'clock, Nikko Littlehales entered the water. Instead of going in over the stern, as divers were supposed to do, he slipped in on the stern quarter. Quickly, before anyone could intervene, the boy was pulled by the current into the propeller and was badly hurt.

Kim Fisher and his crew swung into action; Nikko was brought up on deck immediately. Mrs. Chalmers, a nurse, could see at once that he was gravely injured. The galleon office, notified by radio, called the Coast Guard. Two hours later, a helicopter hovered over the tug, and the boy and his father were taken off. When Bates and Nikko finally arrived at the hospital in Key West, it was too late. The boy had died.

In his log for that day, Kim Fisher wrote: "Today was clouded with tragedy." Mel was desolated. In vain, Deo, Bleth, and the others tried to tell him that his mailbox had only indirectly and accidentally caused Nikko's death. When the *Southwind* returned to port, Mel sent it into drydock. There he had an iron grillwork built around the tug's propellers to prevent any such accidents in the future.

Trouble now piled upon trouble. On August 12, the galleon sank. An electric bilge pump had failed the previous night; by the time the accident was discovered in the morning, the ship's decks were almost awash. City firemen joined Mel's crew in their fight to save the ship, and every available portable pump was pressed into service. Finally, the water flow was checked, reversed, and the long process of pumping out the flooded galleon began. Seawater had soaked and damaged the treasure exhibits in their glass cases below, and repairs and refurbishing took several days.

The office was beginning to return to normal from the sinking when Mel was warned by his attorney that the Securities and Exchange Commission had undertaken a full investigation of Treasure Salvors and its subsidiary, Armada Research. SEC auditors moved into the office and began a complete examination of the companies' stock records. In the meantime, while the investigation went forward, Mel was barred from selling stock or shares in the treasure. His main sources of income had been effectively cut off. This shot—the complaint against the company—had struck home.

Mel made no claims to be different from his treasure-hunting peers. True, some associates had been left unhappy after their mutual dealings. Mel's eyes always remained focused upon his search. In seeking his goal, he was sometimes careless and improvident with equipment, money, and people. Certainly he was a promoter, garrulous and expansive in his claims and promises. But Mel never sought a penny from any investor with any criminal intent or even a mere cynical desire for the money alone. He believed—fanatically, virtually to the exclusion of all else—in the *Nuestra Señora de Atocha.*

Nor was Mel interested for a moment in retribution against the rivals who had done him such harm. He wasted little time in anger, and no energy at all in malice; it just did not interest him. He was bigger than his rivals, and his attention was elsewhere.

By the late summer of 1973 it was evident that the attacks upon Mel's credibility had not only caused him financial problems but had also negatively affected his relations with the state of Florida. As the date approached for the annual renewal of Mel's salvage contract, the correspondence between the company and the state became more and more heated in tone. A continuing dispute raged over the prompt submission of the forms and reports required by the state. Cockrell and Williams also charged the company with more serious infractions: the alleged failure to keep adequate maps of their digging on the site; failure to operate the mailboxes at proper speed at all times; and the removal of treasure items from custody without proper authorization. On one such occasion, when the astrolabe had been taken back out to sea so that the *National Geographic* crew could reenact its discovery, Senator Williams became so irate that he threatened to revoke Mel's contract that very day. Only the intervention of the company's attorney and his promise that the situation would improve stayed Williams's hand.

Bleth realized that the problems of credibility and the disputes with the state of Florida were serious ones; she felt that there were solutions to them. She was certain that the extensive historical documentation about the lost ship and its materials was so conclusive that its general acceptance was only a matter of time. Bleth realized that the state agents on the boats performed little more than

a custodial function, and that very little academic archaeology was being done. There was, in short, a real job to
be done for the company and for the cause of marine
archaeology generally. It occurred to her that Mel should
retain a professional archaeologist. The salvor immediately agreed.

In many ways, the man who took on the job, Duncan
Mathewson, was ideally suited to the task. Mathewson
had done graduate work in archaeology at the universities
of Edinburgh and London; he had worked for many years
on West African sites. Duncan had also served as an archaeologist in Jamaica, where he became acquainted with
Spanish and English materials from Port Royal and Spanish Town. Thus he was well qualified to analyze the materials from the "English wreck"; he was also deeply in-
trigued at the possibilities of the *Atocha* site.

As he began his work with Treasure Salvors, Duncan
Mathewson hit the ground running. As he reviewed the
academic work in marine archaeology, he noted that little
had been accomplished in Florida since the pioneering
efforts of John Goggin and Carl Clausen years before. He
accustomed himself to diving and to the underwater setting; he began to study the materials recovered from the
two wreck sites and set afoot inquiries about their origin
and cultural meaning. In order to help the state with the
cleaning and preservation of the *Atocha* materials, Duncan suggested that Mel also retain Austin Fowles, a skilled
Jamaican conservator whom he had met at Port Royal.

When I finished my dissertation defense in October, I
was free to help Duncan. We made a thoroughgoing analysis of the salvage done on the *Atocha* site to date; it was
obvious that, in the excitement of the previous summer,
control on the wreck site had been haphazard. Although
a number of buoys had been put down and had been used
to locate some of the artifacts, the salvors had only a general understanding of artifact locations on the site.

We utilized all the available records and the recollections of boat captains, crew, and divers to create an arti-

fact location map. Then we made the first inventory of all the recoveries to date. At once we saw that Treasure Salvors had found a substantial treasure. Four pieces of gold bullion—the three bars and the disk—had been salvaged, together with eleven gold coins. In addition, the rosary, the gold cup, a religious medallion of gold, and two golden rings had been found; ten gold chains had also come up from the Quicksands. Silver objects included the three ingots, more than six thousand silver coins, the candlesticks, a ewer, silver spoons, and inkwell, and a silver plate. An arsenal of weapons had been recovered, including twenty-four swords and daggers, nineteen muskets or arquebuses, four stone and almost a hundred iron cannonballs. Hundreds of other objects, many of them encrusted, had come up from the wreck site: a copper ingot, many barrel hoops and ballast stones, a grindstone, and ceramic sherds of majolica and ordinary olive-jar wares. We also possessed a valuable collection of navigational equipment: the matchless astrolabe, four pairs of dividers, a lead sounding weight, and a scaled device that appeared to be a primitive logarithmic scale from an early navigational instrument.

Duncan Mathewson moved to establish better records and stricter artifact control on the wreck site. He began to record the location of each item found, and tied this to a system of numbering for each crater dug during a working day. Major landmarks—the galleon anchor buoy, the "silver bar buoy" over the Bank of Spain, two large state buoys, and other points of reference—formed the grid within which objects already found and future digging would be correlated. Mike Schneidelbach and Kim Fisher flew over the site to get gyrocompass bearings of the main grid lines, and I furnished information about the initial 1622 shipwreck, the second hurricane, and other data from Spanish documents.

In an artifacts storage room that he had built in the hold of the *Golden Doubloon,* Duncan began to study the wreck-site ceramics, with the enthusiastic help of Scott

Hummon and other crew members. Soon, Mathewson was able to advise Mel that a pattern of the shipwreck's scatter was taking shape; he felt that this had resulted from the second hurricane of 1622 and later scatter over the years since. Duncan began to speculate about the possible location of the bulk of the treasure—almost nine hundred more silver bars and a quarter-million coins, plus tons of copper ingots—which he called, in archaeological language, the "primary cultural deposit." Almost everyone else in the company referred to the still-missing treasure as the "Mother Lode."

Perhaps the most important work Duncan Mathewson did was his formulation of a new philosophy for underwater archaeology: a professional archaeologist could work with a commercial salvor and produce data of scientific value. This directly challenged the ideology long cherished by state officials that salvors, per se, were the eternal enemies of underwater archaeology. Duncan also worked with state field agents Larry Murphy and Bill Spencer to prepare a paper to be given in January 1974 before the International Conference on Underwater Archaeology.

In November, Treasure Salvors went en masse to Tallahassee for a meeting before Senator Williams and his advisory commission. Mel, Deo, Preston, Don, Bleth, Duncan, and I attended, together with Bowman Brown, the company attorney from the Miami firm of Shutts and Bowen. The salvage contract renewal for the *Atocha* site had been granted in October; Mel had come to ask for an exploration area to the north and west of the *Atocha*, where he hoped to find the *Santa Margarita*.

The meeting, which lasted almost all day, proved to be a tense one. Dr. John K. Mahon of the University of Florida was commission chairman; applicants came forward with search and salvage requests, and Senator Williams presented the recommendations of his staff on each application. Bob Marx requested and received two search areas off Matecumbe Key—he was still seeking the *Atocha* there.

Other applications were considered, and then it was Mel's turn.

Senator Williams went through a lengthy catalogue of Mel's sins; he summed up by charging Mel with "repeated breaches of the intent of the law." Mel, ordinarily slow to anger, was finally aroused; he rose to speak. In a low, emotional voice, he said that he had broken no laws. The salvor went on to claim that he had done more for Florida history and archaeology than any other treasure hunter. As evidence of this, he pointed to my presence and to that of Duncan Mathewson.

The chairman asked Senator Williams whether he was recommending the search contract. Williams said that Mel was well equipped and able in the field of salvage. Although he had not been "100 percent cooperative" in the past, the senator said, he and his staff did recommend the contract. The commission voted in approval, and we all rose to leave, happy indeed to be departing Tallahassee.

Now the situation in Key West had become critical. Months had passed since the SEC investigation had begun; in the meantime, Mel had been unable to sell percentage contracts or company stock to finance his operations. For many weeks, there had been no money for payrolls. Bills, unpaid and overdue, mounted. "T" Hargreaves, now working as the company's treasurer and accountant, spent hours fending off angry creditors and trying to spread the limited money around. The divers, crew, and girl tour guides in the galleon had to be laid off. Right after Thanksgiving, the power company had cut off service for nonpayment of a bill of $725. This essential service had been restored, but on January 15 the telephones were cut off.

The finding of treasure, it seemed, had only opened the door to trouble. When, Mel wondered, could he get free access to what he had recovered? When (most important of all) could he proceed with his search for the Mother Lode?

X. Conmen, Mystics, and Credibility

In his need for money, Mel Fisher's best asset was still the remaining 1715 treasure. This had been refinanced and moved to a bank in Tampa. Seeking to sell it, Mel began to negotiate with a long series of prospective buyers, often working through agents or others who expected a hefty "finder's fee" if they arranged a sale. Each negotiation in turn reached its crisis point; invariably, what had seemed so hopeful the week before ended in stalemate or failure. To tell the truth, the selling of treasure was a chancy game, and seemed to attract unconventional or even shady persons. The principals who came to see the "Tampa treasure" certainly measured up; they included a bullion dealer from Singapore, a self-styled "country boy" from Alabama who quoted the Bible, and a flamboyant, cigar-chewing promoter who affected green slacks and flaming orange shirts.

I was deputized to go to one negotiation, since Mel had commitments elsewhere that day. I flew from Key West to Tampa and was taken by cab directly to the Marine Bank. There, aided by a letter of authorization from Mel, I began the formalities necessary to release the bullion for viewing. At last, a line of bank employees appeared at the conference room door, pushing wheeled carts loaded with the treasure: gold coins, pieces of eight, and silver wedges. The glittering things, under guard, were placed on the long table, and we waited. At last, two men from overseas appeared with their American lawyer; we were never permitted to know their names. The newcomers began painstakingly to scrutinize the treasure. I later learned that one of the men, a pale, heavyset Englishman, was a London coin dealer; the other, who spoke with a heavy accent, had apparently come from Beirut. After carefully examining each coin, they made a lump-sum offer for the treasure; it was so low that Mel, in spite of his financial need, could not accept it.

And then there was the promoter named Dave. He was well dressed, plausible, and supposedly held the key to bountiful sources of Texas oil money. In his play for the Tampa treasure, Dave offered Mel a cashier's check for two hundred thousand dollars, drawn on a Houston bank. The only trouble was that Dave had not one cent on deposit there. Mel accepted the offer—after all, what could be better than a cashier's check? He deposited the check in the company account, whereupon it promptly bounced; someone in Houston had somehow seen through Dave.

Dave coolly got back in touch with Mel, made his apologies, and set up another deal and another meeting. The parties were to meet in a Holiday Inn in Vero Beach. When the others arrived, they found that the promoter had checked into the motel and then completely vanished, leaving behind only his suitcase. That brought the affair to an end, at least as far as any treasure sale was concerned, but the connection with Dave was far from over. Although Mel repudiated the man, Dave began to represent himself around the country as Treasure Salvors' agent in a bizarre series of incidents. At one point, newsmen from South Carolina called Mel; they had been given a news release noting that the treasure had been buried on a remote farm in the Carolina uplands. The article bore no name but had obviously been inspired by Dave. The story, when investigated, turned out to be false.

In addition to the 1715 bullion, Mel had some other salable assets: a number of "pillar dollars" and some gold finger bars dated 1659. Mel had obtained these from a

site or sites off Florida, outside state jurisdiction, before
the search for the *Atocha* in the Marquesas began. The
coins, some of the most attractive ever produced in the
Spanish colonies, had been minted in Mexico in 1732 and
1733. They took their name from the reverse design, which
featured two hemispheres flanked by the Pillars of Hercu-
les. Mendel Peterson, now retired from the Smithsonian
and acting as an appraiser of coins and underwater artifacts, came to Key West to evaluate the pillar dollars. After
examining the coins, some of which were encrusted in
clumps with shells attached, Peterson certified that they
were genuine and of substantial value. Mel began to try
to sell them or use them as loan collateral to relieve his
financial burdens.

There came, in mid-February, a blow that badly damaged Mel's credibility; a hostile, two-part series, written
by an investigative reporter, appeared in the Miami
Herald. The writer, Robert D. Shaw, Jr., took counsel with
Mel's rivals and repeated all their old charges plus some
new ones. He stated, after his interviews in Tallahassee,
that the Florida officials had agreed that the silver bars
were "suspect." He repeated Burt Webber's denial of the
shipwreck identification and stressed Mel's alleged violation of state regulations. Shaw scored Senator Williams
for what he called a failure to crack down on Mel, and
went into exhaustive detail on the SEC probe then in progress.

It was Shaw's clear purpose to stress any negative aspect
of Mel's activities and the *Atocha* find, while failing to
report any positive matter. He never contacted me in any
way, and did not mention the archival documents that
backed our claims. Although he briefly mentioned the
company's hiring of an archaeologist, Duncan's work on
the Marquesas site was skipped over lightly. From Jack
Haskins, I later learned that Robert Shaw had called him
long-distance in Seville, awakening the salvor in the middle of the night. When Shaw asked Haskins if he thought
the silver ingots Mel Fisher had found had come from

the *Atocha,* Jack answered, "Of course." Instead of mentioning this remark, Shaw wrote that Haskins was dubious about the find. Immediately, I wrote the editor of the *Herald,* protesting the inaccuracies and half-truths of the Shaw article and pointing out the facts disclosed in the documents. The letter was never published or even acknowledged.

To add to our difficulties in the troubled spring of 1974, we accidentally learned that a group had, the previous year, secretly surveyed the wreck-site area with side-scan sonar. We learned of the survey when Don Kincaid called a New Orleans firm to inquire about their service. Immediately, we advised Senator Williams of the illegal act, but had no way of knowing whether or not the clandestine search had succeeded.

My own private nightmare about the *Atocha* began at this point; two treasure hunters, Teddy Tucker and Art Hartman, told Mel that the galleon had been salvaged before. Supposedly, the work had been done by an Englishman within a few years after the hurricane of 1622. I had found in Seville a document from 1688, in which the Spanish House of Trade had listed key shipwrecks of the seventeenth century and in which the *Atocha* was still shown among the unsalvaged as of that date. I felt certain that the Spaniards would know, through their ambassadors in London, if anyone had found the *Atocha.* I checked further, through the Florida and Cuba papers, and found no evidence that the report was true. Still, it was a disquieting rumor, to be stilled only if we found the Mother Lode.

Now Mel Fisher's most modern rivals—Burt Webber and his associates—had begun to work their areas west of the Marquesas. As the April meeting of the State Advisory Commission approached, we learned that Webber had applied for a new search area, close in to our wreck site on its southeast side. This was the very area Mathewson's research had pinpointed as in the line of probable shipwreck scatter.

For the first time, we could deal with the state from a position of strength. We prepared a report summarizing the historical and archaeological evidence behind the ship identification and stressing Mel's prior claim to the area. We asked that Webber's request be denied or modified, as it intruded into our presumed scatter zone. In order to be certain that the commission members got the materials, we sent a copy to each of them independently.

At the meeting, it was evident that Senator Williams was highly irritated. His staff had prepared a large map in color of all the search and salvage contracts Mel had held since 1970. At the senator's request, I held it up against a wall for viewing; I stood there more than fifteen minutes as Williams launched into a diatribe against Mel. The chart, he said, illustrated how little Fisher's data had meant; each time he had applied for a contract, the senator said, Mel had been certain that the *Atocha* or *Santa Margarita* would be found there. At this point our attorney objected, saying that this was prima facie evidence of his client's perseverance; this, he said, should be rewarded, not punished. Finally, the chairman cut Williams's recital short; the commission voted to support our position and to cut the area of projected wreck scatter out of Webber's area. We had won a significant victory, the first official recognition of the validity of Mel's find and of the academic work that supported it.

Now the credibility problems raised by the unfavorable publicity of the past eight months surfaced again, this time in Key West. Without any notice to the company at all, the Key West *Citizen* printed a front-page story alleging that Treasure Salvors had been sued for eight million dollars for fraud and for the counterfeiting of treasure. The newspaper had printed the story after receiving a letter; the same letter had also been sent to the Miami *Herald* and to other newspapers. They did not print it, but the Key West *Citizen* did. Bleth was furious. With Dave Horan, a Key West attorney, she went to the *Citizen*'s office and demanded that the editor investigate the letter. It was then found that no such person as the alleged author of the letter existed in the city from which it came. Clearly, the story had originated with our friend, promoter Dave. Mel told the *Citizen* that he would immediately file suit against the newspaper unless a full and complete retraction was printed in the next issue. It was.

The Chartroom, the bar at the Pier House Motel, is the unofficial center of Key West life. There, all of the current town issues are discussed, and many are settled. It had long since become the custom for the Treasure Salvors faithful to gather there daily and rehash the day. This June evening, however, was neither a happy nor a festive occasion. We had just met Nick Noxon, a noted film director who was considering taking over the *National Geographic* television film, and we were shouting mad.

On first appearance, Noxon seemed deceptively young and mild-mannered. From his first work in television with CBS in New York, he had risen rapidly to a premier position in documentary films. After he was approached by the *National Geographic* about the directorship of the *Atocha* film, he had first of all wanted to satisfy himself as to the project's authenticity. Noxon came to Key West, sought us out, and moved immediately to the offensive. Don, Bleth, Duncan, and I were ranged along the bar when Noxon let fly. He minced no words: "Bob Marx says your silver bars are a plant. He has told us that the ingots were stolen from his Bahamas shipwreck, passed through Nassau customs at a known date, and were sold to Mel Fisher in Miami. He says that Mel then put them down on your site."

I spluttered, "Do you mean that you believe him?"

Noxon retorted, "I looked him up; he has seventeen titles in the Library of Congress card catalogue. How many do *you* have?"

The argument raged. When we had all cooled down a bit, we suggested that Noxon contact the state officials in Tallahassee. We felt that they would surely be able to refute this charge.

Noxon was testing us. He did go to Tallahassee. Eventually he found that Bob Marx's story was just another of his highly imaginative fabrications. The National Geographic Society also commissioned Dr. Alberto Pradeau, a noted expert on the Spanish colonial mints, to come to Tallahassee and examine the *Atocha* coins. We knew that the television presentation and the *National Geographic* article were in a state of limbo; the controversy over the company's credibility had to be settled before they would go forward.

At the same time, Mel's pillar dollars came into dispute. He had sent several of the coins to the evaluating committee of the American Numismatic Association, together with the required fee, for verification of their authenticity and value. After a long delay, Mel received an unfavorable reply. Virgil Hancock, an official of the ANA and well known as a Spanish colonial coin expert, was caustic in his comments on the coins; he labeled them "counterfeits." Perhaps alarmed at the controversy, Mendel Peterson wrote to Mel and withdrew his own certification of the coins' authenticity.

Now the *Virgilona,* the *Southwind,* and the *Northwind* worked alternately on the *Atocha* site from February to May of 1974. The divers were able to sandwich in a number of working days between periods of rough winter and spring weather. Then, as the better diving days of summer came, more intensive salvage began. Both tugs had been plagued with mechanical problems: the *Southwind* had engine and generator trouble, while the *Northwind* had experienced more serious difficulties—her crankshaft had finally to be removed for repair.

The boat crews had changed and enlarged. Pat Clyne had joined late the previous year. His quick intelligence inclined him naturally to an interest in the archaeological and technical side of the salvage; he was also a skilled diver. Pat was also a natural jokester; once he appeared at a semiformal company affair dressed in a tuxedo jacket and dungaree pants! Mike Lucessi, Tim Merrill, and Bill

Allen had also joined the men aboard the three boats. State agent Bill Spencer alternated with Larry Murphy and Bob Vickery.

By summer, Kim Fisher had rejoined the salvors. In April, he had gone to Michigan, where he and Jo Stuart had been married. Now the Fisher family had notably enlarged; it was totally dedicated to the search for the *Atocha*'s Mother Lode.

Under Mathewson's direction, the *Virgilona*'s crew made extensive magnetometer surveys and helped to lay out a comprehensive grid system. The grid area, marked by spar buoys, was checked out thoroughly for underwater anomalies. The tugs then proceeded systematically from area to area to dig for the treasure. By midsummer, a fair section of the Quicksands scatter area had been covered. The work had yielded a few hundred coins, two arquebuses, and a small quantity of ballast stones and ceramics. The divers did, however, discover more golden chains: in June they unearthed a lovely thirty-three-inch chain with massive half-inch links; in July another gold chain, almost seven feet long, had been found.

The work was not without danger. One day, *Virgilona* was returning to the Marquesas after a magnetometer survey. The Navy had been active on the bombing range during the spring, and had sent jet fighter-bombers out that day to fire on the *Patricia,* the stranded target ship that Treasure Salvors used as a theodolite station. As the *Virgilona* crossed the area three quarters of a mile from the *Patricia,* a jet suddenly began a bombing run. It laid four bombs in the water just two hundred yards from the salvage boat's stern. As Don Kincaid noted in the log, the *Virgilona* made a "rapid course change."

It seemed clear that the magnetometer was of limited value in finding further accretions of treasure in the Quicksands. The shipwreck was so old, buried, and scattered that large iron targets were not to be found; usually, in fact, modern objects were turned up when the magnetometer indicated a contact. Treasure Salvors had also carried out a survey by sub-bottom profiler, which re-corded the strata beneath the sea floor; this proved incon-clusive. For years, Mel had sought a "discriminating" de-tector that would locate precious metals. Such detectors had been built, but their range was short and their relia-bility uncertain. Now Arnold McLean, one of Treasure Salvors' original stockholders, had retired from NASA, moved to Key West, and begun to work on a discriminating detector. Captain Re Matheus, an acquaintance of Mel's, also began to research the same project. Obviously, some major breakthrough was needed. The difficulties of the Quicksands site and the all-important question of the loca-tion of the rest of the *Atocha*'s treasure cried out for solu-tion.

In such a circumstance, human nature being what it is, it was only natural that some of the treasure hunters would turn for answers to the occult. Insofar as Mel Fisher was concerned, he had a ready ear for anything that might promise success in his search. After he had received na-tional publicity, many unusual appeals came to him, and he had a number of rather strange visitors. A "map dowser" came to Key West; he believed that his dowsing stick, held over a chart of the wreck site, could point uner-ringly to the Mother Lode. It didn't.

One enthusiast gave Mel and Deo a huge triangular wooden framework. Somewhat on the order of the mystic pyramid, the device was supposed to reveal to its operator the mysteries of the site. The Fishers put it in the office, where it at least made an interesting conversation piece.

A map of the Marquesas was taken to a West Palm Beach woman who was reputed to have extrasensory powers. She was a rather ordinary-looking housewife who lived modestly and took no reward for her services. Once the chart was before her, the woman closed her eyes and went into a state of trance. She spoke of seeing and almost feel-ing the hurricane of 1622; the mystic flinched as she heard the screams of drowning Spaniards. When pressed to pre-dict the possibility of the salvage of the *Atocha,* the woman made a peculiar remark: the *Atocha*'s treasure would not be found, she said, "until a large, rusty, freighterlike ship was anchored directly over the place."

Perhaps the most bizarre use of psychic powers on the wreck site took place in the summer of 1974, when the *National Enquirer* flew Olaf Johnssen, a noted Swedish clairvoyant, to Key West. On June 18, Don Kincaid took Johnssen, Bleth, reporter Mike McDermid, and state agent Tom Gore to the site in the company's fast Mako outboard. In less than an hour they reached the area, then cruised across a part of the site that had not yet been worked. As the boat slowed, the psychic stood with outstretched hands in the bow; suddenly he commanded, "Stop!" Kincaid threw over a buoy to mark the spot and throttled his engines down to idling speed. Olaf Johnssen asked those on the outboard to join hands and form a circle, concentrating with eyes closed as he put his entire attention upon the treasure. The psychic went into a trance, in which he also "saw" the hurricane and heard the cries of the dying. When he came out of his trance, Johnssen told those aboard the Mako that there was metal—treasure—down below. He returned with Mel, the reporter, and the state agent three days later aboard the *Southwind*. The tug anchored over the buoy Don Kincaid had dropped and started her engines. It was there that the thirty-three-inch gold chain, an arquebus, and thirty-six pieces of eight were found.

In mid-August 1974, Mel touched financial rock bottom. Neither the 1715 treasure nor the pillar dollars had been sold. A small sale of 1715 cob coins had brought in some money, but it was just the proverbial drop in the bucket so far as his cash needs were concerned. He had not concluded any other agreement that would enable him to move his enterprise forward. The tension affected everyone. Unhappy with Mel, Don and Bleth quit (they returned in a few days); at one point, for the first time, the crew refused to go out to sea. Clearly, something had to break soon or the whole search would founder.

Then, just as he had done so many times before, Mel found support—important backing that enabled him to go on. The major investor who saved the company was Melvin Joseph, a Delaware contractor; he purchased a half-interest in the 1715 treasure for $315,000. Joseph, a self-made man, also promised to help the company find other buyers and investors. His money paid off the Tampa loan and enabled the repayment of back salaries due to employees and the satisfaction of many other obligations.

While Mel was still in Delaware concluding the contract, however, the company's bad press arose again to haunt him. The two men appeared together on television and issued a press release describing their partnership and discussing all the treasure Mel had found over the years. As the Philadelphia *Inquirer* prepared to run the story, they checked with the Miami *Herald* and got the text of Robert Shaw's February article. The Philadelphia paper then repeated many of the old charges.

Mel returned to Florida to face yet another controversy: a Fort Lauderdale man had filed an action against him for fraud. To bind the man's investment, Mel had given him, as collateral, one of the 1659 gold bars; the investor became convinced that the bar was not genuine. He got into contact with Virgil Hancock over the matter. On the suggestion of the company's attorney, Duncan Mathewson and I began to study the chemical and metallurgical tests needed to verify the authenticity of the gold bar.

But in spite of all his troubles, it appeared that things had turned for the better for Mel Fisher. Not only had Mel Joseph's funds relieved for the moment the financial problem, but the long SEC investigation had come to an end. No charges were preferred against the company, but Mel had to sign a consent decree in which he pledged that he would not sell unregistered securities and would adhere strictly to SEC regulations.

The National Geographic Society issued the book *Underseas Treasures,* edited by William Graves, in late August. It contained a chapter on Treasure Salvors, outlin-

Tug *Southwind* with its deflectors

Southwind's deflectors lowered for digging

One of the *Atocha*'s bronze guns being filmed underwater

The *Atocha* treasure displayed in Tallahassee, Florida, prior to the division with the State in March 1975

"Ralph" the barracuda watches while an archaeologist sketches

Divers raise one of the *Atocha* guns

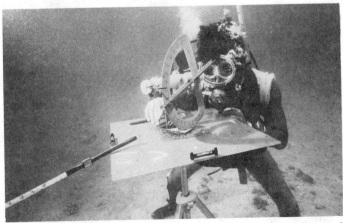

Archaeologist Duncan Mathewson's underwater theodolite and plane table establishes the guns' precise location on the wreck site

Angel and Dirk Fisher, after Dirk had found the astrolabe

The mariner's astrolabe

Northwind's happy crew after the finding of the bronze cannons: *(Left to right)* Jim Solanick, Don Jonas *(behind pole),* Bruce Wisely *(seated),* John Wisely *(standing),* Rick Gage *(behind pole),* Dirk Fisher; *(behind Dirk)* Joe Spangler and Keith Curry

Pat Clyne recovers a Spanish musket intact

Mel Fisher, at the time of the *Northwind*'s sinking

Washington meeting, 1975; a vain attempt to settle claims
between the salvors and the state and federal governments

Pat Clyne finds a silver ingot

Florida State officials are ordered to return the treasure to the salvors

Mel presents the Atocha cannon to
Queen Sophia of Spain

Duncan Mathewson, Mel Fisher, and Gene Lyon match markings on bronze
cannon No. 2499 to the *Atocha*'s gun list

Mel flies out, still seeking the Mother Lode

ing the *Atocha* find. While it was stated that other salvors still felt that the 1622 ships had been lost in the Matecumbes, it gave us full and fair treatment. Next, Dr. Pradeau issued his report on the coins. He affirmed that the *Atocha* coins were genuine, had been obviously recovered from the sea after long immersion, and had substantial value. He went on to say that their dating confirmed the theory of a 1622 shipwreck date. The numismatist was kind enough to call me and advise that he was in complete accord with my findings on the shipwreck.

Insofar as the National Geographic Society was concerned, we had turned the corner on credibility. Their investigations had justified our claims, and from this point on, the society was wholly in our corner—a powerful ally.

By early fall of 1974, we also knew that a forthcoming legal decision could profoundly affect the company's rights in the *Atocha* site and its relations with the state of Florida. Since 1973, the Supreme Court of the United States had been considering the case of the U.S. against the State of Florida, which dealt with the sea boundaries of the state in the Atlantic, the Gulf of Mexico, and the Florida Keys. Earlier in the year, the special master appointed by the court to study the issues in the case had made his report: he determined that the new Florida limits were in error, and recommended that they revert to the older limits. This meant that if the court ruled in accordance with the master's report, the *Atocha* site would no longer be under state jurisdiction. As the date drew near for the court ruling, the state of Florida began to appear more amenable to an early division of the existing *Atocha* finds.

Perhaps best of all, the first tentative proof of Duncan's theory that the Mother Lode of the *Atocha* lay in the deeper water, along the line of wreck scatter, now came to light. One piece of ballast stone and an iron vessel had been found in deeper water on the outward edge of the sandbank. These, we hoped, might indicate that we were on the right track at last.

XI. Gold Shines Forever

Duncan's call in September 1974 came while I was pack-
ing for my trip to Spain. His voice boomed out enthusiastically: "Gene! Good news! They found a fine gold bar from
the *Southwind.* Hank Spinney brought it up, and it has
a number of very interesting markings. Perhaps you can
find it on the *Atocha* registry."

There wasn't time for a Key West trip before my flight
to Madrid, so I got Duncan's promise to send me a photograph of the gold bar and a copy of his artifact data form
on it. The bar had been found deep in the Quicksands.
After the frustrations and controversies of the past summer, it seemed a good omen indeed.

Once in Seville, I began my work, searching for archival
materials on sixteenth-century Saint Augustine, and was
soon absorbed in the quiet routine of the archive.

One day, when the fall had swung into early winter, a
chill rain was falling on Seville. I looked up in surprise
as the *portero* told me I had a visitor. It was Mel, again
arriving unannounced in Spain. Since, as usual, he was
low on cash, he had taken a charter flight from Washington to Torremolinos. There he had taken the rental car
that went with the tour and driven over to Seville. We
went to my *pensión* to talk; suddenly I was brought up
to date on the problems of the treasure hunt.

When I had come to Spain two months before, I had
taken Xavier Calicó in Barcelona a few of Mel's pillar

dollars and a small silver bar; he was to examine them and pass on their authenticity. Mel had come to Spain to retrieve these and to hear Calicó's report.

Mel told me that the Fort Lauderdale lawsuit against him had not yet come to trial, and that a national magazine—*Forbes*—was planning an article that would "roast" him on the issue of the pillar dollars and the 1659 gold bars. He was anxious, therefore, to get a favorable report on them. I also learned that Dirk Fisher had a strong interest in deep-water salvage, and that he would be attending the deep-diving school in Fort Pierce during the winter. After a short conversation, Mel left Seville as quickly as he had come, and I returned to work.

Soon, however, I received a large packet in the mail from Duncan Mathewson. It enclosed a large color photograph of Hank Spinney, his face split by a wide grin, holding the gold bar found in September. A number of impressions showed in the shining gold: in three places, the Roman numeral mark for twenty-one and one-quarter carats; five of the round royal seals; and a small lettered rectangle. The words they spelled out seemed cryptic: they appeared to be *En Rada*. In an old Spanish geographic work, I found that the inner harbor of Cartagena had once been called La Rada, but could locate no other clue as to the mint. It was a puzzle—the bar appeared to be legitimate registry material, for in addition to the royal seals, it had a small notch, the assayer's "bite." I could not, however, find the bar on the *Atocha*'s gold registry, perhaps because many of the bars of that carat rating were lumped together on the records in packages; individual bars and disks were not differentiated by weight.

Duncan also sent me copies of two articles featuring Mel that appeared in national magazines in late 1974. The *Forbes* piece was fully as bad as Mel had feared. Entitled "The One Billion Dollar Hobby," the article warned investors that "bullion collecting, like coin collecting, is a treacherous business." After revealing several frauds practiced upon collectors of modern coins and bars, the writer turned to the subject of Mel Fisher. He described Treasure Salvors' fund-raising methods and then made the charge that "at least six separate authorities who had examined about a dozen coins that Fisher had given investors say roughly half are counterfeit." The writer mentioned the Fort Lauderdale case and quoted from Robert Shaw's Miami *Herald* series. Although the article closed with an admission that the authenticity of Mel's coins and the 1659 gold bars had neither been proved nor disproved conclusively, its tone left a distinctly unfavorable impression.

Behind the attack on Mel in *Forbes* magazine stood the figure of Virgil Hancock. Shortly after the article appeared, Hancock wrote a bitter, vindictive letter to Xavier Calicó, perhaps to attempt to intimidate the Spanish numismatist. He wrote Señor Calicó that tests on the 1659 gold bars at Texas A & M University had shown them to be of modern origin, and went on to repeat Bob Marx's story about the silver bars. The letter closed on a harsh note. "Hopefully," wrote Hancock, "we will be able to put Mel Fisher in the penitentiary before the end of 1975."

Not all of the members of the American Numismatic Association were as hostile to Treasure Salvors as was Virgil Hancock; George Vogt, for instance, felt that Mel's claims about the pillar dollars had validity. In actuality, however, few of the so-called colonial coin experts in the United States really knew much about the details of the minting of Spanish eighteenth-century pillar dollars or about Spanish colonial gold bullion identification. In such a situation, someone in a position of authority like Hancock could make his views loudly and widely known.

The article in *Science* magazine was much more balanced in tone; its writer, Nicholas Wade, had analyzed the controversy objectively and had interviewed all of the principals in it. He spoke with Mendel Peterson, with Bob Marx and Burt Webber, with Mel and Duncan in Key West, Dr. John K. Mahon at the University of Florida, Carl Clausen in Texas, and with Senator Williams and Sonny Cockrell in Tallahassee. Wade's conclusion was that the SEC investigation and Hancock's charges had been "inflated by Fisher's rivals into suggestions of wide-scale fraud which, on closer examination, have no solid basis." To the writer it was less clear whether Fisher and other salvors were irrevocably destroying the archaeological heritage in shipwrecks. The answers evoked by his interviews reflected the deep differences that still existed on that question.

These differences continued to affect relations between Treasure Salvors and the state of Florida. Mathewson had frankly and fully advised Sonny Cockrell of solid archaeological accomplishments at the wreck site and of instances when he had failed to carry out his complete program. Cockrell, however, expressed open contempt of this; he would not acknowledge that Mel had found the *Atocha*. He had told the *Science* magazine writer that he had recommended against the renewal of Fisher's contract, and bluntly said, "I am Fisher's enemy." Fortunately for the company, Senator Williams did not follow his archaeologist's recommendations; Mel's contract for the *Atocha* site had been renewed. Still, it was disturbing to see that, even in Tallahassee, controversy still raged.

One positive thing came of the continuing challenge to the *Atocha*'s identification: it forced us to break new ground. Duncan and I began to study more fully the artifacts the divers had found in the light of our growing knowledge of the site and of the archival documents describing the shipwreck. From Spain, in January 1975, I sent a lengthy analysis of all the data we now possessed for identification of the wreck site.

Slowly I had begun to realize that every lost ship had its own "fingerprints": a unique cultural profile of all that it had carried aboard at the moment of its sinking. To give in-depth knowledge of any one site and to provide a valid identification of it, this profile had to be extracted from the documents and compared with materials found in the wreck.

In addition to the arms lists previously located, I found
a list of the bronze cannon that the *Atocha* had carried
in 1622, designated by their weight in quintals and pounds.
At a small maritime museum in Seville that featured some
seventeenth-century bronze guns, I noticed that weight
numbers had been etched into the metal around the touchhole or carved into the breech rim. I then suggested to
Mel that if we found bronze cannon on the *Atocha* site,
we might be able to identify the site further in this way.
I came across the *Atocha*'s construction contract; in rich
detail, it contained the dimensions of the ship and her
hull and rigging plan.

A most dramatic document had also come to light: the
casualty list of those drowned aboard the *Santa Margarita*
and the *Nuestra Señora de Atocha*. In the long printed
pages were recorded a vast human tragedy. On the soldier's list, the losses were further personalized for me by
the physical description of some of the dead. I learned,
for instance, that the captain's flag-bearer, Jaime de Aranda, had been drowned on the *Atocha*. He was, the register noted, thirteen years old and had "a round face." It
was evident that the crew and passengers of the sunken
galleons had represented a cross section of Castilian civili-
zation: there were high noblemen, members of the upper
clergy, and officials of importance, as well as common
soldiers and sailors. This helped to explain the wealth
of personal jewelry—gold rings and chains, the crushed
cup of gold, and the fine medallions—as well as the gold
coins that had been found on the wreck site.

Obviously what we had found in the Quicksands were
the remnants of a major passenger-carrying galleon. This
knowledge worked its own subtle influence upon me. For
the first time, I began to sense the reality of the *Atocha*.
Now it was almost possible to picture its appearance: its
hull and decks, its sails and cabins, the bronze guns—
but most of all, its people. What had been a ghost vessel,
lost long years before, began to take on the shape of actuality.

Early in the new year of 1975, Jack Haskins came to Seville, bringing a welcome breath of Florida. Jack told me that Burt Webber had ceased operations in the Marquesas Keys and that he believed that John Berrier would also halt his search shortly. Mel's rivals, having found no trace of treasure, had become discouraged and were about to give up the fight.

Other news came from home, and most of it was good. First, Duncan told me that tests made on Mel's 1659 gold bars at the University of Michigan showed that they contained such a high gold percentage that they were evidently older material. Next, I learned that the Fort Lauderdale case had been thrown out of court by the judge. Best of all, it appeared that a division of the retrieved *Atocha* treasure with the state was very near.

Three weeks of intensive work went on in February in Tallahassee to prepare for the division. Mel, Bleth, and Duncan met with Curtiss Peterson and Austin Fowles, the skilled Jamaican conservator now working for the state of Florida. They examined every item in the shipwreck assemblage in an attempt to establish mutually agreed-upon point values for each. Later, state officials were to deny that they chose items of great appeal from the mass of bullion, coins, and artifacts, but that is precisely what they did. Senator Williams especially wanted the finest single item, the astrolabe. Now this was the kind of horse trade that particularly suited Mel, and he realized his chance. In the bargaining, the highest individual value—twenty thousand points—was set for the astrolabe. Actually, both sides thus recognized the great rarity of the instrument. Derek deSolla Price, an expert brought in by Duncan from Yale to study the marine astrolabe, gave it as his opinion that it dated to the mid-sixteenth century and might have been made by one Lope Homem, who made navigational instruments in Lisbon at that time.

The state also chose 33 cleaned silver coins, including one of the rare Santa Fé de Bogotá pieces. They also selected 1,703 uncleaned silver coins and a cross section of other materials, thus fulfilling the state's mission of preserving the essence of each shipwreck for posterity.

For their part, the salvors felt well satisfied with the division. Mel's company received 1,073 cleaned and 3,420 uncleaned silver coins, the 4 gold bars and the gold disk, 2 pieces of gold bars, all 11 gold coins, and more than 20 lengths of gold chain. They also accepted the 3 silver ingots found on the Fourth of July of 1973, the rosary recovered the same day, and 20 of the silver "candlestick holders." In addition, the company received many muskets, arquebuses, swords, daggers, and a fine assemblage of other artifacts. When the salvors took possession of the gold cup, however, they got a shock. It had been skillfully opened and cleaned, but an emerald, visible in a setting within when the cup was turned over to the state, was missing. The only explanation was a terse: "lost in cleaning." They also found that the silver ewer had been damaged during the time it was in Tallahassee.

A major media event was about to occur: the formal announcement of the division and a display of the *Atocha*'s treasure was scheduled for March 4 at the old Leon County jail in Tallahassee. The *National Geographic* television crew had come to record the division; Don Kincaid was prepared to make a complete photographic record of the proceedings; and newsmen were there from all over the country.

For their great day, Mel and all his crew came in the uniform of the day he had prescribed: orange Day-Glo sweatshirts marked with the single word *Atocha*. Many of the stockholders of Treasure Salvors and other members of the public came to view the treasure.

There, behind the bars of the old jail, it lay: a dazzling array of gold objects on a velvet-covered table; thousands of silver coins, displayed in large brandy snifters; the stone cannonballs, the astrolabe, the silver ingots . . .

At the press conference that formally opened the display, Senator Robert Williams presided. He sat with Florida's new Secretary of State, Bruce Smathers, and with Mel Fisher at the front table. Both officials spoke, but Mel was not introduced.

Finally a man in the audience stood and asked, "Who is Mel Fisher?"

Smiling, Mel stood and said, "I'm Mel Fisher."

Afterward, Mel presented Secretary Smathers personally with an encrusted sword. Greatly pleased, the Secretary said, "This is the realization of everyone's childhood dream—to find a shipwreck and sunken treasure."

Among the reporters present at the division ceremony was Robert Shaw of the Miami *Herald,* whose unflattering articles on Mel had appeared just a year before. Shaw had to eat some crow in his new article; after all, the shipwreck had turned out to be genuine, and very valuable, too. How then, could it all have been a stock promotion? Furthermore, it appeared as if it were truly the *Atocha.* In Shaw's *Herald* piece, some of his old charges against Mel reappeared, but the general emphasis of publicity about the treasure division was favorable. Articles about it were printed all over the United States and around the world. Although the state officials still refused to commit themselves as to the identification of the Marquesas shipwreck, they did sign a statement that all of the material divided had come from a Spanish shipwreck of the 1622 period.

From the state's standpoint, the division had come in the nick of time. On March 17, just two weeks later, the Supreme Court of the United States handed down its final ruling on the case involving the Florida boundaries. By unanimous decision, the justices found that Florida's sea borders, as drawn in its 1968 Constitution, were not correct. They found that the boundaries suggested in their master's report the previous year should prevail. This placed the *Atocha* site outside the boundaries of Florida and meant that the state had no jurisdiction over it.

On the day of the Supreme Court announcement, Bleth

called Senator Williams in Tallahassee to ask him what should, in his opinion, be done next. Williams's only comment was "Go on as usual." At that point, Mel Fisher had no other wish himself. He had, in fact, asked Dave Horan (now serving as Treasure Salvors' general counsel) to prepare a new contract between the company and the state. His proposal was that Florida would continue to be the depository, verifying authority, and conservator of the shipwreck materials. Duncan and I strongly concurred— we saw the controversy over the pillar dollars and the 1659 gold bars as evidence that materials without concrete authentication would always be subject to question.

In the meantime, operations in the Marquesas entered a strange period; state agents continued to serve on the boats and to certify the materials recovered, but we kept custody of them in our own vault. Weeks went by, and no reply came from Senator Williams as to the proposed contract that Mel had sent him. We had no way of knowing that serious conversations were under way between the state and federal authorities about the *Atocha.*

Now the treasure company seemed to have within its grasp a great opportunity; they apparently had title to the valuable collection received in the Tallahassee division, the salvors' 75 percent of the *Atocha* treasure. Mel began to consider how to bring about another division: that of the company's share with its investors and stockholders. Sale of the rest could provide long-needed working capital for further search and salvage.

Others in addition to Duncan and myself felt that the concept of authenticity of the treasure was all-important. Lou Tilley, now a member of the company's board of directors, arranged that the treasure received in Tallahassee be deposited, with ample security arrangements, in the vault of a bank in Cape Coral, Florida. Speaking of the validity of the materials, he said, "We may gamble out on the ocean, but we can't gamble on this."

It was further proposed that the company retain Austin

Fowles, the state conservator, who had perfected a process for cleaning encrusted silver coins. Fowles would open his own laboratory in the bank, with guarded access and electronic "frisking" of all entering persons. There he would clean, weigh, and photograph all the coins and produce a certificate of authenticity for each item.

At a lengthy, excitable, and disputatious corporate meeting at Cape Coral on March 21, the stockholders voted to support the authenticity concept and to contract with Austin Fowles to clean the silver coins. Several persons pledged the funds needed to begin the cleaning process; they were to be repaid after individual's coins had been cleaned and a per unit fee had been paid in for this purpose.

Present and contributing to the discussion at Cape Coral was Mel Joseph; he had lived up to his promises by bringing several other major investors into the company. One of these, Dr. Edwin Davis, an Annapolis urologist, was deeply interested in the marketing of the materials; he began to work with a committee Mel appointed to seek the maximum returns from the sale of the treasure.

Don Anderson, a University of South Florida faculty member, had acquired some Treasure Salvors stock by taking ownership of a company that owned it. Concerned with finding the fairest means of dividing the treasure, Anderson seized upon the idea that only a computer could correlate the thousands of coins and artifacts of varying values with the complex stock and percentage interests held by investors. He began to work up a program to carry this out.

Austin, Bleth, and Duncan analyzed the eleven hundred silver *Atocha* coins already cleaned by the state. They found that the great majority were minted during the rule of Philip III—from 1598 to 1621—while about ninety dated from the reign of Philip II—before 1598. Just a few—sixteen—were minted after 1621, under Philip IV. Most of the *Atocha*'s silver coins had been minted at Potosí; a small number had come from the Mexico mint, seven from Santa Fé de Bogotá, a few from Lima, and one from Santiago de Chile. The coins ranged in rarity from scarce to unique—from some known to none known in the world. Clearly the coins were most valuable, and the company's investors hoped that they could all be cleaned within a year and be divided.

On March 24, 1975, a greatly encouraging piece of national publicity appeared. Pete Axthelm, a contributing editor of *Newsweek,* wrote a breezy but penetrating column on the *Atocha.* The *Newsweek* article, the first such to appear after the division publicity, reflected growing public acceptance of Mel's find. Positive in tone, Axthelm's piece pointed out the depth of the company's effort, and singled out Mel Fisher as a successful treasure hunter, "because he was right recently" about the *Atocha.*

When the early spring weather permitted, the salvage boats were again on the site. A late March break in the weather enabled work in the Quicksands, and between the Bank of Spain and the galleon anchor, diver Joe Spangler brought up an object of rare beauty: a golden whistle. Shaped like a more modern bosun's pipe, the whistle had an earwax spoon and manicure set attached. Once cleared of sand, the whistle could be blown and gave forth a piping note; it was attached to a double length of gold neck chain and obviously had been the property of a person of rank on the *Atocha.* Perhaps it had been a pilot's whistle or possibly the symbol of rank for Vice-Admiral Pasquier himself.

The golden whistle became Mel's favorite piece of treasure. Although he estimated its worth at one hundred thousand dollars, he wore the whistle everywhere. When he spoke to the Saint Petersburg Kiwanis Club in May, he blew it for the audience. Describing the whistle to the Kiwanians, Mel said, "The last time anybody blew this was over three hundred and fifty years ago—he was a sailor who is still down there. After all that time, silver turns green, brown, or black, but gold shines forever."

Mel also told his audience of his deepest desire, still

unsatisfied after years of treasure hunting: "What I really want now is a bronze cannon. Every lead on one so far has been a disappointment."

After the finding of the whistle, the *Southwind* and the *Virgilona* moved to a new spot northwest of the galleon anchor. Many of the divers believed that the Mother Lode must lie in that direction. The first fruits of the move confirmed, for them, their belief: Pat Clyne and Spencer Wickens found, close together, two unusual gold bars of a type not before salvaged from the wreck site. Made of very high-carat gold, the bars carried large impressed carat numbers of a style different from those on the gold bar located the previous fall. They also bore small Arabic numbers, evidently of their weight in *pesos de oro*. It was puzzling. The bars had been assayed, but no *quinto* had been paid on them, for they carried neither royal seal nor mint mark. The site of the gold bar find, deemed a good one for future digging, was marked by a new signal: the "gold buoy."

In June 1975 a new security guard, Tom Ford, reported for his first day of work aboard the salvage ships. Tom, a redhead, was a thoughtful, studious young man; he was in the Keys Security Agency's force, retained by Fisher to keep a daily log and to tag independently any objects recovered. Although state field agents were still aboard the boats, they only observed operations and took no part in control of the materials.

On his first trip to the Marquesas site, on June 24, Tom Ford decided, on his off time, to take a dive from the *Southwind*. As he ranged over the sea floor, Ford saw a "little tip of gold, sticking out of the bottom, and grabbed at it." Out of the sand came a long gold bar.

It was perhaps the finest piece of gold yet brought up from the *Atocha*. The bar was larger, heavier, and more ornate than the others; it weighed twenty-four ounces. Eight royal seals and four carat marks were impressed upon its surface, and the mint seal, or *sigla,* displayed the letters *GDRS.* Jarring with the exquisite inscriptions was a large, crude *X X I I* scratched across one end of the bar. Perhaps the assayer who had tested the gold content of the bullion had scraped them to guide the *marcador,* who formally imprinted the carat markings, seals, and other inscriptions.

Now, in addition to the gold disk found two years before, Mel's salvors had recovered seven gold bars, while they continued to bring up lengths of gold chain—thirty to date. The *Atocha* must have been, they thought, literally crammed with gold. Uppermost in everyone's mind was the question: How much more was still out there in the Quicksands? We knew that the ship had carried 161 gold pieces on its registry, but much of what we had found was clearly illegal contraband.

One night at a Key West nightclub, Don, Bleth, Spencer, and I were celebrating the recent successes on the wreck site. We had also come to hear William "Coffee" Butler, a legendary Key West figure. "Coffee," an ageless black musician, was a truly first-rate jazz performer; ignoring the chances of success elsewhere, he had chosen to remain in his native town. On this night, the group was playing particularly well, and the hypnotic beat of the jazz piano rolled on until the hour grew late. The leader began to search the crowd through the haze and smoke of the darkened club, asking for request numbers. Catching sight of the group from Treasure Salvors, "Coffee" Butler called out. "Yeah," he shouted, echoing our exhilaration at winning control of the treasure and the recent achievements. "Yeah," he said. "There's gold in the water."

Since the location of the whistle and the gold bars had heartened the salvors, the company put all possible resources into work on the site as the good diving conditions of 1975 came. By the last week of June, the *Northwind*'s engines seemed to be running smoothly at last. Dirk Fisher had returned from the deep-diving school and assembled his team. Dirk brought with him a new spirit, together with a view about the Mother Lode that differed from that held by many others in the Treasure Salvors crew. With Duncan and me, Dirk believed in the "deep-water theory" of the location of the bulk of the *Atocha* treasure.

Although the newly arrived tug worked for a few days near the gold buoy, by Saturday, July 12, Dirk could wait no longer. He directed *Northwind* out beyond the Quicksands, past the underwater perimeter of bare bedrock, to the place where a new kind of sea bottom began—a dense, hard-packed clay material. At places even the potent force of *Northwind*'s great engines made little impression upon it. A water-jet hose was brought into play to cut into the heavy mud.

At the end of the first day's work, nothing had been found, but Dirk's resolve was not weakened. As strongly as did his father, Dirk believed in the great hidden treasure of the *Atocha.* From behind the mystery that still cloaked it, the Mother Lode beckoned to Dirk; for him it glowed with a special incandescence. He felt certain that he would be the one to find it.

XII. The Guns of the Atocha

When the *Northwind* sailed for the Marquesas in late June 1975, a game for high stakes—legal control of the *Atocha*'s treasure—had already begun, but we did not know it. We had, however, almost despaired of being able to work effectively with the state of Florida. As a result, when Duncan presented our paper on the shipwreck before the Florida Historical Society in May, we had agreed to place the *Atocha* documentation in the University of Florida Library at Gainesville instead of at Tallahassee. By the time I returned from Spain in June, those in Key West were also beginning to lose hope of any cooperative arrangement with the state. Mel had written Senator Williams, notifying him that the *Atocha* site lay in international waters and that state jurisdiction no longer applied; Mel had offered, however, to continue the relationship, referring to the draft contract he had sent weeks before, and about which he had heard nothing.

In truth, Mel Fisher was becoming somewhat weary of the *Atocha*—worn from the years of struggle over it. Those years had brought him little reward, and he felt particularly bound at this time by a number of constraints. News of an undersea discovery in the Bahamas cheered him instantly; it might provide him a way to escape for a while.

The shipwreck, found by lobsterman Rick Magers the year before, lay near Walker's Cay and had sixty-seven iron cannon on its ballast pile. Excited, Mel had written me while I was still in Europe, hopeful that it might be a major treasure-bearing galleon. He applied for a Bahamas salvage contract and planned to begin diving there early in the summer. Unfortunately, I had to advise Mel that his wreck was probably an almost completely salvaged eighteenth-century frigate, not a rich treasure ship. (This later turned out to be the case.) Mel had been disappointed in his attempt to escape the tensions of the *Atocha* hunt.

The new relationship between the company and the state complicated Mel's responsibilities in another way. Now he kept all the treasure recovered since the division in a locked vault on the galleon. An electronic burglar alarm system linked the vault door with the doors leading into the gift shop and office from the main deck. Opening up in the morning and closing up at night had become so difficult that someone would often inadvertently trip the alarm. Quickly the loud ringing of the warning bell would split the air, and within a few minutes the Key West police would be at the galleon. When the mistake was explained, they would patiently return to their patrol. To bolster security, Mel hired one of Keys Security's men to stand guard at the galleon.

Mel and Deo's daily rounds were killing. In the sweltering galleon office, Mel dealt with the growing legal complexities of his shipwreck while continuing the search for money. The pressures were telling on him. After wrestling all day with Treasure Salvors' problems and entertaining a steady stream of visitors, job applicants, and potential investors, the Fishers would adjourn to the Chartroom. There business would continue over a few, or many, drinks; a late dinner was often combined with a meeting with another investor. The next morning, Mel and Deo were up to do it all over again.

No amount of stress, however, could entirely blunt Mel's underlying spirit of fun and raillery. He got some amusement, for example, from the site map. Tacked to the wall over Mel's cluttered desk, it was a large, well-marked chart of the buoys, grids, and chains that formed a street map for operations on the wreck site. It was overlaid with numerous penciled lines and circles, representing mag searches, sub-bottom profile runs, and the excavations of four years.

One day Mel, who well knew the differing views within the company over the Mother Lode location, mischievously took his pen and made a heavy circle on the chart; alongside it he traced a large letter *M.* "There," he said, "put up or shut up. That's where *I* think we'll find it. Bleth, Gene, Duncan—all the rest of you—you put your money on the line and your mark on the map. Let's all bet a week's pay and see who wins." One by one, embodying our hopes in tiny initialed circles, we put our marks on the chart.

Mel was a born practical joker; on the gift shop counter he installed a device that gladdened his heart. To the unwary tourist waiting for a museum tour to begin, it looked like a round receptacle on which there lay a shining gold coin, ready to be grasped. But it was an optical illusion; reaching fingers would close upon empty air. Mel, chuckling, would show that the real coin lay several inches below, protected by thick glass.

Mel had always, however, to return to realities. His formal contract request to Senator Williams had gotten nowhere; nor did verbal proposals to other state personnel yield any result. Finally, Mel had to force the issue. On the morning of June 2, he had sent the salvage boat out without a state agent. When, at three P.M., the state man went to the boatyard where the tug had been moored, and realized what had happened, he immediately got on the telephone to Tallahassee and notified Senator Williams. Enraged, the state official called Dave Horan at once.

Williams, highly excited, accused Mel of breaking the company's contract with the state and threatened to "shut him down." At last the company had the state's attention on the jurisdictional matter; the next Monday, Robert Williams and the Florida State Department attorney, Jack

Shreve, came to Key West to meet with Dave and Mel. The two attorneys decided to continue negotiations, and both parties agreed that while the parleys went on, neither one would contact the federal government. For his part, Mel promised to fly the state agent out to the salvage boat and, for the time being, to leave him there.

Two days after the meeting in Key West, the federal authorities—acting through the U.S. Department of the Interior—formally asserted their jurisdiction over Site 8M0141, where the *Atocha*'s silver and gold had been found. For the first time since the passage of the Antiquities Act of 1906, the federal government claimed that it covered shipwrecks on the outer continental shelf.

In the meantime, in spite of the agreements made at Key West, Senator Williams had made up his mind. Warning Shreve not to notify either Dave Horan or Mel Fisher, he proceeded to apply, in the name of the state of Florida, for a federal antiquities permit on the *Atocha*.

During the night, *Northwind*'s anchors had dragged. Although the very best diving weather had passed, the morning of Sunday, July 13, 1975, was serene; only a gentle chop corrugated the sea surface. Dirk Fisher had gone off swimming to help reset the anchors; now he prepared to dive again, just to have a look at the bottom. It should, he thought, be about the right spot—near the place where, late in the previous season, he had found the ballast stone and the object of crushed iron. Although some had disagreed, Dirk deeply believed that the items had come from the *Atocha*.

The big tug lay at anchor southeast of the Quicksands, in direct line with the bobbing white spar buoys marking major finds of the shipwreck—a northwest-southeast corridor. She was moored near the underwater boundary between the bedrock and the hard-packed mud. Since visibility was poor, Dirk swam deep, almost forty feet down, skimming swiftly over the bottom through milky-green water.

Abruptly, Dirk veered upward; he had almost struck a

tumbled heap of large greenish objects, directly in his path. In complete astonishment, he hung suspended in the water, the discoverer, gazing at what he had found. For 350 years they had lain there, and he was the first to see them—five of the *Atocha*'s cannon. Shock, surprise, and joy possessed him in turn, and propelled him upward like an explosive force.

As Dirk burst from the surface, he shouted hoarsely for attention from the *Northwind,* less than 150 feet away. At first, Angel was alarmed; she thought Dirk had been attacked by sharks. He would not leave his place. Now that he had found his cannon, he didn't want to lose them. At last they understood his shouts and brought a boat and buoy to mark the spot.

While he tread water, awaiting the other divers, Dirk felt a sense of wonder slowly replacing his excitement. Why, he asked himself, had the cannon been found only now? The salvors had worked nearby for four years and must have crossed over the place many times. For a hundred and more years before that, Conch fishermen had frequented the area; their gear littered the bottom. Then he found himself wondering why this had happened to him.

By now it was midmorning. Word of the cannon find had gone out on radio to the galleon office in Key West, creating there a pandemonium even greater than that generated by the silver bars two years before.

When the news came, Duncan was just boarding the galleon; immediately he turned around to return to the trailer he shared with Don Kincaid. There, hastily, he packed the six-foot underwater photographic tower he had prepared for just such an eventuality. Don Kincaid brought all his camera equipment, and everyone converged at the boat: Duncan, Don, Pat Clyne, and the TV newsman from Miami's Channel 4. In a few minutes they had passed out of Key West harbor, headed west.

The boat made fast passage through the small islands, past Boca Grande and the Marquesas to the wreck site.

When they arrived at the yellow tug, a little past noon, they saw that *Northwind* had been moved to a position directly over the cannon. Burning with anticipation, Duncan and the others were soon in the water.

Despite the heat of their emotion, the divers slowed as they approached the cannon group; they were deeply impressed, even shaken, by what they beheld in the quiet below. There lay the unmistakable imprint of death and disaster, three and a half centuries old; a pattern laid down at the moment of the galleon's breakup. Four of the guns were piled together, while one outriding cannon pointed mutely to the Quicksands. Here was the shattered gun battery of a fighting galleon, the blunted power of imperial Spain, cut short in mid-career. A diver guided Duncan's hand to a scrape made that morning on the surface of a gun's tube; the cannon were cast of bronze.

Duncan would not permit the guns to be disturbed until they could be studied, measured, and photographed *in situ.* He and the other divers searched around them, hoping to find fragments of the gun carriages. Their efforts, and a light "dusting" with the blower, brought up a copper ingot from the *Atocha's* Havana cargo, and three bright gold bits, one clearly marked with the royal seal and a carat stamp.

The next day, July 14, Mel and the rest of his family came out to the wreck site. Now the salvors were in hot pursuit of the Mother Lode; they sent *Northwind* running on a zigzag course down the southeast corridor bearing. The tug blasted one hole, moved across the imaginary line, dug another, returned for a third, and then began the fourth excavation of the day. Pat Clyne came up from the hole with poorly suppressed excitement; there were, he announced, more bronze cannon down there! As the cavity enlarged, the whole second cannon feature—four more bronze guns—came to light.

The cannon in this second group lay in a rough west-northwest–east-southeast line, deeply buried in the mud. To the men peering through their face masks in the dim green light, it was evident that the mud cover had beautifully preserved the four cannon. They could see sportive dolphins and intricate shields on the bronze tubes.

Duncan had persuaded the eager treasure hunters to delay the removal of the guns for the necessary archaeological work. After the *National Geographic* film crew, hastily sent on receipt of the momentous news, had taken some underwater footage for the television special, Duncan laid down a baseline to connect the two cannon features. The groups lay just over thirty feet apart. Then the archaeologist took his portable grid and photographic tower below. Bill Spencer and two other Florida field agents aided Duncan in numbering, measuring, and labeling each cannon. Then, through the camera lens in the tower platform, the relative position of each gun was photographed against the grid. Later, Don Kincaid would make a color photomosaic of the whole grouping.

On Thursday, July 17, one gun from each group was brought up. Like all of its fellows, the cannon from the first five was eroded smooth, with no external markings. As it rose, dripping, at the *Northwind*'s stern, the watchers saw that it was strangely distorted—the underside of the tube up to the gun's muzzle was worn away. The divers nicknamed it "Shark Nose." Since a large green turtle had been seen to emerge from the cannon clump, Mel and his divers believed that it had been nesting there. They were certain that its flippers, and those of generations of other sea turtles, had worn the guns down.

After the salvage tug was moved over the second cannon group, the whole crew worked with the tug's winch and the A-frame hoist at *Northwind*'s stern to bring up another gun. Standing on the extreme lip of the fantail, Dirk reached out to steady the cannon as it was swung aboard. Once it was laid on deck and made fast, Mel, Duncan, Dirk, Angel, and the others gathered eagerly around. While the *National Geographic* cameraman recorded the scene, they exclaimed at the markings in relief on the coppery-colored bronze. The cannon carried a simple four-quartered Spanish shield with the castles and lions of Castile and León.

Pointing to another inscription below the shield, Angel said, *"Año* 1607—that must be the year it was made."

Below the touchhole, Duncan spied some incised numbers. Rubbing off the surface stain, he saw the figures *31q 10 L.* He ran for his briefcase and returned with the list of cannon numbers sent from Spain—the gun inventory of the *Atocha.*

"Here it is!" he cried, pointing to the twelfth number on the list. "This is from the cannon list that Gene Lyon sent from Seville. Here it is, *3110.* This is positive identification; this cannon came from the *Atocha!"*

Mel, suddenly pensive, felt a jumble of emotions. For once, his usual garrulity was gone. The impact of the discovery of the bronze cannon had just begun to strike him fully. Finally, he spoke softly. "You know," he said, "I've been looking for one of these a long time. I didn't even know for sure that they really made them, but here they are."

Mel knew that his son had found something rare. In fact, on this one site, more bronze cannon had been located altogether than had been found in modern times in shipwrecks. He knew the guns were valuable. Reverting for a moment to type, Mel said that they were worth twenty thousand dollars apiece. But he knew, as did we all, that something more than monetary value, something more prized than rarity, had been uncovered with the cannon. Slowly, incompletely, a part of the buried past was being unfolded for us, and we had begun to know what it meant; we had thus begun to share in something privileged and precious. The treasure hunt had produced more than loot.

If the discovery of the bronze cannon seemed to bring the hunters closer to the secret of the *Atocha,* it had also brought the search for the first time into the deeper water, which Mel had always instinctively distrusted. He had never wished to work in deep water; this brought very real hazards for divers. Now, for example, they had to begin to observe closely the diving tables, to limit strictly the divers' time on the bottom, in order to avoid the dreaded bends.

Moreover, Mel thought, why not just leave it at that? His long-denied wish for a bronze cannon had been bountifully satisfied. He had the *Atocha* now—the guns proved that—and his company had a substantial treasure to divide. Maybe he had gone far enough. Or had he already gone too far?

Yet Mel's entire career had been a series of gambles, played with ever-escalating stakes until he had reached this, the greatest gamble of his life. Moreover, Mel's inner vision, like Dirk's, linked him with this sunken ship. Somehow its fate, centuries before, was irrevocably tied to his own star. He had to win this gamble. His luck had carried him this far; surely it would take him all the way— all the way to the Mother Lode.

XIII. A Powerful Ocean

"It's a powerful ocean. It takes
people and ships."

—Mel Fisher

Northwind's triumphant return with the two bronze cannon marked a new phase in Mel Fisher's enterprise. Even
before the guns were swung carefully over the museum
galleon's rail to be placed in water-filled boxes on the deck
for the admiration of tourists, the word had gone out. The
discovery was reported locally and then regionally; it
pulsed out through the national wire services and registered in the memory banks of the great American media
system. There, taken together with the story of the treasure division and the Supreme Court ruling, the story had
its impact. Results were not long in being felt.

At the offices of the National Geographic Society in
Washington, the bronze cannon find made it definite: the
story went into high gear. Assistant Editor Ed Linehan
continued with the article while Dennis Kane saw the
film shot on the *Northwind* and huddled with Nick Noxon
over shooting schedules necessary to complete the film.

There was, to be sure, a spasmodic reaction from Mel's
rivals. Bob Marx had a new story this time; now he said
that Mel had brought the bronze cannon from a shipwreck
off Big Pine or Sugarloaf Key (depending on the version
you heard) and planted them off the Marquesas. Any of
the state agents present when the second cannon group
had been dug out of the mud that had covered them for
350 years could have destroyed the tale immediately, but
Tallahassee chose to make no comment. In any event, it

meant little; to the world, the bronze cannon had come from the *Atocha.*

Now a great new eagerness seized the treasure hunters. They saw the cannon as pointers—direct to the Mother Lode. The guns seemed to indicate a major breakup of the ship, and surely, if they dug a little deeper, went on a little farther, the huge pile of coins and bar silver would be theirs. The salvors had paused only briefly to enjoy the fruits of their labors.

Although the company was not all that flush with cash at the moment, expectations were high. Mel paid out a number of bonuses to the *Northwind*'s crew. The highest, ten thousand dollars, went to his son Dirk for locating the five bronze guns. After a short but memorable celebration in Key West, Dirk and Angel went to Miami, where they bought what had long been Dirk's dream: a Porsche. The young couple then returned to Key West to outfit the *Northwind* for its next, and hopefully its most successful, trip.

Ironically, the very week of their celebration and the days of their burning expectation that they might find the bulk of the *Atocha*'s treasure were the very time when Treasure Salvors came close to losing it all.

Since the federal government had announced its claim over shipwrecks on the continental shelf, Bleth had taken a deep interest in the subject. Although she had not studied law, Bleth began to read all the works on Admiralty cases available to her; she also perused the wrecker lore in the Key West Public Library from the time when the city had been the nation's salvage capital. Dave Horan had also been studying intensely the stand his client should take in order to protect this flank of the company's position.

Then, suddenly, Horan heard a rumor that the federal authorities were negotiating directly with the state of Florida over the *Atocha* site. Following the story up, he found that the rumor was true: the state had filed for a federal antiquities permit on the site! He then learned that the permit was, in fact, all ready except for the final signatures. Incensed at what he called "this betrayal," Dave immediately called Jack Shreve in Tallahassee. When he answered the telephone, the state attorney was obviously embarrassed. "I asked him what had happened to our understanding that neither party to the state-company negotiations would go to Washington to deal," said Horan, "and he said that Senator Williams had told him not to contact me—that they would do the groundwork for a permit and then allow Treasure Salvors to work under the state's license."

Horan could see at once that this left his client nothing. After all their toil, trouble, and investment, they would have no security whatsoever; such an arrangement could be easily canceled by the state. This was unacceptable to Dave Horan, a keen, incisive, and aggressive man. He began to seek for alternatives, for a "fall-back position." By the weekend when the bronze cannon were found, Dave was working early and late on the problem. He put all his other legal business aside to concentrate on the Treasure Salvors case.

On Wednesday, July 16, Jack Shreve called from Tallahassee to caution Dave Horan: he should take no action. If he did, the state lawyer warned, the company could lose everything. He promised to fly down on Friday to bring the state's "final offer."

In seeking an alternative for Treasure Salvors, Dave turned over all the possibilities in his mind. Finally he determined that the solution would have to come through Admiralty law, and decided to call in an expert in that field for aid. Fortunately, Joshua Morse, the dean of his own law school, was eminently knowledgeable concerning Admiralty law. On Thursday, Dave called Dean Morse and outlined his problem, stressing that he felt he would have to go into court to establish a negotiating position. That afternoon, they spent almost three hours on the telephone, and neither man slept much that night.

Early the next morning, a rough draft of a lawsuit came by Mailgram to Dave's office, sent by Dean Morse. The two attorneys had agreed on the format: the company would file an old-fashioned salvage action, a wreckers' suit, directly against the sunken galleon.

On Friday morning, July 18—the day the *Northwind* made its rapturous entrance into Key West harbor with the *Atocha*'s two bronze cannon—Jack Shreve came to Dave's office. There he told Dave that, unfortunately for Treasure Salvors, the situation had "deteriorated." The best the state could now offer, said Shreve, was to allow Mel to go on salvaging, under the State's permit, on a month-to-month basis. Dave asked what kind of percentage of find the salvors would get under that arrangement. The state lawyer said that this was not yet clear, that it would have to be negotiated with the federal government, and that Treasure Salvors would just have to accept whatever percentage the state provided.

When Dave asked if that was the state's last word, Shreve told him, "That's all you are going to get, but if you don't take it, you are making a very serious mistake. It's either that or nothing." He added that he would return at one thirty to get the company's answer.

As soon as Shreve had left the office, Dave made his final corrections on the lawsuit draft and had a smooth copy typed. He called Mel, got permission to file the suit, talked awhile, and hung up the telephone. Bleth came in, and they sat and looked at the papers on his desk. Dave, exhausted, put his head in his hands. "My God, Bleth," he said, "what if we lose?"

Dave got on the noon plane to Miami to file his lawsuit; thus he was not in the office when Shreve returned in midafternoon. When Dave's secretary told the state lawyer that the Treasure Salvors' attorney had gone to the Miami District Federal Court to file suit for the *Atocha,* Shreve completely lost his composure. Seeing a sudden serious obstacle in the way of the planned takeover of the *Atocha,*

Shreve shouted, "This is the worst mistake he'll ever make in his life." Then he stormed out.

That same day, four months after the Supreme Court ruling, Mel notified the state field agents that they were to leave the wreck site; he also advised Senator Williams in Tallahassee that their mutual contract on the *Atocha* site was now null and void. Now the fat was in the fire. Against the arrayed might of both state and federal governments, the salvors were fighting for their treasure.

The filing of the lawsuit had capped a whole week of exaltation and strain. Mel, Deo, and Bleth had a few drinks and went to Logun's for a quiet dinner. There, relaxed, Mel and his wife began to recount some of their early treasure adventures—at Silver Shoals, off Tortuga, in Panama. Some of the stories seemed excruciatingly funny; they laughed and laughed. Then, after dinner, they went next door to a little store; it was still open, and Mel bought a leisure suit, in his own private celebration of the discovery of the bronze cannon. Then it was late, and Mel and Deo went off to the Pier House, where they had taken a room to escape the press and the ringing of the telephones.

For Deo, the next day—like most of her days—would be devoted to her family and its enterprise. It was Angel Fisher's birthday, and Deo had baked her a cake. The next morning, she would take it to her. Dirk, Angel, and the rest of the *Northwind* crew had sailed that morning, and Moe Molinar had taken *Virgilona* out to the Marquesas. The elder Fishers wanted to be on the spot when work began the next day. Together, then, they would follow up the cannon—which pointed, they believed, straight to the Mother Lode.

It was not yet seven thirty on Sunday morning, and most of Key West was still sleeping. Far west of there, however, beyond the dark-green outline of the Marquesas islets, the *Virgilona* crew was astir.

Tom Ford, in a bunk below, was brought to wakefulness by a spirited discussion up on deck. Moe Molinar and Spencer Wickens were arguing over the enigma of the morning: *Northwind,* which had been anchored off the atoll at dusk, was nowhere in sight. He heard someone say: "They must have boogied to the wreck site." Since the race for the Mother Lode was on, perhaps Dirk had stolen a march on them.

In a few minutes, they had pulled anchor and *Virgilona* was plowing through an easy swell, headed a little south of due west. As Moe steered with one hand, his eyes were never still. Searching incessantly to port and to starboard, they noted lobster-pot floats, a flying bird on a morning search, the wavering lines of yellow gulfweed. Then Moe spied something very small on the water, some two miles south of the salvage boat. A bright red spot of color caught his attention; someone was waving something red. As Moe turned the *Virgilona* to port to run down south to the object, he felt certain that he had spotted a boatload of Cuban refugees—such craft were often found drifting in these waters.

As *Virgilona* drew closer, the watchers aboard saw that a small figure had been waving to them from a miniature rubber life raft. Clinging to its sides in the water were seven men. To their amazement and then shock, the *Virgilona* crew saw that the boy in the raft was Angel Fisher's little brother, Keith Curry. Counting heads, Moe saw Don Kincaid; Bouncy John Lewis; Kane Fisher; Bob Reeves, a photographer; Jim Solanick; and Donny Jonas and Peter van Westering. Not present were Rick Gage, a new diver—and Angel and Dirk Fisher.

Moe Molinar said, "What . . . ?"

Don Kincaid answered only, "The *Northwind* sank."

Quickly the survivors were helped aboard, given dry clothing and hot coffee. Their exhaustion, their stunned daze shocked the crew of the *Virgilona.* But Don Kincaid had not lost his ability to think clearly. As soon as he was aboard the *Virgilona,* he went to the boat's radio and notified the Coast Guard of the sinking. He told the authorities that *Northwind* had suddenly capsized at anchor at five thirty that morning. He reported further that Dirk, Angel, and Rick had not come up from below and were presumed lost.

While Don tried vainly to raise the company's base radio station, Moe swung *Virgilona* around again to search for the spot where the big tug had gone down. At last Don raised someone on a CB radio: Bob Hall, a friend of Treasure Salvors, who owned the seafood restaurant near the galleon pier, picked up the signal. Hall then telephoned Bleth, who called Mel and Deo at their motel room, awakening them with the news that the *Northwind* had sunk. She couldn't bear to tell the elder Fishers about the missing people, but when Mel went to the Coast Guard office, they told him that his son and daughter-in-law were probably dead.

As Don Kincaid helped guide the boat back to the place of the sinking, he told the *Virgilona* people what had happened. Where the tug had been anchored, the sea had been serene, almost calm; the quiet of the night was broken only by the clattering whirr of the air conditioner outside Dirk and Angel's cabin amidships. After a short party celebrating Angel's birthday, they retired; tomorrow would be a busy, perhaps an epic day. The rest of the crew slept in the divers' cabin, the pilot house, and on the exposed decks.

Before dawn on Sunday morning, Don was startled from sleep by what seemed an insistent voice: "Hey, look out up there!" Instantly awake, he rose, sensing something wrong. As his mind cleared to full awareness, he realized what it was: the *Northwind* was listing heavily to starboard. He went to rouse Don Jonas, who tended the ship's pumps and engines, and they went together to the engine room to find the cause of the list. They found it to be twofold—a leaking toilet valve and the connector valve that maintained fuel balance between the tug's two forward diesel fuel tanks. As Jonas began to work to shift the water that had leaked in from the toilet valve, the fuel oil shifted from port to starboard, and the tug began to lurch toward a steeper angle. Feeling a sudden sense of danger, Don Kincaid shouted a warning to Jonas and the others, and made his way out to the main deck. Suddenly, the salvage tug turned more to starboard, flipped upon its side, and began to sink.

When the *Northwind* turned turtle, several of the crew were caught below—Jonas, Jim Solanick, and Rick Gage, and, in their stateroom, Dirk and Angel Fisher. The others—Don, Kane Fisher, eleven-year-old Keith Curry, Bouncy John Lewis, Bob Reeves, and Peter van Westering—found themselves in the water and scrambled for safety to the bottom of the overturned hull. Solanick made his way to a porthole, squeezed through it, and found the other survivors. After several minutes trapped in the submerged engine room, Don Jonas, breathing from a small air pocket, found a floating flashlight almost miraculously at his hand. By its glow he struggled to the engine-room door, opened it, and swam up to safety on the surface of the black sea. Without their scuba tanks and other diving gear, the men on the steel hull were helpless; they could not dive down to those trapped below.

As the tug slowly settled and began to sink, the survivors found a life raft, uninflated, bobbing in the water. In it, blown up to its full size of only four feet, they placed the boy and then launched out on the still-dark ocean. As they drifted down west toward the Dry Tortugas, the sky brightened with infinite slowness. At length, the sun rose, flooding the sea and the little group of survivors with bright light, disclosing with stark clarity their numb desolation and loss.

After an absence of many years, Bob Moran had come back to work again with Treasure Salvors. On this awful Sunday morning, he and Bleth moved at once to help locate the *Northwind* and bring back the survivors. As it happened, the *Virgilona* found the sunken tug before the Coast Guard did, following a trail of debris back over the sea to the place where an oil slick marked the *Northwind*'s grave. Moe's divers and Don Kincaid went down to the wreck and recovered the bodies of the three young treasure hunters; then they salvaged the diving equipment lost in the sinking.

Bob Moran flew out to the Marquesas in his seaplane to rendezvous with the *Virgilona* and retrieve the survivors, but the wind and waves had begun to rise and he could not land on the sea. A boat from Key West picked up five of the *Northwind*'s crew, and the *Virgilona* began the long trip back to Key West with its sad cargo.

At dockside in early afternoon, Mel, Deo, the Currys, and a small group of company employees and friends met the boat. Tearful, Deo clasped each of the survivors in turn, murmuring to each, "I'm so glad you're here." When reporters pressed Mel for a statement, he could only say, "It's a powerful ocean. It takes people and ships." Before they could leave, *Northwind*'s survivors had to make lengthy statements to the authorities. Then Bob Hall fed them a meal and they all went slowly to their homes.

Word of the *Northwind*'s sinking and the loss of the three young people went out all across the nation to stockholders and friends of Treasure Salvors. It reached Vero Beach, Saint Petersburg, and Daytona Beach; it came to Chicago, Washington, and Annapolis. Bleth, Bob, "T" Hargreaves, and Duncan helped to keep the office going and to deal with hundreds of expressions of sorrow and solidarity. From Spain, Ángeles Flores Rodríguez wrote a compassionate letter, and friends established a fund to memorialize the young divers. When he heard of the accident, Cincinnati Jim Vondehaar came at once to Key West, where he manned the telephones. Out of his own grief, he wrote a memorial poem, "Sail On."

It was a measure of the company's loss that the finest

of the gold bars—the one found a month before by Tom Ford—was lost when the *Northwind* sank; it was counted as but a part of the general distress. The tugs themselves were finished insofar as Mel was concerned. *Northwind* was to be sold where she lay, and *Southwind* would never go to sea again as a salvage craft for Treasure Salvors.

The news reached me on vacation in Georgia, and I hastened home, for the funeral of the young Fishers was to be in Vero Beach. Dirk and Angel were to be buried at the old Johns Island cemetery, near the grave of a family friend whom Dirk had especially admired.

Mel chartered a DC-3 aircraft to fly the entire Treasure Salvors crew up to Vero Beach for the funeral. Arville Renner, the minister who had married the young pair less than two years before, presided at a crowded, emotion-packed service. The couple were buried in the bright clothing they had worn at their wedding, and their fellow divers also wore their wedding clothes.

It had been some time since I had seen Mel or Deo. After the service, I went up to see Dirk and Angel for the last time and passed the older Fishers on the way out the door. I took Mel's hand and tried to say something to his wife, but could not speak. Deo beckoned me closer and said, "Wait until you see them. Wait until you see the beautiful things we have found."

"Do you mean the cannon?" I asked.

"Yes," she said. Deo Fisher knew. She knew the meaning of what Dirk had found, and how great a price had been paid for the discovery.

Before he and Deo went, out of a desperate need to get away, for a short rest at Mel Joseph's country place in Delaware, Mel Fisher swore the search would go on. "I'm sure," he stated, "Dirk would have wanted it that way." But we all wondered if the enterprise had not ended with the sudden loss of the *Northwind*.

We even questioned whether Mel would ever bring up the remaining seven bronze cannons still lying on the sea bottom out beyond the Marquesas Keys; after all, they were wrapped up somehow in Dirk's death and the suddenly altered hunt for the *Atocha* itself.

In just a week, Mel's venture had been greatly, and terribly, altered. The stakes in the game had been raised almost impossibly high. His son's last move had evidently laid the Mother Lode open for the taking. Dirk had proved the deep-water theory, but at an awful cost. Now we wondered if a barrier had not been laid down for Mel, if he had not been told unmistakably, "Go no further." If he did go on, who could know what further tragedy might lie in store?

We wondered, in short, if the *Nuestra Señora de Atocha* might not have won its battle with Mel Fisher.

Sail On

Sail on, sail on, sail on
Across the unknown sea;
Chart the reefs and shoals—
Spot the wrecks for me.

You climbed the highest mountain—
This world became too small;
So you embarked
On the greatest journey of them all.

You have your Angel and faithful crew
To help you find the wonders
That are still ahead of you.

Sail on, I say again—
To some far and distant shore;
Chart the reefs and pick the wreck,
Till we can dive with you once more.

—*James Vondehaar*

In memoriam:
DIRK FISHER
ANGEL FISHER
RICK GAGE

XIV. Courts, Cannons, and Silver

The sinking of the *Northwind* had devastated Mel and Deo. Although they returned to the galleon office after their brief rest in Delaware and attempted to carry on the company's work, it was a terrible time. Other members of the team—Bob Moran (now general manager), Bleth, "T," Moe, Cincinnati Jim—were pillars of strength for the bereaved couple.

Virgilona was sent to the Marquesas to mag, dig, and fill the legal need to protect the wreck site, but seemingly nothing could be decided about the remaining seven bronze cannon. Although they were a valuable prize for anyone to seize, Mel could not bring himself to give the order to have them brought in. In his mind, the guns were all bound up with the death of his son Dirk. While they still rested on the sea bottom, they were a solid bulwark in the shifting wreck-site sands and in the rapidly moving currents of the Fishers' lives. At one point, Mel decided to have a bronze memorial plaque cast and fixed in concrete at the spot, and only then recover the guns Dirk had found, but nothing came of the idea.

Deo's grief for her son was racking and long-enduring. She was corporate secretary and had always attended to many details in the office, but her friends were distressed to see her struggle to carry on her work while clearly unable to free her mind from the dreadful recollections of the disaster. But the rapid march of events would not permit any delay for mourning.

One afternoon, federal marshals appeared on the deck of the galleon museum and approached the wooden boxes that held, in seawater, the first two bronze cannon brought up in July. There, addressing the guns, the officers read aloud a notice of Case #75–1416 in the Southern Federal District Court in Miami: the case of Treasure Salvors, Inc., against the wrecked and abandoned sailing vessel *Atocha.* They then arrested the cannon, the best physical remnant of the ship available, and left them, as the supposed property of the salvors, in our possession.

The state of Florida, after studying the legal position of the parties, decided not to enter the lawsuit; the state officials had privately ascertained that their rights, if any, were marginal. They did, however, join with federal authorities to ask the Coast Guard to expel Treasure Salvors from the wreck site. A Justice Department attorney came from Washington to Coast Guard headquarters in Miami to set up the mechanics of the operation.

In the meantime, however, the company began a high-level publicity campaign to expose the federal activities to the general public and gain sympathy for the salvors' case. Bleth McHaley began to inform senators, congressmen, and other federal and state officials of the planned federal takeover. The salvors reached a presidential assistant in the White House, and through the good offices of many of the company's friends brought their case to high-level attention. Soon we learned that no action would be taken by the Coast Guard to seize the wreck site. We were, however, under continuous surveillance.

Now the federal government formally entered the lawsuit as an interested party, claiming complete jurisdiction over the *Atocha* and its treasures. To counter this move, Treasure Salvors retained Kermit Coble, an attorney with ties to Florida state officials. At this stage, we still believed that the state and the company could act together; perhaps we could negotiate jointly with federal attorneys in everyone's best interest. Under such an arrangement, the state would retain the 25 percent it had received in the March treasure division, the federal government would acknowledge this as a sufficient share, the salvors would get the rest, and the lawsuit would be dropped. In line with this idea and through the help of one of Florida's senators, a meeting was set in Washington for August 15 with all the involved parties.

The federal spokesmen coolly stated the government's position: the entire wreck site and all the materials from it, 100 percent of them, belonged to Uncle Sam. Under existing laws, the spokesmen contended, it would be difficult indeed to divide any of the treasure with the salvors. The most they could hold out was the possibility that Congress might appropriate money to compensate the company for its efforts.

While we sat at the conference table, still stunned over this revelation, Senator Robert Williams stood to speak, representing the state of Florida. As soon as Williams began, we knew that something had gone badly wrong.

After first reciting the role of state agents in preventing salvage divers from ruining the people's heritage underwater, the senator directed his remarks to Treasure Salvors. He launched an attack on Mel and on the company, asserting that since no state field agents were now there to supervise the work, we were "destroying the site." Heatedly he claimed that no archaeology was being done on the wreck site. Williams closed with a dramatic statement that the only way to save anything from the site for future generations was to permit Florida to control the salvage.

We looked at each other around the table, livid with anger. Walking to the table from the corner where he had been photographing the meeting, Don Kincaid stepped up to Robert Williams and said; "That's a bunch of . . . baloney, Senator."

Dave Horan gave the salvors' position, and it was apparent that the parties in litigation were still far apart; certainly no negotiation would be possible with the state of Florida. The matter would have to be fought out in court.

In the aftermath of the Washington meeting, the opposing parties went into legal high gear. Dave Horan was often in Tallahassee, consulting the law libraries there and conferring with Dean Joshua Morse. Bleth learned all she could of maritime law and followed the case vigorously; she continued her publicity campaign with great energy. On August 29, 1975, Mel wrote to President Gerald Ford. In his letter, Mel told the President that Treasure Salvors had invested more than two million dollars, seven hard years, and four lives in the salvage of the *Atocha*. He termed the federal claim to the wreck site "serious government interference in private enterprise."

He learned of a 1969 article written precisely to the point of his lawsuit in an obscure legal journal. Through an influential Southern senator, he gained access to the article, written by a federal attorney. After studying this and other precedents, Horan and Morse concluded that the salvors' case was strong and that the federal government had, in reality, "not a leg to stand on."

For their part, the federal authorities tried to create legal standing for their position. Although no antiquities permits had ever been issued for the outer continental shelf since the passage of the Antiquities Act of 1906, now permits were hastily granted in California, Rhode Island, North Carolina, and Florida. They let a contract (in which Florida officials participated) for a magnetometer search of the Florida Gulf Coast; they set up an Underwater Bureau in the Department of the Interior and staffed it with a director who held a Ph.D. in marine archaeology. All of this was fruitless expenditure of federal monies, however, as far as the *Atocha* case was concerned; when Judge William Mehrtens conducted his pretrial conference, he threw out as evidence anything that the federal government had done after the date when Dave Horan had filed the salvors' suit. Horan, scenting ultimate victory in the case, immediately filed a motion for summary judgment for his client. Judge Mehrtens took the motion under advisement.

They were in new country now. Not only were the salvors working in deeper waters after the cannon find; they were facing a markedly different ocean bottom. Seaward of the narrow bedrock strip lying outside the Quicksands was a material the divers termed "mud." Actually it was a shallow layer of fine gray silt overlying a thick layer of heavy brown clay. Where the layers met, there was a hardpan, very difficult to penetrate. Without the mailboxes of the big tugs, the company needed effective tools to discover what lay beneath the hardpan.

First Fay Feild came to direct extended magnetometer searches in the corridor Duncan had charted: the narrow strip of wreckage recovered from northwest of the galleon anchor through the Bank of Spain to the bronze cannon. In addition to the mag, Mel recognized that other electronic sensing devices should be employed; perhaps the sub-bottom profiler should be used again, this time more systematically. In order to punch holes in the clay and hardpan, the divers experimented with small airlifts and water hoses off the *Virgilona;* clearly, however, they needed a larger working platform than the diesel salvage boat.

Next, a crisis typical of Treasure Salvors occurred: the galleon sank again alongside its pier. After a hectic salvage effort with portable pumps, Mel and Bob Moran devised a huge plastic "diaper" to contain the galleon hull. The divers swam the plastic sheet under the leaky hull, and it was soon fairly watertight again, but the galleon badly needed major shipyard work, for which there was neither time nor money.

In late summer, Mel found a ship that seemed to solve his many problems on the wreck site. The *Arbutus,* a 187-

foot ex–Coast Guard buoy tender, was for sale in Miami for seventeen thousand dollars. It had no motive power engines but had some good equipment and a sound hull. Mel bought the steel vessel and arranged to have it towed to the keys as soon as possible. He foresaw *Arbutus* as a mother ship for stores and salvage crews that could ease some of the headaches of his long supply line from Key West; it could also serve as a direct platform for airlifting and other salvage work—and had another use as well. When, in early fall, the old craft was towed to the wreck site and moored to heavy anchors, *Arbutus* became the official marker of Mel's salvage claim. Under the regulations of federal salvage areas, a vessel had to kept on site at all times to keep the company's legal claims alive.

At the annual stockholders' meeting held in late October, the cleaning, authentication, and distribution of the treasure received in March was uppermost in all minds. Dave Horan had negotiated a stipulation releasing up to 50 percent of the treasure to the company for distribution to its percentage investors and stockholders. Duncan had helped revise the point system to include the items recovered in 1975, including the gold bars, the whistle, and the bronze cannon.

Austin Fowles described how he had moved to Cape Coral, set up his laboratory in the bank, and begun work. He had already cleaned four hundred coins with his reverse electrolysis method. Each object from the shipwreck would be represented by a certificate signed by the company president and secretary, and by the historian, archaeologist, and conservator. Each certificate also bore a photograph of the coin or other artifact, and was thus traceable back to the recovery of the item from the wreck site.

Don Anderson, Division Committee chairman, told the audience what it wished to hear: the computerized system for distribution was ready; soon, when the legal problems had been ironed out, there could be a division.

Plans were afoot to sell the company's share of the treasure. Dr. Edwin Davis, chairman of the Marketing Committee, announced that two specialists in marketing, Elliot Detchon (an investor in the company) and Al Manola, had been retained to seek the best means for a major sale.

From Bleth McHaley, the stockholders learned that a showing of the treasure would be held at the Cape Coral Bank early in the new year. She also noted that the appearance of the *National Geographic* article on the *Atocha* would coincide with a display of the treasure at Explorer's Hall in Washington. I had independent knowledge of this, because I had just been retained by the society to write the article.

Bleth added that the company had other ambitious plans to report; it was negotiating for four and a half acres of Key West waterfront property. The land, an old shipyard, had valuable Gulf frontage; out of her knowledge of Key West's past, Bleth had named it "Wrecker's Wharf." It was hoped that a luxury hotel complex would be built on the property, and a group of stockholders was forming to back the venture financially. Mel added that buildings on the site could serve as an archaeological and conservation laboratory for Duncan and Austin.

Bob Daley, a free-lance writer and novelist, wrote an article for *The New York Times* that appeared on Sunday, November 2. A realistic treatment of Mel's adventure, it featured a touch of the romantic, too. The article caught on at once and was widely syndicated. Later I learned that Bob's investigation had led him to Robert Shaw's Miami *Herald* series, to Bob Marx's remarks, and to other information derogatory to Mel's claims. To check the story out thoroughly, Daley went to Seville and examined my sources at the archive. He was satisfied with their authenticity, and returned to write a story generally sympathetic to the salvors.

It happened that quickly. From a flat calm on Friday, January 30, the *Arbutus* crew watched the weather worsen until by Sunday morning twenty-five-knot winds were whistling around the old buoy tender. Even after the front passed and the winds began to moderate, the ocean swells continued to rise rapidly, from six to nine and even ten feet in height. The first onslaught of the storm had brought down the huge refrigerator in *Arbutus*'s galley; after that, the crew abandoned all thought of diving from the heaving ship, and labored to tie down all loose gear.

It was poor weather for it, but Mel had decided to bring up the remaining bronze cannon, the operation had been planned, and it had to go ahead if at all possible. Mel had chartered the offshore oil-rig tender *Seaker* from Olin Frick, who with John Gasque and other members of his crew came to help raise the guns. *Seaker* was a sturdy, practical craft that carried a heavy crane mounted amidships. She had arrived on the wreck site on Saturday, but put into the Marquesas to await more moderate seas.

In the meantime, Dave Horan had brought Bob Moran, Spencer Wickens, and me out to the *Arbutus* on Sunday; we were scheduled to spend the night and see the operation. Dave had a fine, fast boat—a twenty-eight-foot Cigarette type—and he opened his throttle wide for the trip, but the seas were just too rough. Although we landed Spencer on *Arbutus*'s stern—barely—we could neither unload anyone else nor tie up because of seven-foot seas. As we returned to Key West, we did not realize that the *Cape York,* the Coast Guard cutter, had picked us up on radar and shadowed us all the way in. As far as they were concerned, only pot, cocaine, or gold smugglers would have gone out in that kind of weather.

On Monday, February 2, the operation finally took shape. We returned to the Marquesas on Norman Woods's *Petticoat III,* and I transferred to *Seaker* there for the short trip to the wreck site. There I found that Mel's secretary, Margo McCollum, and Vickie Weeks had played hooky from the office to see the cannon-raising. Their enthusiasm was infectious.

My own excitement was intense enough. I had seen only

two of the *Atocha*'s guns, those brought in the previous July. The divers had told me how beautiful some of the guns still underwater were, and I was eager to see them. But I had a real concern: would all the guns match? That is, would the weight numbers on the other guns match the *Atocha*'s gun list, as those on gun No. 3110 had done? I had brought a blown-up photograph of the gun list with me and hoped that I would have the opportunity to use it.

When Mel arrived with Mel Joseph on Tate Berry's boat, we were ready to go. *Seaker* was positioned over the first of the cannon groups to seaward—the one from which gun 3110 had come. But raising the cannon proved to be a slow and difficult task. Our divers and *Seaker*'s crew toiled for some time in the murky, silted water before they could securely knot their heavy lines around the tube and trunnions of the first gun.

From the deck of the salvage vessel, we could see nothing whatever below; all at once, a diver surfaced to tell us that the lines were fast and the gun could now be raised. Since Mel Joseph had spent his life with heavy equipment, he was the best man to operate the crane; he climbed to the cab and put the crane in motion.

Close alongside *Seaker,* bubbles began to rise in the water. Suddenly the gun rose, suspended over the sea by heavy ropes. I gasped in wonderment; the gun had fine, clean lines; it looked a grim weapon still. The cannon twisted in its hawser as the crane swung it slowly around and inboard. As he began to lower it to the deck, Mel Joseph had to warn me to stay clear; I was that eager to see the markings, if any, on the gun's barrel.

As the gun was being lowered, it tilted in its cradle. Several gallons of seawater spilled out, and a small, radiant angelfish flopped onto the deck. An errant, chilling thought came to me then: Angel Fisher's nickname had been "Angelfish."

When the bronze gun was solidly on the deck, before the lines had even been removed, I was on my knees to examine it. The gun had stunningly lovely markings; they clustered around the after part of the tube. All the shield and breech area was bright, copper-colored; it had been protected by the deep mud in which the cannon had been buried for more than 350 years. Twin Baroque dolphins arched their backs and opened their mouths wide atop the gun tube. Below, a crown surmounted the intricate design of the royal shield. From the shield hung the limp figure of a sheep. This must be, I realized, the symbol of the Golden Fleece, the order of honor founded by Charles V. A device below the shield read: *Don Phelippe III Rei Despana.* Underneath that was an oval *escudo* with the legend: *Don Juan de Mendoza Su Capitan General de la artilleria 1616.* The gun had been cast in 1616! Then, around the touchhole, the incised numbers: *24 Q 99 I* (meaning 26 *quintals,* 99 *libras*)—*2499 pounds.* I consulted the gun list, and there it was: gun No. 2499.

All at once I understood how Dirk and Mel must have felt. The bronze cannon was a messenger direct from the sunken *Atocha.* To me, it spoke directly, freshly, as if it had been run out yesterday on the galleon's gun deck. It spoke of Spain: of hopes and glories, careers, imperial pretensions—all cut short in their prime. I looked at Mel and smiled.

The work was arduous, and efforts lagged as the afternoon wore on. Then, near sunset, with five guns still to raise, Mel Joseph stepped to the rail. He produced his wallet, peeled a hundred-dollar bill from a substantial roll. "Here," he said to the divers. "I'll give the crew a hundred dollars for each gun you bring up between now and the time we quit." Shortly after sunset, all seven guns rested on the *Seaker*'s steel deck. Four of them were worn smooth; they were the cannon found resting on bedrock by Dirk Fisher. The other three, protected by the deep mud, all had shields and other markings.

I returned with Mel on a small craft to Key West after he had arranged for *Seaker* to bring the cannon in the next morning.

Olin Frick rose to the occasion. As *Seaker* rounded the harbor point and turned to Wrecker's Wharf, he fired regular salutes from his brass saluting cannon in honor of the bronze guns. When the ship was tied up alongside the wharf, a celebration began as visitors flocked aboard to see the cannon. Someone brought champagne, served it in paper cups as usual, and the drinks spilled on the deck and over the bronze cannon. Duncan came aboard with Mel, and we knelt to examine the guns carefully in the morning light. All three of the cannon that bore numbers—2499, 3030, and 2711—were found on the *Atocha*'s gun list, as had been No. 3110. The identification of the shipwreck was definitive.

Sherry Leon, puzzled, looked up from the stack of morning mail on her desk. "Mr. Horan," she called through the office door, "what do you suppose this is from the district court? It's an 'Order of Summary Judgment.' "

Dave Horan rushed through the open door to his secretary's desk. He picked up and scanned the document. "My God," he said. "The judge gave us summary judgment. We've won."

Judge Mehrtens had awarded Treasure Salvors the *Atocha* without reservations. In a few words, his ruling destroyed the government's reliance upon the Antiquities Act, the Abandoned Properties Act, and the "sovereign prerogative"; in other words, it destroyed their belief that antiquities recovered by individuals on the outer continental shelf belonged not to themselves but to the government. The decision seemed complete and final. The only question was: Would the federal government appeal? If they should decide to do so, title to the treasure might be clouded.

The Department of Justice had sixty days in which to file an appeal. On the fifty-ninth day, they gave notice that they might appeal. To clarify the situation, Dave Horan and Joshua Morse went to Washington to see the U.S. Solicitor General, Robert Bork. After a discussion,

Bork seemed sympathetic to the salvors' problems but said that since his associates in Justice and Interior pressed for appeal, he would allow it.

"After all," said Bork, "the function of a good general is to stand behind his troops."

"I can remember," said Dave Horan, "when his function was to lead his troops."

Now the case would go to the Federal Appeals Court in New Orleans. Now, obviously, much more time would elapse before the salvors could know whether or not they held clear title to the whole treasure; it might take years.

The federal action attracted the attention of a columnist with clout. James J. Kilpatrick, a well-known conservative writer, first heard the *Atocha* story from his friend Dr. Edwin Davis. Kilpatrick's column about it appeared in the Washington *Star* and around the land. It began with the words: "Pause a moment, if you will, to attend a tale of sunken treasure and greedy government." Kilpatrick went on to describe the treasure hunt and closed: ". . . there is something monstrously wrong when the power of the federal government can thus be used to crush a little fellow and drown his enterprise with the law's delays."

Every writer who deals for the first time with the *National Geographic* must be amazed by the magazine's attention to detail and its dedication to perfection. It was certainly that way with me. I soon learned that preparation of the manuscript of the *Atocha* story and its accompanying illustrations were only the first steps. Before it reached its final form, the article went through six proofs. During that time, keen staff researchers probed every aspect of the story, verified its every word. Over many days, brainstorming sessions were held with Noel Sickles, who did the fine ship and action paintings for the article. Of course, the single thing for which the *National Geo-*

graphic has been most admired for three-quarters of a century is the quality of its photography. Don Kincaid had recorded the story since he had found the *Atocha*'s first gold chain; he had shot probably five thousand color slides. Don's pictures and those of Bates Littlehales and other photographers were diligently canvassed to select the most fitting for the article. By the time the June 1976 issue appeared—in which the *Atocha* article would be featured—the whole presentation would be a perfect whole, the sort of thing that, for year after year, readers of the *National Geographic* have come to take for granted.

In the meantime, the society's television division was going full tilt on the preparation of the hour-long special to be shown in the fall. The producer-director, Nick Noxon, continued to demand nothing less than the deepest truth about the treasure hunt; he pumped us dry of our feelings, our expertise, our knowledge about the *Atocha* enterprise. After reviewing all the previous film shot on the story, Noxon knew exactly what he wanted. In two weeks of intensive shooting, the filmmaker and his crew moved from Key West to the *Arbutus* on the wreck site and up to Cape Coral, where they filmed the treasure in its vaults. Interviews were filmed and recorded with Mel, Deo, Bleth, Bob, Don, and Duncan, and with Austin Fowles and me. Painstakingly, Noxon gathered all the elements of the adventure: he inquired into the cultural meaning of each artifact, probed our individual motivations. I knew nothing of filmmaking, but I knew that a masterful documentary was being created.

The most exciting public event still lay ahead: the treasure exhibit in the Washington headquarters of the National Geographic Society, Explorer's Hall. When it was learned that King Juan Carlos and Queen Sophia of Spain would be in Washington on a state visit in early June, the conjunction of the two events created a glowing inspiration in Bleth McHaley. Why not, she reasoned, give one of the *Atocha*'s bronze cannon to the king and queen at the ceremony? The idea was a natural. Through the Spanish Embassy in Washington, arrangements were perfected with the Spanish crown. The good offices of the National Geographic Society were essential to the project and to its approval by our own Department of State.

Since Bob Moran had brought *Arbutus* and its crews out to the wreck site the previous fall, work aboard the big boat had settled into a regular routine. Two crews alternated duty aboard, and maintained anchor and security watches around the clock.

Pat Clyne, Tom Ford, and other crew created and maintained a map of Treasure Salvors' newly expanded search area, with all buoys, towers, and main wreck-site features tied in with ranges, bearings, and distances. Soon the men became proficient at setting and pulling anchors and in choosing the right ground tackle to carry the ship through the winter storms; at times the wind exceeded fifty knots, and heavy seas often lasted for several days at a time. Since the ship had no engines of her own, she was winched around on her anchors or towed by *Virgilona*. Divers from *Arbutus* surveyed the whole wreck-site corridor and surrounding areas visually, swimming or being towed on an underwater sled. They supported the crews who came to mag the area, and dug and airlifted directly from the big ship. The company's two worn Boston Whalers were in heavy use to set anchors, run messages, and maintain the buoy and grid system on the site.

It was a lonely, uncomfortable, and sometimes downright dangerous life. Radio communication with the galleon base was often unreliable. When, because of storms or money shortages in Key West, the *Arbutus* ran low or even out of food, water, and fuel, the crew did what it could. They swam to the "neighborhood grocery reef" to spear grouper, hog-snapper, or jewfish for supper. They kept in reserve an area known only to the crew—the "lobster condominium." The divers wrestled with balky winches, the compressor, and the generator; they cursed at outboard motors that would not start; they were forever making repairs. Some of the company's equipment was just too worn and needed replacement badly. Although some new gear was sent to *Arbutus* from time to time, it never seemed enough.

To provide better meals for the crews and perhaps to ease somewhat the miseries of being stranded for weeks aboard *Arbutus,* the company worked several girls into the crew changes to serve as cooks aboard.

Sometimes, however, because of equipment failures or lack of supply, the men aboard *Arbutus* felt themselves abandoned by Key West. On two occasions, outboard motor failures left divers stranded in a dangerous place, and they could return to the ship only after long, arduous swims through rough water. The crew captains confided their feelings about these things in the *Arbutus* log—a remarkable, graphic document. Aboard their strange vessel, they were Mel's unsung heroes.

The *Arbutus* crews had extended their visual surveys of the wreck site out to the patch reef where the *Atocha* might have struck on its career to destruction. Then they began to search back northwest, in toward the Quicksands from the cannon buoy.

On March 4, the *Arbutus* crew feasted on hot dogs. Supplies were almost gone, and crew captain Pat Clyne decided that next day they would have to start eating canned meat. It was his twenty-ninth birthday.

Clyne's log for the next day, March 5, reads:

Crew—same. Weather—swells, four to six feet; overcast and rainy. Water is very dirty, limited visibility. Area we are in is right between cannons and corridor. This afternoon we ran visuals south-southwest of the green line between cannons and black spar. We nailed a few grouper down there to complement our canned dinner. Visibility decreased towards evening.

Pat Clyne

P.S. And, oh yes, by the way, we found a silver bar.

Pat Clyne believed deeply in swimming visuals, and it had paid off. While swimming down the bearing from the bronze cannon buoy toward the Bank of Spain, Clyne saw something that looked "just too rectangular" to be a piece of coral. It was the fourth silver ingot found from the *Atocha* cargo.

All the divers' weariness vanished as they brought the bar up to the *Arbutus*'s deck and flashed a message back to Key West: treasure had been found. The old boat had proven worthy of her hire. The ingot, which weighed sixty-four pounds, was a miniature marine garden; it was covered with bright-orange algae, and sprouted a sea fan from one corner.

After Pat Clyne's find, the divers fanned out systematically from the spot with more visual survey runs. Ballast stone and nine cannonballs were found in the immediate vicinity. Then, on March 15, five hundred feet northwest of where Pat Clyne had located his bar, Ron Bennett found a fifth one. This ingot, less encrusted than the other one, bore Roman numerals that totaled 939. Although the bar was not cleaned to disclose all its other markings, it appeared to be one of the Potosí *quinto* bars put aboard the *Atocha* at Portobello.

The silver bars had been found lying on the sea bottom, right along the treasure trail between the Bank of Spain and the cannon. Evidently the disintegrating wreck had continued to spill out valuables all along the way. Where, we wanted to know, would the bulk of the treasure be found? Somewhere nearby?

In order to investigate the site more thoroughly, Duncan called in Dr. Ray McAllister, professor of ocean engineering at Florida Atlantic University. Together they explored the site underwater; then a general brainstorming session was held to study the implications of the historical accounts and the material scatter patterns found to date. Duncan also recruited another scholar whose main interest lay in the cultural importance of the artifacts themselves. This was Claudia Linzee, who had studied at Vassar and the Sorbonne. Claudia, who was completing a Ph.D. in art history at St. Louis University, set to work to study the "poison cup," the rosary, and other religious artifacts and objects in the collection. She became its official curator.

Early in May, with my work on the *Geographic* article completed, I came to Key West to take part in the next act of the treasure drama. Now that the site was better known and marked, it was time to call upon science to attempt to penetrate the mud bottom. Dr. Harold Edgerton, emeritus professor at the Massachusetts Institute of Technology, had used his sub-bottom profiler on the site before, but not since it had been so precisely gridded and marked. Now Mel brought "Doc" Edgerton back for a few days' search.

Doc's arrival had been preceded by that of his four heavy cases of electronic equipment. He followed, retrieved them, and joined Don, Duncan, and me aboard Norman Wood's *Petticoat III.* On the afternoon of May 7, we left for the Marquesas. The trip out through the islands and an evening anchored off the atoll gave us a chance to know Harold Edgerton better. A man of modest, professorial mien, Edgerton was a spare-spoken but likable New Englander; his equipment had created a revolution in the underwater world. With his side-scan sonar unit, a crew had recently located the *Monitor* off Cape Hatteras. He had worked in Vigo Bay with John Potter, off Jamaica's north coast with Bob Marx, and was next scheduled for an assignment in Scotland—to hunt down the legendary Loch Ness monster.

By 8:30 the next morning, we were approaching the wreck site and had established communications with the *Arbutus* and the man in the north theodolite tower, who would help us mark our contacts. Doc Edgerton's bulky equipment was set up in *Petticoat III*'s after cabin and connected to the heavy battery pack he carried for power; the "fish" was ready for streaming, and we were ready to go. We began our first run at 9:00 A.M. The slim detection head we placed in the water could read down to and below the sea bottom to record any distinctive features there.

Now we ran down the buoy line that marked the spine of the treasure corridor as it extended to the little reef southeast of the bronze cannon site: "Candy Stripe," a buoy on the reef; then "Three Stripe," a black buoy; the cannon buoy; a new spar marking the silver bar locations; a buoy on the Bank of Spain; and the oldest, marking the galleon anchor. Beyond was the "gold buoy," where Tom Ford had started the gold rush a year before. Back up and down the buoy line we passed as Norman Woods, steering compass courses, moved over ever so slightly on each pass.

I was recording the runs on a yellow pad, and at 9:43, just as we passed close alongside the cannon buoy, Doc Edgerton paused and said softly, "There's one." On subsequent runs we picked the anomaly up again, and began to chart its general outline on the successive passes. Each time an anomaly was called, we threw over cement blocks with orange buoys attached. Now Dave Hargreaves, acknowledged to be our best theodolite operator, was on the north tower, and he marked the bearings of each marker when it was thrown. Soon the ocean bobbed with orange buoys.

Late in the morning, we looked up from our concentration on a run, startled by high-pitched engine noise. A small, fast boat approached from the Marquesas, pushing ahead of it a white plume of bow wave. "Oh, ho," said Don Kincaid. "Here comes Mel. He'll shake things up."

He did. Mel transferred to *Petticoat III,* looked for a moment at the record of our sub-bottom runs, and started us off in a new direction. Now the turns came more quickly; it seemed as if we were continually turning. Like a wartime destroyer skipper closing in on a U-boat contact, Mel circled us closer and closer around the big anomaly near the cannon buoy. We threw marker buoys until they were gone. Then we stopped for lunch. We replenished our supply of markers from *Arbutus* and continued the search, alternating briefly with a few side-scan sonar runs down the corridor. That night, Duncan and I stayed aboard *Arbutus,* Doc Edgerton and the *Petticoat* went to the Marquesas, and Mel returned to Key West.

The next morning dawned upon an ocean lake—an almost complete flat calm, unruffled by any breeze. As we began our work, the climbing sun rapidly created a broiling heat. When Mel arrived, he had a new idea. Now he moved Doc Edgerton and all his equipment over bodily to *Virgilona,* which was moored with three anchors directly over the anomaly. Mel reasoned that if he suspended the sub-bottom profiler search head right over the anomaly and winched the boat around, he could pinpoint the hot area and perhaps pin down the Mother Lode.

Mel drawled his battle cry as he crossed over to the *Virgilona:* "It looks as if today's the day." Duncan smiled.

As I passed from the immaculate varnished rails of *Petticoat* to the familiar worn bulwarks of *Virgilona,* I struck hands with Moe Molinar. He grinned. "Now we get it, Gene," Moe shouted. "Now we get it."

Adroitly, Moe swung the boat around the anomaly; we heaved and tugged on the anchor lines as the winches creaked, but the *Virgilona* moved as Mel wanted it to. Now, when the recorder noted the anomaly, pipes were hammered by divers into the hard mud bottom to make a mark for later excavation.

As the blazing hot afternoon advanced, I could scarcely bear to watch the divers working in the cool blue water. Finally I could stand no more, stepped onto the dive ladder, and plunged in, clothes and all. When the first delicious shock was over, I floated and looked across the sun-dazzled water toward the galleon anchor, twenty-seven hundred feet away up in the Quicksands.

Suddenly I realized that the bobbing buoy line marked out the *Atocha*'s death ride. Somewhere near here, it was becoming abundantly clear, the dying ship had suffered a traumatic breakup. Dr. Edgerton had warned us that his anomalies might very well be geologic features, but it could just as well be the Mother Lode. Surely we would know before long.

XV. The World's Greatest Treasure Hunter

Like Navy recruits standing our first admiral's inspection, we straightened in our places in the receiving line. Only Mel seemed completely calm; the rest of us cast glances toward the east door of Explorer's Hall, through which the queen would come.

Up until now, we had been busy at concentrated last-minute work, getting the treasure to Washington, helping the National Geographic Society with final details of the exhibit. Now we had to face the really scary part, the presence of royalty. The ceremony was about to begin.

It was apparent, although we had heard nothing officially, that there had been some friction over the gift of the *Atocha*'s cannon to Spain. After all, the gun, with the rest of the treasure, was in litigation. If the government's case was correct, it belonged to the United States. How, then, could the State Department permit Treasure Salvors to present it to Spain? Of course, there were obvious diplomatic advantages in the ceremony: the United States strongly desired good relations with Spain during its critical time of transition after the death of Francisco Franco. But the real answer lay in the National Geographic Society. The man who had broken that deadlock was Dr. Melvin Payne, the society's longtime president, now retiring. He had serenely stated that the ceremony would take place and that was that. And it was.

The first few days of June 1976 had been busy for King Juan Carlos and Queen Sophia. On the afternoon before our ceremony, my family and I had driven past the Pan-American Union Building and seen the royal couple laying a wreath at the foot of Queen Isabella's statue. The next morning, my wife and girls could not take the White House tour because Gerald and Betty Ford were entertaining the king and queen there. This day, they had already opened the "Christopher Columbus and His Times" exhibit at the Smithsonian, presided at the opening of two art exhibits, and dedicated three statues. One of these, a statue of Don Quijote at the Kennedy Center, was a gift of Spain to the United States in its Bicentennial Year. Juan Carlos had another place to go in the late afternoon, the time set for our ceremony; the "Treasures of the *Atocha*" exhibit was to be opened by Queen Sophia.

The Spanish security men, outwardly casual and working with Iberian flair, missed nothing as they scanned the guest lists and checked our credentials. Even though all of them could not be admitted into the area for the ceremony, more than sixty of the Treasure Salvors faithful had come to Washington for the great day; a trainload of divers and office employees was still on its way from Florida.

Mel and Deo Fisher, Dr. and Mrs. Payne, incoming National Geographic Society President Robert Doyle and his wife, Florida Secretary of State Bruce Smathers, Editor and Mrs. Gilbert Grosvenor, Bleth McHaley, and I stood in the receiving line. I had been elected to escort the queen through the exhibit, and felt distinctly edgy about the whole thing.

The National Geographic Society occupies an entire downtown block in Washington. At one end of the block stands the society's new headquarters building, a shining modern structure. Its first floor is called Explorer's Hall and features exhibits of explorations and other scientific matters with which the society has been concerned in its hundred-year history. Our receiving line stood between the treasure exhibit and the outside door, where the queen's honor guard had begun to form in line. Her guard, fifty picked Spanish soldiers, wore the red, gray, and black uniforms of the regiment of Navarre in 1778, in honor of our Bicentennial. At any moment now, the queen would enter.

Then, in the midst of a buzzing crowd of diplomats and Spanish noblemen and noblewomen, Queen Sophia of Spain entered Explorer's Hall. Although poised, the queen seemed youthful, even girlish in manner. As she reached me, her handshake was light but warm, her smile sincere. Sophia was simply but elegantly dressed in white and beige, and wore a diamond necklace and gold bracelets. When the introductions were over, the little group gathered before a lectern, where Robert Doyle gave a short speech of welcome. After responding, Queen Sophia cut the white silk ribbon, and we entered "The Treasures of the *Atocha.*"

The National Geographic Society had outdone itself. A million visitors were expected to see the exhibit before it closed in September, and they would surely be satisfied. We entered through a huge reproduction of a portal of the Escorial, that grim building built by Philip II, the burial place of the Hapsburg kings; it had been blown up to monumental size from a lithograph.

Once inside, we were caught in a hurricane! Whining sounds recorded in a Caribbean storm provided a background while wind (from hidden blowers) and rain (simulated by strobe lights) lashed the hall. The queen picked up an earphone to hear an account of the *Atocha*'s sinking taken from historical documents. At the room's end, dimly seen through the half-light, was a whole wall depicting the *Atocha* as it struck the reef in the Marquesas in 1622— an enlargement of Yeorgos Lampathakis's fine painting.

There was a rich visual and historical setting for stunning displays of gold and silver. The precious things were seen in lighted translucent columns rising from the floor: gold chains draped over quartz cannonballs; gold coins scattered on dead-white sea-bottom sand; disks and finger bars of gold tumbled together. The red and gold of the rosary and the crushed golden cup glittered at us as we passed. The queen viewed the exhibit with interest and appreciation. It was obvious, however, that my role was strictly superfluous; Queen Sophia spoke excellent English, and the crowd was so thick around her that I had little opportunity to use my Spanish.

We passed a wall display of the astrolabe and other navigational equipment from the sunken ship—the state of Florida had lent these and other artifacts to help make the exhibit complete. In other cases were collections of the shipwreck's ceramics, carefully arranged by Duncan Mathewson; the ship's arms, including arquebuses and swords, were shown in water-filled boxes. The queen stopped to exclaim at the dangling, swaying silver coins, still fastened to their filaments; they appeared as they did in Austin Fowles's cleaning procedures. In one special case rested the three silver ingots found on July 4, 1973. They had with them a blown-up copy of the *Atocha*'s registry, from which they and the ship had been identified.

Finally we approached the culminating section of the exhibit—the cannon room. There we paused before Don Kincaid's underwater cannon mosaic mural and watched, on a small screen, film footage of Dirk and Angel Fisher with Mel and Duncan as they recovered the bronze guns. We heard Angel's voice, and Duncan's, and then passed on to the place where the ceremony of presenting the cannon was to take place. There, on a small dais, stood gun No. 2499—we had chosen the finest of the guns to give to the queen. On either side of a small lectern stood the Spanish and United States flags.

The ceremony was a short one. Mel made the presentation, referring to the time when Florida and much of the hemisphere was Spanish. He added thanks for the help of the Archive of the Indies, and stated that he hoped the gun could repose there. The queen thanked Mel and the company for the gun, saying that the relics she had seen were not only wonderful in themselves but were "proof of one of the most fascinating endeavors of our time."

Then Mel did something that was not on the program—something about which he had consulted neither his advisers nor his attorneys. He called, "Hey, Sophie, come over here a minute." The queen smiled and moved closer. From a small jewelry box Mel took a small gold piece on a gold chain. It was the clipped twenty-three-carat gold bit recovered from beneath the bronze cannon. "Here," he said, "we want you to have this," and he slipped it around her neck. She was delighted with the unexpected gift.

A champagne reception followed the exhibit tour and the donation of the cannon, but Queen Sophia could not stay long; she had to be about her busy schedule. But as we chatted briefly, the queen expressed disappointment at not being able to meet the divers—the men, as she put it, who had recovered all the treasure. They had not been admitted to the ceremony, we were told, because of security limitations.

Ed Davis introduced me to James Kilpatrick; I spoke for a moment with Bob Daley. He had already decided to write a full book on the *Atocha* story. Then, in a corner, I saw Mel, talking to a small crowd of reporters. One of them, Vernon Guidry, Jr., from the Washington *Star,* said it the next morning in his paper: "Mel Fisher has, indisputably, arrived."

But Bleth McHaley told me that night, "Gene, Mel's niche is secure, but he wants more. After the party, he asked me, 'Bleth, what are you going to do to top this?' "

In July 1976, Mel's company put out its greatest effort yet to find the *Atocha*'s missing treasure. So many craft, large and small, swarmed over the wreck site that it looked at times like the World War II Normandy landings.

In addition to *Arbutus* and *Virgilona,* another sizable salvage ship came to work the site: *E-Z Livin',* the floating home and workshop of Earl and Nancy Mundt. Mundt, adept at anything marine and mechanical, provided his boat, equipment, and time for a percentage share in the unfound treasure. Arnold McLean had bought the company's fast Mako and worked the site with his nonferrous detector. Ray Dozier brought his boat and magnetometer out regularly. Mel also made a deal for another boat, *Swordfish,* a fifty-four-foot steel diesel crewboat, which he hoped to fit out with mailboxes. And then there was the "Hydra-Flow."

Mel had conceived another invention. Why not, he thought, build a big mailbox independent of a ship's stern? In other words, make a mailbox you could lower all the way to the bottom. In that way, you could avoid the deep-water power loss of a surface-mounted deflector.

Unfortunately, Mel could not afford to build his new dream machine. His whole summer operation rested on a slim financial base. Most of his boats and men were working on speculation, the hope of finding treasure, and there was very little cash available. What little hard money came was spent immediately on the operation. So Mel had to find someone else to build the device. He found a willing firm in Pompano Beach to rent it for cash. On July 4, therefore, the new device, called the Hydra-Flow, came to the wreck site. It looked like a huge section of drainage culvert, but its motor could generate great power.

Rigging the Hydra-Flow was a problem that called forth all the skills of Bob, Mel, Earl, and the whole *Arbutus* crew. Finally they mounted it off the ship by a boom. They lowered the machine until its tube nearly touched sea bottom, started it up, and watched as the Hydra-Flow rapidly dug a crater more than ten feet wide down to bedrock. In the bottom of the hole they found one of *Atocha*'s ballast stones. "Is this," wondered crew captain Tom Ford, "the beginning of the end?"

Now the excitement began to build quickly. The company put out its maximum effort; thirty men and six boats were on site on July 11, when a whole olive-jar base and another ballast stone came to light. When he came out to relieve Ford, Pat Clyne was equally impressed with the new device's digging power. He wrote in the log: "With this powerful new addition to our facilities, there is no reason why this won't be the 'summer of the *Atocha.*'"

Clyne and his crew began systematically to trench out from the cannon site with the Hydra-Flow; they found a six-pound ballast stone one hundred feet out. When Bob Moran took over command on July 20, he began to dig concentric circles around the cannon buoy. By now it was clear that the sub-bottom anomalies were geologic; the Hydra-Flow had dug down through hardpan, clay, and layers of ancient peat to broken coral pieces lying on bedrock. Duncan studied the layering of the holes and sent samples out for carbon dating. It was obvious, however, that the bottom area had been laid down many thousands of years before 1622.

Still seeking and experimenting, the salvors moved the *Arbutus* up into the Quicksands. Northwest of the galleon anchor, the Hydra-Flow took only ten minutes to churn a hole twelve feet deep and fifty feet wide. At one point, they lost control of the blower, and it ran amuck, popping to the surface and doing a tail dance on the water. But soon they learned how best to control the machine. They cut down its speed until a diver could control it from the water and it could uncover the most delicate objects.

Soon *Arbutus* was moved back out into the deeper water, back on the trail of the Mother Lode, for they were running out of time and money. The Hydra-Flow would shortly have to be returned. The salvors dug out south and southeast of the corridor line. A few tantalizing items—ceramic sherds and ballast stones—were found, but they picked up no definite trail.

Treasure Salvors was running out of steam. Without more money, Mel could not maintain the great summer effort. He made a flying trip to the Cayman Islands, where he had promised to meet a Key West promoter named Jerry. Their arrangement was that Mel would deliver a large number of 1715 silver coins and Jerry would turn over cash to him. The plan was based on Jerry's scheme to sell coins to the Miami Cuban community.

Mel put up the coins, but Jerry didn't deliver the money.

Mel was left holding the bag, stranded without funds in Grand Cayman. The company was so broke that it could not send him plane fare home. Finally, Mel pledged a hundred coins to a pilot to bring him home. The "Cayman caper" had not produced the money needed.

The young *Arbutus* crew was still hopeful, however. They had just discovered something new—they could propel their vessel around the wreck site with the Hydra-Flow! By fixing the ship's rudder at the proper angle and running the blowing machine at a low speed, they got *Arbutus* under way. With growing confidence, they "sailed" all around the wreck site. Now Pat Clyne was enthusiastic; it might still be the *Atocha* summer after all.

In the meantime, even though his resources were almost exhausted, Mel took a new direction of his own in the search for the Atocha. It came about through one of those mental illuminations, or flashes of intuition, that characterized him.

Mel had become dissatisfied with the search down the southeast corridor near the Quicksands. He felt that nothing substantial had resulted from all our advice. One day he called me up in Vero Beach to ask me to go over all the documentary evidence again; he was seeking clues as to a possible different location for the Pile, as he now termed the Mother Lode. He listened without comment to my summary of all the sources that described Vargas's and Melián's salvage attempts on the *Atocha*.

Then, just as he had done in 1963, Mel turned to his intuition. "I just sorta saw it, you know, like a vision," he explained to me later. Demonstrating his vision on an enlarged map of the Marquesas, he put his finger down on the outer reef and said, "You see, *Atocha* hit here, and went in, like this, toward Marquesas, and sank in the deep water, about here. Then, a month later, just like the Spaniard's letter said, there came another hurricane. Its winds and waves got stronger and stronger and pulled and tugged and pulled and tugged on that hull under the water. Finally it started to break up; the whole bow section came in on the Marquesas; if we dig there, we'll find it. But the main deck, with all those cannons on it, broke loose and floated like a raft—for weeks, maybe. The currents pushed it right down the Hawk Channel toward where we found the anchor and all the other treasure. So the Pile has to be back up here." And he pointed to a spot many miles east of our wreck site. Mel had dramatically changed the treasure hunt with his dream.

Mel's ability to try his new idea, however, was severely limited. Trouble had caught up with him again. Many of his men, unpaid for many months now, had left. Mel took a small crew of two office girls and one diver out to the new area, but could do little. *Arbutus* moved three miles down the Hawk Channel, there it dug briefly; nothing was found. Then, on September 2, the time had come to return the Hydra-Flow. Pat Clyne reported that the huge digging device had been taken off the *Arbutus,* thus "stripping us of our only hope for the summer."

One more good find was made, from the *Virgilona.* On September 4, 5, and 6, her crew dug with their mailboxes on the southeast edge of the Quicksands. There, along the "treasure trail," they found a fine, twenty-carat gold bar, another copper ingot, three long gold chains, a piece of a miniature barbell, and a few coins and cannonballs. While the new treasure added to the company's inventory and momentarily lifted the salvors' spirits, there was no denying that the summer was over.

On September 26, crew chief Jim Solanick noted in the log that it was a full year to the day since *Arbutus* had been towed to the wreck site. He pointed out that all the hopes current then and since had been dashed: the electronic readings had not yielded great results; the equipment aboard had markedly deteriorated; and the crew was much smaller than "Bob Moran's Army" of the year before. Most important, the Mother Lode had not been found.

When next I saw Mel, he was riding high. As I waited in the office to speak to him, he went busily from one telephone to the other. Articles featuring him had recently appeared in *Newsweek* and *Saga* magazines. He had been termed "a pure entrepreneur" in an article in *Free Enterprise.* Mel and Deo had just appeared as guests on ABC's "Good Morning, America" show. An article in *Paris Match* had just come out, and a reporter from *People* magazine had called. As I sat waiting, I thumbed through the most bizarre of the articles about Mel: one in the "skin-mag" *Adam.*

An elderly Florida couple had just come to see Mel. After they had bought an *Atocha* coin from him, the couple talked about investing in the treasure hunt. Then he told them of his coming venture: the search for Atlantis. They were fascinated.

"You see, Gene," he told me when we were alone, "Atlantis is a natural. You could set up a club, with members putting up so much a week or month; you could bring in a thousand dollars a day—finance the research, the whole operation. None of this money trouble we've had with the *Atocha.* "

Mel explained to me how the coin sales were going. Bleth and Ron Mallory were going in with a company formed strictly to market the coins, with a partner, Bruce Ayres. The marketing would be at high-level conferences in places like Hilton Head, Atlanta's Omni complex, and other places where the clientele could afford a unique artifact, completely authenticated. Dave Horan had negotiated an agreement with the parties to the lawsuit, and the company would get up to 50 percent of the treasure under question. Now the coins would be divided with company stockholders and investors. Don Anderson's computerized lists were completed, and division would take place in December. But Rick Gage's father had filed suit against the company over his son's death, and a settlement had been made. As we talked, Mel signed an agreement to earmark company coins to pay the settlement.

Mel's thoughts next turned to the Cayman Islands. He would like, he told me, to buy a bank there, "Why not?" he asked. "Right there is the future of banking. You should

just see all the banks they have there now, all with numbered accounts, like in Switzerland."

Mel and Deo were leaving Key West. Gulf Oil Company,
which was to sponsor the *National Geographic* television
special on the *Atocha,* was staking them to a three-week
promotional tour, and they were going to New York. After
I saw them off, I reflected that I had just spent two typical
hours with Mel Fisher.

"You know, Gene," Bleth told me when the Fishers had
gone, "finding treasure isn't the end result for Mel anymore. It's the wheeling and dealing, the money-raising
and all of that—that's what he really enjoys." I agreed
with Bleth about Mel's unalloyed enjoyment of his role,
of his fame. But I also felt in this complex man that until
he had found the rest of the Marquesas treasure, he could
never be satisfied.

On the night of December 7, 1976, the *National Geographic* special, "Treasure," appeared on PBS around the
nation. Thanks to the audience following the *Geographic*
documentaries and the publicity buildup given the *Atocha*
show, viewer interest was intense. The special outdrew
any other previous public television performance and
lured many viewers from prime-time network shows.

From the moment of the special's introduction in the
rich tones of Alexander Scourby and the appearance on
the screen of Lampathakis's picture of the sinking *Atocha,*
the documentary's dramatic tension grew. Noxon traced
the story from the Seville archives through the long search
in the Keys and the finding of the first treasure to the
funeral of Dirk and Angel Fisher. He stressed the physical
and mental adventure of the treasure hunt and ended with
the unspoken question: Was it all worth the cost?

As the last closing credits were shown and the image
faded, there was no question about it: Nick Noxon had
created a masterpiece. And there was no doubt about
something else: Mel Fisher had achieved apotheosis. He
was a "legend in his own time." He had become the world's
greatest treasure hunter.

XVI. "Today's the Day"

As Mel must have thought later, 1977 started out well enough. Like ripples in a pond, the publicity impact of the *National Geographic* television special continued to expand outward into the nation. Early in the new year, an article also appeared about the *Atocha* in the New York *Daily News*.

In January, at the Ottawa Conference on Underwater Archaeology, Duncan, aided by Pat Clyne, Tom Ford, and Steve Hamburg, gave several papers on procedures developed on the *Atocha* site. Despite the salvors' failure to find the Mother Lode the previous summer, Duncan told the audience that the Hydra-Flow showed real promise as an archaeological digging tool. In her presentation, Claudia Linzee pointed to the larger cultural meaning of the shipwreck artifacts from the Marquesas. Comparing them with materials in sixteenth- and seventeenth-century European paintings, she stated, could lead to a better cultural reconstruction of shipboard life in those times.

But continued exposure of the *Atocha* story alone could not solve Treasure Salvors' urgent financial needs. On January 7, sheriff's deputies came to seize *Virgilona* for an old, unpaid obligation. Hastily, the boat was put upon the ways in the old shipyard so that it could not be taken away, but the deputy served Mel with an attachment. The veteran salvage boat would be sold on the courthouse steps. A sizable mortgage payment on the Key West property was also overdue, but Mel just did not have the money to meet it.

As Mel puzzled over his cash shortage, there came a reminder of past glories: a letter from the Zarzuela Palace in Madrid. Queen Sophia had sent the company her thanks, and those of Spain, for the gift of the bronze cannon. She promised, further, that Mel's wish would be carried out: the gun would be sent to Seville, to the Archive of the Indies.

When the queen's letter arrived, Mel was in the midst of planning the coming summer's diving. He felt that two things were needed to reach his "dream area," and thus the Mother Lode: first, a vessel more maneuverable than *Arbutus,* with power to move down the Hawk Channel and dig anywhere, and second, better electronic pointers to the treasure's location.

In the absence of cash, Mel had to make another kind of deal. In return for a percentage contract, he acquired a 125-foot ex-tuna clipper, the *West Coast,* which lay in a Florida port. Although the large steel craft needed a lot of work, Mel hoped that its engines would provide the thrust to uncover the missing treasure mass. He also planned, if money became available, to fit out *Swordfish* with mailboxes to help in the digging.

Denny Breese was a man skilled in many kinds of undersea work. A professional diver, he had worked with the Aluminaut submersible and had helped locate the missing H-bomb off Palomares, Spain. Now Breese had developed a new type of electronic detector, which he believed would pick up the presence of buried nonferrous metals under the sea. He believed that it had sufficient range to work in the deep sand and mud on the Marquesas site. Mel also made an arrangement with Denny Breese to search with his equipment.

When Breese came to the Keys, he found changeable weather. However, in spite of rough seas and some technical troubles with his new device, Breese achieved some promising results. Major readings were registered along a bearing out from the bronze cannon buoy, exactly where many of us felt the search should be directed. Mel filed the information away in his mind but was not able to follow up on the readings immediately.

In the meantime, the sale of silver *Atocha* coins was going well, if slowly. The company's share of the money thus brought in did not begin to meet current expenses. Mel, his Marketing Committee, and the sales experts bent their efforts toward a larger sale of treasure. In late January, at a sumptuous Palm Beach home, a showing was held. On a table in a luxuriously furnished room overlooking a Spanish-style patio, Mel spread coins, gold chains, and gold bars, together with copies of the *National Geographic* article. Through the afternoon, we met a representative sampling of American wealth. After a buffet meal in the patio, Mel gave a talk.

At the Palm Beach meeting, some coins were sold and a few thousand dollars raised, but the hoped-for deal— the purchase of the treasure collection by an affluent donor for tax-deductible purposes—failed to materialize.

Mel had another scheme up his sleeve: to raise the galleon anchor, for so many years the center datum point of the *Atocha* shipwreck site. Since the company had no funds for the job, Mel arranged with Long John Silver, Inc., a seafood chain, to lease the anchor for display in return for a small cash fee. Mel then retained Chet Alexander for the raising operation. On February 28, braving four- to six-foot seas, Chet's barge *Aquarius* accompanied *Swordfish* to the site. After some hours, the men managed to secure lines to the ring and shank of the huge anchor. Then Alexander's lifting boom exerted its force; slowly, *Atocha*'s anchor pulled free of its sand bed for the first time since 1622. As the anchor broke water and hung suspended over the barge, watchers saw that its shank was fifteen feet long. Later, they discovered that it measured almost twelve feet across the flukes. As Don and Claudia examined the galleon anchor, they found it in a fine state of preservation. Near the junction of the shank and flukes, they noted cryptic markings. None of us could decipher them, but the marks seemed to have been inscribed at the foundry, and possibly indicated the weight and place of casting. Another mystery, which showed us how far we still had to go in our understanding of Spanish shipwreck artifacts.

None of this raised enough money to meet the company's needs and pay off its obligations. The main problem came, of course, from the legal challenge by the federal government to Treasure Salvors' clear title to the treasure. Until this cloud was fully lifted, no personal or corporate buyer would close a sale.

Dave Horan now proposed a way out of the legal deadlock. Using the point evaluation list that had led to the release of the first part of the materials to the salvors, Horan suggested another attempt to negotiate a final settlement with the government. In his proposal to the Department of Justice, Dave offered on behalf of the company to provide the historical and archaeological data gained from the shipwreck, and further proposed the donation of a representative sampling of the artifacts to the Smithsonian Institution.

To further the negotiation, Duncan, Claudia, Don, Pat Clyne, and I went to Washington to meet at the Smithsonian with institution officials and Charles McKinney of the Department of the Interior. There at the Museum of the History of Science, we were ushered into an upstairs conference room. We presented the academic side of the *Atocha* expedition to a number of scientists and administrators. Although they showed definite interest, and McKinney assured us that the presentation had gone well, nothing was heard further of the proposed negotiation. The lawsuit went on, and no date for a hearing of the government's appeal had yet been set.

The atmosphere at Treasure Salvors' March board meeting was tense. Mel, enchanted as always by movie-making, had signed a tentative agreement with a small film company to do the *Atocha* story. When some objections were then raised, he agreed to bring the matter before the board. In addition to the Fishers, Ed Hirst, and Don Anderson, the directors now included a Washington attorney, Lucille Lambert, and a Florida C.P.A., Jim Maher.

After granting the moviemakers an option on the story (which expired without any action), the board went on to more serious business. Mel reported on readiness for the summer and noted that he had *Virgilona* back—bid in by a friend. Jim Maher proposed a regular budget for the company so that funds could be raised more easily. Bob Moran then advised that Treasure Salvors owed its employees more than $112,000. "Your employees," he stated, "have been underwriting this operation."

But as Dave Horan reported, no solution to the stalled negotiations, to the deadlocked legal case, was in sight.

Neither Mel nor the company could meet the mortgage payments on the waterfront property; nor could they carry out their share of the agreement to build the resort hotel. At this time, therefore, they were divested of their interest in the hotel project. This was a real blow to Mel and to the company, but to the investment group, which wished to proceed with the construction, there was no other way.

Over the next few months, the same mingled hopes and disappointments were played over and over. Mel took the treasure for display in Cincinnati but closed no deal there. Publicity continued to appear: Margo McCollum had written an article about Mel that appeared in the *Argosy* Treasure Annual. In April, Bob Daley's book *Treasure* was published by Random House. The Daley book stressed the tragedy of the treasure hunt and described the deaths of the young Fishers and Rick Gage in poignant detail; reading it must have been painful for the Fishers. Mel was pleased, however, with the coverage the book afforded. He bought a number of copies and began to autograph them, together with copies of the *National Geographic* article, at sales meetings and conventions.

At last, the federal authorities had agreed to another stipulation for further release of treasure, but the appearance of the document itself was delayed and delayed. When, at the end of the spring, it came to Key West, many of the document's provisions were unacceptable to the company. The stipulation was sent back to the Department of Justice, and the matter dragged on.

Meanwhile, the new museum at the R. A. Gray Library and Archives Building in Tallahassee had been opened and dedicated. It contained fine displays of shipwreck artifacts and treasure from Florida waters. Many of the items displayed, in fact, had been recovered by Treasure Salvors. Some of the choicest pieces from the *Atocha,* including the astrolabe, were shown there. None of us from Treasure Salvors was invited to the dedication.

When I visited Key West in midsummer, I could sense deterioration in the company's affairs. The museum ship had lost its foremast in a summer squall. With its missing spar, frayed and trailing ropes, and shredded sails, it looked like a ghost vessel. Nearby, up on blocks, sat *Virgilona.* Even if Moe Molinar had been there to take her out, she was not ready to go. Stranded in the baking heat, the old workboat had opened up in her seams. Considerable work would now be needed to get the craft back into shape.

The company itself was not in much better condition than its boats. The day of my arrival, the Internal Revenue Service impounded all three company bank accounts over a tax dispute. Early the next morning, the city electric crew came to cut off the power for nonpayment of a fourteen-hundred-dollar bill. Mel was able to convince the crew that if they cut off power to the electric bilge pump, the galleon would sink. He persuaded them to accept a small payment on account, promising that the rest would come shortly.

Most of the old crew of the company were gone now.

Bleth had moved to Honduras. Margo had left the office. Duncan and I, involved in other work, had little time to be in Key West. The divers, forced to find paying work, had stayed as long as they could. Spencer Wickens and Tim March were diving now for Chet Alexander. Tom Ford was teaching scuba in Key West. Bouncy John worked at the Raw Bar, which "T" Hargreaves had bought from Bob Hall. John and Elizabeth Brandon had returned to Fort Pierce, where Moe Molinar also lived.

In spite of the apparent penury of his company's condition, Mel seemed as enthusiastic as ever. True, he had some valuable help: Ted Miguel, a retired Navy captain, had come to run *Swordfish*. Bob Moran and Mel had been joined in the office by director Jim Maher, who lent substantial aid in business negotiations and in the attempt to keep together the patchwork finances of the company. Claudia Linzee had by now become deeply committed to the treasure collection. As curator, she was vital to the plan for the Omni exhibit.

Another Omni, a hotel-commercial complex under construction in downtown Miami, was slated to open in late 1977. The operators of an amusement park in the complex had been negotiating to lease the *Atocha* treasure in company hands for display there. Thus the company would have some revenue while the legal snarls were being straightened.

The ostensible purpose of my visit—to help brainstorm the Mother Lode location for 1977 work—turned out to be fruitless. Although we gathered on Earl Mundt's boat to rehash all the known site data, we knew that, as a practical matter, there would be little or no site work that year. Still, some of the old fire was generated as Bob, Duncan, Ted, Pat Clyne, Tom Ford, and I speculated on the mystery of the Mother Lode. The consensus was that we should search out from the cannon area, working back toward the main deposit. Although Mel seemed to be listening intently, he had said little or nothing. Now he gave a brief assent, but then launched upon a repetition of his vision of the *Atocha*'s journey down the Hawk Channel. Mel seemed to be listening to some inner voice; he seemed far from us as our meeting broke up.

As Mel continued to score signal success in his role as the world's greatest treasure hunter, things at home grew worse. True, the Omni contract was finally signed, the treasure went on display in Miami, and an advance against gate receipts was paid and partly distributed to company investors. But the advance money was soon swallowed up in a sea of troubles.

A rash of creditor suits, some of them from unpaid employees, harassed the company. The *West Coast* sank in the port of Miami, partly blocking a channel; Mel had to send a crew to float it again. The galleon, too, sank more or less regularly at its berth at Wrecker's Wharf. Finally, Mel had to close down the museum, and he kept gasoline pumps on hand in the event of a power cutoff or failure. Bob Moran, worn by the strain of recent years, left. From his desk in the galleon office, however, Mel continued to place calls around the nation, to spin schemes for treasure sales, to seek the major deal that so far had eluded him.

To me, two important things—perhaps the most important to have developed out of the *Atocha* enterprise to date—came about in late 1977. First, Duncan Mathewson's thesis on the shipwreck, written for Florida Atlantic University, was finished. When I read it, I was certain that, whatever happened to the salvors' efforts, the basic facts about the ship with which we had all come to identify ourselves so closely would be recorded. Moreover, in the sweep of his objectives, the means of investigation he had chosen, Mathewson had broken significant new ground in marine archaeology. His work was studded with detail; he had meticulously examined the site and the artifacts that had come from it.

In the meantime, one of the precious artifacts that Duncan had described, bronze cannon No. 2499, had slowly made its way to Spain. Evidently it rested for some time in Madrid. In late fall, I received a letter from the *directora* of the Archive of the Indies, Doña Rosario Parra. Doña Rosario told me that the gun had arrived in Sēville at last. Fortunately, she advised, Robert Marx happened to be at the archive at the same time and had volunteered to help by supervising the cleaning of the cannon. Although, as he worked, he continuously declared that the gun could not possibly have come from the *Atocha,* he had done a beautiful job of the cleaning: the gun looked as if it had just come from the foundry. The *directora* added that the gun would be placed on display downstairs, where all entering the archive could see it.

Early in November 1977, underwater interests focused again briefly upon Key West. Working with his university and with a federal grant, Duncan Mathewson had set up a conference on historic shipwreck archaeology. He planned the meeting to allow a frank dialogue between opposing forces in the undersea world; it more than fulfilled his hopes. For two days, an overflow crowd of academics, sport divers, government officials, and treasure hunters listened to long, often angry, exchanges. For the first time, the issues that divided the parties were debated fully and openly.

Carl Clausen and Sonny Cockrell set forth plainly the position of government archaeologists. Clausen bluntly called for an end to all private salvage of historic shipwrecks. Cockrell made an eloquent plea for the preservation of Florida's underwater sites for future generations, but he also revealed his inner feeling about private salvors, likening them to "buffalo hunters." He then pointed out significantly that the state did not have to issue one single salvage contract in Florida waters.

Speaking for the burgeoning federal interest, Charles McKinney was equally frank; he described new legislation planned to place all shipwreck sites on the continental shelf under jurisdiction of the federal government. Speaking particularly of the *Atocha* matter, McKinney gave it as his opinion that if the government lost its legal appeal, federal authorities would appeal further, to the United States Supreme Court.

A procession of speakers represented the private salvors. Art McKee recalled the early days of underwater adventure in the Keys. Jack Haskins spoke briefly but cogently for private enterprise. He stated that virtually all the treasure displayed or stored in Tallahassee and almost all the shipwreck data in state files had been contributed by private salvors. He expressed open doubt that any government agency could ever furnish the drive or investment to locate and recover any important shipwreck.

Dave Horan and Mel Fisher appeared on the platform, and Dave spoke first. He described for the crowd the events that had led up to his filing of the lawsuit for the *Atocha* treasure. Then he scored what he termed the state's "betrayal," which had forced the action.

When Mel rose, he spoke as the dean of treasure hunters; his audience gave full attention. Mel's speech was thoroughly partisan; he called for a "treasure hunters' Bill of Rights"—one that would guarantee anyone the right freely to work shipwrecks. He urged Florida and the United States to adopt Bermuda's plan for the division of shipwreck artifacts: salvors could keep all they found, but the governments involved had first right to buy what they wished, at fair market prices.

Then Mel began to tell the crowd his plans for the *Atocha* collection, and his tone softened. He seemed to be speaking to himself, articulating his dreams. The treasure, he mused, might end up in Madrid's Prado Museum. Then again, instead of selling it for five million dollars, he might turn it into a great traveling exhibit, better than that of the treasure of King Tutankhamen, and tour the world. To many of his listeners, Mel's words seemed out of touch with the realities of his circumstances.

At the Key West conference, few spoke for any middle

ground. Only Duncan Mathewson had made any real plea for mutual cooperation. He insisted that workable archaeological controls were consistent with private salvage in the first stages of the exploration of a shipwreck. But this view found little support. The split was deeper than ever. After the meeting, the salvors met to form an association to protect their interests; they began to build a war chest to fight the federal legislation Charles McKinney had described. Whatever the rhetoric on either side, the battle for the legal rights to sunken treasure was a basic struggle over power and possession. Clearly, it would be long and protracted.

In November, the long-awaited "second stipulation" was finally approved by the parties to the *Atocha* suit. In effect, it guaranteed that the salvors would not receive any less than the materials displayed in Washington, whatever the outcome of the lawsuit. In the same month, Dave Horan had gone to New Orleans to make Treasure Salvors' case before the federal appeals judge. No verdict had yet been rendered, and the unresolved case still clouded the salvors' title.

Mel's crew was now reduced even further. Although Ted Miguel took *Swordfish* out when winter weather allowed, he had only two diver-crewmen left: Don Jonas and Charlie Clyne. The *Arbutus* had become more a derelict than a work vessel. On several occasions, Mel had literally picked a man off the streets to crew her.

Jim Maher had moved back to Palm Beach County to begin his business again. Claudia, Deo Fisher, and two part-time workers manned the office. Mel reopened the galleon; he was short of tour guides and began to take visitors through the museum himself. Although Mel had raised some money and satisfied a few pressing obligations, he had made little headway on the great mass of debt. By now, it was a threat to his company's existence.

The Miami Omni exhibit had proved a deep disappointment. It had not yielded the hoped-for gate receipts and was in fact in danger of closing down. Some encouraging news did come to Key West about the remaining 1715 treasure, now in Mel Joseph's Delaware bank vault; it appeared that it might at last have been sold. Treasure Salvors' share in it had shrunk, however, to fifty thousand dollars. This was all the company now retained, after fourteen years, of the treasure found off Vero Beach and Fort Pierce in the magic years of 1963 and 1964.

The investment group had proceeded with its plans to construct their resort hotel complex at Wrecker's Wharf, but neither Treasure Salvors nor Mel Fisher had any share in it. The bustle of land-clearing and the preparation of the site for construction was in sad contrast to the condition of the battered galleon museum and that of the company it represented.

As long as the company's investors, stockholders, and directors had felt hope in the future—hope in the surmounting of the legal case and in the sale of the treasure, hope that effective search might yet reveal the Mother Lode—Mel's leadership had not been seriously questioned. Now, however, hopes had faded in many minds. As winter turned into a new year and then into spring, the lack of legal resolution and the threatening obligations of the company seemed insoluble. For the first time, severe criticism of Mel's handling of money matters was heard in board meetings.

Then the Fishers received a heavy blow. They learned that Angel's mother had filed suit against Treasure Salvors over her daughter's death. The news brought back to Deo all her memories of the *Northwind*'s loss. It was almost more than she could bear.

The invaders from Key West had achieved complete surprise. On the late afternoon of April 11, 1978, at the new State Library and Archives Building in Tallahassee, Treasure Salvors came for the *Atocha* treasure. Flanked by two federal marshals, Mel and Dave, backed by Don, Claudia, Fay Feild, and others from the company, presented themselves to Ross Morrell. Ross now headed his division, for Robert Williams had become deputy secretary of state. Dave handed Morrell Judge Mehrtens's order to turn over all the treasure the state had received in the 1975 division. The attorney added that they wanted it at once; the marshals assured the state official that he had to comply.

Hastily, Morrell telephoned Senator Williams and Jack Shreve, attorney for the Department of State who had been active in the 1975 negotiations over the treasure. The state lawyer came immediately to Morrell's office and told the group from Treasure Salvors that it was just impossible—the state could not give them the treasure on such short notice. Most of it, he added, was stored in vaults and would have to be removed with proper care. Besides, he said, the judge's order had not been specific enough; the item list that Treasure Salvors had presented was not officially a part of the court order.

When the marshal called the judge in Miami to report that the state had resisted his order, the judge said sternly that the state officials knew very well the materials they had received from Treasure Salvors, and that they should turn them over at once. But Shreve still refused. Morrell, however, assented, and said that in the morning he would begin to obey the court order. Mel and his men could only wait for the morning.

Things had moved fast since March 14, when the federal appeals judge in New Orleans had ruled for Treasure Salvors and against the federal government. Then the Interior and Justice departments had decided that they had had enough; they had declined to appeal the case further. Suddenly the salvors realized that after seven years they had won the fight for their treasure. With this realization, hope reawakened and optimism surged again. The faithful began to gather in Key West. Bleth was already back in the office. Moe Molinar came to put *Virgilona* in digging condition again. Mel and his Marketing Committee began to plan treasure sales based upon secure title. The natural question that next occurred was: What about the treasure in Tallahassee? What about the astrolabe and the rest, now that no government had any right to the *Atocha?* The next move was obvious; Dave Horan went to Judge Mehrtens for a court order.

Early the next morning, state curators began to remove, measure, photograph, and pack artifacts from the *Atocha,* preparatory to obeying the Miami court. At the same time, Jack Shreve and the attorney general's office were feverishly trying to stave off Judge Mehrtens's order. They desperately tried to reach the New Orleans appeals judge who had made the March ruling. At last they made telephone contact, and asked for and received a verbal stay order on turning over the treasure until the state could file a formal action.

During the morning the longtime antagonists—Mel Fisher and Senator Robert Williams—met face-to-face. Williams wore a dark suit, but the salvor was wearing his *Atocha* T-shirt, which depicted the ship on the back. The front of the shirt bore Fisher's battle cry: TODAY'S THE DAY. For his part, Mel was still willing to give a representative sampling of the treasure to Florida for display, provided that the state acknowledge that it was his to donate in order that the salvage company might get a tax deduction for so doing. But the grim-faced Williams had consistently refused to compromise the state's title to the treasure. Now the two men had little to say to each other; it was all in the hands of the courts.

Mel and his party were deeply disappointed at the stay order, yet confident that they would eventually get all the treasure back. They boarded their chartered DC-3 and flew back to Key West. Sure enough, Dave Horan called to advise that the Court of Appeals in New Orleans had dissolved the State's stay order and that Judge Mehrtens had directed the return of the treasure to the company.

July 13, 1979: four years to the day after Dirk Fisher had found the bronze cannons. Mel had chartered a fine salvage vessel, the *James Bay*. In the last ten days, her mighty blowers had uncovered an exciting pocket of *Atocha* treasure — five more gold bars, a small stamped gold disc, an uncut amethyst, and two more gold chains, including one over seven and one-half feet long. his divers had also found arquebuses, pottery, silver coins, and ballast stones.

In the fall, hurricane David raked the lower Keys, stirring the shallow waters with heavy winds and waves. But, as the year came to an end, Mel Fisher had not found his Mother Lode. Today was not yet the day.

Diver approaches ballast pile of Atocha "Motherlode".

Divers picking up artifacts around Atocha timbers.

Silver coin conglomerate as they were found
partially encased in wooden shipping chests.

Color Photos:
Courtesy Pat Clyne / Paradigm Video Productions

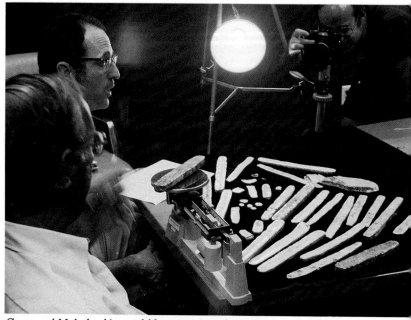

Gene and Mel checking gold bars against the "Margarita" manifest.

The 9 inch gold plate, gold scalloped cup, several gold bars and assorted gold chains.

XVII. The Ghost Galleon

A large group crowded onto John Cryer's porch, overlooking his pool and a canal leading out to sea. As we bent over the sea-chart unrolled on the table, our thoughts, too, reached out to the ocean and the coming season's work in the Marquesas. The previous year's finds were recorded on Mel's operation map, also studded with numbered grid lines, reflecting new technologies he had added to his treasure hunt by 1980.

Now remote sensing devices, such as the faithful magnetometer, were wedded to an electronic navigation system. Accurate to within three meters, it enabled a search boat captain to record the precise position of an anomaly, and later to return to that exact spot. Divers with hand-held pulse-type underwater detectors, capable of distinguishing gold and silver on the sea floor, then tested the target. Radio contact tied the boats to the new heart of the search effort — Treasure Salvors' chart room, where a large-scale map was dotted with multicolored artifact and anomaly locations.

It was that map that now lay on Cdr. Cryer's table, where Mel had called a brainstorm session in January, 1980. His main prize, as always, was the Mother Lode of *Nuestra Senora de Atocha*. But Mel's special emphasis at this meeting was her lost sister ship, the *Santa Margarita*. She had become in modern treasure folklore a "ghost galleon," one reported sunk in many locations, but never yet found. The *Santa Margarita*, it was alleged, lay somewhere deep off Palm Beach, or on Florida's southwest coast, or in the Keys. We knew, of course, of Francisco Melian's salvage work of the vessel near the Marquesas, but in all our searching, we had discovered no trace of *Margarita*. A good part of her valuable cargo should still lie there somewhere for the taking.

Mel now proposed to continue his *Atocha* search, but to set up a special *Santa Margarita* unit. For that purpose, he introduced us to an old associate, Captain Robert Jordan, who had worked with him in the middle Keys fifteen years before. Jordan, white-haired and weatherbeaten, had the appearance of a cagey, cautious seaman. He had contracted to furnish his boat *Castilian* to search the areas designated by Mel in return for food, fuel and $100 a day. The company agreed to furnish him with one of Fay Field's magnetometers, and a marine radio for communication with the Key West office. He would also receive two per cent of any *Atocha* finds and 5% of any treasure recovered from the *Santa Margarita*. In the event he should locate a totally new shipwreck site, Bob Jordan would get from a third to a half of its salvaged cargo, depending on the degree of his support by Treasure Salvors.

As we considered the problem of finding the *Margarita*, Duncan Mathewson described the artifact finds and laid out the wreckage scatter for us. I reviewed the archival documents for the group, and told them about a special puzzle that devilled me. The eyewitness testimony of Captain Bernardino de Lugo, which had helped us find our way to the *Atocha*, had fixed the sinking place of *Margarita* as one league west of that of *Atocha*. Yet, on my last trip to Spain, my former rival and good friend Jack Haskins had provided a piece of contradictory evidence. He pointed to me a letter by Captain Aguilar y Guzman, written after he returned to Spain from Havana in early 1623. From west to east, Aguilar had noted down the resting-places of the sunken 1622 ships. According to his letter, the *Santa Margarita* had been lost to the east of the

Atocha.. Only if the tracks of the two ships had crossed during the time of their travail could these two testimonies be reconciled.

Turning to the map, Mel pointed out two places, both east and west of the *Atocha* finds, where clusters of anomalies picked up in prior years might indicate the resting place of the missing galleon.

Bobby Jordan listened quietly to all that was said. But then, to our surprise, he spoke up suddenly and intemperately, blurting out that he did not believe that we had ever truly found the *Atocha*. Jordan said that we had likely confused the location the two galleons. He went on to say that he relied upon his own research information, in which he had more confidence than ours. As a buzz of comment ran around the room, Mel closed the meeting by directing Jordan to begin his search with the *Castilian* west of the Bank of Spain. If nothing were found there, he should turn back east towards the Marquesas.

By now, another dimension had also been added to Mel's search: a type of funding in keeping with the tax laws of the 1980's — the syndicated limited partnership. Jerome Burke, a New Jersey securities broker, happened to be in Key West on vacation, entered the Treasure Salvors museum, and noted how Mel was financing his treasure hunt with amounts which might come in from individual investors in percentage shares of future treasure. Jerry Burke went to see Mel and the Board, and proposed to syndicate the search with a major underwriting, which would enable Mel to better meet his needs. Mel also approached Vanguard Ventures, a New York investment firm, for money for the search. Burke and Vanguard proceeded to draw up prospectuses for offerings, which neared completion as winter merged into spring in the Florida Keys.

They had been quite ususual, those early months of 1980; the usual sweeping fronts and winter storms were almost totally lacking. It was therefore possible to begin work out beyond the Marquesas keys much earlier. In February, the company boats and Bob Jordan's *Castilian* began their search. After working without success west of the *Atocha* finds, Bobby Jordan turned in March to the area to the east, towards the Marquesas.

The need to find the *Margarita* — fast — was urgent, for heavy pressure was being exerted upon Mel. Serious rivals had again come on the scene, in the persons of Olan Frick and John Gasque, the men who helped raise the *Atocha's* cannons in 1976. Late the previous year they had found substancial backers. Their ships *Juniper* and *Seaker* were outfitted and docked at Key West. Soon Frick and Gasque's boats began to appear in Hawk's Channel, near Mel's operations areas. Next they had intruded into the area injuncted for Treasure Salvors. The previous December five shots were fired by the rivals near Mel's vessels, and in March of the new year, *Virgilona* narrowly escaped being run down by Frick and Gasque. Even though Judge Mehrtens had issued a temporary restraining order against the two rivals within the *Atocha* operations zone, Mel had to move and move quickly or risk losing the *Santa Margarita*.

Castilian, a rugged aluminum oil-patch crew-boat, began to make magnetometer runs in shallow water some six miles west of the Marquesas. On February 18, Bob Jordan and Craig Boyd, his mate, found first indications of a sunken ship. He then located and recovered a hoard of colonial shipwreck materials: a grapnel anchor, a cooking caldron of copper, Spanish ceramic shards, and a ballast stone of the type familiar to them from the *Atocha* site. They also brought in a few silver coins. Don Kincaid, detailed by Mel to represent the company aboard *Castilian*, found matted remnents of indigo. When he examined the shields of the coins at the Marquesas anchorage one evening, he saw that they had been minted at Potosi in the reign of Philip III. Thus they corresponded to that of the earlier 1622 recoveries; from which wreck had they come?

Now *Virgilona* and *Swordfish* hastened to the area, as Mel turned his whole company's attention to the new site.

Acting for Mel, Dave Horan filed for the area in Admiralty with the Federal Court. This would protect the materials until the Judge ruled on their disposition, and allow the salvor to continue onsite work without interruption. But the settled pattern of work on the new area soon changed, and dramatically. As Don said: "from a 350-year-old detective puzzle it became deadly serious...it turned from fun into a curse. The reason: *we found gold.*"

As the divers worked to the north and northwestward from the original area, they found three large and heavy gold bars: the largest weighed more than four pounds! Back at the dock in Key West, the crew celebrated with champagne, using one of the bars as a golden swizzle-stick. But the real effervescence they felt in their viens bubbled up from the joy of their find. As Mel Fisher often says, "gold shines forever," and that night it was reflected in their eyes.

This wrecksite, therefore, was different from the other locations Mel had worked in the Marquesas — richer, and more closely concentrated. On April 12, two more gold bars came up; hundreds, then thousands of silver coins were found. Swords and arquebuses recovered indicated that this was another major vessel.

Now Mel's son Kane came to the fore as a prime mover in the family treasure business. Tall (at six inches over six feet), red-haired Kane had been promoted to boat captain on *Virgilona*. It was soon clear that the veteran treasure boat had not yet finished its career. On May twelfth, Kane set his anchors over the new wrecksite and went overside. There he discovered six silver ingots resting neatly on the ocean bottom; alongside was a large wooden section of the sunken ship itself, more than twenty feet square. The timbers and planks were covered with ballast stones, copper ingots, and other artifacts.

When Duncan Mathewson saw the hull structure he felt immediate, high excitement. Here, he knew, was a unique opportunity to raise and preserve a major part of an early Spanish colonial vessel. Who could guess what might be learned about early wood-joining and Spanish ship construction? Duncan began to lay plans for the careful removal and safe transportation of the structure to a place of conservation ashore.

Nearby, in the next two days, another gold bar, three silver ingots, table silverware, and a silver spur were found. An entire chest of silver coins, almalgamated into one mass, was hauled up with difficulty. Six more gold bars were also picked out of crevices in the rock or from their hiding places in the sand.

A tiny gold ring brought on deck was set with a large table-cut emerald, covering a bubble of sea-water, forced into the setting over the centuries. Mel Fisher termed it as "the world's most expensive carpenter's level."

During this time, I was in Spain, researching again at Seville. One day, the Archive *portero* slipped once more through the purple curtain, came to my desk, and tapped me on the shoulder, making the circular gesture that meant a telephone call. I went out into the lobby, picked up the telephone, and heard the distant, welcome voice of Bleth McHaley. She said "Gene, we've found the most marvellous things — gold bars, silver ingots, and thousands of silver coins. We've got a whole section of ribs and planking: we've opened up another ship, another whole ship!"

My own excitement over these finds matched Mel's, Duncan's, and the crew's. Immediately upon my return, I came to Key West. When I saw the six silver ingots that Kane had found, and compared their markings, five matched the manifest of the *Santa Margarita*!

This particular task, however, meant far more to me than mere ship identification. Ingot number 4718 especially stood out; As I examined it, the bar glowed for me with a personal significance; it was shipped by the merchant Gaspar de Rojas, whose widow's pleadings I had read in Seville. Sent from Lima in 1622, the ingot had reached Panama by way of the South Seas Fleet, was transshipped across Isthmus to Portobello, and was taken aboard the *Margarita* there. The manifest told me that this ingot had been consigned to the Brotherhood of the Holy Cross in Seville. Sure enough, I found Rojas' RX mark and the large S surmounted with a Jerusalem Cross — the sign of the Brotherhood — incised on the bar's surface. Like the merchant himself, the silver ingot had been lost with the *Santa Margarita*. There was no question now as to the identity of the ship. Techniques developed on the *Atocha* site had established it beyond a doubt.

Precious things affect us all, but perhaps in a different ways. For some, the finding arouses a fierce desire for acquisition, no matter the cost. Gold fever had now struck at the Marquesas wrecksite. In Bobby Jordan's case, the disease progressed rapidly. He wanted, and felt he deserved, a greater share. Bobby came to Mel and then to the company Board of Directors, to contend that what he had found was an entirely new wrecksite and that he was thus entitled to half of the treasure. The Board refused, citing Jordan's contract and the definitive identification of the *Santa Margarita*. Bobby Jordan decided to take matters into his own hands. He met with his backers and attorneys, and then filed for the wrecksite in his own name with another division of the Federal Court. He did this on May 21st, without notifying Mel Fisher.

Two days later, after loading and fueling *Castilian* at Treasure Salvors' expense, Bobby Jordan headed out from Key West for the *Margarita* site. Mel had assigned R.D. LeClair and Frank Moody, Jr. to represent Treasure Salvors aboard Jordan's craft. Once over the shipwreck, Jordan set his anchors, put divers overside and found, at the center of the area, a regular bonanza: fifteen gold bars and a large gold disk; more than fifty pounds of gold! They also brought up gold coins, six small silver bars or disks, two copper ingots, and 581 silver coins.

R.D. LeClair, noting that Bob Jordan made no effort to call Mel to tell him of the recoveries, asked permssion to do so, and was forbidden to do so. Jordan laid an M-1 carbine alongside him and strapped on a .22 caliber pistol. He then used the marine radio himself and called his wife. Obviously empolying a pre-arranged code, Bobby Jordan told her he had "found the fish" and questioned whether or not he should "turn it over to the fish farm." Then he pulled his anchors and set course for the Keys.

As *Castilian* approached that afternoon, Key West was strewn with a litter of disaster. The phenomenon called the Cuban boat-lift was in full and chaotic swing. Fidel Castro had briefly uncorked the port of Mariel in Cuba, and allowed his people to emigrate to the United States. The result was one of the largest short-term flood of refugees recorded in our history. In a sea-borne exodus as dramatic as Dunkirk, almost a hundred thousand Cubans swarmed ashore in Key West in a few days. Small boats, often pathetically tiny, were strewn along the island's beaches and in Garrison Bight. No-one knew how many had been lost on the way across the rough Florida Straits. Neither could they tell how many had come ashore unrecorded in the early stages of the boat-lift. Now the Coast Guard was meeting the flotillas of small craft out at sea and escorting them into Key West harbor, where the refugees were carefully checked.

Don Kincaid stood at the Pier House, watching the mad panorama, and scanning the harbor with binoculars. All at once, he recognized *Castilian*, which had just entered the harbor entrance. As he watched, Kincaid noted that the vessel anchored briefly, then set out again, headed east. "Strange," he thought; "why didn't Bobby Jordan come on in and report?"

Jordan had made up his mind what to do. His coded message had set the machinery in motion for a Federal Marshal to come to "arrest" the artifacts he had recovered. This was, of course, to be in his own name and in support of the Admiralty claim he had filed, duplicating Treasure Salvors' prior filing. Jordan proceeded twenty miles eastward from Key West to Summerland Key.

There Bobby Jordan's sponsor boarded the boat and threatened the Treasures Salvors employees, telling them their legs would be broken if they told anyone of the find. They were taken ashore to the backer's large, fenced waterfront estate and confined at the main house. When Jordan's attorneys arrived, the hi-jackers held a celebration over the new-found treasure.

After a Federal Marshal came to "arrest" the treasure in the name of Jordan's salvage claim, LeClair and Moody were released. When R.D. called Mel and Bleth and told them what happened, the company went into high gear to recover the gold and silver.

In a burst of intense activity, Dave Horan prepared the necessary motions. Judge Mehrtens approved, and Bobby Jordan's Admiralty claim was transferred into his court. On June 2, at a hearing on Dave's motion that Bob Jordan show cause why he should not be held in contempt of court, the Judge said:

"...it seems to me inexcusable, really, to be operating under that contract and to charge to Treasure Salvors fuel and food and other things, and go out there. And certainly with the markings that were out there, and with his previous work in that area, I think, really, that he is now embarking upon a course to unjustly enrich himself."

Although Bobby Jordan continued to press his Admiralty claim, the Court removed him from further work on the *Santa Margarita*. On that same day, Judge Mehrtens also heard the Frick-Gasque case. Commenting on the testimony, he called the two rivals, "modern day pirates." The Judge sentenced both of them to five months in jail for unauthorized violation of Mel's Court-enjoined search areas. As Bleth said, "we knew we're safe at least for that day; all the different pirates were gathered together in court."

Then a new threat intervened; the State of Florida moved to claim the *Margarita* site for itself. That summer, Judge Mehrtens died. The *Margarita* cases were then combined under the jurisdiction of Judge James Lawrence King, also of the Miami Federal District Court. While the litigation was being resolved, Treasure Salvors was allowed to continue to work the area.

But this was also a time of struggle for Mel Fisher in other ways. On the same day that Dave Horan filed his motions against Bobby Jordan, Mel's galleon museum sank at dockside at the foot of Front Street. The ship's bottom, patched and re-patched for years, had finally given way to the ravages of the teredo worms. As the ship, heeling at an ever greater angle, settled lower and lower in the mud, crew members crawled along teetering gangplanks to salvage the museum exhibits and office records. Now the company had no choice but to come ashore. Although funds had begun to flow in from limited partnerships, company expenses were greater than ever before.

However, six miles west of the Marquesas atoll, the summer of 1980 was proving a golden one for Mel Fisher. Two parallel stories were enfolding at the same time. While a succession of unique artifacts were rapidly uncovered, we were attempting to find their meanings and the mystery concealed within their scatter. These meanings could help solve the puzzle of the ghost galleon, *Santa Margarita*, and might eventually lead us to the Mother Lode of the *Atocha*.

Once more, Duncan was teaching us his lesson: each item recovered from a shipwreck formed part of a pattern which, taken together, had significance. After our previous experience, we now knew better what to seek. But, still, we were continuously surprised by the lovely things which were brought up onto the decks of the salvage boats.

Now the treasure craft moved northward along the *Santa Margarita's* scatter, sweeping with magnetometers, blowing sand from anomalies, and sending divers to observe the results. Three hundred yards farther along the trail, Larry Beckman dived off *Swordfish* to find a long bronze cannon, its tube surmounted by dolphins. Farther along, they turned up another bronze gun. Although we could not identify the cannons since their markings were eroded away, it seemed likely that they had been the heavy pieces which had once commanded the after section of *Margarita's* gun deck.

For those on the wrecksite, July 8 became the "day of gold chains." Colonial shipwreck material seems to accrue in widely-scattered clumps, and divers were working one such accumulation, where iron cannonballs were mingled with silver coins and other artifacts. Pat Clyne was below, fanning the sand from around a silver ingot, when gold chains appeared from beneath the bar. Suddenly he found that they led to a mass of twisted chain. With Don Kincaid and Stuart Preater he brought up fifteen chains in all. One great chain had 149 huge links. A few days later, Frank Moody, now diving from *Swordfish*, picked out of a sandbank a tiny gold ring set with seven small dark-green emeralds.

On August eighth, Richard Kloudt, diving from *Virgilona*, was struck on the head by an item dislodged from the mailbox stream. He reached out to grasp it and found himself holding a partly-encrusted eight-inch gold plate or salver. Once it could be clearly seen, it proved to be figured with an intricate worked abstract design. It was perhaps the finest single piece to be recovered from either shipwreck up to that time.

On August 23rd, Syd Jones, a keenly intelligent young man

now serving as captain of the *Swordfish*, espied what might have been the contents of a private treasure-box: nine gold finger-bars and eight gold chains, all in a tangle. To Syd the chains looked like a "hive of golden bees."

Among the recoveries the next day was the lid of a small ivory box, upon which were carved the allegorical figures of lions, eagles and other creatures. We later learned that these represented the legend of the first royal family of Ceylon, and were similar to those found on an ivory box in the Victoria and Albert Museum in London, datable to the 16th century. Portugal, under Castilian control in 1622, had conquered Ceylon for Western Christianity. This chest could have come east or west from there, to Europe or to Mexico through the commercial pipeline to the Philippines, heavily threatened by the Dutch. This far — from Ceylon to the Florida Keys — had the wide Spanish Imperial trade extended.

Gentle fanning and digging around the ship timbers of the *Margarita* disclosed to Duncan and Don mementos of the daily life of the people of the sunken galleon: pig bones, chili peppers, and the soles of shoes.

On the 26th, I joined Deo Fisher and others at dockside as *Virgilona* pulled in from the wrecksite. Eagerly we boarded before her crewmen had even finished tying up, and saw her wide cockpit filled with barrel hoops from the *Margarita*, together with many encrusted swords, dirks, and arquebuses. They had also brought another silver bar, and a fused fifty-pound mass of silver coins. While I watched, Mo Molinar, grinning, opened the mouth of a sack and poured twenty-five two-escudo gold coins into Deo's cupped hands. None of these gold coins, we knew, had been minted in the New World. All had come from one mint: the *Casa de Moneda* in Seville. They must have been pocket-money for well-to-do ship's officers or passengers aboard.

Among the finds was a tiny gold boatswain's whistle. When

Mel first put it to his lips, he raised a thin piping sound, the first, he said, to issue from the whistle since the dead Spaniard to whom it had belonged had been drowned. The boatswain's whistle became Mel's favorite toy. He took it with him to meetings and lectures all over Florida.

It was necessary, during the course of preservation of the materials, to raise and deal with many clumps of conglomerate wrecksite materials from the *Santa Margarita*. One of these, which weighed almost two tons, had been located on the hull structure itself. It had to be hoisted up to the salvage ship, transported to shore, and then taken by truck to the conservation laboratory. There the huge clump was carefully cleaned, and yielded more than 250 cannonballs. It also contained a number of other mementos of the human occupants of the lost galleon: coins, beads, glass shards, animal bone — and one rare and significant artifact. From the middle of a clump of coins, which may have been the contents of a leather purse, there appeared a small gold pendant. The item, fashioned in the shape of a scallop shell, featured the cross of Santiago, Spain's patron saint, on both outside faces. Inside was an enamelled blue sky dotted with gold stars, and the letters Y E. I later learned that this was a pendant *venera* to be worn by members of the prestigious military-religious order of Santiago.

Late that summer, Duncan showed me five large bronze mortars, brought up from the *Santa Margarita*. These were decorated with the heads of lions, a Minotaur, Apollo and Satan. The galleon's surgeon had used them, with their pestles, to mix the medicines he employed during the voyage. Then Duncan unwrapped the water-soaked cloth from around a brass sunwatch just brought in for preservation. The watch had contained a small pocket-compass, and was fitted out with a folding gnomon and dial. To tell the time, the owner located north and raised the gnomon to get a shadow which indicated the hour. Instantly, I recalled the Dutch raid on Melian's divers at the Marquesas wrecksite. On June 10, 1627, I remembered, the Spanish salvors had determined the time by a *reloj de sol,* a sunwatch just like this.

At the end of the magic summer, it was time to sum up the Ghost Galleon's treasure. Most strikingly, the divers had brought up gold: bar after bar, chain after gold chain. From the manifest, I had learned that there should have been 24 gold finger bars, bits, or disks remaining after the recovery of the materials found in the Spanish silver-master's floating chest. Actually, we eventually found more than 106 pounds of gold in 54 bars, bits, and disks, forty-three gold chains, fifty-three gold coins, almost 12,000 silver coins and a number of other artifacts.

The gold chains were of many sizes, lengths, and types of workmanship. One design featured extruded gold links like tiny chariot wheels. One pair of solid gold chains, six feet long apiece, were joined together at one link. There were many small finely-worked chains.

The *Santa Margarita's* silver coins were generally in a better condition than those found on the *Atocha* site. They came from a variety of mints: the majority of Potosi, about eleven per cent from the Mexico mint, and smaller quantities from Lima and the Spanish mints of Seville, Toledo and Segovia. The coins from Mexico doubtless included some placed aboard *Margarita* in Havana, after being off-loaded from the New Spain fleet, but probably also represented the substantial intercolonial trade.

As on the *Atocha,* the coins which interested us the most were the rare pieces from the Santa Fe de Bogota mint. Thirty-seven were salvaged from the wreckage of the *Santa Margarita.* We now held the only such coins known in the world. In Seville I had discovered a letter from Turillo de Yebra, the mintmaster, in which he acknowledged not only that he had minted coins in Bogota at that time, but that some of his funds had been lost on the galleons which had sunk.

The effort to preserve, examine and classify the new treasure was as important as the recoveries themselves. A division committee, with membership including major interest groups, was set up to begin the work of coordinating the evaluation of the treasure. Moreover, a talented team of specialists was ready at hand to aid Duncan Mathewson in dealing with these artifactual riches. The company invited Professor John Hayward, a noted British specialist in antique Renaissance and Early Modern artifacts of every sort, to come from England to appraise the materials. This soft-spoken expert carefully studied each item, established a reasonable value, and even advised that Mel had underrated the asking price of the gold chains. So much for the "Fisher factor!"

Duncan Mathewson approached Dr. Barbara Mullen of the Hispanic Society of New York to examine the gold plate, and she rendered it as her opinion that it was of a type not generally known, but its design might indicate Italian origins. Even though the salvaged materials from the *Santa Margarita* were still tied up in the litigation, Mel got permission to prepare an exhibit of the most striking items. With this, in March, 1981, the company travelled to San Diego, where Howard Ruff had scheduled a convention. More than five thousand persons were in the San Diego Convention Center at any one time, and they filed through the treasure exhibit. Howard Ruff introduced Mel Fisher to a large auditorium of his followers, where the treasure hunter made a tremendous impact upon those devoted followers of free enterprise and precious metals. The exhibit of silver bars, gold and silver coins, and artifacts proved to be the hit of the meeting.

At this point, one could still draw a striking comparison between Mel Fisher and the other salvor of *Santa Margarita:* Francisco Nunez Melian. Like the Spaniard, Mel had found the sister galleon while looking for the still-missing *Almiranta*. Although the *Margarita* had yielded him much, an estimated twenty million dollars' worth, and he had transformed it from "ghost galleon" into golden reality, he had still to fulfill his deepest desire: to reach the *Atocha*. Would he, like Melian, die before this wish could be realized?

Now Treasure Salvors, that unique company, began to approach its own peculiar peak configuration. Although from outside appearances it seemed a loosely-organized firm, in reality many remarkable people blended their abilities to accomplish company goals. Mel, as leader, was unusually accessible for a corporate president. He had no door on his office; often people with something to say would just walk in and say it. Mel would listen, at least if he were not talking into one of the telephones. Deo was always nearby. Although she was corporate secretary, Deo also served us all as intercessor and mediator. Her moderating influence on Mel was vital. If she represented the family in a family company, she also was one to whom anyone could appeal.

It would have been difficult to imagine Treasure Salvors without Bleth McHaley and Don Kincaid. Key figures in the enterprise, they took lively interest in the yeasty day-to-day excitement which always boiled up in the office. Don and Bleth relished the controversies which resulted from the nature of the treasure hunting, and had particular expertise in presenting the public face of the company to the world. While Don continued to record the treasure hunt for posterity, Bleth acted as company spearhead in its lengthly litigation.

Claudia Linzee, already experienced in the study of the company's shipwreck artifacts, sketched and recorded the recovered materials. Jerry Cash, a diver and fine artist, worked with Duncan and Claudia in the depiction of the detail of the jewels, weapons, and other artifacts. Larissa Dillin later joined Jerry in the art department. Preservationist Jim Sinclair, newly-arrived from New England, began to set up the tanks and electrolytic apparatus needed to clean the coins and other artifacts. Consultant Curt Peterson aided him very much in building the company's facilities and establishing good preservation procedures.

Onsite, Treasure Salvors and Duncan were fortunate in having several archaeological-minded persons: boat captain Syd Jones, master diver Tom Ford, and diver-photographer Pat Clyne. Duncan, Jerry and Don Kincaid joined them in mapping the new finds. Aided by Dr. Ray McAllister of Florida Atlantic University, they used Dimitri Ribikoff's underwater vehicle, *Pegasus,* to create a photomosaic of the gridded wooden ship section and the main part of the site. A huge fiberglass receptacle, dubbed the "hot tub," and measuring more than twenty feet square, was fabricated in Key West to be used in the planned recovery of the *Margarita's* timbers, when weather permitted. Bill Muir, a skilled and careful draftsman and wooden-ship buff from Key West, began to draw the *Margarita* timbers. Using the *Atocha* contruction contract which I had found in the Archives of the Indies, Bill began to sketch out the appearance of the other 1622 vessel as well. Kelly Bernard, a graduate student from the University of Notre Dame, was of great utility to Duncan and the company in curating and understanding the whole artifactual collection.

Treasure Salvors had an unusual and effective family in the Miguels, Ted, Leah, and Holly. Ted Miguel wrought mightily, keeping the boats at sea and ensuring that equipment and supplies flowed to the onsite crews. For some time, he had also served as Operations Director offshore. Leah was curator to the collection, and bore the responsibility of several transfers of the valuable materials from bank to bank and exhibit to exhibit. Holly Miguel worked with K.T. Budde, a young woman who became a fine diver, in classifying and categorizing the coins found on the *Santa Margarita.*

Bob Moran later assumed the jobs of onsite Operations Director, and thereafter spent much of his time at sea, searching with his fine new boat *Plus Ultra.* When Bob married, his wife Marisha served at sea with him as an active member of the team.

An unusual and essential helper was Steve Candela, who

owned a large welding shop on Stock Island in Key West. Steve literally kept the operation together by his services through many years when the company had no money to pay him. But Steve Candela had an obsession — bronze Spanish guns. In return for his help, he received bronze cannon from the firm or bought them from individuals who had received them in division. Steve then built huge containers to hold the guns, which he began to preserve by electrolysis.

The Treasure Salvors office was well served by a succession of secretaries: Caroline Cash, Caroline Herman, and finally by Judy Sojourner. Surely they had to produce more contracts than any normal corporation, as Mel made or proposed deal after deal, many of which never got beyond the draft stage. And the visitor and telephone load at the office was always heavy. Mirroring the work habits of Mel Fisher, office hours were often the reverse of those in a normal office. Meetings tended to last through the lunch hour, sometimes taking place on weekends; work might begin later in the morning but could last until late in the day. Marjory "T" Hargreaves had long held things together in the accounting office of the company. Now she worked with Rose Chibbaro, a New Jersey C.P.A., who brought the internal tax filings up to date for the first time in years. Rose, short, smiling and dynamic, helped "T" prepare Treasure Salvors for entry into the modern corporate world. Finally Rose Chibbaro left her northern practice and moved south to establish herself in Key West.

Taffi Fisher married strapping Jose Quesada of Key West, and the newlyweds took over the operation of the Museum Gift Shop, which sold coins and other artifacts from other divisions. When the exhibit went to other cities, they took the shop on the road as well. Sherri Culpepper, who had worked for Treasure Salvors years before, returned to work in the gift shop.

The company cartographer, Ed Little, carefully recorded and mapped all the wrecksite "hits" recorded by electronic remote sensors. There was now mutual feedback between the chart room, Mel, and the boat captains directing the search. This connection was not always precise, for a spirit of freedom permeated Treasure Salvors' operation. At any time, Mel might interrupt a line of search to follow a sudden impulse. Often the men at sea also showed a degree of independence. Still, the use of the electronic navigation system and the regular charting of finds gradually narrowed the search by elminating unfruitful areas.

Now the time had clearly come to return to the quest for the *Atocha*. Duncan Mathewson still wrestled with the deepwater theory he had developed more than five years before. Others in the company believed that the main treasure must have gone up into the Quicksands with the ship itself, during the second hurricane of 1622. Their belief was encouraged by the rich, if fragmentary finds already made there. But important evidence had been found in mid-July of 1981. Bob Moran on *Plus Ultra*, searching far out on the deeper water of Hawk's Channel, uncovered three anchors, which *Swordfish* and *Dauntless* freed from the mud. They ranged in size from six and a half to twelve feet long. One anchor bore the crudely cut number 1618, and had probably been cast in Vizcaya at that date. Duncan and I both felt that the anchors, clearly colonial in origin, must relate to *Atocha*. Duncan testified for the court that the anchor finds encouraged him in his hypothesis that *Atocha's* main deposit must lie somewhere in the vicinity, in Hawk's Channel.

This deep-water search was put on hold after a series of important recoveries led the boats and their divers back to the Quicksands again. Thanks to a technology just coming into general use, we were enabled to locate precious metal artifacts which the magnetometer could not easily find. The pulse-type detector, used in the successful *Concepcion* finds at Silver Shoals in 1978 by Jack Haskins and Burt Webber, had particular utility on the edge of the Quicksands.

John Brandon and his crew had developed special skill in the use of the new detectors during their work on 1715 shipwrecks in the murky waters of Florida's Indian River coast. Now they moved to the Keys for the summer of 1982, and began to probe the rocky margins of the big shoal, north of the bronze cannon area.

It takes great patience for a diver to search for hours among crevices for faint signals from a hand-held detector; in this case the effort was repaid. An anomaly resulted in the recovery of a small item, shining with fresh gold color. Another, then several, finally twenty-four exquisite gold segments of a jewelled belt were found; some were many inches deep in fissures in the rock. The pieces were of two different designs, and were alternately set with pearls, rubies, and diamonds.

Almost the exact same belt was pictured in a portrait of Philip II's daughter, the Princess Isabel, by the Spanish painter Coello, which hangs today in her bedroom in the Escorial. In another painting by a Spaniard, Juan Pantoja de la Cruz' portrait of Anne of Austria, Philip's wife, a similar jewel appeared, in the form of a necklace. It certainly seemed that the belt was a copy of a piece in vogue at the highest level of Court society.

These new finds on the *Atocha* site spurred Mel to try again to solve his old Quicksands problem — how to move the deep sand. He contracted with the owners of *James Bay,* a large, deflector-equipped tug. She followed a systematic digging plan, and began to uncover valuable caches of treasure. Twenty gold finger bars were brought up from one spot. These bars were unique in the salvage, and were evidently contraband, for they bore no Royal seals. Also, they had scratched on their surface numbers indicating their weight in *pesos de oro,* the first we had seen.

In July came a breathtaking find. The event began in quite a commonplace manner, as diver Rico Ingerson remounted the deck of *James Bay* with a small nondescript oval box in his hand. It looked modern, like some rusty piece of World War II hardware. Other observers thought it a kind of large sardine can, made perhaps for kippering herring. In fact, it was suggested that Rico toss it back overside and go down again to look for some real treasure. But an impulse prompted him to open the can, and what wonders the bright sun shone upon! There lay a gold cross with fourteen large deep-green Muzo emeralds — more than forty carats of stones altogether. On the reverse of the cross were two religious figures. Later in Spain I learned that it was a pectoral cross, intended to be worn by a Bishop or by an even higher prelate. George Spruck, a devoted specialist in Catholic symbolism, told us four years later that one of the figures was *Nuestra Senora de la Leche*, representing the well-known devotion to the Virgin suckling the infant Jesus. Within the box was also a large gold ring with a fine ten-carat emerald, a perfect match for the cross. It would appear that the ring was intended for the same use as the cross, being so large that it would best fit over the glove of a high cleric.

Later a silver medallion was found nearby, which read: "Alabado sea el Santissimo Sacramento." This meant "May the most Holy Sacrament be praised." On its reverse, there appeared a stylized communion wafer, displayed in a monstrance. We had uncovered a pocket of significant religious artifacts, precious in their own right, but of particular interest for our knowledge of the rich Baroque culture of the church.

The renewed offshore activity was reflected in action ashore. That same summer, the company moved its offices twice; from an old Conch house on Caroline Street, it relocated to the former Admiral's office on the Navy base. From thence, Mel moved again to Building 41, an ex-warehouse on Mallory Square, at Whitehead and Greene Streets. This was a much better setting for the museum exhibit, near the heavy tourist traffic which flowed around the Aquarium and the Conch Train station. Soon, the museum and offices were installed. Bleth, who possessed a natural flair for the decorative arts, designed and supervised the installation of the new exhibit. It featured hourly showings of the National Geographic film, "Treasure," and a unique lighting system, where cases of gold bars draped with many gold chains drew viewers. In other display areas, dead-white coral heads were studded with bright gold coins and rings set with emeralds. An especially popular item was a large gold bar set in a heavy plastic holder, where visitors could reach in and helft the bar themselves. Set apart in its own special case, the gold plate shone. On a bed of white sand, Bleth had arranged the gold jewelled belt, with a reproduction of the princess' portrait alongside. Another tubular column displayed the emerald cross and the ring. It was set so that the light struck the emeralds and illuminated them.

Then, amid this busy time for his company, mortality seemed to place its hand upon Mel Fisher. Distressing symptoms led him to undergo medical tests, and then to the removal of polyps in his bladder. These were discovered to be malignant, and Mel began a long, painful series of chemotherapy treatments. Although he neither complained nor attempted to keep his condition a secret, the news was hard for us to accept. Mel Fisher had seemed as indestructible and eternal as the sea which he had battled for so long. His very persistence was such a part of his being that it seemed impossible that he might not live to see the end of his search. Now the quest for the *Atocha* seemed distressingly sharpened, like a game in which the player's time is running out.

To add to Mel's frustration, a web of legal actions still surrounded his treasure hunt. Dave Horan's slim legal staff faced the State Attorney's office and large private law firms opposing them. Bleth McHaley was of inestimable help in these battles, for she acted as Dave's paralegal, but served as far more than that. As corporate representative, Bleth was always at the counsel's table for Treasure Salvors. As she rapidly learned legal procedure and system, Bleth kept track of testimony and evidence. The legal team was, moreover, strongly backed by Joshua Morse and Bill VanderCreek.

The large opposing forces of lawyers could grind out the masses of documents required in the paper war. But this was not always an advantage. At one point, Bleth had to type up an answer and get it off immediately to the 5th Circuit Court of Appeals in New Orleans, when that Court agreed to hear the case on very short notice. In that event, less was more; Dave stole a march on his unwieldly legal opponents. The court's decision denied Federal ownership of the *Atocha*, despite the United States' contention that the Antiquities Act, the Abandoned Property Act, and the Outer Continental Shelf Lands Act should apply. Another 1981 ruling affirmed the supremacy of Admiralty law.

The decisions made in the *Atocha* cases also affected the 1715 disputes involving Mel's other company, Cobb Coin. Cobb had filed for many of the old 1715 sites in August, 1979, in Federal Admiralty Court, ignoring the State statute. On one of the sites, the so-called "Corrigan's Wreck" near Johns Island in the Indian River area, salvaged materials were duly "arrested" by a Federal Marshal. The cannon Mel brought up embroiled him in controversy; the local officials issued a warrant for his arrest in the name of the State of Florida. The State had intervened in the case, with a salvor who possessed a State permit. Again in 1981, Mel's contractor in the Indian River was threatened with arrest by State agents. When he ruled on the case, Judge Sydney Aronivitz followed the precedent of the 1981 decision on the 1622 galleons. He ruled that traditional Admiralty principles should prevail within Florida waters as well. Further, he noted, Florida's claim for protection of the Eleventh Amendment of the Federal Constitution did not bar Federal jurisdiction in the case, since that Amendment only applied to cases in which money damages would be required from a State treasury. This meant that the State law, under which Florida had regulated salvors for years, was probably invalid, where challenged in court.

Nevertheless, a compromise was reached which recognized

the salvors' rights and the State's interest in preserving a portion of the underwater heritage for its citizens in future years. Cobb Coin Company and its former enemies agreed to cooperate in the salvage of a number of the 1715 sites, each party furnishing what it was most uniquely fitted to provide. Although recoveries which might be termed "treasure" were not large, the results were indeed impressive. Duncan set up a twelve-person party, headed by archaeologist David Moore to provide professional services to salvors on all the 1715 sites. Mapping, site analysis, and artifact preservation furnished more data on these sites than had been amassed in all the previous years of salvage under State control. Moreover, the State had its pick of the artifacts for its own museum displays.

In January, 1982, Dave Horan presented his case to the United States Supreme Court. Dave came before that notable Bench on crutches, having virtually destroyed the ligaments of one knee in a skiing accident in Utah a few weeks before. But this did not prevent Dave from making a masterful appearance. When the Court's decision came the next summer, it was neither overwhelmingly favorable nor definitive. It affirmed the principle of Admiralty law. Although the decision did agree that the Eleventh Amendment could apply to such a case, the Court ruled that Florida had failed to utilize it properly. Effectively, the attempted take-over by both levels of government had been effectively halted, at least until new legislation might override the constitutional Admiralty guarantees.

The formal legal opposition Mel had faced was compounded by open hostility from many persons and institutions opposing private shipwreck salvage. This had grown through the past several years among the academic and governmental community. It found its most important focus in the Council for Underwater Archaeology, an organism affiliated with the Society for Historical Archaeology. The most extreme proponents, such as Sony Cockrell of Florida, preferred that there be no private enterprise salvage at all.

Alarmed by the precendent in the *Atocha, Santa Margarita* and 1715 cases, these forces began to unite their efforts. They now included persons on the Texas Antiquities Committee, and at Texas A & M University. Since the courts had consistently ruled for Mel, the opponents' only remedy was to try and bypass the duly constituted Admiralty rights of salvors by Federal legislation which would suppress those rights. As the coalition built, political due bills were called in. Members of the Texas Congressional delegation, powerfully influenced by the anti-salvor nuclei in that State, joined with a North Carolina Representative and Congressman Charles Bennett of Florida. They prepared legislation which embodied their views, and which would have virtually put an end to private salvage of historic shipwrecks. When a hearing was held in Washington on their bill in mid-July, 1982, Mel Fisher went to testify, and cited all the efforts, expenses, and sacrifices of salvors, which had made the finds possible. He demonstrated the benefits that had accrued to the whole public from those recoveries.

Waxing eloquent, Mel heaped scorn upon the State of Florida: "For twenty years the State has insisted that the private salvor do their work for them. They have used the funds, the equipment, the technology, and most important, the knowledge of private enterprise in the name of public interest. In the name of the public interest they subjected the private salvor to threats, economic harrassment, personal slander, degredation, and even jail, when we attempted to exert our rights in the Federal Courts. The coffers of the State have been filled through the efforts of private enterprise. What has the State of Florida accomplished in that 20 years? They have amassed a great collection of material of which they have very little knowledge, and by their own admission cannot tell which item came from which shipwreck! They have done no original research, published very, very little, discovered no heretofore unknown shipwrecks in their waters, and now through this Bill would prohibit private enterprise from filling the void." The bill did not pass the Congress, but that did not stop its proponents. They gained rather than lost in strength and vociferousness.

My own first experience with the opponents' power had already come. In February of 1982, the *National Geographic* article on the *Santa Margarita* appeared, and I was truly pleased with the beauty of its layout and photography. But the article brought trouble in its train. Shortly after its issue, I received a telephone call from an anthropologist. He had acted as chairman of a New Mexico conference, where I had jointly presented a paper on Spanish maritime contraband the year before. Without mincing words, he told me that he was withdrawing the paper from publication in the conference proceedings. This angered me, since he had enthusiastically accepted it just a few months before. When I asked the reason for his seemingly unjust action, he said that he could see from my *Geographic* article that I supported treasure hunters, and therefore did not deserve to have my work published with that of professionals. I had to go abroad to get the paper in print.

But the Purgatory Ducan Mathewson had to endure was far more severe and long-lasting than my own. After his professional group, the Society for Historical Archaeology, printed an extract of Duncan's progress in recording and analyzing the *Atocha* and *Margarita* site data, it was forced to deny him any furture space. The Council for Underwater Archaeology had applied pressure to keep any favorable mention of salvage operations from the Society's newsletter. Finally, at conferences or in the printed word, Duncan found himself virtually blacklisted by his own profession.

In the meantime, the all-important Jordan case was not yet decided. Division of the *Margarita* treasure was still held up until it could be resolved. Finally, in August, 1982, more than two years after the finding of the shipwreck, the matter came to trial at the Courthouse in Miami. I suggested to Dave that we get the Judge's permission to remove three silver ignots from the vault in Key West, bring them to Miami, and to the court. There we could introduce them into evidence, and I could testify as to their provenience — that they were on the manifest, and that we had indeed found the *Santa Margarita*. The three heavy silver bars — Nos. 821, 1096, and 4718 — were brought from Key West to Miami in the trunk of a rental car, and turned over to the clerk. When the room was called to order and Judge King began the proceedings, a perspiring bailiff trundled them into the courtroom on a cart. When I was called to testify, Dave asked me to describe how I had identified the galleon from her silver ingots. With pages from the manifest I demonstrated how the numbers of the bars themselves and those on the document matched. Judge King took an intense interest in this testimony, and leaned over his desk to question me himself. There now seemed no doubt about the strength of Treasure Salvors' legal position, for the case was skillfully handled by Dave and all the legal team. Jordan's position, on the other hand, was woefully weak. He was shown to be nothing more or less than a claim jumper on a legally authorized salvage operation. The judge heard the evidence that the company had properly filed a prior claim on the shipwreck site, had duly recovered materials from it, and had identified these as from the *Santa Margarita*. The trial ended, and we confidently awaited judgement.

When the Judge King's decision came, it was almost worth the three year wait. Without reservation, the company was awarded the treasure of the *Santa Margarita*. Bobby Jordan's share would indeed have been substantial. Instead, he had chosen to take a questionable action to try to get a larger share, and ended with no treasure at all. Jordan even had to pay all the legal fees and court costs.

At division time for the Margarita treasure, investors celebrated at a Duval Street restaurant. Jerry Burke's investor group had done well, even though they had suffered a long and anxious wait until the end of the Jordan case. Don Kincaid was especially happy to have received the golden scallop shell pendant as his share in the division.

Our joy over the division of the *Santa Margarita* treasure was dashed by the sudden death of "T" Hargreaves. We could all remember her committment to the search, whether on her brother's boat, in patching up the tattered money affairs of Treasure Salvors, or in mothering us all. After a time of transition, tall, efficient Sandy Dunn brought her expertise to the office and presided over the accounts. With her came the all-pervading computer.

Soon it was time for Mel's sixtieth birthday, celebrated at a notable surprise party at the Pier House. Hundreds of friends appeared to make it a "This is Your Life" occasion. From Washington, Dennis Kane came to speak to Mel's accomplishments. One after another, his friends rose and praised or "roasted" him. The Pier House commemorated the night by announcing the naming of a part of its restaurant the "Treasure Salvors Grill." In one corner, the restaurant placed a special table; imbedded beneath its clear surface were photographs, replica Spanish coins, and other mementoes of Mel's treasure hunt. On the nearby wall, an appropriate plaque announced that Mel was forever entitled to a lifetime meal at that table, on the house.

At the same time, by mutual consent, many friends and assocites of the Fishers formed the idea of establishing an enduring memorial of Mel's lifework. It would be something which would continue to inform and educate the public about the epoch of the galleons, the era of sail.

Thus the Mel Fisher Maritime Heritage Society was founded and became a growing non-profit association. Rose Chibbaro, Duncan and I, Mel and Deo, and Joan Langley of Key West were among the founders, and the membership grew rapidly. Soon the Society issued its own newsletter, reporting to its members on the historical and archaeological side of the 1622 salvage. It began to accumulate books, aided by the gift of Don Kincaid's substantial maritime library.

Meantine, far northwest on the *Atocha* site, the late summer of 1984 brought a fresh interest to those holding the

Quicksands theory of Mother Lode location. Fay Field spotted a large bronze cannon while being towed by Bob and Marisha Moran behind *Plus Ultra*. On September 10, 1 mile and a half beyond that, the Morans found a second cannon. This led to the immediate dispatch of Tom Ford and the *Swordfish* crew and Kane Fisher and the men in *Dauntless*. When two additional anchors were found even farther northwest, intense excitement was created. As the divers scoured the ocean bottom, a small quantity of treasure was found — then no more. The Main Pile remained a mystery.

Still thwarted, Mel Fisher sought other ways to break out of the *Atocha* deadlock. Two of Mel's alternatives to the regular electronic sensing and navigation equipment seemed bizarre to outside observers. First, Mel contracted with a trainer to provide two porpoises for $25,000. The porpoises were to be turned loose on the wrecksite, and would hopefully swim direct to the silver pile, followed by the eager salvors. Unfortunately, the trainer had not allowed for the effect of open ocean conditions on his charges. When they were released, the porpoises became disorientated and the trainer was lucky indeed to recover them. They had found no silver or gold.

Next, Mel began to develop an electronic device of his own, a type of gradiometer which he termed "Squarkometer." He was certain that "Squark" readings would spell out that unknown spot where the Main Pile lay, and insisted on the use of the gadget from his own Hatteras cruiser, *Bookmaker*.

On the legislative front, both opposing sectors had now drawn their lines of battle. The coalition favoring the end of private salvage was now met by an organized group composed of sports divers, treasure hunters, and those few academics who agreed with their point of view. This organization, called the Atlantic Alliance, had been founded with the help of Duncan Mathewson, Dan Koski-Karrel, another marine archaeologist, and the very welcome support of Charles McKinney. McKinney's aid pointed up the enlightened nature of the new coalition; it's purpose was not to destroy, but rather preserve the maritime heritage through the cooperation of professionals and amateurs alike.

As the new bills proposed made their way rapidly through the Congress, the extremists imposed their influence until, in the last edition, virtually all shipwrecks on the Continental shelf were to become the property of the United States. The Federal government might then delegate its authority over the sites to the several States. Admiralty jurisdiction over shipwreck salvage, a feature of Federal law since the founding of the Republic, was to be severely curtailed.

Near the end of the Congressional session of 1984, this newest version of the shipwreck legislation approached its moment of truth. Leaders of the Texas delegations, Congressman Bennett of Florida, and other partisans brought strong pressure to bear to force to another set of bills through the Congress. The House version went to the floor and was passed. Despite the usual logjam of last-minute bills, it appeared that the Senate might also vote its approval. But one Senator, Paula Hawkins of Florida, stood firm. She stated: "(the) attitude on the part of government, that it is entitled to all or part of every effort by its citizens, is in my judgement one of the primary evils of modern political life. It is foreign to our traditions." Senator Hawkins refused to be stampeded. She stood firm in opposition, and the anti-salvage legislation failed once again.

But now another concern arose, that might have halted Mel's efforts through the destruction of his company.

Bob Moran had long and valuable service on Treasure Salvors' Board of Directors. He had helped Mel, Deo and the other members of the Board provide for improved accounting and inventory practices in the company, and took part in all the struggles which the firm had experienced in recent years. Perhaps encouraged by the find of the Quicksands cannon, Bob and Marisha Moran began to feel that they, better than

Mel Fisher, held the key to the Mother Lode. Feelings became increasingly strained between the Morans and other Treasure Salvors personnel. Marisha Moran was evidently convinced that only she and her husband could re-direct the company on its proper course. She proposed a list of "reforms" which were not warmly received by the Board majority. It was not the items proposed, some of which were valid suggestions and had already been implemented by the company, as the manner in which they were presented, that aroused dissension.

As the time approached for the December, 1984 stockholders' meeting, the Morans decided to challenge Mel Fisher in a proxy battle for control of Treasure Salvors.

First, they gathered material from office files that they felt might support their case. Without company authorization, they copied the stockholder list and began calling to solicit proxies in Bob's name, following up with letters written on company letterhead. The burden of the Morans' message was that mismanagement ruled at Treasure Salvors, and that Mel Fisher was no longer fit to direct the company. Bob Moran asked that he be elected President. When Bob called me, I urged him to stop his campaign, telling him that this proxy fight could seriously disrupt, even destroy the company. Later I found that Bob had called some of my friends and told them that I supported his efforts.

It was very near the meeting date before the Board majority learned of the Morans' scheme. We then immediately issued a letter to the stockholders, denying Bob and Marisha's right to do what they had done, and asking for fresh proxies from all the shareholders. As the battle mounted in intensity, and at just the right psychological moment, Bleth McHaley who had been gone for many months, returned to take part in the fight.

When the annual meeting began on December twelfth in a large meeting room at the Casa Marina, the camaraderie of past years was missing. There are a few dissident individuals in every group, and Treasure Salvors is no exception. But those stimulated by the Moran's calls and letters, had now joined together and had united with some larger stockholders to mount a serious challenge to Mel Fisher. It seemed that faith in Mel's ultimate success had worn thin. As the stockholders crowded around the meeting room entrance, Rose Chibbaro officially recorded those entering, collected proxies, and noted the proxies which had been sent by mail.

The Board majority had decided, after seeking legal advice, that the only way to handle such a thing was to face the issue of control head-on. This meant making the first order of business the election of a new Board. Mel, an easy-going chairman at any meeting, throughly disliked such a chore, but it had to be done. Loud, angry protest arose from the audience when the decision to vote first, without discussion, was announced. Marisha Moran came forward to complain. Bob stood up in his seat at the head of the table to ask his own election as president.

As the roll was called, many old associates' votes were cast against Mel and the Board majority. But there were also loyal supporters, who added their votes to those of the Fishers. The final tally, Rose Chibbaro announced at last, was five to three in Mel's favor.

Bob Moran, defeated, had to vacate his seat. Jud Chalmers, highly successful in business and of able and equable judgement, was the choice to fill the chair. But, as the meeting broke up, a bitter taste was left in many mouths. During this hard-fought proxy battle, many had openly questioned Mel Fisher's leadership. Mel and Deo must surely have been heartsick at all they had heard at the meeting, even though the final vote was in their favor. After that kind of experience, we all wondered, could the company possibly unite again to realize their goal?

XVIII. The Mother Lode

On the *Saba Rock*, it was Memorial Day, but there was no holiday from the unceasing pace of the diving. Since the weather had cleared, the treasure hunt had picked up momentum and changed its course once more. The giant tug was moored in Hawk Channel, more than a mile south of east from the bronze cannon, for Mel Fisher had again pushed the *Atocha* search out in that direction. Ed Stevens, skipper of the tug, worked with Captain Chip Clemons on *Bookmaker* to make detection runs at the end of the artifact trail. Soon Kane, commanding *Dauntless*, joined the group with a whole heart: he belived strongly in the deep water location of the Mother Lode. They had been led to the spot by a sparse trail of ballast stones, and had recently recovered barrel hoops and a single spike. But now many empty holes had been dug with nothing but modern debris to show for their effort. Still the work went on.

As Susan Nelson, Ed Steven's fiancee, told it, she was weary of diving day after day; Susan really did not want to suit up and work on Memorial Day. But once she had entered the water, she began to look around for Andy Matroci, who had preceded her dive by five minutes. Before she could locate Andy, her eye was caught by something on the bottom: it looked, she noted, like a "piece of yellow plastic." At once, the thought struck her that it must be a gold bar. She began to breathe rapidly in her excitement, rapidly using her air, almost hyperventilating. Then Susan spotted another bar, and another, and another. Immediately, she swam over to seek Andy; she brought him to the place to share her delight. In a rush they came to the surface to climb up aboard the *Saba Rock* and spread the word. Before dark the divers found thirteen gold bars.

Mel had heard the news on the radio, and hastened from Key West to the place by fast speedboat. He could instantly see the significance of the find — it could be a pointer back out to the Mother Lode. Thinking for a moment of something else, Mel asked the divers to keep a sharp lookout for emeralds.

No sooner suggested than found. The next day Syd Jones and K.T. (now his wife) then uncovered four small but dazzling pieces of gold jewelery of different designs, set with sixteen fine emeralds. More than four hundred silver coins were also fanned out of the sand.

That same day, Susan Nelson saw another glimpse of gold color, and put her mask down close to examine the find with more care. It was an exquisite gold chain, and she enjoyed its beauty awhile without disturbing it, wishing she had a camera to photograph it on the bottom.

Using the site as springboard, Mel sent his boats forward. As had so often occured in the past, however, the new energy generated out of the recoveries of Memorial Day did not endure, for the artifact trail petered out and died. The seekers' impetus seemed to ebb away. Some urged Mel to abandon his outward southeast thrust, return to the place where the Memorial Day finds were made, and re-establish the trail. An echo of Quicksands theory still hung in the air; after all, many, many valuable recoveries had been made there. One long-time company hand even voiced the opinion that *Atocha* must have gone right over the Quicksands into the Gulf, and that the search should be re-directed there.

But Duncan clung to his belief in the deeper-water theory, as did Mel and Kane. Mel refused to change his course. *Dauntless*, *Swordfish*, *Virgilona*, and *Saba Rock* continued to work their way to the southeast. Now they were in mid-Hawks Channel, heading for the far-distant outer reef. Passing northeast of the place where the outlying anchors had been found, they dove on anomalies charted in previous searches. The means of verifying the electronic contacts was meticulous and difficult: the circle search. This involved anchoring the salvage craft over the contact coordinates, and sending divers down. A two-man team then explored the radius around a block or other marker laid on the ocean floor, using hand-held pulse detectors. There were many of these anomalies to check out, unfortunately almost all of the wrong kind.

Time after time the targets proved to be crumpled, shell-encrusted World War II practice bombs. The bombs lay in eel-, manatee-, or turtle-grass over sand, or in hard mud bottom, but each one had to be checked out. Very few artifacts that might have been Spanish were found — a ballast stone here, a small shard there, a long ship-nail. I went twice to Spain that early summer; between my trips, Mel called me to inquire about the origin of a spike he had found on the trail. For identification purposes, I sent him a paper I had written on Spanish colonial nails. However, the evidence in hand was, in the eyes of many in the group, scanty. The trail, if it was indeed a trail, seemed very thin. But Mel never lost faith in it.

As the men and women in the boats labored on, the summer's best diving weather began to pass. Clear, calm water was replaced by choppy seas, as squalls and thunderstorms regularly appeared. One day a lowering cloud hung over the area of the search. As Tom Ford, now Captain of *Swordfish*, looked ahead, he saw it spawn one, then two waterspouts. From the cloud's belly they reached slim grey tendrils down to the surface of the sea. One column appeared to hang directly over *Saba Rock*. *Dauntless*, true to its name, moved closer to get a better look, while a third spout formed.

On July 18th, Mel sent Kane out to pursue the trail. The same day, *Swordfish's* men dived on a strong contact and found a heavily-encrusted iron mass. When they brought it on deck, they could at once see that it was an iron swivel-gun. Nearby, the divers located cannonballs and other ship relics, of the period of the 1622 ships. At the news of this, radio traffic between ships and their shore base became more intense. Back and forth across the miles Mel, his ship captains and Ed Little turned their attention to the scattering of other anomalies which lay further to the southeast. What was the meaning of this find, which lay far southeast beyond the Memorial Day area of discovery?

Now *Saba Rock* had gone into port with an engine casualty, and was stationed at dockside in Key West, where her bridge watch listened with frustrated interest to the stepped-up radio communications. Onsite, *Dauntless*, and *Swordfish* were engaged in taut competition as they hopscotched step by step down the trail.

The next day, almost a half-mile past the place where the swivel-gun was found, Kane Fisher leapfrogged the rival boat to follow a thin line of ballast. He directed *Dauntless* to the DelNorte bearings of an anomaly. As Kane and Steve Swindell were doing circle searches, they sighted a large, sixty-pound ballast stone of the Spanish colonial type. Then they detected barrel hoops and saw five copper ingots on the bottom. Next, they struck a pocket of almost a thousand silver coins. Very late on the evening of that day, as the light was rapidly fading, further "dusting" on the anomaly disclosed a sight that stopped the divers' breath, the sight they had been waiting for years to see: the telltale of a colonial shipwreck, a great mound of ballast stones, five feet high.

Back at the office, Ed Little asked Bleth: "Would you like to see the *Atocha*?" "Oh sure, sure, Ed," replied Bleth. But he brought her into the map room, and pointed to a sub-bottom profiler anomaly recorded long before. "There it is," said Ed.

"That is right where Kane is digging. He's on the Mother Lode."

Meantime, Kane had been trying to reach home base. *Dauntless'* radio had been tuned to the normal operating channel, but was too far away to raise Key West in those atmospheric conditions. *Swordfish*, still close by, had run out of ice and groceries, and was heading in. Kane therefore asked Tom Ford to relay his message. Tom tried, but could not reach Mel at the office or at his home; next he called Ted Miguel, who had a radio unit at home, and told him about the ballast pile. Leah, Syd and K.T. were also listening when the call came in, and Tom heard them shout together: *"What did he say?"*

Once refueled and supplied, *Swordfish* headed right back out.

The morning dawned in Key West with squalls of rain. Saturday, July 20, 1985 — ten years to the day after the deaths of Dirk and Angel Fisher and Rick Gage. When Mel came into the office, he called me in St. Augustine. After learning that I had not yet returned from Spain, he asked my daughter Beth to give me Friday's news, and said the divers were now east of the line the *Margarita* must have travelled.

Mel expressed his thought: the documents had told a story which now made sense — Bernardino de Lugo had looked east to see the *Atocha* sinking. Moreover, the depth in which Kane was working was about the same as that measured by Gaspar de Vargas. The Mother Lode must be nearby now.

Meanwhile, almost thirty miles from the office, operations began early despite the poor weather. The DelNorte navigating gear on *Dauntless* was not working well, and Kane Fisher had difficulty relocating his finds of the evening before. Other boats now arrived to help, and *Swordfish* had returned, joined by *Bookmaker* and *Virgilona*. When the spot was found again,

Tom Ford asked and received permission to tie up alongside Kane and take part. As his lines were made fast, a powerful squall line ran through the area; a hard rain pelted the little nest of salvage boats.

Greg Wareham, 26 years old, of Dubuque, Iowa, pulled on his wetsuit, shrugged into his airtanks, placed the regulator in his mouth, and dived from *Dauntless*. Water visibility was limited, but as Greg approached the bottom, fifty-four feet down, something filled his whole field of vision. He saw heaps of oblong objects, stacked high in a thirty-foot long mass. He drew closer. The metal detector hung from his wrist screamed. The objects were, he suddenly realized, silver bars. Hundreds and hundreds of silver bars. "There," he said, "was a big pile of silver. It was what I expected to see, but I was surprised that I found it." Bringing his fellow diver, Andy Matroci, over, he pointed out the silver reef to him. Exulting, both men then popped up from the water shouting, trying to get someone's attention. "We found it! We found it!" they cried.

Kane Fisher, picking up the microphone, told home base: "Throw away the charts — put the charts away — we've got it! Silver bars — we've got it!" Then everyone from all the boats who could dive went into the water. Down they went, into the place where Gaspar de Vargas had sounded on the sunken *Almiranta* three hundred sixty-three years before, sinking into fifty-four feet of water.

Putting down the micorphone at the office, Mel felt a swirl of emotions. The missing segment of *Atocha's* last ride, the resting place of her main treasure mass, was now known. The Mother Lode had been found. He told a reporter: "Today it looks like we came to the end of the rainbow and saw the pot of gold. It's been a gigantic 16-year jigsaw puzzle. The feeling today is...like when you put in the last piece."

Almost instantaneously, news of the Mother Lode radiated outward from the Treasure Slavors office through its three telephones to wire services, the television networks, the National Geographic Society, and to scores of friends, investors, and stockholders. At the same time, the radios were closely monitored to keep track of the latest word from the boats offshore.

When, shortly afterwards, Kane radioed his father again to ask permssion to "bring up a couple of bars," it was clearly a crucial point. Concerned about disturbing the integrity of the site, Bleth had an immediate reaction: "No." Mel, however, overruled her and gave his assent. What resulted at the site, however, was quite different. Between the feverish glow which the treasure pile induced in those who saw it, their haste to bring it up, and competition among the salvage boats, divers actually brought up more than a hundred of the ingots. Proper procedures for the recording of data *in situ* were largely forgotten. Even if Duncan had been there to try and impose some kind of order, it might not have been possible. The excitement was too intense.

On Sunday, a day between storms, water clarity improved, and the outside world descended upon the site of the Mother Lode. Early in the morning, Mel sped out to the Marquesas, taking with him everyone who could be spared from the office, thirty-two bottles of champagne and a case of plastic champagne cups. As he approached the salvage vessels tossing at anchor over the Mother Lode, Mel could see that they were outnumbered by a whole bobbing squadron of small craft. The little boats had been chartered by media representatives, eager to see the treasure at first hand. When those aboard the ragtag fleet saw Mel about to board, he was welcomed with shouts and cheers such as few victorious Admirals have ever received from their assembled ships.

Duncan Mathewson, who had come with Mel, quickly suited up to dive. As he prepared to go overside, Duncan was thrilled, but somewhat aprehensive. He, too, knew the heady feeling of victory after long struggle. But he also realized that the

Mother Lode represented a one-time opportunity for archeology. At this moment of chaos and triumph, could the opportunity still be realized, or was it already too late?

As Duncan and a host of other observers dived and fanned out above the Mother Lode, they could begin to see the whole site in more detail than was possible the day before. They saw a section of large wooden timbers from the sunken galleon. Next to the ballast pile was the silver reef — estimated at thirty tons and more of silver bars. To the suspended watchers, said Tom Ford, the bar mass looked like "the foundations of a building — the ingots were laid in regular patterns." They could discern where some divers were working to recover ingots and, beyond that, where others were fanning out multiple thousands of silver coins. These areas were successively oriented along an axis which ran roughly north-northwest by south-southeast.

Still farther inshore on the site lay hundreds of copper ingots tossed carelessly by the 1622 hurricanes, lying among large ballast stones. Studded in the mound were two intact Spanish olive jars, once used for oil, wine or water by the crew, soldiers, or passengers of the *Atocha*. For his part, Duncan was struck and overwhelmed with the responsibility for the task. How and where could he best begin?

Mel could immediately see that the weight of recovered silver was almost too much for the *Dauntless* to hold. He gave orders that some of the silver bars be transferred to *Swordfish* and other vessels, pending their shipment to Key West.

Then a boat carrying Jimmy Buffett came alongside the nested salvage ships. Jimmy, long a friend of the company, had come to see the treasure and celebrate its finding. The singer climbed to the deck, while Mel called to the crewmen to help build twin thrones of silver bars for Buffett and himself. Jimmy played for the crew their triumph song. As the guitar rang out, champagne spilled on *Dauntless'* rusty deck, over the bare feet and the silver. Mel at once knew the mystery solved, the circle closed between his own time and that of Francisco Nunez Melian. Now the promised treasure lay open before him, as massive and valuable as he had always believed it would be. It was his. Raising his glass, Mel repeated again and again the only words he could muster: "Fantabulous! Fantabulous!"

That afternoon, I was just returning from Madrid to St. Augustine, where we now lived. Since my flight home from New York was delayed, I stayed Saturday night at a motel near Kennedy airport. When I finally arrived home Sunday, I had heard nothing about the finding of the treasure. Beth greeted me downstairs, and asked if I had heard any good news. When I replied "No," she told me to go upstairs where her mom would have some to tell me. Dot took the greatest pleasure in saying: "Mel has found his Mother Lode at last." A powerful emotion poured over me: overwhelming thankfulness that the effort had ended in victory for Mel, and for us all. Immediatey I called Key West, where Deo recounted all that had happened. Even while I tried to grapple mentally with the sheer size and drama of the find, some intuition told me that the seekers had now entered another, far different phase. In this new dimension, the *Atocha* was sure to disclose to us wider, richer meanings than we had yet seen.

Down in Key West the mood of exaltation spread. Other reactions came: Don Kincaid said "I'm a millionaire!" John Brandon, who had cut off his long hair to fulfill a long-standing vow about the Mother Lode, stood to gain as much as Don. Dave Horan, quoted by the Key West *Citizen*, said that he would now pay off the mortgage on his new home. Many other mortgages were paid off in imagination that night. Near the museum, the Two Friends bar hosted a nonstop Treasure Salvors party, where the song until dawn was: "We're in the money!"

"Cincinnati Jim" Vondehaar, who had called Key West every single day for years to check on the progress of the search, wrote another poem, in mingled joy and recollection:

"Disappointment, heartache, sorrow and tears;
Just part of the price Mel paid through the years."

While the wire services thrummed out the astonishing headline: "Mel Fisher finds $400,000,000 treasures," all the major network evening news programs prepared to feature the *Atocha* story. Mel was scheduled on the three big morning talk shows, but the first, the "Today" show, did not turn out quite as planned in New York. The arrangements, Bryant Gumbal assumed, were all in place to pick Mel up live at the Treasure Salvors office early on Monday, July 22. But none could find him. While the anchorman stalled for time on live broadcast, staffers desperately searched throughout the building. Finally Mel came on camera, seated on silver bars in front of a bronze cannon at the entrance to the museum. As Mel attempted to answer questions, it was apparent that he was still half awash from the all-day and all-night celebration. The interview was mercifully short. But the publicity blitz had just begun.

The Mother Lode story became a frenzy, a media madness. There were *New York Times* headlines, then front page stories for three days. Articles immediately went forward for early release in *Time*, *Newsweek*, *U.S. News*, and *Life*. One of Earnest Hemmingway's granddaughters was commissioned to write an article for *Playboy* magazine. It was virtually impossible to raise anything but a busy signal in any of the company's multiple phones. Bleth even pressed reporters into service to man them.

Nicholas Wade, who had written about Treasure Salvors for *Science* magazine years before, composed a piece for the Editorial Notebook of the *New York Times*. Reviewing the whole adventure, Wade pointed out how Mel had fought many court actions against acquisitive governments, and had prevailed. Most of the sharks Fisher had encountered, Wade concluded, were to be found on land. He closed with the statement "Against many odds, Philip IV's loss has become the public's gain." Dr. George Bass, the noted marine archaeologist, was quoted as saying: "From what I've heard it sounds like a spectacular find. It is a special thing to find an intact cargo that can give a picture of 17th century exploration in the New World."

As the publicity spread locally and nationally, visitors thronged the museum by the hundreds, then by the thousands.

Despite the frenzied office activity, wrecksite operations enjoyed a respite the next two days, for on Monday and Tuesday the area was swept by the winds and rains of Tropical Storm Bob. While the boats were in port, a welcome breathing spell afforded time to better plan the operations, free of the silver fever that had raged at the wrecksite on the first two days.

To help him deal with the massive challenge of the *Atocha's* main deposit, Duncan had to assemble a team of additional archaeologists, and quickly. It would not be easy to find professionals ready to risk their reputations by collaborating with a treasure salvor. But Duncan was able to persuade Dr. James Bellis of the University of Notre Dame, and Dr. John Dorwin, an archaeologist from Indiana who had a consulting firm, to come to Key West. Moreover, Walter Zacharchuk, highly experienced in underwater archaeology through work with Dr. George Bass and Parks Canada, also agreed to help. Nancy Demyttenaere, a very able conservator from the American Museum of Natural History, came to aid in the massive conservation effort which confronted Duncan and Jim Sinclair. Duncan added Bill Schwicker of Big Pine Key to his group, since Bill, a boatbuilder, could contribute greatly to the interpretation of wooden artifacts from the *Atocha's* hull structure. Michael Marken, a Californian who was in a doctoral program at St. Andrew's University in Scotland, arrived to undertake a study of the galleon's ceramic collection.

Duncan's game plan was to assemble a grid to use on the wrecksite; the first one built proved to be too large and awkward for use where many divers from several boats were working busily on the Mother Load. After some heated discussion on the salvage boats, in which Mel had eventually to take a hand, it was agreed that proper archaeological standards should be imposed. A smaller grid and a baseline were prepared, and airlifts were used on the Mother Lode instead of the more destructive mailbox.

On Friday, July twenty-sixth, some of the divers spread out over the shipwreck mound and encountered eight intact silver coin chests. The fused coin masses in several of the chests were enclosed with their cedar sides: one of them still had its intact wooden lid. Further down the ballast pile, they discovered 13 gold bars, bits and discs in a heap. Meanwhile, those divers engaged in raising ingots from the silver reef had struggled to bring up the heavy bars one by one to the surface. To correct this, Steve Candela worked late to fabricate heavy-gauge steel baskets; he had them onsite the next day. Now the workers could haul up silver bars and chests of coins much more quickly and safely.

Boatloads of silver bars and buckets and ice-chests of loose coins were sent inshore. To reach more items on the site the divers brought out a wheelbarrow to trundle the cumbersome ballast stones underwater down a plank runway to clear the site.

As Bill Moore of *Dauntless* held the mouth of his bucking airlift to an area rich in barrel hoops and other artifacts, it began to suck a dusty cloud from around a stack of objects. At first they seemed a pile of sticks but, as the sand arose in a cloud around them, Bill realized that they were gold bars. He had found what must once have been a chest of gold, with seventy-six bars! When I saw the company people after these finds, I reminded them that what we were to look for now was emeralds. There seemed little else that the *Atocha* might yield.

Now Donny Jonas, who had barely escaped with his life from the sinking *Northwind*, had come onsite with the steel ship *J.P. Magruder*; Dick Kloudt was his first mate. R.D. LeClair soon joined in *Virgilona*.

In Washington, on Monday, July 29, 1985, Senator Paula Hawkins entered a statement into the *Congressional Record*. For her Florida constituents and for all Americans, she expressed her pride in Mel Fisher, and went on to say "My interest in all this lies less in the fact of Mel's success — although he surely deserves his rewards — than in the realization that our Nation still has such people, and that we still permit determined men and women to pursue such dreams, to success or failure."

It soon appeared that a challenge was to be laid down to the Mother Lode. Richard Lightner was the last of the litigants who sought to claim rights in or near the remains of *Nuestra Senora de Atocha*. His case, filed some time before, had been continued and now came before Judge Sydney Aronovitz of the Federal District Court. We felt the case came at an opportune time, and welcomed the test. Dave, his partner Rick Bannon, Bleth, Josh Morse and Bill Vandercreek felt it advisable to put the challenges to rest for once and for all.

During the first hearing at the courtroom in Key West, Judge Aronovitz expressed his wish to see the silver bars in person, to obtain an idea of the nature and extent of the treasure on which he would have rule. Eager to see the Mother Lode recoveries, I had come to Key West and, late in the morning of July 29, I hastened to the office. There Taffi gave me a list of the ingots which had been cleaned, and their markings as she had deciphered them. I went to the museum's main exhibit room, where an immense pile of silver ingots, more than three hundred blackened bars, lay on the floor. There I labored to move and examine other bars to record their marks and compare them with the cargo manifest. As I peered at the markings of the blackened ingots and rubbed the edges of the marks to make them clearer, my notebook was smudged with sooty fingerprints.

In the afternoon, Judge Aronovitz, Dave Horan, and Lightner's attorney came to the museum. We gathered before the silver pile amidst a buzzing crowd of tourists, photographers and reporters. As camera flashes flared, I demonstrated how the bar markings disclosed their serial marking, silver fineness, and origin and destination, and how these tied to the manifest of the *Atocha*. Pat Clyne recorded the scene on videotape. The next day, in court, I testified much the same: that the Mother Lode bars were identical with those that had been loaded aboard the *Atocha*. With my copy of the translated manifest in hand, I noted the matches on the bars — numbers 3885, 1090, 4794, 3709, 523, 4176, 4884; the last bore the famous Arriola mark, and was shipped by Lorenzo de Arriola himself. It was then brought out that both ends of the long treasure trail had contained similarly verified ingots; the *Atocha* had been definitively identified by marks inscribed on the ingots she bore.

After exhaustive pleadings, in which Dave Horan laid out the case with all his drive and skill, Judge Aronovitz ruled for Mel Fisher and Treasure Salvors, granting an exclusive right for two years to the entire six-mile-long wrecksite.

When the decision was announced, Bleth realized that the Lightner case marked the end of ten years of litigation. It was, she told me, "the most fascinating period of my life...but it was fun." It was also, she could have added, ten years of travail. From the County Court to the Supreme Court, it had been ten years of hearings, motions, trials and judgements.

For Mel Fisher, however, it was time to have some fun. He had been invited to appear on the Johnny Carson show, and flew to Hollywood. Onstage, after the call: "Heeeeeeeerre's Johnny!" rang out, the star appeared, bowing to the applause. When Mel had also been introduced, and had taken a seat alongside Carson, he proceeded to upstage the master. After putting a gold chain around Johnny Carson's neck, Mel replied to his host's question about the value of the treasure by saying it might pay Carson's alimony for one month. Then he launched a homespun plea that his viewers notify their Congressional representatives to protect private enterprise treasure salvage. As an aftermath to his appearance, Mel invited Johnny Carson to come to Key West and dive on the *Atocha*, which he did the following month.

Shortly after the Carson show, Bleth master-minded Treasure Hunt Week, a major national promotion for Key West. As prizes, Mel Fisher put up one of his own gold bars from an earlier *Atocha* division, and a local jeweler provided an emerald worth $10,000. Many clues were furnished for the entrants, and a number of persons joined in to find the treasure. But celebration was about to come to an end, as a kind of treasure backlash began.

In a situation very nearly like our experience in 1973, the Mother Lode discovery elicited an eventual negative reaction from a variety of sources. These second thoughts included an article in *McLean's*, where *Newsday* writer Fred Bruning presented Mel as a creature of media hype, a type of audacious hero now in vogue. He was portrayed as a huckster who cared not one whit for the scholarly values which Sony Cockrell had expressed to the writer of the article.

Next, a Miami *Herald* article pointed to the delay that might take place in the division process with investors, and described the many types of investor that Mel had dealt with over the years. Then *Money* magazine printed an article, heavy with innuendo about Treasure Salvors. It implied that Mel Fisher had practiced chicanery in funding his salvage, and featured a full-page picture of a grinning Mel, festooned with loops of gold chain. It was if this writer were saying: "Would you buy a used shipwreck from this man?"

Shortly after that, the news came that the Florida State Banking Board and the Securities and Exchange Commission had opened inquiries into Mel's financial operations. Mel, Deo and the other directors could also sense the approach of a substancial tax problem, which might affect the corporation as well as the ultimate recipients of the treasure. Treasure Salvors again retained John Dougherty of Hogan and Hartson to advise and represent them on tax and securities matters.

As the fall and winter weather approached, Duncan and his staff came to examine the remaining hull of the *Atocha*. Bill Schwicker swam slowly over the timbers, examined them at close range, and studied the scale drawings which detailed their dimensions. He could see that the galleon had been a broad, deep-draft vessel, of relatively short length relative to her wide beam, and with a flat deadrise. He saw evidence of the terrible trauma of the shipwreck and the second hurricane which had wrenched the hull apart: he observed keel-bolts sheared right off, but no keel was found. It was if, said Bill Schwicker, the vessel had been "gutted with a knife like a mackerel."

The archeologists decided to protect the hull timbers of the *Atocha* against the winds and rains to come, and covered them with a shroud of heavy plastic. At first, it appeared that the bulk of the treasure had come up. But then a tiny gold falcon was found, six more gold bars, and another two silver ingots. The *Atocha* had still other surprises for us: the cargo which might eventually characterize the *Atocha* more than any other precious thing found. In a small area, less than a hundred feet square, the men began to find small oblong green crystals. At first, these looked so ordinary that only the experienced divers, who had seen them before, relized what they were — uncut emeralds. First they located a few, then a number, and finally a great number. Now the divers began to fan the sand gently by hand, in order to avoid missing the small objects. Mel now recalled that he had once seen a document, he believed shown him by Art McKee, mentioning a chest of emeralds loaded aboard the *Atocha*. I told Mel that they were certainly not listed on the legal manifest of the galleon.

In four short, stressed months, the company had wrought

incredibly to recover, enumerate, preserve and prepare to divide, a vast treasure. By November, Treasure Salvors had spent hundreds of thousands of dollars to meet security needs and expand its preservation facilities.

At Judge Aronovitz' direction, Federal Marshals had to come to Key West to dictate requirements for the security of the treasure operations. Since the treasure was the Court's responsibility until adjudicated, the Judge wanted no slip-ups. The Marshals studied the situation at the wrecksite, and suggested that the company provide an armed escort craft to transport the recovered treasure back to Key West. They made particular recommendations for its security there.

Now Mel's museum building was surrounded by a high chain-link fence with barbed wire; two guards patrolled its perimeter twenty-four hours a day. Inside, more guards kept watch and tended a sophisticated electronic alarm system. In early November, I visited Key West and was ushered into the offices, which had been relocated to provide for higher security. Like any visitor who penetrated the outer layers of protection, I was under surveillance. In the laboratories, in rows of tanks, I saw coins, ingots and silver pieces being cleaned by electrolysis. At the door of a third-floor room I entered the Holy of Holies, a sanctuary of treasures, protected by its own guard outside the door. Inside, the most precious things were kept in their own vault, and removed only for listing, photographing, or study.

Preservationist Jim SInclair carried a heavy load, but approached his duties with zest. He remained in fascination at the variety of artifacts which had come in from the wrecksite. Colonel Robert Green, a Key West resident who was a specialist in antique silver, had also lent his considerable talents to the analysis of the silverware. Jud Chalmers presented a newly-published Spanish work on colonial Hispanic silverware to the company, and I ordered other works for Col. Green from Madrid. Henry Taylor, a Spanish colonial coin expert who had worked on the *Concepcion* finds seven years before, was now aiding the company in setting up the momentous task of cleaning more than a hundred thousand coins. Pat Clyne photographed each and every item. Elsa Pedersen and Sandy McKinney studied each gold or silver coin as it was cleaned and ready for classification and grading.

To manipulate this mass of treasure, the sheer quantity of which had not been experienced before by any salvage firm, it was necessary to have recourse to computerized handling. Mel signed a contract with Michael and Mark Carlson to provide a system of entry and control of the recovered *Atocha* artifacts. This program also generated certificates of authenticity, and provided for an audit trail for tagged materials from salvage boat logs through the preservation process until their final delivery date to their ultimate owners. Soon and entire bank of computers were clicking and whirring as the treasure moved securely from the cleaning area into company records. As items were recorded, the smallest and most precious were then placed in the adjoining vault sanctuary. By the time of my visit, they had carefully processed and stored one hundred ninety-nine emeralds.

Ah, the emeralds! Michael Marcial, an expert from Colombia now resident in Key West, had examined each of them meticulously. He pronounced them to be of superb quality, from the Muzo mines of Colombia, where clarity and deep color reigned as the chief criteria of value. "But," as he explained to the Board of Directors, "these stones do not sparkle like diamonds, with outer light reflecting from cut facets; emeralds' fire arises from within. Many of those who see them develop a *la fiebre verde* — the green fever — do you feel it?"

Marcial explained that the *Atocha* collection was so valuable that, if we continued to find emeralds on the site, they might soon surpass the gold and silver in value. To date, the largest of the stones weighed 77 carats, but the finest, of 27 carats, might yield a cut emerald of perhaps 15 carats, which could be worth half a million dollars. If, said Marcial, you covered your palm with smaller stones, you held in your hand more than a million dollars' worth.

When I asked Kane Fisher how he could recover such tiny precious stones from the sands of the *Atocha*, he merely laughed, saying that he had developed a "green thumb."

The changes taking place in the company were evident at the meeting of the Division Committee on November fourteenth. Although Mel was present and took active part, it was clear that the new generation of Fishers were coming into their own. Taffi and Kim served on the Committee, which Taffi directed very effectively. Also present were staffers of Treasure Salvors, and representatives of the major investing groups whose funds had made the venture possible. The aim of the Committee was to devise means for the fair distribution of the *Atocha* treasure; this involved many complex questions, including that of the rights of the company stockholders, and the possibility of holding together enough of the artifacts to provide a viable museum collection.

As the Division Committee examined the lists which Taffi Fisher presented, the mass of the Mother Lode took shape before us. Since the first of January, a very great treasure had been recovered.

Buoyed up incredibly by the location of the Mother Lode, Mel Fisher appeared now to have no bounds upon his spirit. Even though he had found the main body of his treasure, it seemed impossible for Mel to turn off his proclivity to wheel and deal. He was vied from every side. Where no backers or studios would consider it a few months before, a major studio and a large network had battled for the right to film his life story. It was finally decided that CBS would do a for-television movie, and Mel received a large lump-sum payment for the rights to use his name and life story in the film. He sold an interest in his share of the treasure for a substantial sum. Mel had been interviewed by *Rolling Stone* magazine, appeared in the *Saturday Evening Post*, had received a proposal to lend his name to a floating casino, and had been approached to be a partner in a Caribbean resort. He and Deo had travelled to Peru to examine treasure possibilities there, and had appeared in Rome on Italian national television.

As December drew to a close, over 300 emeralds had been brought to Key West from the salvage boats. Word came in that another nearby ballast area was uncovered. It yielded more copper ingots and silver coins. Perhaps more would still be found; we estimated that a number of ingots and coin, together with a quantity of gold still remained undiscovered.

The new year of 1986 began, the seventeenth of the search for the *Atocha*. Although the Mother Lode had been found, Mel's boats and divers had continued to ply the area. They had in fact surpassed their previous working schedules, keeping on site through much of the fall and part of the winter of 1985-1986.

The company stockholders who gathered in Key West in January came in a far different mood than at the end of 1984, their last meeting. Because of the finding of the Mother Lode, they were all sharers in Mel Fisher's fame. They heard reports from Mel and others. They viewed a videotape of the silver reef as the divers had first seen it the previous July.

Now the problems confronting Mel's company were those which attended sudden and great prosperity: the likely tax liability. John Dougherty of Hogan and Hartson, told the shareholders of the options open to them. A new director took his place at the Board table: Doug Douglas, a young Chattanooga builder who had come to live in Key West, fallen under the spell of Mel Fisher, and invested in the treasure enterprise. At the meeting's end, Charles Luria, a substancial Virginia businessman, rose on behalf of the other stockholders to propose a resolution of tribute to Mel Fisher for the success realized.

Filming of the CBS movie began in the Virgin Islands in the spring of 1986. Cliff Robertson and Loretta Swit portrayed Mel and Deo, while the figure of Moe Milinar became an important one in the drama. At the same time, another film, made by the National Geographic Society, was released. This television performance, which utilized some of the footage of the original Geographic movie of 1976, was entitled *Atocha: Quest for Treasure*. Its preview took place in Key West on March 19. Since it was the first of the National Geographic series to appear on the Turner Broadcasting network, it appeared on WTBS nationwide three times, later in March. This film was magnificently done, and was reported later in the year to be in line for an Academy award, since it was shown at a number of film festivals.

But the outstanding event of the New Year was the immense job done by the whole staff in processing nearly one hundred fifty thousand items — the whole of the 1985 treasure. In little over a year the artifacts had been salvaged, recorded, preserved, studied, photgraphed, and entered into the computers at company headquarters.

The division committee, meeting seven times under Taffi's leadership, had prepared the vast treasure for division with the investors. As a committee member, I watched as strong points of view expressed by the diverse interest represented were substancially reconciled. After many months of hearing appraisals and discussing the relative values of the different categories of treasure, we finally agreed on point values. Touche, Ross and Co., a major accounting firm, was retained to supervise and audit the 1985 division, which was to be done by computer selection for randomly selected investors and stockholders. What was this treasure?

115 gold bars, disk, and bits — more than two hundred pounds of gold.

Twenty gold chains, or parts of chains.

Sixty-seven gold coins.

Six pieces of gold jewelry, some set with emeralds.

A quantity of bezoar stones in a small chest, two set with silver.

The emeralds — 315 of them, ranging in size from 1/2 to 77 carats. These had now been appraised by five separate experts, and their quality and characteristics were well known: the famous Muzo emeralds from modern Colombia, the colonial Nueveo Reino de Granada.

The coined silver was impressive, both in quantity and quality. There were a hundred fourteen thousand loose silver coins of two, four and eight. Eleven large coin masses, still encrusted into the form of the chests which originally held them, were to be divided as they were. It was estimated that these held an additional twenty-two thousand silver coins.

The coins came from many mints, some struck as early as the 1550's. Two hundred coins had been set aside as types of all varities in the collection. A number of these rare coins were unique in the world. More than 1600 were rare in the assembalge of *Atocha* coins.

969 silver bars constituted the heaviest mass of treasure — thirty-two tons of ingots. Some were ninety pounds in weight. As these bars had been cleaned of the sulfides which coated their surfaces, additional markings had come to light. As Mike Riccio studied the bars in the laboratory and compared them with the manifest book my brother Homer had created, he was able to identify the large majority of ingots. The connections these identifications made permitted the seventeenth century to live again, as they vividly embodied the rich fabric of personal, commercial, governmental and religious transactions in the Spanish trans-Atlantic trade.

Three hundred five copper ingots had been recovered, The irregularly shaped slabs had been furnished to the Spanish Crown by contractor Juan de Eguiluz, brought by small craft around Cuba from Santiago, and shipped on the *Atocha* from Havana. They had come from the same copper-mining area where the apparition of Cuba's patron saint, Caridad del Cobre, had first been seen, and where her shrine now is. One should rather say of her shrines, for the exiled Cubans in Miami have now built another, pending that day in which they might return to their homeland.

We had found 599 artifacts of other kinds. There was a large quantity of silverware, some gold-plated: bowls, candlesticks, sanders, beakers and pitches, salt-cellars, winebottles, alter- and other religious ware. There I was particularly struck by the fragile beauty of the *Atocha's* silverware. Classic lions chased each other around the rim of delicate beakers; lovely gold-plated tableware vied for a viewer's attention with two perfectly-preserved sets of wine and water cruets for the Mass. Althuogh some plates had been irreparably damaged by time and the sea, many were almost new in appearance. A gilded plate bore a motif of Paramus and Thysbe, two lovers from the tales of Ovid.

One silver plate, in excellent condition, became for me a vibrant recollection of the human dimensions of the *Atocha*. On its reverse was scratched the name "Dona Ysabel." The name seemed a familiar one; searching I found it on the manifest of silver plate shipped on the galleon. Dona Ysabel de Pernia had sent thirty-five pounds of silverware from Portobelo, consigned to herself in Spain. Although she had not sailed the *Atocha*, this noblewoman's own prized table plate had been lost in the Marquesas, along with that of other wealthy or titled persons: Martin de Salgado, Lorenzo de Arriola, and the Marquis of Oropesa.

Colonel Green pointed out to us that Spanish religious and secular silverware from the early 17th century was rare to a point of non-existence in the world of collectors, and that the *Atocha* silver was therefore almost priceless in value. Jim Sinclair began to study the Inca influence visible in some of the Peruvian silver found in the galleon.

The religious artifacts reflected the rich diversity of the Catholic Church at that time — and its almost bewildering number of religious orders, confraternities, personal and corporate devotions. They spoke of a Counter-Reformation Church, led by a renewed Papacy strengthening itself for its tasks. We were particularly fortunate at this juncture to have the aquaintance of George Spruck of Cincinnati, who took special pains to examine and interpret the religious materials in the collection. In turn, he put the company in touch with the Sacred Museum of the Vatican, which expressed an interest in the artifacts.

In addition to the 1985 treasure which was shortly to be divided, the *Atocha* site had yielded much more in the new year. Late in April *Dauntless'* divers brought up a small wooden box, some five inches square, from a spot near the Mother Lode area. Mel brought it to New York, where it was opened with great ceremony on the CBS morning news show. Gently Mel and Cliff Robertson raised the lid, to find it crammed with five tangled gold chains. In each of the four corners of the box, the Spanish owner had packed a stack of silver coins.

On the site, additional silver and gold bars and gold chains were also found, with several thousand more pieces of eight. Up northwest, near the 1985 Memorial Day site, more precious items of gold jewelery turned up in one day — fifty-eight brooches or pins, set with emeralds. Many other artifacts of interest were also found, including a lovely tiny gold spoon, with the likeness of a woman's head upon it. The major story of the year, however, was the bonanza of late May, 1986, which was to lead to the great emerald find.

Back southeast, a short distance to the south of the place where the silver pile had been, divers recovered a large wooden chest that was almost intact: only its cover was missing. They concluded that it must have been the sea-chest of the *Atocha's* drowned pilot, Martin Jimenez, for it held a wealth of navigational instruments. Within was another fine astrolabe, in virtually perfect condition, together with five sets of pilot's dividers, a sunwatch with an ivory face and a cross-staff. The chest also contained a large, high quality emerald, 1400 silver and eight gold coins, and two long gold chains. Nearby on the ocean floor lay three more astrolabes! Two of the navigational instruments were dated and in virtual mint condition. It was generally believed, says Bleth, that what was located next may have also come originally from the chest, for it was all found within a compass of a few feet.

Only a week remained of the month of May when Donny Jonas manuevered the *Magruder* over the ocean floor and anchored. Her men began to stir the sands on the bottom with an airlift. Since they had found more than two hundred emeralds the day before, their attention was riveted upon the smallest things which might appear amid the swirling sands. All at once, the divers found themselves in a green rain, as emeralds showered down upon them from the top of the airlift tube. The head had struck a large pocket of the precious stones. When they had all been gathered, 2,300 had been found that day, bringing the total of emeralds recovered on the wrecksite to more than three thousand. When they were brought to Mel in a filled quart jar, he chortled with delight.

These and other riches recovered led to continued consideration of the question of tax liability for the company and its stockholders. After study, attorney John Dougherty recommended to the Board that we consider the dissolution of the corporation. Otherwise, he warned, the total tax that might be levied upon the treasure would be virutally confiscatory — it could conceivably take three-quarters of the materials. The Board approved this recommendation, and the stockholders verified it in a special meeting in June.

The dissolution of the corporation certainly met with Mel Fisher's approval. He had succeeded in his goals, was throughly tired of the burdens of the company he had operated for so many years, and was ready to turn his attention elsewhere. But the decision brought other questions in its train. There remained the issue of continuing to preserve those materials not yet completely through the conservation process. It also highlighted the problem of the museum collections: should they be parcelled out to stockholders along with the other company assets, or should an exhibit be formed to display the *Atocha* artifacts for a period of time?

As the possible end of the corporation approached, Duncan and I here became increasingly concerned with future public access to the treasure. We wished to make it possible for the recipients of artifacts to donate them to museums, in Florida and elsewhere. It was also suggested that the *Atocha's* ceramic collection — more than nine thousand items — be donated to a Florida museum. Mel himself made the largest single donation: he transferred a full one per cent interest from his share in the 1985 treasure to the Mel Fisher Maritime Heritage Society.

Late in the summer Duncan's book *The Treasure of the Atocha* was released. This significant book represented many things. Duncan's success in the analysis of the shipwreck trail back to the Mother Lode and his justification in the war between academics were emphasized in the publication of this perceptive work. It served as source document and textbook in marine archaeology. The book also produced the best record of the salvage effort: all those who had worked with Mel, the boats which had sailed out of Key West for the Marquesas sites, the office staff, the exhibits they had produced — all were listed. The book's color reproductions were indeed lovely, constituting the most full and meaningful view of the treasure yet presented to a national reading audience.

The weekend of September 13 was special for Mel's investors. They had been invited to Key West for a premier showing of the CBS film "Dreams of Gold." Boatloads of friends and investors were ferried to the wrecksite on a specially chartered boat where they watched divers working the Mother Lode, over closed-circuit television. They flocked to the museum, where they could see the whole treasure for the last time before the division. That night, the Martello Towers historical museum and gardens were turned over to Treasure Salvors for a premiere party.

The film was screened at the new Tennessee Williams theatre on the Community College Campus. Before the lights went down, Mel came on stage to address the audience. He told the viewers that he had seen the movie, and that he had both laughed and cried during the performance. Mel added that he thought that the viewers would enjoy it as much as he had. "Dreams of Gold" featured the story of Mel, Deo and their children and their family treasure adventure. It proved highly dramatic, particularly in the scenes which recounted the death of the young people in 1975. After the showing the next week in the Kennedy Center, the movie was scheduled to air on CBS television on November 15. Mel would see the fulfillment of his long-held dream: he and Deo would be portrayed by Hollywood stars in a nation-wide television movie.

As the time approached for the division, a legal challenge arose, as a long-forgotten claim surfaced. In North Florida, an attorney obtained an injunction to halt the company's find of the Mother Lode. Dave Horan and Mel made a settlement, and the division could proceed.

On Monday, October 13th, 1986, Mel, a large crowd of employees, investors, and media representatives filled the computer room at Treasure Salvors' office. Cake and punch were served, and Mel prepared to begin the division. The he stepped aside, and motioned for Taffi Fisher to do the honors. At 2 P.M., she pressed the key that began to run the largest treasure division in modern times. Now the computer would grind at top speed for sixteen hours to apportion out the 2,500 page inventory of precious artifacts. To print out the recipients' division sheets would take more than three days. Slowly, the crowd dispersed, leaving reporters and camera crews to get individual interviews to fill out their stories. They all wanted Mel, but he had gone. Where was Mel Fisher? "Has he wandered away again,?" asked Bleth.

Mel had indeed gone, through the side office door, across the storeroom, and into the museum by a rear entrance. Quiet for once, the museum was empty except for the guards. Mel's gaze flickered over the silver ingots stacked along the walls, the treasures displayed in lighted cases — the gold belt, the golden salver, the emerald cross, the shining bars and chains, the emeralds, glowing dull green. All this. So hard won, so lately found, so soon to be dispersed. He sat heavily in the ticket-takers chair, unseeing. In imagination he made the journey once more. Again he left the harbor, traveled the look-alike islands, passed Boca Grande and started across the wide channel to the Marquesas, shining olive-green in the sun. Beyond, he knew, lay the outer reef and the big shoal, where the sea had swallowed so many people, so many ships. He recalled the loss: more than five hundred...Garcia de Nodal, Lorenzo de Arriola, the merchant Rojas...Dirk, Angel and Rick. Before him appeared all the seekers — Vargas and Cardona, Melian, Webber and Haskins, Holloway, Ted, Bob. In tortuous remembrance he retraced the journey of fifteen years, his path from the great sandbar to Dirk's cannon, out to Kane's trail to the Mother Lode.

Mel shook his head, as if to shake off those years, to clear his mind forever of those things. Far too long they had bound him to the Marquesas, tied him to the galleons of 1622. Now that he had found them, it was finished. It was time for him to move along. He could go now to that Caribbean island where Montezuma's treasure lay; Art McKee had almost died down there looking for it. He would go back to Peru, to the lake near that cave, and find the lost gold of Atahualpa. Surely he would get a contract to salvage the rich wrecks of Spain. He could dive on the Colossus of Rhodes. Why, all the world was his. Tomorrow would be the day.

The waning late afternoon sun spread golden light across the choppy water, as winds from an early cold front pushed breaking waves over the wrecksite. Three buoys tugged at their lines, bobbing over the place of the Mother Lode. At a short distance, a green spar marked the emerald bonanza of four months before. Unseen, almost four miles away to the northwest, was the spot where Dirk's bronze cannons had lain; beyond that, the Bank of Spain in the Quicksands. Perhaps the treasure that the galleons had carried had been largely found and excavated. But it was more likely that great wealth still remained, scattered beneath the waters where the *Nuestra Senora de Atocha* and the *Santa Margarita* sank. It was certain that other men would continue searching for those precious remnants of the 1622 galleons. Driven by their fantasies of silver and gold, they would recklessly invest their money and their lives in the pursuit. Doubtless they would also battle rivals seeking the same treasures.

In the library of the archives of the Indies I sat scanning through a book on Spain's fleet system. As I flipped pages in a chapter on notable explorers, I came to the reproduction of a title-sheet from a book dated 1621. Blinking, I looked closer: the book was about Bartolome Garcia de Nodal's voyage to Cape Horn. On the left side of the page was an engraved portrait: the likeness of the soldier who had drowned on the *Nuestra Senora de Atocha*, dressed with high ruffled collar and armored breastplate. Looking out impassively at me was a stearn, mustachioed and bearded face. Here I could directly see the visage of the Galician who had directed his King's troops on the galleon and who was lost off the Marquesas. I asked myself: was this only a drawing on a page, or could we truly discern this man, understand his life, reconstruct his time?

Then the answer came: we could try, with substancial hope for success. By pooling all our skills, together we possessed the tools to comprehend the man and the world he knew. We could fix a date from a shard, examine passenger's status in a jewel, discover minting technique from a coin, reconstruct commerce out of the markings on an ingot of silver. We could definitively identify a vessel by numbers cast in bronze cannon. We could learn much of the art of shipbuilding from the joining of frames and planking and from comparison with the ship's construction contract. But the whole was far greater than the parts. A vanished culture, society, and empire could be extrapolated from the microcosm of this tumbled and scattered shipwreck. And our glory was this: for whatever motives, we had been led to uncover these precious things. We had also found the documents which gave them more meaning. And, like the partaking of a sacrament, we had shared the adventure of the finding and the joy of the learning.

Thanks to Mel Fisher and all who had labored with him, the galleon had been located at last. Her material riches might be divided, but knowledge about the ship was universal. Men might personally hold the recovered things but none could possess the *Atocha*. Thanks to Duncan Mathewson and those who worked to understand their meaning, she now belonged to everyone. It would take years to examine her heritage fully. That study might well outlast our lives, but we begun the task. Looking beyond the single-minded passion of the searchers and heated disputes of the academics, the final result was sure. The future would be the gainer. The long efforts and monies expended, the lives lost over more than three centuries would not have been spent in vain.

THE END

THE 16th CENTURY MAN

Eugene Lyon

Eugene Lyon had himself stretched across 500 years. His head was in the 16th Century but his hand was on a slick new computer, tethering him to the 20th.

"It's great to be alive and in the 16th Century," he said, happily.

He lives across the street from a 17th Century fort and works in an office faithfully reconstucted from 18th Century plans.

He walks to work down a narrow old street in a city that flourished as a resort late in the 19th Century and early into the 20th, one that set the Florida pattern.

The man feels as though he has come home, to where his heart is — the mother lode of Florida history, St. Augustine — the oldest city in North America.

Lyon became research director for the St. Augustine Foundation, which specalizes in the Hispanic beginnings of this country.

To him, at least, those beginnings seem to be undergoing a revival now as they never have before.

He cites international plans for the approaching (in 1992) Quincentenary — the 500th anniversary of Columbus' discovery of the New World — plus recent archaeological discoveries, here and elsewhere, that add dimension to what we know of those times.

"Suddenly, the whole Hispanic mission system, world and cities of the 16th Century are just coming alive. It's really fascinating," he said.

St. Augustine is one of Florida's distinct jewels, a city of 12,000 being pressured by the population boom, a place ancient and Hispanic at its core (founded by Pedro Menendez de Aviles in 1565), but radiating outward in urban spangles.

By any exact reckoning, St. Augustine should always have been a place swarming with historians panting for more information. But in comparison with the resource, for years there were surprisingly few.

The nature of Florida never seemed to encourage a sense of history, only a mild curiosity, so that the truly facsinating colonial past of St. Augustine rarely has gotten full appreciation. In the past decade, for example, tourism showed a decline.

By any realistic measure of value in terms of heritage, St. Augustine also should be an attraction point for Florida's large Hispanic population. But, considering their numbers, it is not.

Lyon laments past inattention. But he recognizes it as a puzzle not created by lack of merit. For him, in fact, it provided a disguised opportunity.

Lyon, a native Miamian, once was a career local government administrator. He worked for Dade County's Metro government in its early days; later he moved on to Vero Beach as city manager.

A combination of events propelled him backward into the 16th Century: the perils of the city managing business; an interest in treasure hunting; an acquaintance with professional treasure hunter Mel Fisher, plus those tricky crosscurrents that come with a sense of midlife crisis.

At 38, he returned to the University of Florida for a Ph.D. in Latin American studies, focusing on 16th Century Florida, and at that time he became aware that he was entering a study subject to odd prejudice.

He was advised that many in the field consider the Spanish period to be something of a dead end, not a mainstream current of U.S. history. He stayed with it, anyway.

Work on his dissertation took him to Spain and the Archive of the Indies in Seville. His friend Fisher had asked him, while there, to stay alert for information about shipwrecks off the Florida coast during the 16th Century.

Out of that trip came not only the Ph.D. but a book (*The Enterprise of Florida*, a study of the founding of St. Augustine) and a controversial but rewarding involvement as a researcher for Fisher's marine treasure hunts. They led to a second book (*The Search For The Atocha*).

Meanwhile, he had become a free-lance historian and writer, teaching at Indian River Community College, becoming assoicated with National Geographic and increasingly drawn to St. Augustine.

For 11 years, he was one of three historians who put together plans for a 16th Century museum village of the St. Augustine Restoration Foundation (the "Restoration" now has been dropped from the title).

Finally it was decided that, although the necessary information and money was in hand, it was not feasible to bring in enough actors to make a living museum function and pay its way.

Instead, the foundation produced two films on the period: the first, *Struggle to Survive*, concentrated on life style; the second, recently completed, centered on Pedro Menendez de Aviles himself. Both have regularly scheduled public showings.

These, plus nine blocks of old St. Augustine streets still functioning as laid out by the Spanish (not buildings, just the layout), make up the visual 16th Century history that any visitor can see.

They complement the 17th Century Castille de San Marcos and the many 18th and 19th Century buildings that have been restored or reconstructed under the auspices of the Historic St. Augustine Preservation Board.

So there sits Eugene Lyon, the 16th Century man with a computer, comfortably stretching across history as through it were an old Hispanic hammock.

From an earlier column in TROPIC by Al Burt.

APPENDIX A

Paper delivered to:
Society for Historical Archaeology
by Eugene Lyon

Atocha: What Documents Told
January 9, 1987

Seven years ago, Professor Paul Hoffman of Louisiana State University addressed this Society and discussed concerns felt by historians working in ethnohistory. (1) Professor Hoffman concluded that archaeologists need historians less for general history and chronological data, where secondary materials already exist. Hoffman stated a belief, however, that when more complex questions arise: those of social status, demography, and sources for information on material culture, it is often advisable to go into primary materials. Then, due to their peculiar knowledge of sources, and their ability to manipulate and interpret manuscript materials, historians' skills may be useful.

This morning I would like to discuss the utility and confines of the historian's craft when primary materials are employed in the study of Spanish shipwreck sites. I will use the *Atocha* search and salvage for illustration. There are, I believe, three levels of such utility. First is the limited and discrete usefulness primary documentation holds for salvors. These obviously include data directly leading to the location of lost vessels, information on their cargos and the degree of previous salvage, if any; and the essential matter of identifying the shipwreck materials found. One might also add that a deeper knowledge of materials gleaned from contemporary documentation tends to authenticate the artifacts and may add measureably to their material value.

Secondly, some of these same concerns also affect archaeologists. With a site-specific orientation, they often share a lively interest in the location of the loss and the enhancement of knowledge about individual artifacts or assemblages. Thus they may welcome primary documentation about the shipwreck.

The third step, also shared to some degree by both historians and archaeologists, is to advance our studies toward the entire cultural meaning of a shipwreck. This must involve the comparison of recovered items and assemblages with data gleaned from primary documentation and secondary historical sources in order to open their context into the widest possible compass. It is about this third step, it is in the interest of stimulating such broadened thinking that the following remarks are offered.

A Caribbean hurricane caused the fleet disaster of September sixth, 1622, bringing eight Spanish vessels from the combined Guard and *Tierra Firme* fleets, together with a small Cuban coastguarder, to grief in the lower Florida keys. Over 500 lives were lost with over a million and half pesos' of cargo of the eleven million the fleets carried. Two of the ill-fated ships, *Nuestra Senora de Atocha*, and *Santa Margarita*, have been located and salvaged over the past sixteen years. (2) The *Atocha*, upon which we concentrate here today, and the artifacts recovered from her, are directly tied with seventeenth-century Spain and its empire and the complex of cultural entities extant pertaining to those entities. They may be connected with the colonial trade of Iberia and reflect the condition of worldwide war during which the galleon was sunk.

Spain's deepening involvement in the Thirty Years' War led to heavy expenditure to support her armies in Europe. Their success in Germany seemed to be near, but required increasing committment. Spain had also to shore up Imperial defense around the globe, as Dutch assaults battered Spanish ships and positions from the Orient to the West Indies. (3) This speaker would agree with Pierre and Huguette Chaunu that Spain's commercial peak and the concomitant beginning point of her real economic decline likely occurred at this particular time. (4) To support the indispensable bridge of ships between the hemispheres, merchants in the *Carrera de Indas*, the Indies trade, paid for their own defense through the *averia* tax and other imposts on the trade. The Crown share of incoming Western cargoes was never enough to satisfy interest and principal payments on past debts and carry the burdens imposed by statecraft. Nevertheless, when the Dutch truce expired in 1621, foreign policy hard-liners in Spain, including young King Philip IV, determined to press on to uphold the military honor and religious position of Spain. They refused to consider renewal of the truce. In that same year, the Dutch West India Company was founded to act as spearhead against Spain the Western Hemisphere. It was in 1622 that Don Gaspar de Guzman, later created Conde-Duque de Olivares, first came to power as the Royal favorite; he was destined to lead the nation even further into the morass of war and debt.

In the meantime, the tax-farmers of the *averia* had contracted for four new war-galleons to reinforce the royal Guard fleet; Alonso Ferrera of Havana delivered the last of those ships, the *Atocha*, in 1620. Her construction contract and associated lawsuits furnish substantial detail about her dimensions, manufacturer, spars and rigging. (5)

As I began to study problems of the *Atocha* location in Seville in 1969, I went to a source rich in general information about the fleets, the *Papeles de Armada*, in AGI CT. *Legajos* 2987 and 2988 contain a wealth of data for the 1622 ships, about supplies, rations, ship repairs, cargoes, muster and pay rolls, and fleet movements. I learned that the *averia* contractors had appointed an administrator to receive funds due from the tax, and to make payments for the needs of the Guard fleet. They had agreed to furnish eight galleons, three *pataches*, 1100 seamen and 900 soldiers, plus all their arms and supplies. For the Guard fleet commander, the Marquis of Cadereita, the difficulties and costs of outfitting, arming and supplying the 1622 ships were considerable. (6)

After arming and loading, *Atocha* and the other ships in the two fleets crossed the Atlantic and made the round of the Indies ports of Portobello, Cartagena, and Havana, where they discharged their European cargoes and took aboard the lading of the Indies. When they began their last voyage, the galleons carried bullion, coin, and tobacco and copper from the Royal monopolies. (7)

In first seeking location data about the sunken 1622 ships, it was necessary to seek a fresh approach. Although this was a shipwreck disaster much discussed among treaure hunters, and some of these had commissioned research in Spanish archives about it, the information they had gathered had led them to the area of Upper and lower Matecumbe in the central keys. While researching other material, the serendipity of primary research disclosed to me documents in which the words "cayos de Matecumbe," were indeed used, but which added those of the "cayos del Marquez," named for the Marquis. Map comparison led to the hypothesis that these were the modern Marquesas keys. The location I suggested was only a general one, near the Marquesas, for two documents gave seemingly conflicting information about the relative places of loss of the several sunken ships. (8) Further information came through reading the descriptions of salvage attempts by the Spaniards from 1622-1679. (9) After many years of unsuccessful salvage attempts, the Spaniards believed that the *plan*, or lower hull of *Atocha*, with the ballast mass and silver pile, still lay in the 54′ depth in which the galleon had originally sunk.

The salvor, Mel Fisher, moved his operations from the central Florida keys to the area of the Marquesas in 1970 and, the next year, discovered a colonial anchor and other shipwreck artifacts, including Spanish utility ceramic ware. He continued to work the site, located upon the Quicksands, a large sandbank extending westward from the Marquesas atoll. Now the shipwreck found had to be identified. This problem was compounded by an atmosphere in which it was difficult for either rivals or State officials to accept a judgement based upon empirical evidence. Soon, in fact, the matter was in litigation, which made definitive identification an even more vexed and crucial question.

True, a number of silver and gold Spanish colonial coins had been found on the site. These coins pointed to a 1622 dating and had an unmistakeable *Tierra Firme* bias. (10) But coin dating, a traditional means of shipwreck identification, is limited by its ability to distinguish a site only generally and not specifically. It was therefore necessary to seek other data for a more definitive determination. In examining the aggregate of artifacts located — a number of arquebuses and muskets, swords, daggers, and quartzite stone cannonballs — it appeared that a major war galleon with an infantry company, and not an ordinary merchant vessel, had been found. The artifacts were analagous, in fact, with those on the arms list of the *Atocha* and the other 1622 Guard ships. (11)

At this point, it appeared to me that one could posit a hypothesis that each ship once had its own distinctive profile, made up of its hull, rigging, equipment, cargo, and personal possessions aboard, by which its remains may best be identified. Documents could, I reasoned, help establish such a profile. If this were true, therefore, every vessel's "fingerprints," would be identical with its own unique cultural image. As a holistic entity, it is more than the simple sum of its parts. Among the actual artifactual finds onsite, however, no significant anomalies from the documented profile should exist.

In addition to the *Papeles de Armada*, one may seek data about westbound cargoes from the manifests listed in the AGI *Contratacion* series, or found in some *legajos* of AGI *Indiferente General* (hereinafter IG) or the *Audiencia* papers in the AGI as well as some materials in the *Consejo de Hacienda* section of the Archivo General de Simancas (hereinafter AGS). In the case of *Atocha*, I began with the *averia* accounts and then studied AGI CT 2211, the homebound manifest of the vessel from all three Indies ports.

These manifests, documents of great socio-economic interest, tie to many personages and institutions of the time. The manifest, a collection of sworn bills of lading with supporting materials, had the force of law. The key figure was the ship's silver-master, bonded to receive the goods registered aboard, and sworn to protect them and ensure their safe delivery to the House of Trade in Seville. It was thus a peculiar paradox that reliably registered cargo co-existed aboard the ships with large amounts of smuggled, undeclared and contraband goods. (12) Once I learned that one could generally rely upon a manifest, I believed it possible to identify a site through the correlation of recovered artifacts with discrete items once registered aboard.

Since the Indies trade, yoked to scheduled fleet sailings and annual fairs, tended to produce regular pulses of coin and ingot manufacture, ingots shipped were usually tied to a discrete numerical series of those cast in a short period of time. The serial numbers were cut into the bars. Their silver purity was also regularly tested, and the *ley*, or measure of fineness, was cast or encised upon the bars against a 2400 scale. Some of those, moreover, were Royal *quinto* bars, representing the Crown bullion fifth. Those, in 1621 and 1622, carried date and place markings. (13)

The finding, on July 4, 1973, of three silver ingots on the Marquesas wrecksite afforded an opportunity to test the theory. Upon examination, the bars bore numeric markings in cursive Roman script, and other symbols. Little work had been done on Spanish colonial ingots; Darby McNickel had discussed a bar found at Gorda Cay in the Bahamas. He pictured but could not explain the ingot's markings. It seemed clear that the three bars carried their serial numbers as well as the *ley*, or silver fineness number. I located first bar No. 4584, which had been loaded at Cartagena, and then the other two on Atocha's manifest. One of those, number 569, was a multi-point match; its serial and *ley* numbers coincided with the manifest data, and the shipper/consignee marking in the document, a crossed J topped with a Z, was also inscribed upon the bar. (14)

This seemed, therefore, evidence toward an identification of the *Atocha*. When in 1980, the *Santa Margarita* was found, the same procedure was used for her identification, and was accepted as definitive by the Federal Court. In July, 1985, at the time of the finding of the main deposit of the *Atocha*'s bullion, large runs of ingot correlation with the manifest verified the earlier identification. This was also entered into evidence in other litigation before the Admiralty Court, to demonstrate the extreme ends of the wrecksite. There were on both vessels, of course, some contraband ingots which were not manifested. (15)

In 1975, another, corroborating means for identifying the *Atocha* arose, when Dirk Fisher and Pat Clyne found nine bronze cannons just off the Quicksands on the *Atocha* site. These guns, the major weapons system of their time, were cast in Spain, Havana or Flanders or captured in the wars of Charles V and his successors. Prized and carefully accounted for, the cannons were listed by a weight number cast or incised in the vent field or on the breech rim of the piece. Due to the non-standardized methods of bronze casting in that time, duplicate weights, even among thousands of cannon listed in the Seville archives, are almost never found. The *Atocha* guns were measured and photographed *in situ*. All those cannon which bore markings matched the weight numbers on *Atocha*'s list of bronze guns. (16)

After the basic data needed by the salvor had been located, and artifactual material of great cultural richness began to be recovered, it was possible to examine the documents for information of a more broad cultural interes.

The first of this related to the men, women and children aboard the *Atocha*, of whom only five of 265 survived. These included Vice-Admiral Don Pedro de Pasquier y Esparza, Silvermaster Jacome de Vreder, Pilot Martin Jimenez, Augustinian visitor to Peru Fray Pedro de la Madriz, and Captain Bartolome Garcia de Nodal, noted explorer and infantry captain aboard *Atocha*, and the only person aboard whose likeness we know through a contemporary engraving. Data about the officials may be gleaned from the fleet papers through muster-rolls and passenger lists, and relations of the drowned. Another means of following up individual noblemen or career officials is through their "merits and services," filed in many parts of the Spanish archives. It is advisable to look years downstream for full data about an individual, normally given near the time of this retirement. (17)

Two streams of military culture converged aboard *Atocha*; a long maritime tradition met with that of the "Queen of Battles," the Spanish infantry. The list of Nodal's company of soldiers on *Atocha* includes young noble cadets, veteran non-commissioned officers, and many regular soldiers seasoned in the wars in Flanders; the list furnishes age, personal characteristics, parentage, and identifying marks of the men. (18) Another list features *Atocha*'s sea-officers and mariners, all those whose combined skills carried forward the traditional knowledge of the sea: pilot, quartermaster, guardian, cooper, carpenter, diver, caulker, surgeon, trumpeter, ordinary seamen, and ship's boys. (19)

Other lists described artillerymen, chaplain, passengers, and, at the bottom of the scale, servants and slaves, "persons of no importance." (20) One of those, Diego de Illescas, was listed as *"mestizo."* *Atocha* was, therefore, a substantial cross-section of Hispanic society, emphasizing how class barriers existing in Spain and the Indies were present aboard ship. Wealthy merchants in the Peru trade, such as Lorenzo de Arriola and Miguel de Munibe, were drowned together with the cargoes they shipped. The *corregidor* of Cuzco, Governor and justice over the lives of many Peruvian Indians, Diego de Guzman, died on the galleon. Martin Salgado, a *letrado* who was secretary of the Audiencia of Lima, was a upper-level functionary returning to Spain with his family and the savings of a life's labor.

Social stratification aboard *Atocha* was not only evidenced by rank and office, but was substantiated by the placement of individuals in living and sleeping quarters on the ship. *Atocha*'s sterncastle section held the aura that surrounds "officers' country" in a modern US Navy warship or was found in the area of the first-class cabins of, say, the *Lusitania*. In the stern-castle dwelt Vice-Admiral Pasquier, Captain Garcia de Nodal, the Silvermaster, the pilot and other important ship's officers, and the wealthy passengers. Less favored persons slept on the gun deck level or, when weather permitted, on the weather deck. The fine plate, jewelry, and religious artifacts found on the wrecksite are not random items; they reflect the status of the former possesors. The kind of possessions held by the nobility was represented by a large and ornate piece of silver table plate found on the shipwreck site in 1985. It bore the mark "Dona Ysavel" and likely belonged to Dona Isabel de Pernia, who shipped thirty-five pounds of silverware on *Atocha*. (21) Fifty-eight pieces of gold-and-emerald jewelry located in one spot in 1986 point to an owner of substantial wealth.

Many of the salvaged artifacts are tokens of the sanctioning power of religion. The very name of the ship itself — that of one of Spain's most important shrines, Our Lady of Atocha in Madrid — indicates the overarching influence of the Catholic Church. A salvaged lead Papal seal, likely from an indulgence — or other bull, may well stand surrogate for the resurgent power of a Counter-Reformation Papacy. The year of 1622, in fact, brought important advances for the Church as new fervency gripped the Catholic nations. Pope Gregory XV founded the Propaganda Fide to advance the faith around the world. The whole array of religious artifacts recovered from the galleons — altarware, medallions, rosaries, crucifixes, *veneras* of the religious-military order of Santiago — reflect the complex sociology of Tridentine Catholicism. (22)

The emerald cross located in 1982 in the Quicksands area, found together with a large emerald ring, likely was a bishop's pectoral cross. (23) It bears upon the obverse an engraved likeness of *Nuestra Senora de la Leche*; an ancient and vital devotion in Spanish life. As the *Atocha*'s muster rolls note, seculars, Augustinians and other regulars were present aboard the ship. A medal dedicated to the Eucharist may have been related to a sodality or confraternity of that name. Many of the rartifacts also point to the intensity of personal devotion and specifically to Spain's great consecration to Mary. The Marian tradition of the rosary is linked over time with the Dominican Order and with it, to the preservation of orthodoxy. Thus those who used the rosaries recovered on the *Atocha* site celebrated the mysteries of intercession while they acknowledged the cleansing fires kept alight by the Holy Office.

Many contraband gold bars, chains, and over three thousand emeralds have been found on the *Atocha* site. In addition to such proof of illicit ladings, there appeared among *Atocha*'s recovered artifacts other evidence of the darker side of Hispanic society. The unified Portuguese and Spanish slave trade brought blacks to Cartagena. In 1622, some 1400 entered the port, survivors of the tortured voyage across the Middle Passage from Angola. (24) *Atocha* carried funds homeward from the Crown's head tax on this human traffic, as well as gold bars and disks from the Cauca valley and Popayan mines and foundries, where slaves furnished the main labor force. The vast mass of the silver in coined or ingot form aboard the *Atocha* had come from the mines and refineries of Potosi and Oruru, where thousands of Peruvian Indians toiled under the *mita*, a system of forced labor approximating wage slavery.

In sum, then: the matrix of primary documents from which we may draw knowledge about the 1622 shipwreck disaster, and about *Nuestra Senora de Atocha* in particular, provides valuable knowledge of the climax time of a world empire. Archival materials were also important in the search for the location of the sunken galleon's remains, and provided means to definitively identify the ship. Their greatest usefulness, however, lies in their being a connecting link between artifacts and artifact assemblages found on the wrecksite, and the personages, events, beliefs, institutions, technologies and other cultural riches of the seventeenth century.

For more than all else, the artifacts and the documents speak of *interchange*, a great exchange carried out over more than two centuries by means of the Spanish fleet system. Across one road and one road only came westbound the products of Europe — fine cloth, iron tools and weapons, and sugar cane, with smallpox, measles, and other disease to decimate the native Americans. Westward also came the technology of ideas: powerful belief-systems of religion, organized, absolute government, with a conquering language, literature and liturgy, art and music. Back to the Metropole went chocolate, the potato, maize, tobacco, precious metals and, arguably, syphilis. Two worlds met across the ship-bridge and were changed forever. As the Spanish Empire expanded further, products of the Orient and the Pacific Basin also entered the ship stream. The artifacts from the *Atocha*, therefore, can best be vested with their fullest cultural meaning when seen in combination with historic documentation.

In sum, on this and other shipwreck sites, there exists an immense ethnohistorical challenge. We must attempt to extrapolate a vanished time from the documents and from those microcosms of the period found in buried and scattered ship remains. To meet this charge, all our skills, blended in full cooperation, are needed. We must look beyond the single-minded passion of treasure hunters and fruitless disputes over academic and bureaucratic turf. Ownership of such riches cannot be disputed, for in truth none can possess a ship like the *Atocha*; she belongs to all. Cooperation can be our only strategem in attempting to validate this ownership.

We now know that the entire first museum collection of *Atocha* and *Margarite* artifacts will remain intact, available to the public, together with many of their other artifacts. It is hoped that the *Atocha* ceramic collection will be housed at the Florida State Museum. Where items have been distributed to individual owners, full data has been recorded about them. Years of work lie ahead but, thanks to the salvor, Mel Fisher, to our forum chairman, Duncan Mathewson, and the others who will be speaking here today, it appears probable that the enduring values of the *Atocha* will remain.

1. See Paul E. Hoffman, "Clio and the Diggers, or how one historian views the role of the historian in Historic Sites Archaeology," Society for Historical Archaeology, Albuquerque Conference, January 11, 1980. The paper was later published as "The Historian in Historic sites Archaeology," in Albert E. Ward, compiler, *Forgotten Places and Things*, (Albuquerque, Center for Anthropological Studies; Contribution to Anthropological Studies, No. 3, 1983) pp. 37-47.

2. See Eugene Lyon, *The Search for the Atocha* (New York, Harper & Row, Publishers, 1979). Second edition, Florida Classics Library, 1986. Revision in press. An excellent appreciation of the cultural side of the shipwreck is found in R. Duncan Mathewson III, *Treasure of the Atocha* (New York, Pieces Books, 1986).

3. Dutch East India Company forces had founded Batavia in 1619 and were forcibly attempting to enter the China trade directly, after having taken other former Portuguese bastions. Portugal in 1622 was, of course, in the Spanish empire. An absorbing account of events in Java and the Far East at this time is in Leonard Blusse, "Jan Con, Batavia, and the Dutch China Trade," *Itinerario* (Journal of the Institute of European Expansion, University of Leiden, IX, 2 [1985]), 3-41.

4. See Huguette and Pierre Chaunu, *Seville et l'Atlantaique*

(Paris, 8 vol., S.E.V.P.E.N., 1955-59), *Le Trafique*, 1614-1630. Some of the reasons for the decline in Spanish shipping may be seen from the losses for the decline of the 1622 combined *Tierra Firme* and Guard fleets and also the 1622 New Spain fleet; these have been totalled in a report by the administrators of the *averia* found in Archivo General de Indias (hereinafter AGI) *Contratacion* (hereinafter CT) 2.988, and dated 1623.

5. Descriptions of the *averia* and other maritime imposts are found in Guillermo Cespedes del Castillo, *La averia en el comercio de Indias*, (Seville; Escuela de Estudios Hispano-Americanos, 1945), and Ismael Sanchez-Bella, *La organizacion financiera de las Indias* (Seville; Escuela de Estudios Hispano-Americanos, 1968). Discussion of the previous *averia* contract, under which the building of *Atocha* was authorized, is found in AGI IG 2687. The *averia* accounts about the four galleons are summarized in *AGI* CT 3003, and discussed in detail in AGI IG 4545. The construction contract for *Atocha* and the other galleons is found in AGI *Santo Domingo* (hereinafter SD) 132. In the same *legajo* is found, at No. 21, a description of how the anchors and fastenings for the galleons were brought to Havana from Vizcaya by ship. More details on the outfitting and acceptance of *Atocha* are found in AGI CT 4844 and CT 4859. Translation of the construction contract, by Eugene Lyon, is available in unpublished typescript at the St. Augustine Foundation, St. Augustine.

6. See the Marquis de Cadereita's letter dated at Cadiz on 14 April, 1622, describing the urgencies of various needs for comestibles, powder, and other supplies; this is in AGI CT 2987. See also "Autos y visita fechos sobre el apresto de lost galeones de la plata que el ano que biene de 1622 an de yr a tierra firme a cargo del general Marques de Cadereita" from the same *legajo*. The *averia* administrators had borrowed 100,000 ducats from the probate deposits at Seville to help finance the expense; see Administrators of *averia* to the Crown, 1623, from AGI IG 2688.

7. Sources for the lading of the *Atocha* are discussed in the text below. Payment for the tobacco, raised along the coasts of New Granada in *Tierra Firme*, was made on July 31, 1622, in Cartagena; see the acknowledgement before the Royal Treasury Officials of that date, from AGI CT 2988. *Atocha*'s lading of valuables is totalled in "Relacion de la plata y oro...embarcada.," from the same *legajo*. 581 copper ingots were loaded on *Atocha* at Havana; see AGI CT 2211, ending page of *Atocha* registry.

8. The letter of Pedro de Aguilar y Guzman, Seville, 1 Feb. 1623, from AGI CT 90A, gave a ship-by-ship location of the lost vessels, from *Rosario* on the westernmost of the Tortugas to eastward. This conflicted with Captin de Lugo's eyewitness testimony in the Cadereita letter (Marquis of Cadereita to Crown, December 12, 1622, Havana, from AGI SD 132), until excavation of the vessels gradually marked out the incoming ship tracks; then the two accounts were reconciled. The key words came from Francisco Nunez Melian's salvage accounts in AGI CD 1112. One of the most useful maps was that of Miguel Hurdel de Montellon of 1733, found as *ramo* 200, *seccion cartografia*, Biblioteca Nacional (Madrid).

9. Gaspar de Vargas' initial work on the wrecksites is described in AGI CT 2987; another description of his tasks is found in Governor Francisco de Venegas' statement, dated at Havana April 5, 1624, from AGI CT 2988. The efforts of Nicolas de Cardona are detailed in his manuscript, "Descripciones Geographicas E Hydrographicas de Muchos Tierras y Mares," (1636, dedicated to the Conde-Duque de Olivares) Seccion de manuscrito, Biblioteca Nacional (Madrid). The accounts for Francisco Nunez Melian's salvage of the *Santa Margarita* and search for *Atocha* from 1625-1631 are found in AGI *Contaduria* (hereinafter CD) 1112. Later salvage work is described in the Merits and Services of Lazaro Fanex de Minaya, June, 1645, from AGI SD 134, No. 61, and in the petition of Isidro de Mayorga, 1679, AGI SD 140.

10. The *Atocha* coin assemblage is a most interesting one. It demonstrates as its major emphasis the Peru trade, since coins from the Potosi and Lima mints are in the majority. Of particular numusmatic interest within the assemblage are the coins from the Santa Fe de Bogota mint in the Nuevo Reino de Granada, modern Columbia. The earliest coins minted there by mint operator Alonso Turrillo de Yebra were found on this site, and on that of the sister galleon *Santa Margarita*. See letter, Turrillo de Yebra to Crown, received at Madrid, 23 September 1623, from AGI *Santa Fe* 192. The *Atocha* coin assemblage is generally described by N. Neil Harris in "Coins of the *Nuestra Senora de Atocha*," in *The Numismatist*, XCIX, No. 10 (October, 1986), 2017-2040. The presence of some ten per cent of coins from the Mexico mint stand as proof of the proscribed, but sizeable intercolonial trade.

11. See "Relacion de los pertrechos de artilleria, armas, y muniziones que son menester para armar los ocho galeones y tres pataches...," 1622, from AGI CT 2988.

12. See Eugene Lyon and Barbara A. Purdy, "Contraband in Spanish Colonial Ships," *Itinerario* (Journal of the Institute of European Expansion, University of Leiden), 6, No. 2 (1982), 91-108.

13. The *quinto* bars are listed in AGI CT 4784.

14. Ingot 4584, sent from the Royal Treasury, represented the payment of head taxes for black slaves received at Cartagena; it was found on the manifest, AGI CT 2211, fol. 488vto. Ingot 569, sent from Diego de Leon to A. Sierra, was also loaded at Cartagena and is described in AGI CT 2211, fol. 506vto.

15. For information about contraband ingots aboard the *Santa Margarita*, which totalled some 19% of those recovered by Francisco Nunez Melian in 1626, see *Cargo*, AGI CD 1112.

16. The gun list for the 1622 ships is found in AGI *Indiferente*

General (hereinafter IG) 1144. For one of several general lists of bronze cannons see the *Mayordomo de Artilleria*'s listing in 1624, from AGI IG 2688.

17. For instance, information about D. Pedro de Pasquier, *Almirante* of Tierra Firme, drowned aboard Atocha, the Marquis of Cadereita, and Captain Miguel de Chazarreta, also an official in the 1622 fleet, is found in AGI IG 2535.

18. See "Relacion de los oficiales y soldados de la compania del capitan Bartolome Garcia de Nodal que yba embarcada en el galeon nobrado *Nuestra Senora de Atocha*, almiranta de la flota que se perdio en los cayos de tortuga en 6 de septiembre de 1.622.", from AGI CT 2987.

19. Relacion de la gente de mar que yba embarcada en el galeon nombrado *Nuestra Senora de Atocha*, AGI CT 2987.

20. See "relation of the private persons drowned in the two silver galleons lost in the storm of September 5," Havana, 12 December 1622, from AGI CT 5116.

21. See AGI CT 2211, fol. 428vto.

22. A *venera* of Santiago, found on the *Margarita* site, was likely worn by a cavalier or comendador of the Order. See Archivo de los Condes de Revillagigedo (hereinafter ACR) *Canalejas* (hereinafter CAN) 47, No. 22; Pedro Menedez de Aviles wore such a *venera* on a gold chain at the neck.

23. See similar emerald crosses in the Diocesan Museum, Cuenca, and the Cathedral Treasuries of Granada and Palencia.

24. For an excellent delineation of this trade, see Enriqueta Vila Vilar, *Hispanoamerica y el comercio de esclavos. Los asientos portugueses.* (Sevilla; Escuela de Estudios Hispano-Americanos, 1978)

APPENDIX B

Communication from Marquis of Cadereita to the Crown, Havana, January 10, 1623, from AGI *Santo Domingo* 132..

Having left the bay of Cadiz with Your Majesty's armada on the 23rd of April (as I wrote Your Majesty), following my voyage, the weather was so favorable that Grand Canary came into sight on the third of May, and at the end of it (the voyage), the islands of Dominica, from which I dispatched a private patache the same day to Havana. (I did this) in order that the governor (of Havana) might have the two galleons prepared which Your Majesty ordered outfitted in that port. And the armada went carrying out its voyage to Cape Huza, where I found some gales so fresh that I was delayed there seven days without being able to pass until the wind eased to a breeze, with which it entered Cartagena the fourteenth of June. (We) delayed in that port until June 22, and left for the port of Portobelo, where I entered on July first, and found the Tierra Firme fleet there. (It was) in such poor state of readiness, as in past years, that during the interim until the silver of Your Majesty arrived, the galleons *Nuestra Senora de la Candelaria* and *Nuestra Senora del Rosario* were careened, so that they were staunch and of the best in the armada. And because of the word I had by letters from the Governors of the Tierra Firme coast, that 36 urcas of (Dutch) enemies had been seen there, which left (the salt-pans of) Araya, it seemed proper that I convene in a junta the President of (the Audiencia of) Panama, the General of the Tierra Firme fleet, and all the other ministers of Your Majesty in Portobelo. Having conferred among all these about what might be best to do in this case, it was resolved that since the galleon *Nuestra Senora del Rosario Candelaria*, which had gone out as a merchant ship in the said fleet, should then be armed for war, as was done, she being very well-fitted for it, and having previously served as Almiranta of the armada, so that the treasure might come with more security and the risks be better divided. And having loaded in it and all the other (ships) of the Armada, and the Capitana and Almiranta (*Atocha*) of the fleet, all which came from the Kingdoms of Peru, I left for Cartagena on July 22. I entered there on July 27, and was detained in gathering that which proceeded from the (New) Kingdom (of Granada) and that province, and the tobacco of Your Majesty until the third of August, when I left for Havana. And with the many fair winds and calms I was delayed until the twenty-second, when I entered in its port, where I found the galleon named *San Juan Bautista*, of Vice-Admiral Tomas de Larraspuru, finished with its yards raised. (It) was armed the same day, and its registered silver and the precious merchandise which was alloted to it, and it serves as Almiranta (of the Guard of Armada).

And, preparing that which was necessary in order to sail, on the 25th of the same month I received Your Majesty's Royal order of May 23rd, which came sent in the courier ship to Cartagena and was remitted by its Governor to Havana. And on the 26th (of August) I convoked a junta (with) Don Francisco Venegas, Governor and Captain-General of this island of Cuba, and all the officials of the armada and fleet, in order to advise them how Your Majesty had ordered that the two galleons *Nuestra Senora de la Candelaria* and *Nuestra Senora del Rosario* carry neither silver nor precious merchandise, despite the fact that they had been careened.

And, all having conferred about what should be done, and, seeing that those careened in Portobelo remained very strong and staunch and of the best in the armada, it was resolved that the treasure which they brought not be taken out of them, but that they might carry it to Spain. And having also conferred on the same junta about the day in which it would be best to depart to sail from this port for the Kingdoms of Castile with the said armada and fleet and by which latitude and course they must make the voyage, it was agreed that they should wait until one day before the (planetary) conjunction of September, and, if the weather was fitting, they would sail that day, and that they might go by 37 to 38 degrees (of latitude) until arriving at the islands of the Azores, and that they might pass on the south side, withdrawn from them, if the weather permitted. With which I agreed, since it appeared to me very fitting to the service of Your Majesty, and I had all the vessels of the armada examined and had embarked in them the supplies, munitions, and equipment necessary, in the manner which is customary.

And, everything being arranged, on the following fourth of September, the day dawned so serene and cloudless, and the north-east wind so moderate and fitting that all the pilots felt that it would be a great success to go out to sail. And, having communicated it with them and the other experienced and satisfactory persons in things of the sea, with the opinion of all who could give it, the armada and fleet and other ships of their escort, which were altogether 28 sails, were unmoored and, at seven in the morning, I sailed on a NNW course until until three in the afternoon when it was changed to ESE until sunset. (When), the armada finding itself ten leagues east of Havana with a ENE wind and (the weather) appearing good, I turned on a northerly course, until the following Monday at seven in the morning, when there came upon (us) a great hurricane and storm of northeast wind, which obliged the armada and fleet to bring down topmasts and pull off bonnets. And, not being able to remedy things in this manner, at three in the afternoon of this day, they scudded before the sea with only foresails on the SW course until five when, the weather having worsened with such rigor and having carried away the foresails of many vessels, they laid to. And others, through not being able to steer and lacking their mainmasts, (did the same?). Thus, at nightfall I found myself alone with the Capitana, and went running a WSW course and to the West until midnight when, the wind having veered to the South with much violence, it took the fore(sail?) and both were thrown into the sea. And thus it was until Tuesday, September sixth; at ten, the (weather) having cleared to the South, the fore and mainsails were set, and (we sailed) on the WSW course until Thursday morning when the wind went SE and we found ourselves able to steer South until seeing the Havana coast. And having reconnoitred it, I turned outside on a northerly course, seeking the armada and fleet ships and, not having found any (of them) by Monday, the twelfth of the said month (and) judging that they would have put in at the port of Havana, where I would find them, I turned on its (Havana's) course. And, having entered and anchored, I found it in ten ships of those of the convoy: the three silver galleons *Nuestra Senora del Rosario*, Capitana of the fleet, *Santa Ana la Real*, and *Nuestra Senora de la Candelaria*, all dismasted and making much water, and seven ships of the fleet, five dismasted and all very badly used.

And (I saw) Don Bernadino de Lugo, Captain of soldiers and seamen of the galleon *Santa Margarita*, one of the silver (galleons), and having asked him about it and the other missing ones, he said that the day of the storm he followed the Captana on the SW course until nightfall, when the wind carried away her foresail. Being at cross purposes, the galleon broke its mainmast and the whip-staff of her rudder and her tiller was shattered. Not being able to carry sail and seeing some lanterns nearby, she remained thus until Tuesday, the sixth of September. Then at dawning, they took soundings and found forty arms of water. Loosing the sprit-sail which they had lashed to the foremast in order to go about on the other tack, the wind carried it away. It now being full daylight, they loosed another which was lashed on, but the same thing happened. Then the force of the wind and the currents impelled the galleon to a depth of ten arms of water where she anchored. Dragging her cables, she was lost upon a bank of sand which is to the west of the last key of Matacumbe, close to the *Cabeza de los martires* of the Florida coast. At seven of the morning he saw, one league to the east of his galleon the one named *Nuestra Senora de Atocha*, *Almiranta* of the *flota*, dismasted of all her masts except the mizzen-mast. While he watched, she went down and sank in such a way that nothing could be seen of the ship, nor any other thing than half of her mizzenmast. Then, about ten o'clock in the morning, the great seas tore his galleon apart. The greater part of her crew drowned. One blow from a heavy sea washed him out of the wreck and he found himself floating and swimming upon a plank until five o'clock in the afternoon. Then, since the weather had moderated, a shallop from a Jamaica ship picked him up. Having entered into the shallop, he buoyed in a cannon a yard and other poles with a pennant wrapped around them to serve as a mark and signal of the place where the two galleons had been lost. Thus they might be found and the treasure and artillery aboard could be recovered.

On Tuesday, the 13th of September, in the afternoon, the galleon *San Juan Bautista* entered the port of Havana. She had all her masts and was in good order, with nothing lacking. With her came eight other ships of the convoy, all dismasted. Having asked the Admiral about the missing ships and what course they had taken, he responded as follows: on the day when the storm came upon them, he was following the *Capitana* until, with the great spray and obscurity of visibility, he could see it no longer. He remained fighting the seas until mid-day Tuesday when, conditions having moderated, he made sail and went in search of the armada. While searching for it on Thursday, the eighth of the said month, in the place of Tortuga, he saw grounded upon one of its keys the ship named *Nuestra Senora del Rosario*, a private merchant ship which had sailed from Cartagena in the convoy of the *flota*. He saved fifty-four persons which had been in her. Those people and persons from other ships told him that, on the afternoon of the storm, they saw running before the wind with spritsail and foresail the ship of Gaspar Gonzales de los Reyes, close-reefed(?), and she capsized without their being able to help her nor save anyone from her crew. Thus also the same day they had seen another ship, the one of Juan de la Torre Ayala, which could not steer itself nor carry sail, and they felt sure that the same thing had happened to it and that she was lost.

Thus on the fifteenth of the same month, I called a meeting of the Governor of the land and all the ministers and pilots of the armada and *flota* in order to confer on the best thing to do for the service of Your Majesty; whether it be most fitting that, after re-masting the ships and repairing the destruction caused by the storm, the ships should be set sail for the Kingdoms of Castile or whether it might be best to winter in Havana. Also discussed was the recovery of the treasure, artillery and other things which had been lost in the two galleons mentioned above and the efforts which would be well to put forth to do this and to serach for the missing ship, *Nuestra Senora del Rosario*, of which Miguel de Chacarre (?) was captain. Having conferred about these matters, it was resolved that the armada and *flota* would sail again, if the things necessary for this had been provided. In the meantime, while this was being done, Captain Caspar de Vargas would go (with the instruments and equipment which I had provided) to recover the two lost galleons and search for the missing one through the keys of Tortuga, Matecumbe and the coast of Florida. He sailed out to carry out this mission on the 16th of September with three *pataches*, and two shallops. having arrived at the place where they were lost, he discovered the mizzen-mast of the *Almiranta*. Close alongside it he anchored and, embarking in a shallop, sounded the depth in which this galleon is. He found ten arms of water. Even though he put divers down to try and enter the silver storage-room, they could not do so because the hatches were battened down and the decks were still whole. Thus they could do nothing until the weather and water should break up the wood, or until instruments could be made to do it. Having salvaged two pieces of artillery (though not finding any more above the principal deck, he buoyed the galleon with a cable and a spare yard to serve as a signal, if the mizzen-mast should be missing. From there he went to seek the galleon *Santa Margarita* and the buoy which the captain left there and found neither one during two days of search. Since, with the (astronomical) opposition of the moon, a great storm came down upon him, he was at the point of being lost and grounded, he could not remain in that place and went on course to Tortuga searching for the galleon *Nuestra Senora del Rosario*. He found it grounded on one of the keys on the 24th of September, and found on land all its people. On another cay, close by, he found the *patache* of the *flota*, from which he saved all the people. Having reconnoitered the galleon, he saw that nothing could be salvaged from it until the main deck and everything above the water was burned. He put this plan into execution and with divers and instruments which he carried he salvaged all the silver and twenty pieces of artillery. He also recovered four pieces of artillery from the *patache*. He recovered many cannon-balls and supplies. He remained in this work until the 17th of October, when he entered this port to advise of the many storms which took place in the whole moon. While he was on that island there came a storm so strong (with the astronomical conjuction of the fifth of October) that they key, even though it was 1½ miles long was totally submerged, and there remained above water no more than one high point on which he could gather the people and the silver.

Having asked the captains of the galleon and patache how they were lost, they said that on the day of the storm they followed the *Capitana* until nightfall when, with the great spray and obscurity and the wind having carried away their foresails, they lost sight of its lantern. Then they were struggling with the sea until dawn on Tuesday, the sixth of September, when the great seas, wind and currents impelled them onto the keys of Tortuga. At the sight of these, they anchored. When the anchors dragged and the cables broke, they were lost on them. On the 13th of October I sent Don Pedro de Ursa *Caballero* of the order of Santiago from this port with three *pataches* two shallops and some canoes with many drags, grapnels and other instruments, in order to seek the galleon *Santa Margarita*. The pilot saved from her and other persons who knew of the place where she was lost went along.

Fearing with these delays that the armada's supplies might not be conserved, I caused that the ships be surveyed and visited. This being done, it was found that they were in such bad condition that in no way could they endure or go out to sea. The sea-biscuit, which is the main staple, was getting old and beginning to rot and the other supplies in the same condition. Thus it was impossible for the armada and *flota* on the 23rd of October. having conferred at length about these matter, and seeing that it was not possible to carry out what had been decided in the meeting of September 15 (that it go out to sail after the conjunction of October). That conjunction and all the moon of that month had been such bad weather that when the fleet might have been ready it couldn't have sailed. In addition to this, when the generals prepared to work on the ships' sides, they were found to be so badly damaged from the storm and making so much water that it was essential to careen them. They are presently in careenage and have been for many days. Neither have the masts, which we are waiting for from the back country, going to arrive (for some time), since the whole island is inundated from the heavy rains. It was resolved, therefore, that aid be sent for from New Spain, which is the nearest place from which supplies, munitions and equipment can come. In the meantime, moreover, while these are coming, that Captain Gaspar de Vargas should go to the keys of Matacumbe with the new instruments — irons, drills, chisels, petards and the other things prepared in order to blow up or break open the decks of the *Almiranta* and pull out the treasure and artillery from her and the ship named *Margarita*, with the divers who are carried for this purpose. Because this will not be done with as much brevity as in Spain, and so as not to cause Your Majesty and all your vassals in recovering it and in sending notice of what took place, I dispatched a dispatch-boat, and for this purpose I prepared a new frigate, fast and of those of the convoy, which is the vessel most fit for the purpose among those here in this port. I also caused to be prepared two other frigates. I sent one of them on November first to New Spain with a person of care and diligence with the dispatches necessary, in order that the Viceroy of that kingdom and General Don Carlos de Ybarra might give him all the supplies, munitions and equipment that was asked of them, which is what we need in order to sail out of here. I notified them that only the lack of supplies detained this armada; thus I hope that they will start them coming in such a way that they will be here shortly in this port. I also sent from here on the sixth of December the other frigate to the port of Porto Bello, and I gave notice of happenings to the Viceroy of Peru, in order that next year and the years to come the sending of the silver might be speeded up, in Potosi as well as in Lima. In this lies the secret of good success and arrival on the coast of Spain in summer. I sent this notice in duplicate by way of New Spain, and also gave it to the President of Panama, in order that when the silver arrives at the port of Perico, it be brought down to the *castellos* in Port Bello. I sent to ask him and the Governor of Cartagena the registries of the treasure and other things which had been loaded into the two galleons, since what they carried had been lost in them.

On the seventh of December Captain Don Pedro de Ursua arrived at this port, damaged by a storm, since he could not repair his ships in the keys of Matacumbe, where he says that he had such bad weather that he could not search for the galleon *Santa Margarita.*

Having arrived at the place where the *Almiranta* was lost, he could not see her mizzen-mast nor any other sign. Judging that the storm of the conjunction of October and the great storms of all that month had broken it up, he went seeking through all the keys of Matecumbe to see if he could find any sign of it. On one of the keys he saw half the sides (hull) of the said galleon *Almiranta* from a mid-ship section one-eighth of the way back up to the stem at the bow, with all its four wales and 5½ feet below that. According to this, he judged that both decks had become separated and that only the keel and floor timbers and in it the silver, artillery and other weighty things remained (where she went down). In order to go and salvage it Captain Gaspar de Vargas had been prepared; the bad weather had detained him in this port until the 18th of November, when he sailed out with one *patache* of the armada, two fregatas, and two long-boats and all the instruments and divers needed to search for and salvage the silver in the two galleons. The same day he sailed, a storm came upon him and forced him to take shelter in the port of Marien, which is seven leagues to leeward of Havana, where he had bad weather until the eighth of December, when he returned to Havana to re-stock his supplies. With these and the other necessaries, he sailed for the keys of Matacumbe on the eleventh of December to carry out the program of salvage. Due to his experience, care and devotion which he brings to the service of Your Majesty, one may expect the same good results which he had in the galleon *Rosario*. In consideration of this and of his many services, and in view of the fact that he has on this voyage lost two galleons in the service of His Majesty, he is deserving that he be made a *merced*, honoring and advancing him, in order that others be brought to do the same, as I supplicate Your Majesty. I also ask that on the first possible occasion you order sent to this port two tartans together with the people who can sail them, and a quantity of nets, so that if all the lost silver and artillery are not found, the rest can be dragged up with them.

In the seven vessels which were lost, five hundred and fifty persons were drowned. I judged that 1,500,000 of *pesos de a ocho reales* was the quantity the two lost galleons *Almiranta de flota* and *Santa Margarita* carried. Included in this were 254,000 pesos for the account of the Royal exchequer of Your Majesty, in gold, silver, tobacco and copper, with that of the last two types which was lost in the galleon *Nuestra Senora del Rosario*. In order to carry the people, silver and artillery which is salvaged and reinforce the armada, I have armed for war the new ship which Captain Esteban Delgado made in this island. It is finished in every way, very strong and seaworthy with the second careening which was given it for this purpose.

With a ship which arrived here from New Spain with flour, General Don Carlos de Ybarra sent me notice of how his *flota* had safely arrived at the port of Vera Cruz on September 12, and he remained with concern until knowing that the *flota* of the charge of General Fernando de Sousa might have arrived, and what happened to it in the September storm. Rodrigo Madera, who went with his ship in his convoy, came to this port. I learned from him that the stormy weather which struck them in the place of Bermuda was so strong it left his ship in such bad condition that it was necessary to abandon her, saving himself in a small boat with only 19 persons.

Since the General of the *Tierra Firme* fleet, Juan de Lara Moran, died after his arrival at this port and his Admiral Don Pedro Pasquier had drowned, and nothing remained of the *flota* except two small ships, because the rest had gone ashore, it seemed best fitting the service of Your Majesty to combine it with the armada, as was done. In order to avoid costs and other inconveniences, the same was done for the galleon which served as *Capitana*.

Lorenzo Bernal, chief pilot of the armada, remains a prisoner for not having carried out that which was resolved in the agreements about the sailing of the armada from this port and having set sail from it on the day on which he left, contrary to that which I had ordered. Because of this, I have charged him, and am proceeding against him juridicially. In his place, I have named Marcos de la Cruz as chief pilot; he held the same post in the *flota*. This appointment was made in the meantime, while word is waiting of what Your majesty might order in it.

From the ship which just arrived here from San Juan de Ulua, I have learned that there is no sea-biscuit in that port.

That which I asked for the armada must be made in Puebla de los Angeles. This cannot be done with so much brevity so as to arrive here until the end of January. For this reason, and because the whole month of February is very stormy and the worst of the year, I judge that I cannot sail until the month of March. Conforming to this, Your Majesty will order things to be done as might most convene, since the year is so far advanced. Those in this port have been so bad that it is now more than a month since this notice is dispatched, and it has not been able to go out before now, which gives me very great concern and care, for that which Your majesty and all your Kingdoms shall have. May God guard the Catholic Royal Person of Your Majesty for the many years for which Christianity has need. From Havana, December 12, 1622.

Up to this point is a copy of that which I wrote to Your Majesty with the first notice which I sent from this port on December 13. According to the weather which afterwards we have had I judged him to be in a good place, and I wait hour-by-hour for news from the keys of Matacumbe of the good success of Captain Gaspar de Vargas. If it be what is desired, I will give account to Your Majesty. This will go with a *patache* which I have prepared for this purpose, and in that which Don Carlos de Ybarra sends with news of his arrival it seems well to me to duplicate this dispatch, without having any more news of which to advise Your Majesty until today.

10 January, 1623.

The Marquis de Cadereita

APPENDIX C

Communication from Don Luis de Cordoba to Crown Havana, Dec. 10, 1622; A.G.I. *Santo Domingo* 132

Junta, on 21 March
Count of Castile
Don Pedro Pachaeco
Solorzano
Marmolejo
Valdes

Lord

Since the Admiral of the Tierra Firme fleet had been drowned in the storm on the fifth of September, I succeeded in the position, as Your Majesty had given it to me as a royal favor, according to your royal decree of March of this year — until, when General Juan de Lara Moran died on the third of November, the command of his fleet devolved onto me. What I can advise Your Majesty about the events of the voyage is as follows: having sailed from the Bay of Cadiz with the Capitana, Almiranta, one armada *patache* and five merchant ships (eight sails in all), with a fair wind we sailed on March twenty-third. On the 30th, we came in sight of Grand Canaria and on the 24th of April, the islands of Dominica. The fleet entered Cartagena on the second of May, and remained there until May 16, when it sailed for Porto Bello. Entering that port on May 24, it took until June 30 to unload the merchandise on land and ready the fleet ships. On June 30 the galleons entered. The sale opened with such low prices (as in the past years) that all was finished by the 22nd of July when the armada and flota sailed for Cartagena. In Porto Bello, they left behind one of the merchant ships, since it was in no condition to make the return voyage to Spain, and another ship was armed as a silver galleon.

The fleet entered Cartagena July 27 and left for Havana August 3rd. Due to the fair weather and calms it did not enter this port until August 22. Here it waited until September 4, when it sailed for the Kingdoms of Castile. On the fifth a great hurricane and storm came upon them of violent northeast wind, in which the galleon Nuestra Senora de Atocha, Almiranta of the fleet, was lost, and all her people were drowned, without their being able to save more than five seamen. (Also lost) were two other silver galleons, from one of which everything she carried and her artillery were recovered. (Also lost was) the fleet armada *patache* and another (of a private person) grounded in Tortuga and (also lost were) two moderate-sized ships of the convoy, which capsized in the force of the weather. All the other ships were dismasted, and the main one, named Nuestra (Senora) de la Balvaneda, had opened up to such an extent that it was urgently necessary to ground her in this port, as was done. She had arrived in this port together with the Capitana of the flota, and two merchant ships, which were those which remained of the fleet, and many others which had joined with it in the Tierra Firme ports to come in convoy with the fleet when the Marquis should arrange the departure. The Marquis, being in charge of the fleet since the third of November when its general died until the 19th of November, attempted to take twenty-five soldiers and a sargeant from the Capitana of that fleet and put it into his own guard corps. Because Your majesty has ordered, by cedula of November 25, 1620 that no galleon general nor any of his subordinates should meddle with the companies of soldiers embarked in the fleets even if they be of his regiment, I warned him of this and asked that he honor the cedula. The Marquis became so angry that he arrested all my officials and issued a statement in which he announced that he had reformed the fleet, and that which remained of it should be gathered together. In carrying this out, he pulled out of the Capitana my company and assigned the company of Capt. Miguel de Chacarreta, to whom he turned over this galleon ..... since he had lost his. He put my company in the Capitana of the armada. Although I protested in writing of the senselessness and injustice of this action, which he had done in ignoring the decrees of Your Majesty (this matter was properly in my jurisdiction, since I was not only Admiral of the said galleon but also governor of the said fleet, through being the senior captain of it), he did not wish to reply. He ordered all of his head officials and those of the flota that no-one should let me take any role whatever nor give me any testimonies. To someone with whom I tried to accomplish something, such threats and menacing, fright was given that he did not dare to do anything. The Marquis should give the reasons for his making such moves against me, without my having done anything more than serve Your Majesty with sincerity and satisfaction for more than twenty-two years, in Flanders and in this Carrera (de Indias). Being inheritor of the many services of General Don Geronimo de Portugal y Cordoba, my cousin and also inheritor of the hatred and enmity which the Marquis bore him... this matter has greatly dispirited me. I am not at all certain that Your Majesty, as such a great Christian, would cause me to be thus aggravated; it is, however, sure that the Marquis does this through the power he has from Your Majesty. My qualities are so well-known, as is advised by the testimony and information which is enclosed, that I supplicate that Your Majesty see fit to do me the favor to honor me with the title of Captain-General of this fleet, and order that I be paid the salary of that office since the day when the former holder of the position died. May God guard the Catholic royal person of Your Majesty, as Christianity has need and your servants desire. From Havana, 10 December 1622 years.

Don Luis de Cordoba

APPENDIX D

Communication from Gaspar de Vargas, from "this key," January 9, 1623

I wished to send in this ship 500 more bars I promise that it has not been possible (to do) more than the labors which are going on here. I do not know how to describe it — as Your Lordship knows, I am better at doing than saying. Advising of what, up to now, has been done — I have seen that every day we leave this key with the two *barcos* and we leave at four in the morning and it took us until seven to arrive the time before and other times even later. We work until two o'clock and it takes us all the rest of the time until ten at night to get to land. Once we stayed out at sea because we couldn't get to land and the men were exhausted from wandering against the wind. Seeing how much we worked I determined to take the *patache* which Your Lordship sent me to the waters where I had marked the ship when, on September 26, I removed the two pieces of artillery. We went searching there Tuesday the third of January and Wednesday, Thursday and Friday (day of the Three Kings) the drag caught within a few feet of where the patache was anchored. I sent down the diver Andres — he came up saying "give me the reward for good news." He stated that the ship is there; I and all the others were delighted.

The other diver, Diego Martin, went down and said that it seemed doubtful to him. Cabrera, a man to whom you pay more attention, went down and said that it seemed to be rocks to him. Andres went down again and came back to re-affirm that "it is the ship." They had a little argument about the matter, and I tried to make peace among them and said to them that they should let it go until another day. On Saturday at nine in the morning Adres went down and said again "yes." Cabrera said "No." Finally they could not untangle the lines and (?) it was necessary to break them, as I did. Well, having been all the night anchored to a (?) they (either, neither) lacked nor did they come supplied with rocks (for weight?) as they had come before — as if they might be attached to weights made of cedar-wood with which they weighed themselves down for the diving. That which was said to Your Lordship is that all the divers are exhausted and tired; well, they just do not have the spirit to do anything on the Almiranta, because it is in 10 arms of water). I would be most happy to be a diver, in order to be able to send Your Lordship the truth about the matter. I, senor, came to search for the Almiranta, and am certain that it is what I say, because it is in the same place which I marked, as mentioned above, and in a little less than ten arms. Within the area where the drag was caught is (an area) of 7½ arms, which could be the length of a ship. Sounding within the 7½ arms with the deep-sea lead, I did not bring up any sand, mud or rock — it was clean. This is the truth, as I say to Your Lordship. Everyone else is of this opinion except Cabrera. Having seen this, I buoyed it with two buoys, the best that I could for the present. The first day of good weather I will take another buoy which I have here. This is done now; when Cabrera saw that he had no way to cover (up?) his weakness, he asked me to write to Your Lordship (as well as the others) that they could not dive down to the Almiranta, and that Your Lordship should decide upon finding some one who could do it. It is winter, it is cold, and there are heavy seas. Until now, they are quieter about it than I have already said. Although Cabrera does not say so much, between one and the other, senor, they will not do anything now, nor in the summer. Even if I advise Your Lordship of all, in order that divers be sought out, and do your good wishes and concern and the great amount which Your Lordship has labored — today Cabrera has said to me that it seems to him a certain thing to send to Margarita for divers, whom he believes can dive in 10, 12, or 14 *brazas*, (for?) a sunken thing. Today, as you know, in the present circumstance, I confess it as in accordance with what he says, he and others also; it does not seem to me a difficult thing to send for them with brevity which the occasion requires. The summer is coming and there will not be delay. Your Lordship will see and agree to what is most fitting as someone who understands what to do with the whole affair.

I only say, senor, that the relation which I write is true, and that many things do not (cost, suffer?). Thus I have determined to advise Your Lordship, and I have also ordered Don Pedro to go in person, and vocally (to explain) all this. If in case Your Lordship might send to Margarita for the thirty divers, or the number which Your Lordship (might deem fitting?), of that which also will be, as Don Pedro has been — he finds and knows the Governor and the keeper of the Negroes. I am certain (???) for he served His Majesty with love and zeal, while as to others I do not know what they will do. I supplicate Your Lordship to observe the brevity, quickness, haste which seems necessary to me. I am certain that Your Lordship will see and order what is needed. To the divers I have said, let's go and look for the Margarita, which is in shallow water. They said to me. "well and good," and thus it will be done, even if the weather is not ideal. But I fear that we will not do anything until summer-time, which is far away, and (?) of the pleasure...At last, Your Lordship might advise me as to what suits you, that I might not take out this frigate — it is sunk with water. Even if I send it to Your Lordship, if I determine that it might be, send me another. It is important, for if some day we cannot make the keys, we will have some aid in it. That

God might bless Your Lordship with the health and increase of life which I desire. From This Key, 9 January 1623.

Gaspar de Vargas

APPENDIX E

Communication from General Don Francisco Venegas, governor and captain-general of the island of Cuba and the city of San Christobal of Havana, for the King Our Lord.

I certify that I know Captain Gaspar de Vargas, who is captain of the Spanish infantry aboard the Royal Armada guarding the Indies for the King; and that he has served him since 1588 (in the journey to England headed by the Duke of Medina-Sidonia as captain-general — Vargas was in one of the galleons of that Armada of which I was the captain of infantry) until today in different posts of the Royal Service. He has served with the great approval of his superiors, and has always given the good account which was expected of him. During this time, he has renedered very particular services to His Majesty which, due to his great experience, could only have been entrusted to him. He has always come to his duty with zeal.

Finally, the Armada in charge of the Marques de Cadereita having left this port for Spain the year of 1622 — a great storm came upon them in the mouth of the Bahama Channel, and three galleons were lost. These contained the treasure of His Majesty and private individuals which was lost along with many people. The said Marques having arrived at this port with the rest of his ships, he charged the said Captain Vargas with the responsibility of going to seek the said three lost galleons with broad powers; thus he could, if the ships be found, do what the circumstances required, leaving it to his industry and experience. As it worked out, having left this port with four ships and the galleon *Nuestra Senora del Rosario* being found on the key of Tortuga (Capt. Vargas was owner of this galleon), sunken — Vargas found it possible to salvage a quantity of equipment of a value of more than six or seven thousand ducats. Instead, he did not, taking first things first, and proceeding to save the people and treasure which went in the ship. This he did so that some storm might not come along, break up the wreck, and bury the treasure in the sand (as happened with the other two). Then he began the operation of salvaging the silver, first setting fire to the galleon, to burn it down to water-level. In this way he recovered all the treasure, artillery, and copper which she carried and brought it all back to this port together with the people who were saved. Then he went ahead to seek the others, and found a patache of the said armada lost on another key and saved the people and six pieces of bronze artillery which were in her. Further on he found the Almiranta of the Tierra Firme fleet, sunk in 10 brazas of water, and he recovered four bronze cannon. Because she was lost in such a depth and he could not recover the silver, he returned to this port and after having made some instruments for the salvage, he returned with them to the key where the said Almiranta was lost. There he found the wreck blotted out by the second storm — afterwards there appeared in different places pieces of her planking. Having dragged with (grappling-hooks or grapnels?) and searched with divers to seek the floor-timbers of the said galleon Almiranta, he found them, but could not continue his recovery, as she was buried under one braza of sand and ten of water. Due to his considerable diligence in searching the sea around those keys, he recovered two bars of silver, a chest of *reales*, many muskets, arcabuzes, cannon-balls, swords and more than 100 silver plates. He was working at this during the time the Marques of Cadereyta was in this port — always in the keys of Matcumbe. After the Marques left for Spain, Capt. Vargas remained to see if, during the coming summer, the recovery of the silver could not be accomplished. Vargas told me of the intolerable labors he underwent, being many times on the point of losing his life as a result of some storms which came upon them in those keys, for he was there with two small craft in such a dangerous place without any other shelter whatever. General Don Antonio de Oquendo arrived with his armada at this port and found the said Captain Gaspar de Vargas there at that time; he presented him with the order the Marques had given him. Relative to this, they held a meeting to decide what should be done from that point on relative to the water. With myself concurring in it, it seemed best to excuse the expenses caused to date since there remained a marker where the Almiranta was lost, for what the King (His Majesty) had been pleased to order — and that the said Captain might go to Spain to give account of it all to His Majesty. Having arrived and departed, the Armada had to return and spend the winter in this port. During the course of this time, the said Captain has gone to check on the buoys in the said keys of Matecumbe every time that he was ordered to do so. Thus, during 18 months, he has continually undergone the labor which he devoted himself to considering — this is the time that I assisted in this ministry here. I gave the present document at his request in order that by it it might be advised what he merits, and in order that His Majesty honor him and make him a *merced*, bearing in mind his most particular and well-known services. It is also well-known how he lost his property on this voyage, as the Capitana of the same armada which was lost upon leaving the bar of San Lucar was also his. Thus he served His Majesty with two galleons and both were lost. Signed with my name and sealed with the seal of my arms and submitted by my secretary in Havana on 5 April 1624.

*Octōber — E.L.

APPENDIX F

UNITED STATES DISTRICT COURT
SOUTHERN DISTRICT OF FLORIDA

Case Nos. 79-1381-Civ-JLK
80-1205-Civ-JLK
(Consolidated)

TREASURE SALVORS, INC., a
Florida corporation,

    Plaintiff,

vs.

THE UNIDENTIFIED, WRECKED
AND ABANDONED SAILING
VESSEL, et al,
    Defendant

_____/

MEMORANDUM OPINION
CONTAINING FINDINGS OF
FACT AND CONCLUSIONS
OF LAW

_____

ROBERT JORDAN,
    Plaintiff,

vs.

THE UNIDENTIFIED, WRECKED
AND ABANDONED SAILING
VESSEL, et al,
    Defendant

_____/

The ultimate fare of the SANTA MARGARITA, a royal galleon of the Spanish Tierra Firme Flota of 1622, is the subject of this opinion.

As this magnificent six hundred thirty ton galleon cleared Havana Harbor on Sunday, September 4, 1622, she carried one hundred eighty-eight persons on board, one hundred forty-three of whom sailed to a rendezvous with death in the tragedy to follow.

The SANTA MARGARITA also carried a treasure of gold and silver ingots, bars, discs, coins, chains, and precious jewelry of such magnitude as to be almost beyond the imagination of modern man.

FINDINGS OF FACT

THE SHIPWRECK

The drama that unfolded during the trial of this case commenced on a clear and beautiful day 360 years ago. Dr. Eugene Lyon[1] described it thusly in *The Search for the Atocha:*[1]

Sunday, September 4, 1622. Slowly and majestically, flying all their flags, the ships of the combined fleets passed one at a time by El Morro at the Havana harbor entrance. With Guard Fleet galleons and escorts, Tierra Firme vessels and small craft, twenty-eight ships filed out into the open sea. They sailed a good six weeks behind schedule.

At dawning the day had been so serene, so clear, that Lorenzo Vernal and the other pilots had unanimously recommended that the fleet sail. If the morning before the conjunction of September were so fair, what possible danger could the nest day bring? When he heard the pilot's recommendation, the Marquis of Cadereita felt reassurance, but still he hesitated. At last, the decision had to be made; he determined that the fleet had to sail. Too much was at stake, at home and abroad, to do otherwise. At seven in the morning, the Marquis had given the order to weigh anchor.

It took more than an hour for all the ships in the unwieldy convoy to clear the port and form into sailing order. Then the Guard Fleet capitana led off on a north-north-west course. As almiranta of the Tierra Firme ships, the Atocha brought up the rear of its fleet. Having gotten safely offshore by midafternoon, the fleet then tacked to the eastward of Havana to enable the ships to sail easily northward with the wind to the lower Florida Keys. There, where the current was strongest, the fleet would enter the Gulf Stream, which would boost them strongly homeward.

At sunset, Lorenzo Vernal estimated that the fleet had reached a point thirty miles to the northeast of Havana. Accordingly, he ordered a turn to the northward. Although the wind had changed little in strength or direction since morning, Vernal knew the weather had altered. The strikingly lovely deep-red sunset was disquieting in itself; its vivid colors were reflected in a thin veil of cirrus clouds that had overspread the sky. And Vernal saw how the sunset tint lit a towering bank of cumulus piled high in the southeast. At dusk a stronger breeze began to blow.

Through a night of steadily rising wind, the fleet held its course. Toward dawn on Monday the ships entered the center of the Gulf Stream current. The tossing motion of the vessels brought discomfort, then uneasiness, then wholesale seasickness to many passengers and crewmen of the fleets. Early morning disclosed that a strong northeast wind was raking the opposite-flowing current of the Gulf Stream, rising vicious cross-seas.

The ships reduced sail to weather the storm. Seamen went aloft to bring down the topmasts and reduce the windage there. All objects on deck were strongly secured and hatch covers firmly lashed down. As the morning passed, the day darkened and the weather worsened. The wind rose to a whole gale. The height of seas around the convoy mounted to more than ten feet, and flying spray torn from wavetops by the shrieking wind obscured the horizon. Visibility fell until pilots and lookouts on the ships could scarcely make out the vessels on the convoy's edge.

Now the ATOCHA'S waist was almost continuously awash, as great seas swept around the overloaded ship. The pilot ordered the mainsail lowered so that the ship could go forward more easily under foresail alone. The sailors who struggled to comply with the order clung to the mainyard, battling lashing canvas, as the extreme ends of the yard dipped regularly into the boiling sea. What most disturbed the men at work, however, was what they had seen near the ship's stern: the fins and the upper bodies of two great gray sharks, following the ATOCHA through the storm

Even with reduced sail area, the ship plunged wildly and became increasingly difficult to control. The helmsman could no longer steer properly, so the whipstaff was disconnected and the tiller lashed in place. At each heavy blow of the sea the ATOCHA'S hull shuddered and her masts creaked in their steps. Crashes below told of shifting cargoes and broken wine and olive jars.

By the end of the long afternoon, many of the ships in the convoy had lost their mainmasts. Some had no steerage-way whatsoever, for their rudders had been shattered by huge following seas. One small ship, the BUEN JESUS, had lost both masts and rudder; she fell farther and farther behind the other vessels and was finally lost to sight. Watchers aboard the ATOCHA saw the little NUESTRA SENORA DE LA CONAOLACION struggling along under a close-reefed foresail. To their horror, they saw the small craft suddenly capsize and vanish into the angry ocean. They could launch no boat in the wild seas, nor could they turn their own ship to go to the aid of those on the stricken vessel. The gnawing feeling grew among those on the ATOCHA that the same fate might well await them all.

Long before sundown the world grew dark, and the chief pilot, Vernal, lit the Guard Fleet capitana's stern lantern. He could not tell at that point if any other ships survived to follow the lantern's gleam; as far as he could see, the capatana now sailed alone. Any protective sense of being in convoy had now gone, and each ship still afloat struggled in its own lonely battle against the hurricane.

Aboard the SANTA MARGARITA, silvermaster Gutierre de Espinosa called his aide, Aguirre, to his cabin. Bracing against the plunging motion of the ship, Espinosa opened his official truck and asked Aguirre to help him take out some treasure.The two men removed eight gold disks and six gold bars, three small gold pieces, a silver bar, and some silverware; they placed it in Aspinosa's personal sea chest. The silvermaster then locked the chest and bound it with rope. He had made his own private preparations for disaster.

Meanwhile, below decks in the SANTA MARGARITA, Captain Bernardino de Lugo shouted for silence; frightened cries and groans of despair faded, then died. Holding for support to a ringbolt, the captain motioned to the pale cleric beside him, and told his men that Chaplain Ortiz was ready to begin confessing them. He added that the two Jesuit priests aboard were in the cabin above, taking the confessions of the officers and passengers; they would also come to the gun deck to help there when they were through. Even greater than his dread of drowning at sea was a Spaniard's fear of dying in a state of sin. That could mean the loss of his soul for all eternity. The men crowded forward.

By the time the wind shifted to the south, both capitanas and nineteen other vessels of the combined fleets had passed to the west of the Tortugas and this out of danger of grounding. Five unlucky ships - Vargas' ship the ROSARIO, the fleet patache (tender), the Portuguese slaver, the SANTA MARGARITA, and the ATOCHA, playthings of the wind - were swept irresistibly toward the Keys. A small Cuban coast-guard vessel was also caught up in the ill-fated group.

To Spanish mariners, Florida was an evil name. Scores of shipwrecks dotted the sea bottom along its coast and in the Keys. In the isolated area that lay ahead of the six ships, Spain's writ scarcely ran. For more that fifty years, expeditions sent there from the Spanish capital at Saint Augustine had never succeeded in making lasting settlement. Sailors lost in the keys had to run a double gauntlet: if they survived the ruin of their ship, they still had to face the untamed ferocity of the Keys Indians, who often killed shipwrecked men.

The first light of dawn on Tuesday, September 6, revealed an awesome sight. As the Spanish ships came into more shallow waters, the seas became even steeper. The few men left on deck beheld a sea covered with huge rollers, their fifteen-foot crests whitened by the gusting wind. Lookouts on the three westernmost of the ships saw vaguely ahead the outline of low islands - the Tortugas. The sailors heaved over their anchors to halt the ships' onward course to disaster. One by one their anchor lines broke, and the ROSARIO, the slave ship, and the fleet patache were grounded, wrecked in the shallows, battered by incoming storm waves.

Meanwhile, forty miles to the east, the SANTA MARGARITA and the ATOCHA approached a place where the trough of each passing wave bared the reef in a welter of foam.

Only the stump of the MARGARITA'S mainmast remained; her rudder was gone and her foresail had blown away. When sounding showed rapidly shoaling water, three seamen crept forwrd to set a scrap of canvas on the foremast and attempted to claw back away from the reefs ahead. The makeshift sail blew out. When their anchors began to drag, the crew was helpless. The ship was pushed inevitably toward the place of danger. At seven in the morning, the SANTA MARGARITA surged across the reef on the crest of a wave. As the ship swept on, Captain de Lugo looked to the east. There to his astonishment, he saw the hull of another crippled galleon. It was the ATOCHA.

Fifty-five feet deep, off a wide shoal west of a stormswept circle of mangrove islands, lay NUESTRA SENORA DE ATOCHA. With her, frozen in time, lay seventeenth-century Spain.

The southern sky had cleared. Except for fitful gusts, the wind had dropped, and the afternoon sun burned down fiercely on the place of disaster. With nightmare clarity, it revealed a churned and littered sea, its surface heaving with the refuse of shipwreck. The little merchant ship SANTA CRUZ had weathered the hurricane; it picked its way through floating planks and spars in the waters off the great sandbank. The small ship was already crowded with sixty-eight survivors of the SANTA MARGARITA, including Captain de Lugo and twenty of his men. Shortly after the sinking of the ATOCHA, the MARGARITA had grounded against the sandbar. By midmorning, battered by the waves, the ship had begun to break up. Only those who could keep a hold on floating wreckage had survived. Gutierre de Espinosa and all the passengers had perished. One hundred forty-nine persons had drowned.

Spanish Salvage of The Santa Margarita

The Spanish governor lost no time in commissioning Gaspar de Vargas to find and salvage the lost ships. Vargas sailed September 16, 1622 with five vessels for the lower Florida Keys. He found the wrecked galleons SANTA MARGARITA and ATOCHA lying six and ten miles respectively southeast of a low circle of wind wracked mangrove islands later to be named "Keys of the Marquis". A subsequent hurricane on October 5, 1622 and the 55 foot depth of the wreck site prevented meaningful salvage.

In 1624 an influential Havana politician, Francisco Nunez Melian, obtained a royal contract to search for and salvage the galleons and by June, 1626, Melian's crew, in a bronze diving bell, found the main ballast pile of the SANTA MARGARITA.

Melian's salvors brought up 199 silver ingots, more than 30,000 silver coins, silverware and slab of rough copper. After retreating to avoid hostile Dutch ships, Melian later returned to the Keys, and salvaged an additional 151 silver bars, great masses of blackened silver pieces of eight, a large anchor, eight bronze cannon, copper slabs and silverware. Of the total of 350 silver ingots, 67 were discovered to be contraband not listed on official manifests. Nearly twenty per cent of all treasure during this phase of salvage was contraband.

Salvage auditor Juan de Chaves later told of arduous salvage work in perilous currents under pitiless sun, amid occasional heavy squalls. One diver, Juan Martinez, died at the wreck site in August of that year.

The 1627 diving season began less auspiciously. On Thursday, June 10, the salvors reached the wreck site just after dawn. They moored their longboat securely as morning light turned dark waters translucent blue, and set to work. By the salvage master's hand-held sundial it was eight o'clock when lookouts shouted, "Sail! Sail!".

The Dutch enemy had reached the Marquesas. Cutting their mooring lines, the Spaniards fled over the quicksands into shallow water where the Dutch could not follow. The Spanish salvors escaped to Havana, and treasure salvage was discontinued for that year. The following year 37 more silver ingots and 3,000 silver coins were recovered.

Before the 1629 season could begin, Francisco Nunez Melian was appointed governor at Caracas, and left the salvage of SANTA MARGARITA and the search for the ATOCHA to other, less successful hands. In 1644, while Melian was reviewing his troops, his horse reared and he was killed. An audit of his accounts of the SANTA MARGARITA salvage was sent to Spain to repose finally in the Archive of the Indies.

The Spaniard's efforts in salvaging the vessels during the 17th Century were only partially successful and were finally abandoned through the passage of time. An immense fortune continues to rest upon the ocean floor a few miles off the coast of Florida, covered by the shifting sands and mud of the southern reaches of the Gulf of Mexico.

Modern Salvage

All but forgotten, the remains of the 1622 Golden Galleons were subjected to the process of nature which eroded the structure of the vessels and diminished the possibility that the unsalvaged portions of her fabulous cargo would ultimately be returned to the mainstream of commerce. Although identified as a "wrecked vessel", the SANTA MARGARITA is more accurately termed a wreck site, for what the teredos and the passage of time have left for salvage is cargo scattered on and under an expanse of ocean floor. Remarkably, a substantial section of ribs and planking of this once great ship has sonmehow survived the passage of time and the ravages of the sea to be recovered. The timbers are of white oak, fron the north of Spain and not found in the Caribbean.

In 1968, 324 years after Melian's death, the plaintiff, TREASURE SALVORS, INC., and its President, Mr. Mel Fisher embarked on a modern search for the lost galleons of the 1622 Fleet. Working with Mr. Fisher was Dr. Eugene Lyon, a Colonial Spanish Historian hired by the plaintiff corporation to research in the Archives of the Indies in Seville, Spain. By 1971 Fisher and his group had followed the leads provided by Dr. Lyon from the SANTA MARGARITA'S salvage audit and had located a great anchor from the NUESTRA SENORA DE ATOCHA. Over the next nine (9) years, Fisher's company, TREASURE SALVORS, INC. incurred great expense in its lengthy battles to protect and retain funds from the ATOCHA. Mel Fisher and his wife, Dolores, suffered personal tragedy in the loss of their son and daughter-in-law at sea during the salvage of these lost galleons of the 1622 Tierra Firme Fleet. These legal battles are extensively documented. The litigation against the United States for title to the NUESTRA SENORA DE ATOCHA is reported at 569 F.2d 330 (5th Cir. 1978) hereinafter referred to as *Treasure Salvors I*. The litigation against the State of Florida with regard to portions of the salvage, is reported at 621 F. 2d 1340 (5th Cir. 1980) hereinafter referred to as *Treasure Salvors II*.

Competing salvors appeared on the scene commenced to observe the ongoing salvage activities of the Fisher organization at the ATOCHA site. Fearful that others would find SANTA MARGARITA before him,

Mr. Fisher decided to increase the pace of the search by adding more men and equipment.

The documentary evidence of the MARGARITA'S location was less than precise with Bernardino de Lugo's statement placing the MARGARITA one league *west* of ATOCHA or just over three nautical miles away. Mr. Jack Haskins, a modern salvor and skilled researcher had told Dr. Lyon about an ancient letter he had discovered written by Captain Aguilar Y Guzman, stating that the MARGARITA lay to the *east* of the ATOCHA.

Emphasizing the contradiction, Mel Fisher's searchers had recorded magnetometer contacts both east and west of th ATOCHA wreck site in earlier searches. Mr. Fisher ordered continued exploration in both east and west areas. Urgency impelled him, for he feared that rivals might reach the SANTA MARGARITA first.

On March 13, 1979, Case No. 79-1381-Civ-WM and no. 79-1382-Civ-WM were filed in the United States District Court for the Southern District of Florida. The original wreck site description in Case No. 79-1381-Civ-WM was west of the ATOCHA wreck site. The original site description in Case No. 79-1382-Civ-WM was southeast of the ATOCHA wreck site. Both of the cases were filed on the available information and belief that the SANTA MARGARITA was either three miles east, or three miles west, of the ATOCHA wreck site and upon remote sensing data which had previously gathered showing the exIstance of shipwrecks in both locations.

A well-financed competitor had moved in and begun operations near where Fisher was recovering the scattered remnants of the ATOCHA. In a hauntingly similar reenactment of the Dutch against Melian's men, three and one-half centuries earlier, five shots were fired by the competitor and (in a subsequent incident) the competing vessels almost ran down a TREASURE SALVORS vessel, the *Virgilona*. The history of these modern-day pirates is reported at 640 F. 2d 560 (5th Cic. 1981) hereinafter referred to as *Treasure Salvors III*. On July 2, 1982, the Honorable Sidney M. Aronovitz issued a preliminary injunction protecting the right of the extensive wreck site of the NUESTRA SENORA DE ATOCHA.

In January of 1980, Fisher called a meeting at Commander Cryer's house for the purpose of sharing the information gained from years of ocean searching and research in Spanish archives. All of the Treasure

Salvors captains and other principles of the company attended for the purpose of pooling their knowledge in the search for the SANTA MARGARITA. Those present heard Dr. Lyon describe the Spanish Archival evidence gathered over years of research. Captain Robert JORDAN was present and participated in the meeting. At this meeting archival documents were shown to JORDAN and copies were later given to him. He subsequently was furnished a number of confidential company documents reflecting magnetometer readings, maps and charts of the search area. At the conclusion of the meeting JORDAN, archaeologist Duncan Matthewson, salvors/photographers Don Kincaid and Pat Cline, and Melvin Ficher all marked on a map their best estimates of where they thought the MARGARITA lay.

In early February of 1980, Melvin A. Fisher, on behalf of the plaintiff, TREASURE SALVORS, INC., submitted a proposed contract to JORDAN, who over a period of days consulted with advisors (including Mr. Finley Ricard) and altered the contract prior to its execution. The contract, executed February 5, 1980, was signed by Captain JORDAN and by TREASURE SALVORS, INC. through its President, Melvin A. Fisher.

In addition to affording Mr. JORDAN the privilege of working the wrecks claimed by TREASURE SALVORS, the contract provided that he was to receive food, fuel, and lubricants for the M/V *Castillian* and $100.00 for each work day of four (4) hours or more at the wrecksites for Mr. JORDAN"S labor and the use of his vessel.

TREASURE SALVORS made payment to Mr. JORDAN under the Agreement and, in addition, provided him $50.00 extra per work day at the wrecksites. Mr. Kincaid gratuitously provided winches valued at $1,500.00 for Mr. JORDAN'S vessel to better stabilize it at anchorage and TREASURE SALVORS ;loaned Mr. JORDAN an extra radio. Mr. Finley Ricard (a financial backer of Mr. JORDAN in other salvage ventures) provided other money for operation, dive equipment, detection gear and the cost of having the M/V *Castillian* hauled out and repaired when the crankshaft was damaged during the course of salvage operations in March, 1980.

To do the magnetometer work that was required, Captain JORDAN was provided an extremely expensive, one-of-a-kind, prototype precision, proton flux-gate magnetometer developed exclusively for TREASURE SALVORS by Faye Field. During the search carried out pursuant to the February 5, 1980 contract, this magnetometer provided by TREASURE SALVORS was used by CAPTAIN JORDAN on board his salvage vessel, *The Castilian.*

Winter weather in the Keys, often stormy, was cooperative in 1980. After a few days of fruitless magnetometer search west of the ATOCHA site, JORDAN took the *Castillian* to the eastern area where, at the edge of a wide sandbar, the instrument registered a concentration of electronic targets. JORDAN positioned his craft and found a small grapnel anchor, and then a very important discovery: a six foot diameter copper cooking caldron. Thereafter three small colonial anchors were found.

Don Kincaid, another employee of TREASURE SALVORS and a marine photographer who had first found the ATOCHA treasure, came aboard *Castillian* to help direct the search as salvage director. Following an electronic trail northward the crew found ballast stones covering the sea floor, Spanish pottery, indigo, and a clump of four encrusted silver coins.

For nearly a year, Case No. 79-1381-Civ-WM and No. 79-1382-Civ-Wm had lain dormant with no process having been served on a defendant vessel and no substantive litigation *in rem* or *in personam* having been pursued. After finding and salving the anchors, copper pot and other artifacts, TREASURE SALVORS, on the 10th day of March 1980, amended the defendant vessel's described location under Case No. 79-1381-Civ-WM to an area being within 3,000 yards if coordinates located at N. Latitude 24 degrees 33.3 minutes and W Longitude 82 degrees 17.0 minutes.

A witness testified that it was at this point that many of the participants started to believe they had, at long last, found the SANTA MARGARITA, The coins found in March had been taken into the Marquesas anchorage and, after cleaning, discovered to be Spanish pieces of eight, minted in the 1621 period of the reign of Phillip III - the same vintage as those from the ATOCHA. The shipwreck, however, appeared different from the ATOCHA in at least one respect; much of the material lay exposed on the bottom

On April 4, 1980, in the shallow water along rocky outcrops northwest of the first finds, *Castillian* divers suddenly found three large heavy gold bars. One bar was more than eleven inches long and weighed over five pounds. The treasure was brought into Key West and delivered to TREASURE SALVORS, INC. by Captain JORDAN where joyous divers broke out magnums of champagne and used one of the gold bars as a swizzle stick. Captain JORDAN entered into his log that the first gold of the MARGARITA had come to the surface.

TREASURE SALVORS, INC., at approximately 10:00 a.m. April 4, 1980, caused the portions of the defendant vessel that had been salvaged to be arrested pursuant to admiralty law by a Deputy United States Marshal. This arrest of April 4, 1980, gave the United States District Court for the Southern District of Florida, *in rem* jurisdiction over the ongoing salvage of the defendant vessel. The court finds that Captain JORDAN was present in Key West on April 4, 1980 and had knowledge of the action taken by TREASURE SALVORS to effect the arrest, by the U.S. Marshal, of the articles salvaged.

After the discovery of the gold, Captain JORDAN became dissatisfied with the terms of his contract and consulted Mr. Fisher, President of TREASURE SALVORS to obtain a better division of the salvage. Mr. Fisher discussed this request with the Board of Directors of TREASURE SALVORS, INC. where it was denied.

On May 5, 1980 a second amendment to the wrecksite description was applied for by TREASURE SALVORS. This Court's order of May 12, 1980 allowed the amendment to the pleadings. The amendment of the wrecksite description of May 5, 1980 was based on site salvage data that was being originated on a daily basis not only by the *Castillian*, but also by the TREASURE SALVOR vessels, *Virgilona* and *Swordfish*.

On April 12th, two more gold bars were found. Pot shards, bones and lead sheathing came up as the salvage progressed. Except at slack tide, vicious currents ran across the wrecksite, making, as the 17th Century Spaniards had earlier discovered, " ... the diving task very difficult." On May 9th, the *Castillian* turned into TREASURE SALVORS a rich variety of artifacts: broken pottery, hundreds of clumped and single silver coins, and an eleven pound ship's bell, silver plates, a sword, and a fragmented mariner's astrolab.

A few days after the *Castillian's* May 9th find, Mel Fisher's son Kane dove on the site and found six silver ingots evenly spaced in two rows nesting directly on bedrock. That was not all that met his eyes in the clear green water: he saw a great section of the remains of a wooden ship. It was twenty-three feet long with the ribs and planking capped by ballast stones and a conglomerate of encrusted artifacts.

Working the surrounding area, divers uncovered a gold bar, two more large (and one small) silver bars, silver bowls; an ink well and sand shaker, a candle stick and plate, and a silver spur. A one hundred and five pound mass of silver coins was brought to the surface still welded into the shape of the wooded chest that had long ago rotted away. One especially precious prize was a diamond cut emerald set in a gold ring. Beneath the green stone floated a seawater bubble forced in by the pressure of years beneath the ocean.

Dr. Lyon compared the markings on the silver ingots with those listed on the SANTA MARGARITA'S manifest. Five of the silver bars matched. The centuries dropped away as Dr. Lyon found ingot No. 4718 and the true significance of this modern day saga was brought into focus. Dr. Lyon's research established that the silver bar had been shipped at Portobelo, intended for Seville and the Brotherhood of the Holy Cross by the drowned merchant, Caspar de Rojas. Cut into the blackened surface of the bar were Rojas's RX mark and S topped with a Jerusalem cross. Five of the other bars had markings and numbers identical to the manifest. The sunken vessel was unmistakably the SANTA MARGARITA!

THE TROUBLE WITH TREASURE

Captain JORDAN'S first-mate in March and April of 1980 was Mr. Craig Boyd. Captain JORDAN told Mr. Boyd he was dissatisfied with the February 5th contract between himself and TREASURE SALVORS, INC. and that he was thinking of breaking the contract. Mr. Boyd advised Captain JORDAN to comply with the contract.

In May 1980, Captain JORDAN consulted attorneys regarding his rights under the employment contract and his entitlement to a larger share of the treasure being recovered from the *SANTA MARGARITA*. Up to this point in time , all of the salvaged artifacts had been brought by Captain JORDAN to the TREASURE SALVORS dock in Key West, Florida and delivered to the court appointed substitute custodian (TREASURE SALVORS, INC.).

On May 21, 1980, Captain JORDAN'S attorneys filed suit in the United States District Court for the Southern District of Florida (80-1205-Civ-SMA), claiming salvage rights to the treasure. The suit was consolidated for discovery and trial with the pending case previously filed by TREASURE SALVORS and Mr. Fisher (79-1381-Civ-JKL). After signing the complaint on May 21st, the intervening claimant, ROBERT JORDAN, returned to Key West and loaded the *Castillian* with supplies and fuel charging the fuel to TREASURE SALVORS and requesting and receiving a TREASURE SALVORS check to pay for the groceries for the upcoming trip. On May 23, 1980, the *Castillian* set sail from Key West carrying on board, Robert LeClair and Frank Moody, Jr. who were employees of TREASURE SALVORS. Mr. Robert LeClair had received orders from Melvin Fisher, to keep watch over JORDAN'S activities.

In addition to the proton magnetometer on board the *Castillian* was a marine Radio Telephone provided to JORDAN by TREASURE SALVORS, INC.

Near the center of the SANTA MARGARITA site on May 25th, *Castillian's* divers hit a bonanza. Their excitement built as they recovered eleven large gold bars, four smaller ones, and a magnificent ten pound gold disc. In total fifty pounds of gold bullion was recovered. They also found five gold two-escudo coins, six small silver bars or discs, two ingots of Cuban copper, a quartzite stone cannonball, and 581 silver coins. The historical significance and uniqueness of the artifacts and items of treasure make valuation difficult. Many of the items are priceless. Trial testimony ranged from estimates of six to thirteen million dollars of treasure yielded so far from the grave of the *SANTA MARGARITA*.

On the evening of May 25, 1980, R.D. LeClair was prohibited by Captain JORDAN from using the radio telephone to inform TREASURE SALVORS of the finds. However, Captain JORDAN used the radio telephone to call his wife, with whom he had arranged a secret code in order to prevent the court's substitute custodian, TREASURE SALVORS, or anyone else, from learning about the salvage recoveries. The secret code worked and arrangements were made to have the bonanza arrested under the newly filed *in rem* action. *Robert Jordan vs The Wrecked and Unidentified Sailing Vessel, et al*, No. 80-1205-Civ-SMA.

On May 26th, the *Castillian's* captain pulled her anchors and left the wrecksite. Captain JORDAN paused briefly at Key West Harbor, making another call on the radio telephone to find out whether he should turn the treasure over to the court's duly appointed substitute custodian (Treasure Salvors) or continue up the Florida Keys and meet with his personal advisors and financial backers. He chose to do the latter. Next, Captain JORDAN turned the *Castillian* into Hawk Channel and proceeded easterly up the Keys to Summerland Key, approximately thirty miles east of Key West. During the trip up the Keys he disclosed to R.D. LeClair that he intended having a "confrontation" with his employer, TREASURE SALVORS and its President, Melvin Fisher.

Upon arriving south of Summerland Key, the *Castillian* was met by a smaller boat piloted by financial backer and advisor, Finley Riccard. After coming to the dock at Finley Riccard's house, the TREASURE SALVORS' employees, Moody and LeClair, were told that they should not attempt to contact TREASURE SALVORS. Soon thereafter, Captain JORDAN"S attorneys arrived at the Riccard house. Photographs were taken of the salvaged treasure and a celebration ensued.While the *Castillian,* laden with treasure, remained the night of May 26th tied up to the dock at Finley Riccard's house, TREASURE SALVORS' representatives made several calls to the Riccard residence in an attempt to find out whether treasure had been discovered and why the *Castillian* and her crew had disappeared. No information was given to Mr. Fisher or his representatives. The next morning, Captain

JORDAN took the *Castillian* back out into Hawk Channel to a point where it was hidden from view from the mainland. The treasure was still aboard. When Deputy United States Marshal, Peter Craig, arrived at Summerland Key, the *Castillian* was at anchor at Hawk Channel, and he had to be ferried out to the larger boat. When the marshal went on board to carry out the *in rem* arrest under Case No. 80-1205-Civ-SMA, the deputy marshal was not told that he was arresting MARGARITA treasure or that the treasure he was arresting was from the same lost vessel that he had executed *in rem* warrants upon earlier (April 14, 1980).

After the marshal's arrest of the treasure out on the water, Captain JORDAN brought the *Castillian* in (for a second time) to the dock at Finley Riccard's house. The TREASURE SALVORS' divers, LeClair and Moody, were told they could now contact their employer, TREASURE SALVORS and they were allowed to leave the premises of the Riccard estate.

Prior to the voyage of May 23rd through May 26th, 1980, intervening claimant, JORDAN, had regularly turned over objects of salvage to the court's duly appointed substitute custodian, TREASURE SALVORS, and he knew prior to May 21, 1980 that TREASURE SALVORS had filed an *in rem* action which claimed the defendant vessel.

The activities described above provoked a flurry of intense litigation. The late Judge William O. Mehrtens issued an ancillary warrant approving the transfer of the gold and silver to TREASURE SALVORS as the court's legal custodian and at the same time, Captain JORDAN"S case was transferred from Judge Aronovitz to Judge Mehrtens. The return of the treasures of the MARGARITA to the court's substitute custodian, TREASURE SALVORS, was accomplished by motion for warrant of arrest *in rem* as to the defendant vessel which was filed May 28, 1980, executed on May 29, 1980 and filed with the court on June 6, 1980

TEMPORARY RESTRAINING ORDER, PRELIMINARY INJUNCTION AND MOTION TO SHOW CAUSE

On May 28, 1980 the plaintiff, TREASURE SALVORS filed an application for a temporary restraining order without notice and motion for preliminary injunction. It also filed a motion to show cause why ROBERT JORDAN should not be punished for contempt. A rule to show cause and a temporary restraining order were issued on May 28, 1980, by Judge William O. Mehrtens. An evidentiary hearing on the preliminary injunction and rule to show cause was heard June 2, 1980. At the conclusion of the lengthy hearing, the court found as follows:

> Gentlemen, it appears to me that I find Mr. Jordan, at the time he went out there was under contractual relations to Fisher, and he owed Fisher a duty and obligation certainly that would exist between a normal employer and employee.
>
> I find, of course, that he was unhappy and dissatisfied with his contract and was desirous of obtaining more.
>
> On these particular days in question when an exceedingly lucky find was made, I find it was within the area covered by the Order of this Court, as amended.
>
> I would be less inclined to find that Mr. Jordan had willfully violated the Order of this Court if he had taken some, to me, firm action in disowing contractual relations with Fisher.
>
> But it seems to me inexcusable really, to be operating under that contract and to charge Treasure Salvors fuel and food and other things, and go out there. And certainly with the markings that were out there and with his previous work in that area, I think, really, that he is now embarking upon a course to unjustly enrich himself.
>
> . . . I am going to make it a preliminary injunction, unless you gentlemen want to stipulate that you do not have any further evidence to offer on the matter . . . .

But meanwhile, the temporary injunction has been made a preliminary injunction and I find him guilty of the willful and deliberate violation of my order.

If there is any question as to jurisdiction, I also find that I have had and do have jurisdiction over the parties and the res and the subject matter of the law suits.

Since the preliminary injunction was issued on June 2, 1980, Captain JORDAN has provided no salvage services and has remained away from the SANTA MARGARITA wrecksite, carrying on other salvage on the reefs south of Sugarloaf Key and Marathon, Florida.

THE SALVAGE CONTINUES

On the 6th of July, the salvage vessel, *Swordfish,* was at anchor over an area which at the time was on of the northernmost areas of the wrecksite to be salvaged. A sharp wind shift caused the *Swordfish's* anchor to drag, and when it finally held, diver Larry Beckman swam down and discovered, lying on bare bedrock, a bronze cannon. Twin decorative dolphins rode its great tube. On the SANTA MARGARITA'S arms list it appeared to have been one of the galleon's heaviest guns, at just under two tons.

July 8th could fairly be named "the day of the gold chains". TREASURE SALVORS divers had followed an artifact trail to a large clump of cannon balls. Two silver ingots and various coins were found amid rich shipwreck material. As salvor/photographer Pat Clyne fanned around one ingot with his hands, a large gold chain popped up, then another and another, all attached in a tangled golden mass. All together there were fifteen chains recovered, the largest had 149 great ornate links. The salvage vessel *Virgilona,* moored nearby, uncovered six more gold bars and a disk of gold.

Duncan Matthewson, TREASURE SALVORS' Marine Archaeologist, began an extensive study of the SANTA MARGARITA wrecksite and the material recovered from it. Mr. Matthewson, along with Dr. Lyon, compared Melians' records with the present site in order to discover how the ship had broken up. They concluded the grapnels may have been lost by Spanish salvors; one might even have been the anchor abandoned when the Dutch threatened Melians' salvage in 1627.

The wrecksite displayed a wider range of ceramic pipes and silverware than the ATOCHA, but to the archaeologist, the single most exciting thing was the large section of the ship itself. It was among the oldest and largest remnants of a Spanish ship ever found in the western hemisphere. It provided substantial physical evidence concerning Spanish Colonial ship construction.

Archaeologist Matthewson delayed raising of the hull structure until the remnants of the galleon could be properly mapped in situ, preparatory to its conservation. A photo mosaic of the structure was made using 132 separate pictures pieced together. During the work on the hull structure, the sand around the timbers was removed by gently fanning for artifacts. Just beneath the structure, they found pig bones, several chili peppers, and two pieces of shoe laces, relics that spoke of the living beings once aboard the SANTA MARGARITA.

Perhaps the most valuable single item turned up while one of the *Virgilona's* divers was working a sand crater's edge. As the boat's tubular mail boxes deflected the prop-wash downward, digging the crater deeper, a round object emerged and struck the diver a glancing blow on the forehead. Before it could vanish in the current, he reached out and took into his hands a beautiful golden plate. The eight inch plate, an artifact of exquisite beauty, displayed an intricate pattern of neo-Moorish design.

On August 23rd, Syd Jones, Captain of the *Swordfish*, saw a treasure mass on the ocean bottom. Lying together were nine more gold bars and eight chains! The same day the divers found the lid of an ivory box, decorated with delicate incised figures of mythical animals. Research later disclosed similar designs on an ivory box from Portuguese Ceylon. Thus far did the network of Spanish imperial trade extend.

On August 25th the *Virgilona* returned to Key West with her priceless ancient cargo of barrel hoops, swords, an arquebus (a memento of Bernardino de Lugo's company of soldiers), a 50-pound clump of silver coins, and an ingot of silver. The skipper of the Virgilona, Captain Mo Molinar, poured from a sack a stream of twenty-five gold two-escudo coins.

As of the present time, it is evident that the SANTA MARGARITA has yielded a very great treasure. The treasure has been recovered along a scattered path of more than 4,000 feet long. The gold bullion alone, in 56 bars, discs, and bits, weighs more than 118 pounds. Mel Fisher and his men also found 180 feet of gold chain and 54 gold coins. It is the largest amount of gold bullion salvaged from a Spanish Galleon in modern times. The divers have recovered nearly 15,000 silver coins and 18 silver ingots with a number of other valuable artifacts.

In artifact value the treasure is worth millions of dollars but the knowledge that will be gained from the shipwreck in ceramic dating, marine construction, and Hispanic culture generally will prove to be of much more enduring value than the bullion.

These findings of fact not only provide a comprehensive background for an understanding of the history of the wrecksite which led to these complicated events between the parties in modern times, but also provide the framework within which the governing law may be applied for determination of the parties' rights in this proceeding.

II CONCLUSIONS OF LAW

JURISDICTION

This Court has jurisdiction over the subject matter pursuant to the Constitution of the United States, Article III, Section 2, Clause 1, 28 U.S.C. §1333, and Rule 9 (h) Fed. R. Civ. P., as a case involving an admiralty and maritime claim. Claims arising out of salvage operations are unquestionably within the admiralty jurisdiction of the Federal Courts.

There are several persuasive factors which lead the Court to the conclusion that it has qualified jurisdiction *in rem* over the wreck and wrecksite of the SANTA MARGARITA. First, thousands of artifacts from the wrecksite have been brought into the physical possession of the United States District Court. Second, through the Court's substitute custodian, TREASURE SALVORS, INC., there is a physical presence and control of the wrecksite by vessels, divers, equipment and otherwise and it could be said that this Court has the wrecksite *in custodia legis.* See *Treasure Salvors I,* fn 5 at 335. Third, the wrecksite lies wholly and exclusively within the waters of contiguous zone of the United States in the Atlantic Ocean. Under the convention of the territorial seas and the contiguous zone, the coastal state has certain custom, fiscal, immigration and sanitary authority within the contiguous zone. See *Treasure Salvors I,* fn 14, at 338; *U.S. v. Gunnar Williams,* et al., 617 F. 2d 1063, 1096 (5th Cir. 1980). The contiguous zone is considered the functional equivalent of the border and therefore affords an area of limited United States jurisdiction.

As between the parties to this litigation, it is conceded that this Court has *in personam* jurisdiction, by virtue of process duly served, to adjudicate the dispute between the parties as to all those objects from the wrecksite whose ownership is in issue. The Court has *in personam* jurisdiction of the parties to determine the validity of a contract between the parties and any rights conferred thereunder. Jurisdiction is also conferred based upon *in personam* principles to adjudicate and protect the rights of these parties on a continuing basis to complete the salvage of the wrecksite now before this Court.

Finally, this Court has in rem jurisdiction, coupled with *in personam* jurisdiction, over the parties to dispose of all artifacts brought up from the site of this wreck during the pendency of the lawsuit. *Cobb Coin*

Company, Inc., v. The Unidentified, Wrecked and Abandoned Sailing Vessel, etc., 525 F. Supp. 186, 194-197 (S. Dist. Fla. 1981); *Treasure Salvors, Inc. v. The Unidentified, Wrecked and Abandoned Sailing Vessel, etc.*, 569 F 2d 330, 333-336 (5th Cir. 1978); *Treasure Salvors v. The Unidentified, Wrecked and Abandoned Sailing Vessel, etc.*, 640 F. 2d 560, 567-568 (5th Cir. 1981).

An *in rem* action for a salvage award against artifacts recovered from the remains of a centuries-old shipwreck states a claim within this Court's admiralty jurisdiction, governed by the judicial doctrine of finds and the principles of maritime salvage. *Cobb Coin*, 525 F. Supp. at 203 *citing Treasure Salvors, Inc. v. The unidentified Wrecked and Abandoned Sailing Vessel*, 569 F. 2d 330 (5th Cir. 1978) (*Treasure Salvors I*); *Cobb Coin*, 549 F. Supp. at 548; *Eads V. Brazelton*, 22 Ark. 499 (1861); *Wiggins v. 1100 Tons, More or Less, of Italian Marble*, 186 F. Supp 452 (E. Dist. Va. 1960); *Brady v. S.S. African Queen* 179 F. Supp 321 (E. Dist. Va. 1960); *Nippon Shoson Kaisha, K.K. v. United States*, (E. Dist. Va. 1960); *Brady v. S. S. African Queen* 179 F. Supp 321 (E. Dist. Va. 1960); *Nippon Shoson Kaisha, K.K. v. United States*, 238 F. Supp. 55 (N. Dis. Ca 1964); *Rikard v. Pringle*, 293 F. Supp 981 (E. Dis. N.Y. 1968); *Treasure Salvors, Inc. v. The Unidentified ,Wrecked and Abandoned Sailing Vessel, etc.* 569 F. 2d 330 (1978); Volume IIIA, M. Norris, *Benedict on Admiralty:* The Law of Salvage, 11-14 (7th Ed. Rev. 1980); *Platoro Limited, Inc. v. The Unidentified Remains of a Vessel*, 614 F. 2d 1051 (5th Cir. 1980); *Treasure Salvors, Inc. v. The Unidentified, Wrecked and Abandoned Sailing Vessel, etc.*, 640 F 2d 56; and *Herner V. U.S.*, 525 F. Supp. 350 (S. Dist. N.Y. 1981).

ANALYSIS OF THE RIGHTS OF THE CLAIMANTS

The State of Florida initially claimed title to the treasure as an aspect of sovereignty, contending it had the right to protect the archaeological heritage of the shipwrecks. TREASURE SALVORS, INC. claims title by virtue of having furnished Robert JORDAN the fruits of its years of extensive research as to the SANTA MARGARITA'S location, supplying him with equipment, provisions, and crew; and contracting with JORDAN to find the wreck. Robert JORDAN claims title to the treasure as a first finder not under contract of employment by TREASURE SALVORS, INC.

CLAIM OF THE STATE OF FLORIDA

The Complaint in this cause was originally filed on March 2, 1979. The State answered on April 5, 1979 admitting that the coordinates given in the Complaint placed the wreck outside the State's territorial waters. On April 10, 1979, the State moved for elimination of requirement of security for stipulation of costs, reciting it in its supporting memorandum of facts and law:

> Pursuant to the applicable rules of the court the STATE filed an answer to the Complaint in admiralty served upon it. The answer does not claim an interest in the unidentified, wrecked and abandoned sailing vessel, but in effect disclaims any interest in the wreck located at the coordinates stated. The answer specifically admits that the stated coordinates are outside the State of Florida.

Based upon the State's representations, this Court entered an Order on May 5, 1979 granting the Motion.

Although the coordinates contained in Plaintiff's Complaint have been amended since the filing of the action, the present coordinates (like the ones initially filed) are outside the State territorial waters.

The seaward limits of the sovereignty lands of the State of Florida were established by the United States Supreme Court in *United States v. Florida,* 425 U.S. 791 (1976). In that case, the Supreme Court states in pertinent part:

1.   As against the State of Florida, the United States is entitled to all the lands, minerals, and other natural resources underlying the Atlantic Ocean more than three geographic miles seaward from the coastline of that state and extending seaward to the edge of the continental shelf, and the State of Florida is not entitled to any interest of such lands, minerals, and resources. As used in this decree, the term "coastline" means the line of ordinary low water along that portion of the coast which is in direct contact with the open sea and the line marking the seaward limit of inland waters, as determined under the convention on the territory sea and the contiguous zone, 15 U.S.T. (Pt. 2) 1606.

In the early stages of this litigation, the State took the position that it would not assert a claim to the shipwreck here involved if it developed factually that the vessel was located outside the State's territorial waters. It is undisputed that the SANTA MARGARITA does not lie inside State territorial waters as established in *United States v. State of Florida, supra*. Once the State was satisfied, concerning the proof of location, it voluntarily withdrew its claim.

CLAIMS OF TREASURE
SALVORS AND ROBERT JORDAN

Each party seeks to be declared owner of the Defendant wrecksite, under the general law of "finds" and, alternatively, each seeks a salvage award for services performed on the wrecked vessel under the maritime law of salvage.

This Court holds that it is appropriate to apply both the law of "finds" and salvage in this action to determine rights to the remains of the wrecksite stipulated to be the SANTA MARGARITA.

The MARGARITA is indisputedly an abandoned vessel whose location has been lost throughout the centuries and whose original owner is not in existence.[2] Under the law of "finds", title to ancient and abandoned vessel vest in the person who first reduces that property to his or her possession. *Treasure Salvors, Inc. v. Unidentified, Wrecked and Abandoned Sailing Vessel, Etc.*, 569 F. 2d 330, (5th Cir. 1978).

As a general rule, under the law of finds, a finder acquires title to lost or abandoned property by "occupancy", i.e., by taking possession of the property and exercising dominion and control over it. It is well established that a finder does not acquire title merely on the strength of its discovery of lost or abandoned property. *Treasure Salvors, Inc. v. Unidentified, Wrecked and Abandoned Sailing Vessel, Etc.*, 640 F.2d 560, 571 (1981). Cobb Coin Co., Inc. v. *Unidentified, Wrecked and Abandoned Sailing Vessel, Etc.*, 549 F. Supp. 540, (So. Dist. Fla. 1982).

Once in possession and control of an identifiable wrecksite, the exclusive right to recover on a continuing basis depends upon the intent of the salvor to do so and his proven capacity to continue the recovery. *Hener v. United States*, 525 F. Supp. 350 (S. Dist. N.Y. 1981). The rights of a salvor who continues uninterrupted operations on an identifiable wrecksite are dependent upon his demonstration of that degree of dominion and control which is appropriate under the circumstances. *Cobb Coin v. Unidentified, Wrecked and Abandoned Sailing Vessel, Etc.*, 549 F. Supp. 540, citing *Eads v. Brazelton, supra; Treasure Salvors III, supra; Brady v. S.S. African Queen supra; Hener, supra.*

This Court holds that the wrecksite containing the scattered remains of the SANTA MARGARITA is abandoned property that was first discovered by employees of Plaintiff **TREASURE SALVORS, INC.**, who were employed by the Plaintiff for that specific purpose, and **TREASURE SALVORS** is therefore entitled to all rights of a first finder under the law.

TREASURE SALVORS, INC. has, through its agents and employees been in continuous possession and control of the wrecksite and the defendant abandoned sailing vessel since it was first discovered. The Plaintiff, **TREASURE SALVORS, INC.** has carefully and systematically brought the discovered artifacts and treasure of the SANTA MARGARITA into the custody of the United States District Court for the Southern District of Florida. The Plaintiff has preserved the archaeological provenance of the shipwreck and has clearly demonstrated its competence to satisfactorily salvage the remains of this magnificent vessel. Title to the recovered treasure of the SANTA MARGARITA is therefore vested in its first finder in possession and salvor, **TREASURE SALVORS, INC.**.

ANALYSIS OF THE CONTRACT

In teaching the conclusions set forth above and in analyzing the rights of the parties, the Court must examine the relationship between the claimants. In this case, there are two relationships. First, **TREASURE SALVORS** and **JORDAN** were parties to the February 5, 1980 contract and stood in a contractual relationship to each other. Even without the February 5th contract, however, the parties, as employer and employee, existed in a relationship as principal and agent. Thus, the Court must apply principles of contract law and principal/agent law to resolve the parties' dispute.

The claimant, **ROBERT JORDAN**, presents three theories in support of invalidating the contract of employment signed on February 5th by **JORDAN** and Mel Fisher, president of TREASURE SALVORS: misrepresentation of face, mutual mistake of fact, and failure of consideration. These three theories rise and fall on **JORDAN**'s contentions that (1) Fisher told **JORDAN** that Fisher had located the remains of the MARGARITA prior to the signing of the contract, and that (2) the first sentence of Paragraph One of the Agreement was an untrue statement when made. That sentence reads, in part, "Salvors is the sole owner against all claims of the sailing vessel 'Nuestra Senora de Atocha,' Margerita [sic], ..."

JORDAN claims that the statement in Paragraph One constituted a misrepresentation of a material fact as did Fisher's alleged statement that he knew the exact location of the MARGARITA. Relying on these representations, **JORDAN** agreed to be compensated[3] by a much smaller percentage of the treasures and artifacts of the MARGARITA than he would have demanded if he had known otherwise.[4] **JORDAN** argues that his reliance on the misrepresentation made the contract voidable, and that he successfully avoided the contract beginning on May 27, 1980, when he delivered salvaged items from the MARGARITA to the United States Marshal pursuant to his own recently filed claim in Case No. 80-1205-Civ-SMA.

A contract created by two parties is not made in a vacuum. To understand the contract, the Court must view it in the context of the events and circumstances from which it arose. The Court must, above all else, give effect to the parties' intentions.

Pennzoil Co. v. Federal Energy Regulatory Com'n, 645 F. 2d 360, 388 (5th Cir, 1981). "Such intentions are to be drawn as much as possible from the language of the agreement, but where, as here, the agreement is silent on the issue, the Court may turn to extrinsic evidence for support." *Valley Cenent Indus. v. Midco Equipment Co.,* 570 F. 2d 1241, 1242 (5th Cir. 1978). The Court must give due consideration to all surrounding circumstances including those during the negotiation period. *Morris v. Federated Mutual Inc. Co.,* 497 F 2d 538, 540 (5th Cir. 1974).

The Court finds, for reasons stated *infra,* that the evidence presented clearly reveals the parties' intention in entering into the contract of employment was to allow **JORDAN**, as a **TREASURE SALVORS'** employee, to explore and begin salvage operations east and west of the ATOCHA with the hope - nay, the expectation - of pinpointing the exact location of the MARGARITA.

Mel Fisher and ROBERT JORDAN were certainly not strangers to each other; they had been acquainted for fifteen years. They had contracted before on several other occasions concerning the same type of exploration and salvaging contract as the instant one. In the mid 1960's, for example, JORDAN had worked for Fisher south of Marathon, Florida, on the 1733 fleet vessels. In 1979, he had worked for Fisher off the beach at Ft. Pierce, Florida, on 1715 fleet vessels. These undertakings were pursuant to the direction and control of Mel Fisher as JORDAN"S employer. The history of the relationship of the parties, therefore, suggests the intention of the parties on February 5, 1980, was to enter into another contract of employment for purposes of exploration and salvage.

Events just prior to February 5th, during a period of pre-contract negotiations, however, are even more indicative of the parties' intentions. JORDAN was given $600.00 by Mel Fisher to haul his boat, the *Castillian,* out of the water for repairs and to bring it down to Key West. When JORDAN arrived, he was asked to be present at a meeting at Commander John Cryer's house in late January. At this meeting, exclusive and extensive information based upon years of archival and on-site research was presented by Dr. Eugene Lyons, TREASURE SALVORS' historian and archival researcher, and others concerning the possible locations of the MARGARITA and other ancient Spanish wrecks. Captain JORDAN, in fact, was given over one hundred pages of translations of documents for his own reference and use. Results from TREASURE SALVORS' prior explorations at various sites were discussed. It was learned that archival research and magnetometer readings had suggested the MARGARITA wrecksite lay east or west of the ATOCHA.

At the end of the meeting, a large map of the area surrounding Key West was produced and the participants each marked their best guesses" on the map as to the location of the MARGARITA and the rest of the ATOCHA based upon all the information which had just been presented. Mel Fisher, Captain JORDAN and others indicated their "best guesses."[5]

Several days after this meeting, the parties signed the Agreement in question. This Court finds, based on the events and circumstances preceding the signing of the contract, and based on the credibility of the testimony of the witnesses, that the intention of Mel Fisher and Captain JORDAN was to turn their "best guesses" into a reality by employing JORDAN to perform further exploration and salvaging in specific locations (i.e., east and west of the ATOCHA until the wreck of the MARGARITA could be pinpointed.

JORDAN'S course of performance during the existence of the contract supports the Court's finding concerning the intention of the parties. "Where an agreement involves repeated occasions for performance by either party with knowledge of the nature of the performance and opportunity for objection to it by the other, any course of performance accepted or acquiesced in without objection is given great weight in the interpretation of the agreement." *Restatement (Second) of Contracts* (1981) §202 (4). Captain JORDAN was directed to several locations to explore and salvage over the course of his employment from February 5th and thereafter. If he truly thought that Fisher had already pinpointed the location of the MARGARITA, he had the opportunity to object when he was directed to areas where his salvage operations yielded nothing. Yet JORDAN chose not to do so . Therefore, the Court finds that JORDAN's course of performance from February 5th and thereafter is consistent with the intention of the parties in forming the contract.

Although there is no claim to the contrary, this Court specifically finds that JORDAN and Fisher, as president of TREASURE SALVORS, entered into the contract of employment freely and voluntarily and with mutual assent. As previously mentioned, Fisher and JORDAN were not strangers to each other, having known each other for some fifteen years. They had contracted before on several other occasions concerning the same type of contract as involved here. The language of the instant contract was pieced together from the previous contracts between the parties. Prior to February 5th, JORDAN took the proposed contract for 4-7 days to his financial backer, Finley Riccard, for consultation and advice. In addition, the signing of the contract was preceded by several days of discussion and negotiation of each sentence by the parties. The contract, in fact, was altered by both parties prior to the signing, thus evidencing a negotiated instrument.

Keeping in mind the intention of the parties informing the contract, the Court now turns to a consideration of the claimant's claims that the first sentence of Paragraph One of the Agreement was untrue when made and that Fisher had represented he knew the exact location of the MARGARITA and that these constituted misrepresentations of fact. As previously stated, the statement in question reads, in part: "Salvors is the sole owner against all claims of the sailing vessel 'Nuestra Senora de Atocha,'Margerita [sic], ..." In order to render an otherwise enforceable contract voidable, a material misrepresentation of fact must be relied upon, and the contract must be disaffirmed, Calamari, *The Law of Contracts* §9-13-15 (1977); *Classic Bowl, Inc. v. AMF Pinspotters, Inc.* 403 F 2d 463, 466 (7th Cir. 1968).

The Court finds that based on the evidence presented and the credibility of the testimony of the witnesses, there was no misrepresentation to Captain JORDAN concerning the status of ownership or the location of the MARGARITA wrecksite. TREASURE SALVORS had generally located the vessel as a result of its previous research and salvage efforts in the area. In March, 1979, it had filed a claim to the wrecksite in Case No. 79-1381-Civ-WM. The coordinated were based on the then available information and belief, including positive readings from remote sensing data showing the existence of a shipwreck, and were located east of the ATOCHA. [These coordinates were later amended on March 10, 1980 and again on May 12, 1980 to reflect recently discovered artifacts].

The task of locating ancient wrecksites, especially those such as the MARGARITA whose treasures and artifacts have been widely scattered by shifting currents and storms over the years precludes absolute precision in establishing exact coordinates which contain the wreckage.

Since the purpose of the contract was to pinpoint the location of the MARGARITA either east or west of the ATOCHA, this Court finds, and indeed the claimant stipulated on the opening day of trial, that the remains of the vessel discovered east of the ATOCHA on February 13, 1980, by Captain JORDAN and the TREASURE SALVORS crew on board the *Castillian* to be the MARGARITA as contemplated by the parties in their contract.

This Court also finds that the more credible testimony, considering the intention of the parties in forming the contract and the events at the January meeting, to be that Mr. Fisher never represented to JORDAN that he knew the exact location of the MARGARITA. It is clear from the nature of the meeting that the whole purpose of the meeting was to enable the participants to formulate educated theories as to the specific location of the wreck. JORDAN was aware that Fisher had, at best, a "best guess."

This Court further finds that JORDAN knew the purpose of his employment was to *ripen* TREASURE SALVORS' ownership in the MARGARITA wrecksite by pinpointing the location through further exploration and salvage efforts. This Court therefore finds that there could have been no misrepresentation concerning ownership of the wrecksite to JORDAN[6].

Even if this Court had found there was a misrepresentation, which it has not, JORDAN must still establish that he reasonably relied to his detriment on that misrepresentation.

This Court finds the evidence shows JORDAN had not demonstrated such reliance. He knew TREASURE SALVORS had not yet found the wrecksite and that such was necessary to prove possession and control essential elements of ownership. His course of performance subsequent to the signing of the contract supports this finding. JORDAN made no objection to Fisher when directed to areas where no artifacts or treasures were found - if he had relied upon Fisher's alleged representation that he had pinpointed the location, he would have questioned Fisher's directions.

Finally, this Court finds that even if there were a material misrepresentation and that JORDAN had reasonably relied upon it when contracting, JORDAN affirmed the contract by accepting the benefits and thereby lost the right to disaffirm the contract.

A party operating under a material misrepresentation has the power to avoid the legal relations created by the contract. The power of avoidance, however, is lost by ratification of the contract and acceptance of the benefits. *Restatement (Second) of Contracts* §7 (1981). In the instant case, after the signing of the contract of February 5, JORDAN was an employee of Mr. Fisher and TREASURE SALVORS. From that date on, Mr. JORDAN and his crew were paid daily wages by TREASURE SALVORS. Food and fuel for the *Castillian* were also supplied. The crew, in fact, were TREASURE SALVORS employees. Captain JORDAN, therefore, accepted these daily benefits for a period of more than one hundred days before attempting to avoid the contract by not delivering treasurers and artifacts to TREASURE SALVORS, the lawful substitute custodian.

Even more than the daily benefits of food, fuel, wages, and crew, however, was the benefit to JORDAN of the wealth of information and knowledge about where to search for the MARGARITA which had been provided to him at the January meeting at Commander Cryer's house. TREASURE SALVORS had invested hundreds of thousands of dollars worth of both archival research of ancient Spanish documents and on actual site work. This information was freely given to Captain JORDAN.

This Court finds that JORDAN used the information extended him by TREASURE SALVORS and relied upon documents provided by TREASURE SALVORS during his employment by the company.

Much of the equipment on board the *Castillian*, essential for a successful salvaging operation, was provided by TREASURE SALVORS. In addition to hoists and wenches, used to retrieve artifacts and treasures from the ocean floor, TREASURE SALVORS provided the VHS marine radio with ship-to-ship and ship-to-shore communications. The most important pieces of equipment, however, was the highly sophisticated one-of-a-kind proton magnetometer. This enabled JORDAN to specifically locate treasure once his boat was in the general location as directed by Fisher.

In summary, this Court finds that JORDAN affirmed the contract of employment through his action - by accepting and making use of the benefits of salary, food, fuel, crew, information, and equipment from February 5, 1980 and thereafter. JORDAN also affirmed the contract through his regular course of conduct in turning over all artifacts discovered prior to May 25, 1980, to TREASURE SALVORS, the court-ordered substitute custodian of the treasurers of the wreck. Therefore , even if there had been a material misrepresentation and detrimental reliance, which would have made the contract voidable by JORDAN, the power of avoidance was lost by JORDAN's ratification of the contract and acceptance of the benefits.

This Court notes that even if it were to find the February 5th contract of employment void *ad initio*, it would still find that based on the parties' course of performance from February to the end of May 1980, there was an enforceable implied employment contract between the two parties, and that JORDAN was to receive a daily salary and, in addition, 5% of the treasurers and artifacts recovered from the wreck of the MARGARITA as an employee of TREASURE SALVORS in return for his exploration and salvage efforts. *See Bloomgarden v. Coyer, 479 F. 2d (D.C. Cir. 1973).*

This Court now turns to the arguments of the Plaintiff, TREASURE SALVORS. The plaintiff argues Captain JORDAN, as an employee of the company. breached its fiduciary duty to TREASURE SALVORS and breached the contract of employment by failing to deliver treasurers and artifacts from the MARGARITA to the court appointed custodian on May 25, 1980 and thereafter and by establishing his own claim to the wrecksite.

An agent owes a duty of the utmost loyalty to his principal. *Laub v. Genwasy Corp.* 60 F.R.D. 462 (S.D.N.Y. 1973). This is a fiduciary duty with respect to matters within the scope of the agency. A fiduciary is held to "the punctilio of an honor the most sensitive." *Meinhard v. Salmon,* 249 N.Y. 458. 464, 164 N.E. 545, 546 (1928) (Cardozo, C.J.). An agent must "act solely for the benefit of the principal in all matters connected with his agency." *Restatement (Second) of Agency* §387 (1958). He must not compete with his principal concerning the subject matter of the agency, Id. at §393.

> Everyone, whether designated agent, trustee, servant or what not, who is under contract or other legal obligation to represent or act for another in any particular business or line of business of for any valuable purpose must be loyal and faithful to the interest of such other in respect to such business or

purpose.He cannot lawfully serve or acquire any private interest of his own in opposition to it. This is a rule of common sense and honesty as well as of law. The agent is not entitled to avail himself of any advantage that his position may give him to profit beyond the agreed compensation for his services. He may not speculate for his gain in the subject-matter of the employment. He may not use any information that he may have acquired by reason of his employment, either for the purpose of acquiring property or doing any other act which is in opposition to his principal's interest.

McHaney v. McHaney 209 Ark. 337, 1909 S.W. 2d 450,454 (1945). *See B.J. McAdams, Inc. v. Boggs,* 439 S.Supp. 738 (E.D. Pa. 1977).

The relationship of TREASURE SALVORS and Captain JORDAN was in a fiduciary relationship to TREASURE SALVORS. JORDAN owned a duty to his employer to act with the highest degree of good faith and loyalty. He owned a duty to TREASURE SALVORS not to act for an adverse party *or himself* in any transaction within the scope of the agency.

This Court finds that JORDAN breached his fiduciary duty to TREASURE SALVORS when he did not deliver salvaged treasures and artifacts to the lawful custodian on May 25, 1980, and based on the events which transpired thereafter. The discovery on May 25 of an immense fortune in gold and silver, beyond man's wildest dreams, caused JORDAN to pursue his own selfish interests instead of those of his employer. The surreptitiousness of the events during the days of May 25 through 27 during which two TREASURE SALVORS' employees were prevented from communicating with their employer, lends credence to the Court's finding that JORDAN breached his fiduciary duty.

For the above-stated reasons, and based on the evidence produced at trial and the credibility of the testimony of the witnesses, this Court finds that Captain JORDAN breached his contract of employment and his fiduciary duty beginning on May 25, 1980, when he did not deliver treasures and artifacts found that day to the lawful custodian. By his actions and conduct in attempting to establish a claim to the MARGARITA while under the salaried employ of TREASURE SALVORS and while using the company's information, fuel, food, crew, and equipment, this Court further finds that JORDAN forfeits any right he might have to equitable consideration, under the theory of quantum meruit, for services rendered May 25, 1980, and thereafter.

ANALYSIS OF THE RIGHTS OF
TREASURE SALVORS UNDER
THE LAW OF ADMIRALTY

The court holds, first, that TREASURE SALVORS, INC., is entitled to a salvage award for the articles it has retrieved from the SANTA MARGARITA wrecksite. The three elements of a salvage claim are:

1. that marine peril exists;
2. that the service was voluntarily rendered; and
3. that the effort was successful in whole or in part.

Platoro Ltd. v. Unidentified Remains of a Vessel, 518 F. Supp. 816, 820 (W. Dist. Tex. 1980), citing *Legnos v. M/V Olga Jacob*, 498 F. 2d 666,669 (5th Cir. 1974), *Cobb Coin, Inc. v. Unidentified Wrecked and Abandoned Sailing Vessel*, 549 F. Supp. 540, (S. Dist. Fla 1982).

It is established in this Circuit that a marine peril exists in an ancient, abandoned shipwreck for purposes of meeting the requirements of a valid salvage action. *Platoro Ltd. v. Unidentified Remains of a Vessel*, 614 F. 2d 1051, 1055 (5th Cir. 1980); *Treasure Salvors I*, 569 F. 2d 330, 337 and n. 13 (5th Cir. 1978), quoting Norris, The Law of Salvage § 185 (1958).

The Plaintiff has satisfied the second and third elements of salvage claim as well. There is no dispute that TREASURE SALVORS voluntarily rendered the salvage service. [7] It was under no pre-existing duty to save the vessel and its cargo and apparel pursuant to , e.g., a contract or provision of law. Further, the Findings of Fact entered above by this Court amply demonstrate that TREASURE SALVORS successfully saved property of considerable historic, archaeological, and monetary value.

SALVAGE AWARD

As this Court has previously held, the public policy underlying salvage awards in the Admiralty Court is to hold out a "continuing incentive to undertake the physical and financial risks entailed in salvage operations and to bring the property thus recovered into court for a salvage determination." Cobb Coin, 525 S. Supp. at 207, Cobb Coin, 549 F. Supp.540. The elements considered by the Admiralty Court in determining a salvage award are:

1. the labor expended by the salvors in rendering the salvage service;
2. the promptitude, skill and energy displayed in rendering the service and saving the property;
3. the value of the property employed by the salvors in rendering the service and the danger to which such property was exposed;
4. the risk incurred by the salvors in securing the property from the impending peril;
5. the value of the property saved;
6. the degree of danger from which the property was rescued.

Cobb Coin, 549 F. Supp at 557, *Cobb Coin*, 525 F. Supp at 207, n. 15, *See Also* Norris, 3A Benedict on Admiralty, The Law of Salvage, 7th ed §244.

The services rendered by TREASURE SALVORS, INC., with respect to each of these elements, have been discussed in the preceeding portions of this opinion. The Plaintiff has clearly demonstrated its entitlement to a salvage award.

As this Court has held in previous decisions, the appropriate form of award in a case like this should differ from traditional awards. It should be given *in specie* because the property saved is uniquely and intrinsically valuable beyond its monetary value. See *Cobb Coin*, 525 F. Supp. at 198. The Court therefore holds that the plaintiff, TREASURE SALVORS, Inc., shall be awarded all the artifacts it has recovered since the inception of this lawsuit, as compensation for its expenses and an award for superlative salvage services.

The Court further holds that TREASURE SALVORS has established a right to the protection of this Court to conduct further salvage activities, for as long as it demonstrates the requisite diligence and success in its efforts.

The Court therefore retains jurisdiction:

1. To protect the Plaintiff's valid salvage operations on the defendant wreck, and to adjudicate its rights vis-a-vis competing salvors who may assert a superior right to salve the defendant wreck, the area described in these pleadings, and

2. To Adjudicate the Plaintiff's claim to a salvage award on a periodic basis. The plaintiff shall file in this Court, beginning on January 1, 1984, and on January 1st of each subsequent year, its claim stating with specificity the value of the salvage services performed and cataloguing the artifacts saved in the previous calendar year. Any failure to file by that date will constitute *prima facie* evidence that it has abandoned the defendant wreck site, and the plaintiff will have thirty days to attempt to rebut that presumption, through appropriate pleadings, after which this case will be closed.

INJUNCTION

The June 2, 1980 order temporarily enjoined the agents, employees, and attorneys of rival claimants from interfering with Plaintiff's ongoing salvage operation. That injunction is hereby made permanent now that the plaintiff has succeeded on the merits of its claim under federal law.

CONTEMPT

Mr. Robert JORDAN was held in contempt on June 2, 1980 by the Honorable William O. Mehrtens for violation of the Court's order appointing TREASURE SALVORS substitute custodian of the recovered artifacts of the SANTA MARGARITA.

The Court accepts Mr. JORDAN'S statement that he was motivated by a desire to obtain a Court ruling on his dispute with Mr. Fisher and TREASURE SALVORS, INC., over the terms of his employment contract. Fully recognizing that his methods were unorthodox and could have resulted in loss or destruction of priceless historical artifacts;

ATTORNEY'S FEES

The award of attorney's fees and costs in admiralty is discretionary and specifically permitted in salvage cases. *Compania Galeana v. M/V Caribbean*, 565 F. 2d 358 (5th Cir. 1978), *Cobb Coin Co., Inc. v. Unidentified, Wrecked and Abandoned Sailing Vessel, etc.*, 549 F. Supp 540 (S. Dist. Fla 1982). The Plaintiff has succeeded on the merits and is therefore entitled to an award of fees and costs from Robert JORDAN. It is, therefore

ORDERED, ADJUDGED and DECREED as follows:

1.   TREASURE SALVORS, INC. is hereby awarded all artifacts and treasure recovered from the wrecked Spanish galleon SANTA MARGARITA lost September 5, 1622 and delivered into the custody of the Court.

2.   The Court retains jurisdiction to protect the Plaintiff's valid salvage operations within the area described in this case and to adjudicate its claim to a salvage award on a periodic basis for those artifacts hereafter recovered.

3.   The claimant Robert JORDAN, his agents and employees are permanently enjoined from interfering with the Plaintiff's ongoing salvage operations, its officers, agents or employees.

4.   The in rem admiralty action, *Robert Jordan v. The Unidentified, Wrecked and Abandoned Sailing Vessel, et al.* Case No. 80-1205-Civ JLK, is hereby dismissed with prejudice.

5.   The Plaintiff is entitled to recover reasonable attorney's fees and costs. The attorney for the plaintiff shall file his affidavits for fees and costs within twenty (20) days of the date of this order.

DONE and ORDERED in chambers at the United States District Courthouse, Miami, Florida, this 18th day of January 1983.

JAMES LAWRENCE KING
U. S. DISTRICT JUDGE

cc: David Paul Horan, Esq.
Michael T. Callahan, Esq.
Ronald W. Brooks, Esq.
Gerhardt Schreiber, Esq.
Linwood Anderson, Esq.

FOOTNOTES

1. E. Lyon, *The Search for the Atocha* (Harper & Row, 1979).

2. The modern day government of Spain has expressed no interest in filing a claim in this litigation as a successor-owner.

3. In addition to 5% of the recovery of treasures and artifacts from the wreck, JORDAN was paid a daily salary all the time while under the employ of TREASURE SALVORS.

4. This is JORDAN's argument for failure of consideration.

5. Fisher's "best guess" later proved correct, JORDAN's proved considerably off mark. As discussed *infra*, this Court finds that Fisher at no time prior to the signing of the contract represented to JORDAN that he had anything better than a "best guess" as to the location of the MARGARITA.

6. Based on the foregoing analysis, the Court rejects the claimant's theory that there was a mutual mistake of fact or failure of consideration.

7. TREASURE SALVORS has expended considerable sums of money, vessels and manpower, to establish possession and control over the wrecksite of the SANTA MARGARITA. Prior to 1971, TREASURE SALVORS, interested in the recovery of the ATOCHA and MARGARITA, had explored sites in the Atlantic Ocean, off the Florida Keys, in the Bay of Florida along the Gulf of Mexico boundary of the Florida Keys, including Matecumbe Key. It is equally clear that Mel Fisher and TREASURE SALVORS made the first major, primary effort to direct their attention to the exploration in the Marquesas Keys area as a result of Dr. Lyon's discovery in the Archives of the Indies in Seville, Spain. On a trial and error basis, TREASURE SALVORS spent many months and years in areas east as well as west of the Marquesas. During the time it finally isolated a promising, productive and responsive area now known to contain the wrecksite of the NUESTRA SENORA DE ATOCHA and the SANTA MARGARITA. In excess of 7.1 million dollars was spent by the plaintiff in this effort, *Treasure Salvors v. Unidentified Wrecked and Abandoned Sailing Vessel, etc.*, 546 F. Supp. at 925 (S. Dist. Fla 1981).

APPENDIX G

TRACKING THE ATOCHA

by

**JOHN P. CRYER
CDR. USN/RET.**

SEPTEMBER 15, 1986

Archeometeorology - Dr. Jim Bellis of Notre Dame coined the phrase. We had met as part of a group going to observe the wreck site of the Spanish galleon Nuestra Senora Atocha which has recently been located by Mel Fisher's Treasure Salvors.

In 1973, at the urging of Duncan Mathewson and Dr. Eugene Lyon, I developed the track of the Spanish fleet that had departed from Havana, Cuba on September 4, 1622 and was overtaken by a storm and wrecked on the Florida Keys. This Tierra Firme Flota commanded by the Marquis of Cadereita consisted of 28 ships. Among the galleons, the Santa Margarita was designated as Capitana and the Nuestra Senora de Atocha as the Almiranta of the Flota which meant she would be rear guardship. A copy of this track was reproduced in R. Duncan Mathewson's book, "Search for Nuestra Senora de Atocha" published in 1983. The location of this site, much to my personal satisfaction, proved to be where I had located it in 1973.

My methodology, which has been dubbed "archeometeorology", was basically to gather all the meteorological information I could pertaining to the ill fated voyage of these ships, and from this data reconstruct the storm and storm track and its effect on the armada.

Most of this information was derived as a result of Dr. Eugene Lyon's research in the Archives de Seville, Spain. His thorough work in uncovering and translating letters written in 1622 from the Cadereita to the Crown were invaluable. These letters were based on the testimony of eyewitnesses to the voyage and the final sinking of both the Atocha and the Margarita. They provided me with enough information to reconstruct what historians have been calling a hurricane, but which I now believe to have been a strong tropical storm by meteorological definition. A hurricane is specifically defined in present terms as having winds of over 65 knots. However, I must explain that before the world became so technically precise, the Spanish had picked up the word hurricane from the Caribbean Indians, the word was "huracan" which meant "evil spirits". The word was gradually assimilated into the Spanish language and eventually became hurricane.

In order to develop this track, the first step was to make a chronological list of all wind reports. Now you may say, where are you going to get meteorological reports in chronological order in 1622? The answer is to be found in the testimony given by survivors. For example the statement that "the day dawned so serene and *clear* and with such a *fair northeast wind* and so fit for the purpose, all the pilots felt that it would be a very great success to set sail." From this we can infer that the winds at sailing time were Northeast 10 to 15 knots. Further information was derived from the following: "At seven in the morning I set sail on a NNW course until three in the afternoon when a change was made to ESE until sunset. Then the armada found itself with ENE wind and changed course to North until the following Monday."

"At seven in the morning a great hurricane and storm came upon the fleet pushing out a NE wind."

"Not being able to carry on in this manner at three in the afternoon, they scudded before the sea with only foresails on a SW course until five o'clock. At that time the weather became so vigorous that the foresails of many ships were carried away."

"Thus at nightfall I found myself alone with only the Capitana and went running WSW and W until midnight." [ships are being driven by the wind which is gradually veering from ENE to East.]

"Around midnight the wind shifted to South with such violence carrying away the foresail and putting both of them in the sea."

At this point we can surmise that the eye of the storm passed very close and wind velocity was close to hurricane force. My estimate was 50 - 55 knots.

With the wind information laid out in chronological order we can start to see the pattern of the storm.

If we extract all the information regarding wind direction and force and lay it out in chronological order we can use this to develop the pattern of the storm. See Figure 1.

We now apply Buy Ballots Law, which states "If an observer in the northern hemisphere faces the wind, the center of low pressure (the eye of the storm or hurricane) is toward his right somewhat behind him." Applying our information on wind direction we can locate the center of the storm.

First we must draw a model storm from a meteorologists' standpoint as shown in figure 2.

The lines around the center are called isobars or lines of equal barometric pressure. In a cyclone or low pressure system the lowest pressure is in the center and the wind pattern is counter clockwise around the center. The winds also called gradient winds converge at an angle of from 10 - 15 degrees towards the center from the isobar lines.

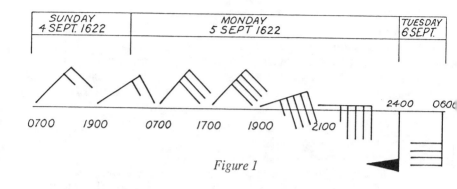

Figure 1

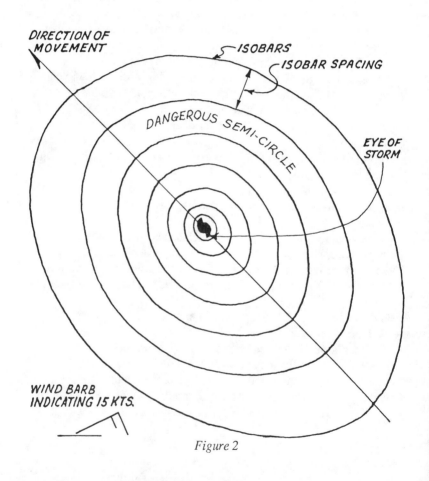

Figure 2

Thus the winds in a cyclonic storm converging towards the center and the spacing between the isobars is called the gradient. The closer the isobaric spacing the higher the gradient and the stronger the wind. Now we can plot on our model storm the various winds that we have previously obtained from our analysis of the survivors statements. See Figure 3. The lower wind velocities will be located further from the center where the isobaric spacing is greatest, conversely the higher winds are nearer the storm center. This shows us two things, where the ship was in relation to the storm center and conversely where the storm center was in relation to the ship.

Now we are ready to start our plot to determine the track of the armada. The process will involve reconstructing a navigational track using all the information available, such as:

1. Courses
2. Speed
3. Set and Drift
4. Wind speed
5. Leeway
6. Times of course changes
7. Sea state
8. Material conditions (i.e., dismasted or only foresail up, or bare poles)

Courses were given in magnetic vs true heading and no allowance was made for variation or deviation.

Speed - The speed of 17th century galleons has been derived from the study of many logs of voyages as well as writings of the times. The speed of a galleon can be reckoned as two knots in a light breeze, four knots in a fresh breeze and six knots in a strong breeze.

Set and Drift - The set of the current is defined as the direction in which the water is moving and the speed at which it is moving is called drift.

Leeway is the leeward or down wind motion of a vessel due to the wind. They could not sail much closer to the wind that 55 - 60 degrees and their speed was in the 3 - 5 knot range Lack of a good keel and high freeboard makes leeway a considerable factor These factors are very important when we consider the sailing characteristics of the Spanish galleons.

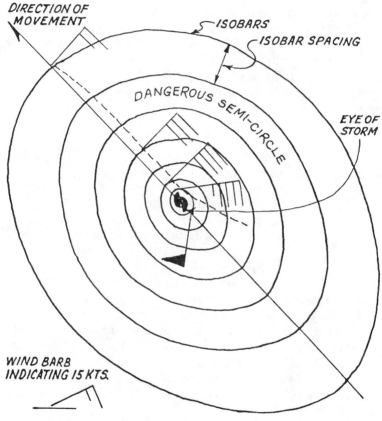

Figure 3

Times of course changes can be determined by such statements as sunset or sunrise or the hour. Time was kept on board galleons by means of hour and half hour glasses, and the sounding of the bell for watch changes and prayers. It was checked using the astrolabe for local apparent noon and the nocturnal for obtaining the time at night by using the relationship between the pole star, Polaris, and the position of the "guards i.e. Kochab, part of the dipper that rotates around Polaris, the north star.

Sea State is obtained by the description of the narrator. "The day dawned serene and clear and with such a fair northeast wind ..." Sea state would be between 0 and 3. Whereas a statement such as, " . . . not being able to carry on in this manner, at three in the evening they scudded before the sea with only foresails." might indicate a sea state of 4 or 5, and the statement, "At five o'clock the weather became so vigorous that the foresails of many ships were carried away." and later, " . . They could not steer and lost their mainmasts." would indicate state 5 to 7.

We now have a good picture of the sea conditions the armada encountered. The storm center as it approached the armada and engulfed it with ever increasing winds and seas passed just to the southwest of the armada as noted by the sudden shift of the wind from the *south*, which carried the Margarita and Atocha helplessly northward on to the reef.

Soundings - Depth was determined from statements of the survivors. One of these statements was made by Don Bernardino de Lugo, troop captain of the galleon Santa Margarita. When asked about the sinking and about missing ships, he said the following: "On the day of the storm his ship followed the Capitana on its southwest course until nightfall, when the wind carried away her foresail, being at cross purposes, the galleon broke its mainmast and whip staff of her rudder and her tiller was shattered, not being able to carry sail and seeing some lantern nearby she remained thus until Tuesday, the sixth of September. Then at dawning they took soundings and found forth arms of water . . ."

From the statements of other survivors we know, " . . . this day at six was lost the galleon Nuestra Senora de Atocha, Almiranta of the flota, with such quickness that within an hour she sank . . . it is understood she sank through their having her cable cut with which they had anchored in three or four brazas of water where they had no choice but to cut it." Another statement " . . . having struck before dawn on a "rise" (reef) opened up from below in such a way that with the short distance which it went it sank in ten arms of water (55 ft.)."

With this wealth of information we can now put it to good use by plotting the track. For the first leg we will use:

> Course ....NNW or 337° 30"
> Speed.................................4 knots
> Set & Drift of Gulf Stream .....095°   2.2 knots
> Wind................................NE 10 - 15 knots
> Leeway Factor ....0.4 knot

The resultant track is shown on the chart in figure 4. The same process was repeated for each course change, or as in the case when they lost all steerage control the effects of the wind and sea are used. The resultant track was terminated using the intelligence gleaned from the testimony of the survivors. i.e. "The Admiral of the entire fleet (Almiranta) ran northward all night . . . suddenly she came to shallow water and in short space ran herself aground in two fathoms of water plus a little more (12 - 15 feet) where her beak broke in pieces . . ." ". . .it is understood that she (Atocha) sank through their having cut a cable with which they had anchored . . ." and, "the Almiranta of the Fleet followed its course . . . and having struck before dawn upon a rise, opened up from below in such a way that with the short distance which it went it sank in ten arms of water (55 feet)."

From the foregoing testimony it becomes apparent that the Atocha on seeing the pounding surf on the reefs ahead of them and sounding 40 arms of water let go their anchors. When the anchors finally held and with all the cable out the anchor would have been some 1200 feet from the ship since sheet anchors usually carried two cable lengths of line. In this position (see figure 5) with storm waves of some 10 - 15 feet, it would have caused the ship, when at the bottom of the trough, to pound on the reef, and lift off on the crest and back down into the trough. Realizing their perilous plight we can surmise they immediately cut the anchor line as stated in the testimony, allowing them to drift off the reef. However, it was too late, with the damaged beak head they were

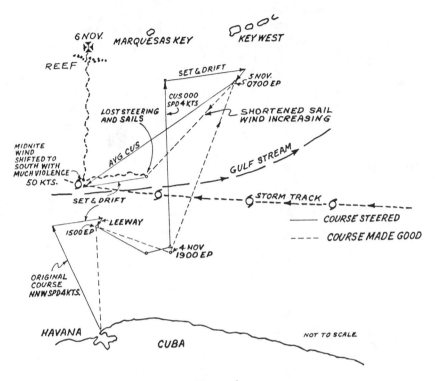

Figure 4

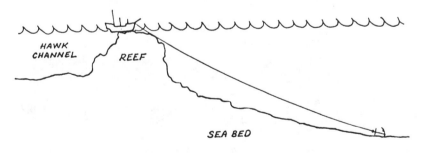

Figure 5

taking on water at an alarming rate and as they were now free of the anchor they were driven northward by the winds and seas and she quickly sank. As the Spanish salvor Vargas stated in his salvage report, when he found the Atocha, she was in ten arms of water (55 feet). Knowing this we can now project our track along the course over the reef to terminate in 55 feet of water depth. This was done as noted on my original track developed in 1973* Treasure Salvors searched the area back then with a magnetometer and missed the big pile. The later search by Kane Fisher in 1985 finally located the "big pile" right in my location circle of highest probability.

Bibliography

Bowditch ....American Practical Navigator

Chapelle, H.I.....................................Search for Speed Under Sail

Harding & Kotch.............................Heavy Weather Guide

Lyon, Dr. Eugene.............................Miscellaneous research material

Mathewson III, R. Duncan..................The Search for Nuestra Senora de Atocha

Petterssen ....Heavy Weather Guide

Waters, D.W. ....The Art of Navigation in Elizabethan & Early Stuart Times

John P. Cryer   Commander, USN Retired

Spent thirty-six years in the United States Navy as line officer. Held billets as commanding officer, executive, operations, weapons, ASW, navigator and staff meteorologist, port captain and various other billets. Since retirement in 1977 he has teamed up with Dr. Eugene Lyon and has utilized his techniques in locating many other ship wrecks around the world. Attended Rutgers University, University of Kansas and U.S. Navy Postgraduate School, Monterey. Holds a B.S. in meteorology.

*The original track chart was printed in R. Duncan Mathewson's book, "Search for the Atocha" published in 1983.

APPENDIX H

GUNS OF THE 1622 SPANISH GALLEONS
(A PRELIMINARY STUDY)

BILL MUIR, DESIGNER   January 12, 1988

Artifacts that provide positive verification of early seventeenth century Spanish two wheeled marine gun carriage configuration and proportion have been recovered in the Florida Keys westerly of Key West, Florida. They were found in deep overburden southwesterly of the Marquesas Keys. The remarkable underwater finds were among many recovered in recent years by underwater archaeologists in cooperation with treasure recovery divers on the site of the Spanish galleon NUESTRA SENORA de ATOCHA and from the trail of the Guard galleon SANTA MARGARITA. These were two of eight galleons, merchantmen and patches that were dashed into the reefs and shoals of the westernmost keys ranging from the Marquesas to the Tortugas chain during the severe hurricane of 1622. The Tierra Firme and Plate fleet Armada of 28 sail were on their way through the Florida Straits returning to Spain from the West Indies when the disastrous tempest took its heavy toll of the treasure laden fleet.

Ten of the original twenty-two bronze guns from ATOCHA have been recovered, and appear to be broadside mounts. They range from 6 pounder sacres and 10 pounder quarto cañon (cannon) to 18 pounder tercio cañon. The period of manufacture appears to be from several years prior to the Spanish Armada campaign (of 1588) to 1616, perhaps even 1621, judging from dated escutcheons showing the Collar of Golden Fleece insignia on several, and from astragal and ring configurations on others. The tercio cañon shown in the accompanying drawing has the escutcheon of Philippe II (reign 1556-1598) and is dated 1592. One sacre and one cañon carry the Philippe III escutcheon (reign 1598-1621) with the Collar of the Golden Fleece insignia. The weights range from approximately 2000 pounds to about 3200 pounds, and the tube lengths vary from 7'-7" (35.83 cm) to 9' - 8" (45.67 cm). The sacre is dated 1616, and is now on display at the Spanish Archives in Seville, Spain. One of the 10 pounder cañons has a Royal Coat of Arms and is dated 1607.

Two bronze stern chase guns recovered from the trail of the SANTA MARGARITA were also recovered some years ago from near the Quicksands region westerly of the Marquesas. One of these is tentatively identified as an 18 pounder tercio de culebrina of 3750 pound weight and its length is 10' - 2" (48.03 cm). The other is a 16 pounder tercio de culebrina of 4300 pound weight and length of 10' -7" (50.00 cm). Both have Royal Coat of Arms crests which are still under study.

Four relatively complete sets of capsquare irons, vertical carriage cheek forelock bolts and horizontal through bolts with peened iron plate fasteners and through ring bolt irons from broadside marine carriages were recovered from the ATOCHA site, together with miscellaneous other scattered carriage irons. A vertical forelock bolt with the foreward cheek iron encompassing a foremost portion of wood cheek, (in a manner that clearly defines the carriage cheek height as being 18") was an extremely interesting find. It was located in an area that made positive identification from either vessel uncertain. This assembly was certainly from a stern chase marine carriage. The proportions of cheek size, wheel sizes proportioned to provide the needed elements for compatibility with stern gunport specifications stated clearly in the ATOCHA shipwright contract. A few wood cheek remnants were preserved by metallic oxide and conglomerate protection, and analysis of a sample is currently being made to determine wood species. (The carriage irons of the four broadside marine carriage sets indicate a height of cheek of 13", and is also positively compatible with the broadside gunport specifications stated in the contract).

Of the four relatively complete sets of broadside carriage mount irons, the capsquare iron on one side of each set is undamaged and positioned much as it would have been on the carriage cheek. The other capsquare iron in each set however, was badly askew and bent back on itself, to indicate clearly that a violent withdrawal of the bronze guns from the carriage occurred in a direction at right angles to the broadside lay of the guns.

Survivors' reports to the Spanish Crown in 1622 indicated that the ATOCHA grounded violently on the outer reef or an inner patch reef shoal, snapping the bowsprit and carrying away the foremast and main topmast. This almost instant cessation of forward motion of the vessel would certainly have caused the heavy bronze guns to be propelled relentlessly toward the bow due to the inertia of their heavy masses. Shearing of the forelock wedges on each side of the trunnion nearest the bow would not be hard to visualize, and once free of trunnion sockets and capsquare fastenings they then would easily have snapped the large breeching cables and become terrible creatures of destruction on the rolling gun deck. With the vessel surging wildly in the towering waves, the one to one and a half ton bronze guns undoubtedly rolled and skidded forward, back and athwartship in a destructive rampage crushing all in their paths, delivering wrecking ball blows to hull framing members, strakes and fastenings. The terror brought on by the hurricane thus was compounded many fold by the terrible havoc wrought on the gun deck after grounding, to ultimately be stilled only when flooding of the gun deck started as ATOCHA began rapidly sinking as she sought her final resting place.

The iron swivel gun shown in an accompanying drawing was located about a mile westerly of the ATOCHA main site and southerly of portions of the SANTA MARGARITA trail. The swivel piece is a short barrelled large bore breech loading gun that bore the name 'murtherer' by the English in the seventeenth century. Used mainly as an antipersonnel weapon during boarding skirmishes, it was loaded with iron nails, tacks, bits of iron and stone, lead balls and other forms of deadly material called 'langrage'. One interesting variety of this 'langrage' was found on the ATOCHA site and consisted of small lead discs wired together with bronze wire to form swivel joined discs that would open outward into a whirling missile when fired from the swivel gun at enemy boarding parties.

This small gun was recovered with an iron shackle through its breech, with fifteen feet of heavy iron elongated link chain, and swivel connected rings at both ends. This obviously was the 'cañon' referred to in survivors' reports to the Spanish Crown indicating that the two sunken galleons were buoyed with a spar connected to a 'cañon'. The swivel gun could have been recovered from the prop rail of the ATOCHA since that rail would have been barely 3 to 5 feet below the surface of the channel after she sank and heeled over slightly, with her mizzen protruding above the surface. The Jamaican rescue vessel could then have merely drifted westerly with the prevailing counter-current to drop it at an advantageous point to mark both vessels by means of compass bearings and ranges from the spar buoy. Or, perhaps it is just as feasible that the swivel gun came from the small Jamaican sloop that rescued some of the few survivors of ATOCHA. The chain would have acted as a shock absorber to dampen the pull of the spar buoy in rough seas and to prevent 'walking' of the anchoring cañon.

BIBLIOGRAPHY:

Garcia de Palacio, Diego, *Instruccion Nautica*, 1587, Mexico. Translation by J. Bankston, 1986, Bisbee, Arizona.

Mainwaring, *Seaman's Dictionary* (1625/1644).

Manucy, Albert, *Preliminary Study of Artillery at the Fort of St. Augustine in 1580.* (Unpublished report dated 1975, St. Augustine, Florida.

Martin, Colin, *Full Fathom Five*, 1975, New York.

Muckleroy, Keith, Gen. Editor, *Archaeology Under Water.*

Simanca Archives (GA 405, M y P XVIII-47, 48, 49). Communication Dr. Eugene Lyon (relating to the two wheel marine gun carriage).

McDonald, David & Arnold, J. Barto, *The Documentary Sources for the Wreck if the New Spain Fleet of 1554*, 1979, Austin, Texas.

Cannon 2499 Nuestra Senõra de Atocha discovered in July, 1975 and identified from Atocha's gun list.

AGI Contratación 2,211, Fº 488VO The first silver bar identified, Nº. 4,584. (See Manifest)

AGI Indiferente General 1,144 page 1 gun list of Nuestra Senõra de Atocha. (see no. 24q99L) This is the gun that was donated by Mel Fisher to Queen Sofia of Spain. It is now in the Archives of the Indies, Seville, Spain.

AGI *Indiferente General 1,114 Page 2 of the Atocha gun list.*

Photos of manifest courtesy of the author.

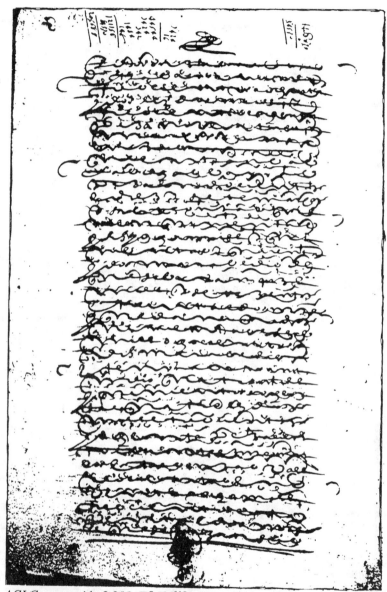

AGI Contratación 2,211, F<u>O</u>488<u>VO</u> · From the Atocha Manifest Note at the lower part of the page entry for bar 4,584 - the first identified.

AGI Contraduría 1,112 (the Melian salvage accounts, 1626-1631) see the words, "El Cayo del Marquez" on line 11.

AGI Contratación 4545. First page of construction contract for Atocha with Captain Alonso de Ferrera (1616) to build four war galleons, including the Atocha.

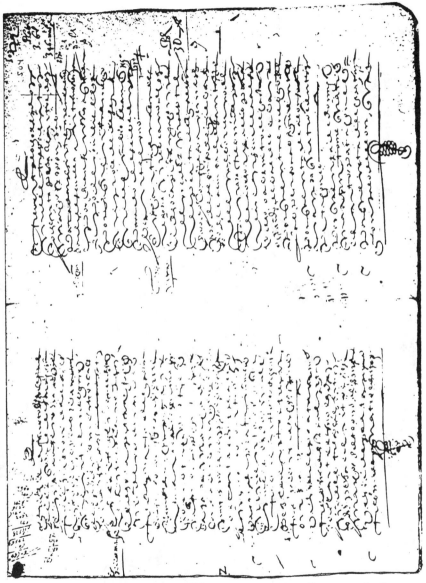

AGI Contratación 2,211, Fᵒ 506ᵛᵒ.. Atocha Manifest, Cartagena Lading,
Bar No. 569 - middle of the left page

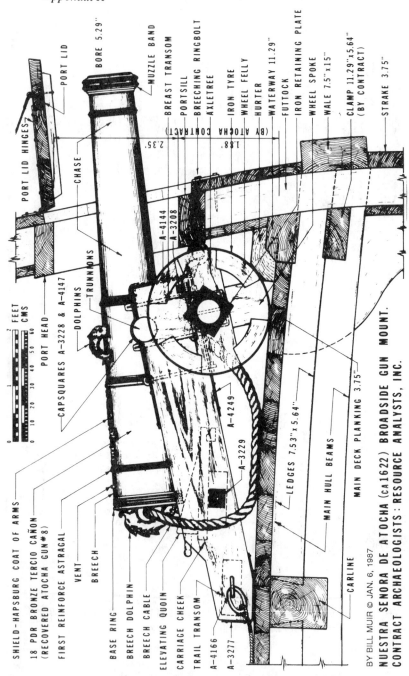

BY BILL MUIR @ JAN. 6, 1987

NUESTRA SENORA DE ATOCHA (ca1622) BROADSIDE GUN MOUNT.
CONTRACT ARCHAEOLOGISTS : RESOURCE ANALYSTS, INC.

Labels (clockwise/around diagram):

PORT LID
BORE 5.29"
MUZZLE BAND
BREAST TRANSOM
PORTSILL
BREECHING RINGBOLT
AXLETREE
IRON TYRE
WHEEL FELLY
HURTER
WATERWAY 11.29"
FUTTOCK
IRON RETAINING PLATE
WHEEL SPOKE
WALE 7.5"x15"
CLAMP 11.29"x5.64" (BY CONTRACT)
STRAKE 3.75"

PORT LID HINGES
CHASE
PORT HEAD
(BY ATOCHA CONTRACT)
2.35"
1.88"
A-4144
A-3208

SHIELD-HAPSBURG COAT OF ARMS
18 PDR BRONZE TERCIO CAÑON (RECOVERED ATOCHA GUN#8)
FIRST REINFORCE ASTRAGAL
VENT
BREECH
CAPSQUARES A-3228 & A-4147
DOLPHINS
TRUNNIONS

FEET
CMS
0 1 2
0 10 20 30 40 50 60

BASE RING
BREECH DOLPHIN
BREECH CABLE
ELEVATING QUOIN
CARRIAGE CHEEK
TRAIL TRANSOM
A-4166
A-3277

A-4249
A-3229

LEDGES 7.53"x5.64"
MAIN HULL BEAMS
MAIN DECK PLANKING 3.75"
CARLINE

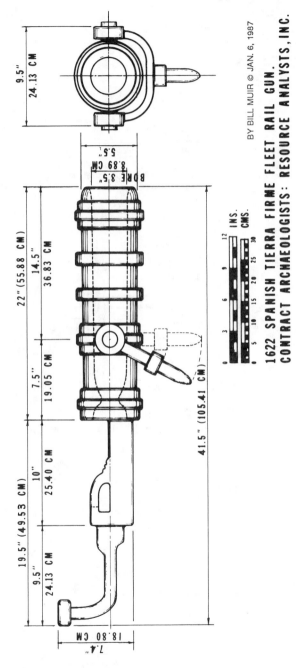

9.5"
24.13 CM

BORE 3.5"
8.89 CM
5.5"

22" (55.88 CM)

14.5"
36.83 CM

7.5"
19.05 CM

41.5" (105.41 CM)

19.5" (49.53 CM)

10"
25.40 CM

9.5"
24.13 CM

18.80 CM
7.4"

12   INS.
CMS.

9   25   30

6   15   20

3   10

0   5

BY BILL MUIR © JAN. 6, 1987

1622 SPANISH TIERRA FIRME FLEET RAIL GUN.
CONTRACT ARCHAEOLOGISTS: RESOURCE ANALYSTS, INC.

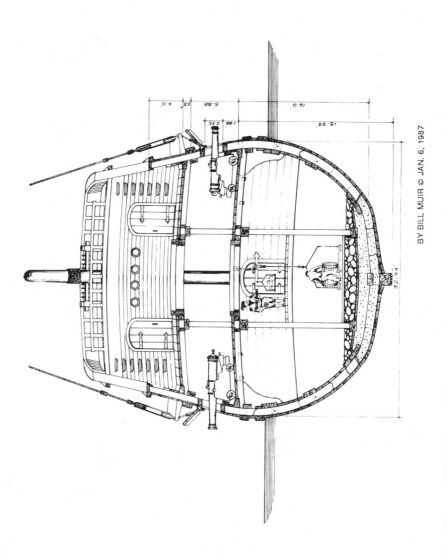

Cross section of vessel showing gun deck.

APPENDIX J

100TH CONGRESS
1ST SESSION

S. 858

IN THE HOUSE OF REPRESENTATIVES

DECEMBER 20, 1987

Referred jointly to the Committees on Marchant Marine and Fisheries and Interior
and Insular Affairs

AN ACT

To establish the title of States in certain abandoned shipwrecks,
and for other purposes.

1   *Be it enacted by the Senate and House of Representa-*

2   *tives of the United States of America in Congress assembled,*

3   **SECTION 1. SHORT TITLE.**

4   This Act may be cited as the "Abandoned Shipwreck

5   Act of 1987".

6   **SEC. 2. FINDINGS.**

7   The Congress finds that—

8   (a) States have the responsibility for management

9   of a broad range of living and nonliving resources in

10   State waters and submerged lands; and

1   (b) included in the range of resources are certain

2   abandoned shipwrecks, which have been deserted and

3   to which the owner has relinquished ownership rights

4   with no retention.

5 **SEC. 3. DEFINITIONS.**

6   For purposes of this Act—

7   (a) the term "embedded" means firmly affixed in

8   the submerged lands or in coralline formations such

9   that the use of tools of excavation is required in order

10   to move the bottom sediments to gain access to the

11   shipwreck, its cargo, and any part thereof;

12   (b) the term "National Register" means the Na-

13   tional Register of Historic Places maintained by the

14   Secretary of the Interior under section 101 of the Na-

15   tional Historic Preservation Act (16 U.S.C. 470a);

16   (c) the terms "public lands," "Indian lands" and

17   "Indian tribe" have the same meaning given the terms

18   in the Archaeological Resource Protection Act of 1979

19   (16 U.S.C. 470aa–470ll);

20   (d) the term "shipwreck" means a vessel or

21   wreck, its cargo, and other contents;

22   (e) the term "State" means a State of the United

23   States, the District of Columbia, Puerto Rico, Guam,

24   the Virgin Islands, American Samoa, and the Northern

25   Mariana Islands; and

1   (f) the term "submerged lands" means the

2 lands—

3   (1) that are "lands beneath navigable

4   waters," as defined in section 2 of the Submerged

5   Lands Act (43 U.S.C. 1301);

6   (2) of Puerto Rico, as described in section 8

7   of the Act of March 2, 1917, as amended (48

8   U.S.C. 749);

9   (3) of Guam, the Virgin Islands and Ameri-

10   can Samoa, as described in section 1 of Public

11   Law 93–435 (48 U.S.C. 1705); and

12   (4) of the Commonwealth of the Northern

13   Mariana Islands, as described in section 801 of

14   Public Law 94–241 (48 U.S.C. 1681).

15 SEC. 4. RIGHTS OF ACCESS.

16 (a) ACCESS RIGHTS.—In order to—

17   (1) clarify that State waters and shipwrecks offer

18 recreational and educational opportunities to sport

19 divers and other interested groups, as well as irreplace-

20 able State resources for tourism, biological sanctuaries,

21 and historical research; and

22   (2) provide that reasonable access by the public to

23 such abandoned shipwrecks be permitted by the State

24 holding title to such shipwrecks pursuant to section 6

25 of this Act,

1   it is the declared policy of the Congress that States carry out

2   their responsibilities under this Act to develop appropriate

3   and consistent policies so as to—

4   (A) protect natural resources and habitat areas;

5   (B) guarantee recreational exploration of ship-

6   wreck sites; and

7   (C) allow for appropriate public and private sector

8   recovery of shipwrecks consistent with the protection

9   of historical values and environmental integrity of the

10   shipwrecks and the sites.

11   (b) PARKS AND PROTECTED AREAS.—In managing the

12 resources subject to the provisions of this Act, States are

13 encouraged to create underwater parks or areas to provide

14 additional protection for such resources. Funds available to

15 States from grants from the Historic Preservation Fund shall

16 be available, in accordance with the provisions of title I of

17 the National Historic Preservation Act, for the study, inter-

18 pretation, protection, and preservation of historic shipwrecks

19 and properties.

20 SEC. 5. PREPARATION OF GUIDELINES.

21   (a) In order to encourage the development of underwat-

22 er parks and the administrative cooperation necessary for the

23 comprehensive management of underwater resources related

24 to historic shipwrecks, the Secretary of the Interior, acting

25 through the Director of the National Park Service, shall

1 within nine months after the date of enactment of this Act

2 prepare and publish guidelines in the Federal Register which

3 shall seek to:

4   (1) maximize the enhancement of cultural re-

5   sources;

6   (2) foster a partnership among sport divers, fisher-

7   men, archeologists, salvors, and other interests to

8   manage shipwreck resources of the States and the

9   United States;

10   (3) facilitate access and utilization by recreational

11   interests;

12   (4) recognize the interests of individuals and

13   groups engaged in shipwreck discovery and salvage.

14 (b) Such guidelines shall be developed after consultation

15 with appropriate public and private sector interests (including

16 the Secretary of Commerce, the Advisory Council on Histor-

17 ic Preservation, sport divers, State Historic Preservation Of-

18 ficers, professional dive operators, salvors, archeologists, his-

19 toric preservationists, and fishermen).

20 (c) Such guidelines shall be available to assist States and

21 the appropriate Federal agencies in developing legislation

22 and regulations to carry out their responsibilities under this

23 Act.

1 SEC. 6. RIGHTS OF OWNERSHIP.

2   (a) UNITED STATES TITLE.—The United States asserts

3 title to any abandoned shipwreck that is—

4   (1) embedded in submerged lands of a State;

5   (2) embedded in coralline formations protected by

6   a State on submerged lands of a State; or

7   (3) on submerged lands of a State and is included

8   in or determined eligible for inclusion in the National

9   Register.

10   (b) The public shall be given adequate notice of the loca-

11 tion of any shipwreck to which title is asserted under this

12 section. The Secretary of the Interior, after consultation with

13 the appropriate State Historic Preservation Officer, shall

14 make a written determination that an abandoned shipwreck

15 meets the criteria for eligibility for inclusion in the National

16 Register of Historic Places under clause (a)(3).

17   (c) TRANSFER OF TITLE TO STATES.—The title of the

18 United States to any abandoned shipwreck asserted under

19 subsection (a) of this section is transferred to the State in or

20 on whose submerged lands the shipwreck is located.

21   (d) EXCEPTION.—Any abandoned shipwreck in or on

22 the public lands of the United States is the property of the

23 United States Government. Any abandoned shipwreck in or

24 on any Indian lands is the property of the Indian tribe

25 owning such lands.

1   (e) RESERVATION OF RIGHTS.—This section does not
2 affect any right reserved by the United States or by any
3 State (including any right reserved with respect to Indian
4 lands) under—

5   (1) section 3, 5, or 6 of the Submerged Lands Act
6   (43 U.S.C. 1311, 1313, and 1314); or

7   (2) section 19 or 20 of the Act of March 3, 1899
8   (33 U.S.C. 414 and 415).

9 **SEC. 7. RELATIONSHIP TO OTHER LAWS.**

10   (a) LAW OF SALVAGE AND THE LAW OF FINDS.—The
11 law of salvage and the law of finds shall not apply to aban-
12 doned shipwrecks to which section 6 of this Act applies.

13   (b) LAWS OF THE UNITED STATES.—This Act shall
14 not change the laws of the United States relating to ship-
15 wrecks, other than those to which this Act applies.

16   (c) EFFECTIVE DATE.—This Act shall not affect any
17 legal proceeding brought prior to the date of enactment of
18 this Act.

Passed the Senate December 19 (legislative day, December 15), 1987.

Attest: WALTER J. STEWART,
                                    Secretary.

Description of the Spanish Salvors Chart of 1623

The Head of the Martyrs (*Cabeza de los Martires*) is the east-west point of Florida, on a north-south line with the port of Havana. It is a latitude of a little more than 25 degrees; which place is so dangerous that infinite souls have drowned in it, that for this reason they call it The Martyrs--or because of the innumerable keys which are thus clustered together. They are of sand and shifting in the rigors of the weather. Some are large, with mangroves or other kinds of trees, and there are settled on them some fisher Indians, since there is water (for drinking).

In the years of 1623 (Note error), three silver galleons under the command of the Marquis of Cadereita were lost, and other fleet vessels (in) which there perished many souls and fortunes. The *Almiranta* of *Tierra Firme (Atocha)*, with more than a million (pesos), was lost, according to opinions, in nine *braza* (54.5′); the galleon *Margarita* in five (27′) on a rocky outcrop; that of General Chazarreta in three *brazas* (16.2′ on Tortuga, and other private ships.

This year the Viceroy of Mexico, the Marquis of Gelves, sent me from the port of Acapulco in the South Sea with 14 black divers and instruments to aid in the search for this treasure. Going in company with the Marques of Cadereita, Captain Gaspar de Vargas, and Don Pedro de Ursua in the keys of Matecumbe (note misspelling Motacumbe) and sandbanks, searching for it. And even though we found traces of the two galleons and took from them many muskets, barrels of balls, ballast and some silver bars, it was not possible to come up with the main deposit due to bad weather, even though the work was done with the greatest care. Afterwards the silver of the galleon *Margarita* was found, due to the directions I gave to Pilot Govea and Francisco Melian, citizens of Havana---as my certifications advise. And it is certain that, if diligence be practiced, the missing silver and that from the *Almiranta* of *Tierra Firme* --- will appear, because it is a pity to leave for lost more than a million in such little depth, as it must be.

A. The Armada patache which the Marquis of Cadereita used to recover the people who went seeking the silver.

B. The lost galleons.

C. The launch in which the Marquis was embarked with his divers.

D. The Keys of Tortugas, where the galleon of Chazarreta was lost.

E. The launch in which Captain Nicholas de Cardona was embarked, with the divers whom he][transported from][the South Sea.